Captured

The Japanese Internment
of American Civilians
in the Philippines,
1941–1945

Captured

FRANCES B. COGAN

The University of Georgia Press | *Athens and London*

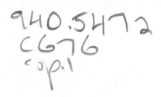

© 2000 by the University of Georgia Press

Athens, Georgia 30602

All rights reserved

Designed by Kathi Dailey Morgan

Set in 10 on 13 Electra by G & S Typesetters

Printed and bound by Maple-Vail

The paper in this book meets the guidelines for
permanence and durability of the Committee on
Production Guidelines for Book Longevity of the
Council on Library Resources.

Printed in the United States of America

04   03   02   01   00   C   5   4   3   2   1

Library of Congress Cataloging in Publication Data

Cogan, Frances B.

    Captured : the Japanese internment of American civilians
in the Philippines, 1941–1945 / Frances B. Cogan.

        p.   cm.

    Includes bibliographical references and index.

    ISBN 0-8203-2117-6 (alk. paper)

    1. World War, 1939–1945 — Prisoners and prisons, Japanese.

    2. World War, 1939–1945 — Concentration camps — Philippines.

    3. Prisoners of War — United States — History — 20th century.

    I. Title.

    D805.P6C63   1999

    940.54'7252'09599 — dc21   99-30959

                                                CIP

British Library Cataloging in Publication Data available

Dedicated to

My husband, Daniel J. Cogan

and

My daughter, Elizabeth B. Cogan

One purchased my academic freedom for six months and listened to every rewrite

The other pulled books from shelves and listened even to notecards

Both made finishing this book possible

Contents

Acknowledgments

I owe thanks to many people and organizations. I would like to thank the Center for the Study of Women in Society for its summer grant when I started working on this project. I would also like to thank the Social Science Research Council for its seed-grant for another summer's work. I owe the University of Oregon and the Honors College gratitude as well for granting me a paid sabbatical for winter and spring terms in 1996—during which time I actually finished the book I started seven years earlier.

I especially would like to acknowledge the help and encouragement—as always—from my parents, Clarajane and George Browning. My father gave me my organization, and my mother proofread chapter after chapter, asking the questions that needed to be asked for the sake of clarity. Both have done all they could to aid me during the writing of this book, and I am so very grateful. My brother, Tom Browning, went out of his way as well to help—searching used bookstores all over the state to purchase me copies of internment diaries published in the 1940s and 1950s and out of print. My gratitude is also extended to my cousin, Steve Stivers, whose continuing interest in all my projects has always been deeply appreciated.

I would also especially like to thank two scholars who corresponded with me, answered my questions, suggested books and articles, and even went so far as to write recommendations for me for several grants.

The first of these is James Halsema—not only a former internee of Baguio (Hay/Holmes) camp but also, over the last thirty or more years, the author of two books on internment and the true godfather of internee scholarship, texts, and information. He has been more than generous, allowing me to see (and use portions of) two private diaries he kept during internment, as well as correcting my errors. If there are any mistakes in facts, they are all my own, not his.

The second scholar is Professor Lynn Bloom of the University of Connecticut (Storrs) English Department. She is the editor of two of the most important women's internment diaries (Sams and Crouter) from the Philippines. She is also almost the only one to write any academic articles on internment and its effect on women, as well as the most lucid, the least jargon-filled, analyses of diary narrative and its limitations and its strengths. Her theories and explanations of the pattern of various first-person narratives helped me develop my own historiographic analysis of the first-person accounts as accurate historical sources.

I would also like to thank my editor (now the director of the University of Georgia Press), Karen Orchard, who suggested the project to begin with, assured me that, indeed, I had the skill to do the book, and managed to get me a provisional contract.

I also owe a number of internees many thanks for all the help and interviews they gave me so freely. Primary among these is Grace Nash, to whom I wrote out of the blue after reading her book (*That We Might Live*) and who actually called to talk to me. She consented to several interviews, and more important, she made a point of getting the names and addresses of a long list of ex-internees who were attending the Las Vegas reunion. Through her, I was able to distribute and get back questionnaires, as well as find out about other books.

I owe special gratitude to Professor Martin Meadows, a former teenage internee at Santo Tomás, who offered me invaluable prints of pictures taken by the Signal Corps—pictures now extremely difficult to locate in the newly relocated Bureau of Still Pictures in the National Archives. In addition to the pictures—and a copy of the first propagandistic *Tribune* picture spread of the camp—Professor Meadows shared his memories, choice anecdotes, and facts about the effects of internment after the war. He also generously reviewed reels of movies, which, by index description, were pertinent to my work.

Among those other internees who graciously answered my questions and offered further sources I would like to thank especially Dr. Jay Hill, who loaned me his father's (Alva Hill's) manuscript and his mother's book of poetry from before the war and during internment. He also granted me several phone interviews and put me in contact with the Center for Civilian Internee Rights. The director of that organization, Gilbert M. Hair, receives my gratitude for sending bibliographies, news clippings, and a newsletter that kept me informed on the progress of the bid to receive reparations from Japan.

Several other internees whom I would like especially to mention include Frieda Magnuson, Susan (Magnuson) DeVoe, Alice Morton Hill, June (Darras) Alden, Teedie (Cowie) Woodcock, Margaret (Sherk) Sams, Peggy (Peters) Read, and Henry Sioux Johnson. All were generous with their time and their knowledge and suggested further contacts. Their anecdotes and encouragement meant a great deal. Angela Collas-Dean, whose memories of the Philippine liberation were particularly valuable, provided another contemporary source.

Finally, I would like to thank a couple of colleagues and friends who helped in a variety of ways, not the least of which was taking me out for a beer or serving as a friendly ear: Professors David Frank and Max Grober. I would also like to thank another internment scholar with whom I traded information, Dr. Theresa Kaminski. I would also like to thank Professor Louise Westling of the English Department for her continuing support and friendship. I want especially to thank once again Professor of U.S. History (Emeritus) Richard Maxwell Brown, my first and foremost model of a professional historian and colleague. I am grateful especially to my friend Dr. Claudia Hardwick for her professional and personal attention to me and mine. I would also like to thank the Eugene chapter of Zeta Tau Alpha for its constant interest and warm support. I would like to acknowledge as well the invaluable, continuing professional support of Professor Paul Csonka, current director of the University of Oregon Honors College, where I teach; his interest in this project has been gratifying and sustaining. Finally, let me add a short but definite thank you to Colby Stong, my light-handed and deft copyeditor, who somehow managed to keep the sense and cut out the nonsense, despite my additions in purple, red, or blue pen at various awkward points.

Captured

Introduction

A number of years ago, just before I actually began writing this book, I remember friends and various family members asking me quizzically why I became so heated over the subject of American internees in the Philippines. What was it to me? they asked. I had been born two years after the internees' release and could, therefore, have no contemporary historical interest. My friends asked if I had a family member who had been interned. (I didn't.) My family wondered why I would involve myself with something so remote and so depressing. At that time I didn't have a coherent answer for them — I just knew it was a project that demanded I take it up and follow it.

I now have an answer. It was and is the need for greater public awareness. I was appalled to discover that such a piece of American history had apparently been forgotten. Few have any idea that over 5,000 American civilians in the

Philippines were interned by the Japanese in camps during World War II and held for three years in what steadily devolved into starvation conditions.[1] That the United States also shamed itself by interning thousands of Japanese-Americans during that same war is a sad but familiar fact; that they were not the only American civilians to suffer such indignities (and worse) is not so well known.

To understand the internment experience is to understand something about American values, strengths, and weaknesses. Although Americans were by no means the only nationality represented in the Philippine camps, they were by far the most numerous (the British were next). So many Americans lived in all the camps that one could make a strong case that American expectations, institutions, and ways of doing things dominated camp life. It is for this reason that I have restricted myself in general to discussion of Americans in the internment camps.

The camp populations also seemed to reflect a looser, less class-structured American society rather than one adhering to rules of caste and family. Even before the internment, the Americans in the Philippines were primarily college-educated, middle-class people, not society trendsetters or nobility. On the other hand, neither were most of the Americans rough and ready pioneers. Though both rich and poor were among the American population in the Philippines (and therefore in the camps), the majority of internees were middle-class. They played bridge, they liked to go to club dances, they were both white-collar workers and skilled laborers, they raised their families or they lived as single career people, and they worked at a variety of American occupations. The Japanese dragnet of civilians made this evident; it included bank presidents, missionaries, teachers, company vice presidents and their wives, teenagers from private schools, veterans from the Spanish-American War, newspaper editors and reporters, doctors, military nurses, housewives, children, musicians, writers, prostitutes, engineers, chemists, plumbers, electricians, administrators, society belles and Rotarians, college professors, clergymen, nuns and priests, and even professional entertainers. Here for the first time in anyone's memory what amounted to an entire small town was interned. It was as if someone had taken 1940s Ames, Iowa, or Rumford, Maine, or Newport, Oregon, and forcibly confined all the inhabitants to several crowded camps for over three years, at first denying them freedom of movement, then refusing to repatriate them, and finally starving them. What conditions they faced, how they dealt with imprisonment, their ingenuity when beset by need, their reactions to captivity, the nature of life in camp, and their release should be a part of our common consciousness and heritage. It could serve certainly as a model in the future of how a civilized people behave when placed in a horrific situation for a long period of time. This model illustrates what both communities and individuals can accomplish, even short of resources, weakened by illness, and made captive.

This work represents a narrative social history, carefully taking into account individual camps both on and off Luzon. By this means I intend, perhaps for the first time, to provide a *representative* idea of what life was like for an average American civilian captured and interned in the Philippines by the Japanese during the war, rather than a picture of life at any particular camp.

This is not to deny scholarship exists about the internment camps. Several excellent secondary historical works on the American internment experience exist already: Anthony Arthur's *Deliverance at Los Baños* (1985); James L. Halsema's *The Internment Camp at Baguio*, edited by Michael Onorato (1987), as well as his *E. J. Halsema, Colonial Engineer: A Biography* (1991); Michael P. Onorato's *Forgotten Heroes: Japan's Imprisonment of American Civilians in the Philippines, 1942–1945—An Oral History* (1990); and finally, Van Waterford [Willem F. Wanrooy]'s *Prisoners of the Japanese in World War II: Statistical History, Personal Narratives and Memorials concerning POWs in Camps and on Hellships, Civilian Internees* (1994). Added to this are a variety of trenchant articles by Lynn Z. Bloom, analyzing diary accounts of internment, which, incidentally, are almost the only scholarly articles dealing with the experience. One might add to this list the critical introductions to three key diary or retrospective accounts: Natalie Crouter's *Forbidden Diary* (1980) and Margaret Sams's *Forbidden Family* (1989)—both edited and introduced by Lynn Z. Bloom also—and Elizabeth Vaughan's *The Ordeal of Elizabeth Vaughan* (1985), edited and introduced by Carol M. Petillo. One should note as well Vaughan's later sociological study of internment, *Community under Stress* (1949), written after the war.

Although these works provide an understanding of individual camps and the experiences in them, as well as, in the case of Arthur, of one of the most dramatic rescues in the history of the war in the Pacific, they are not particularly comprehensive. They deal usually with only one (or at the most two) internment camps. There were, however, at least ten individual camps in the Philippines (Waterford, 258–260), though some of them were small (Iloilo, Cebu, Tacoblan), and several sequentially housed the same population (Hay, Holmes, Bilibid). Arthur's work focuses primarily on the rescue at Los Baños camp and the earlier life at Santo Tomás for internees before their transfer to Los Baños camp. Halsema's work puts the two different "Baguio" camps (Hay and Holmes) into perspective; Onorato provides a critical introduction to a series of oral histories he wrote about camps on Cebu and Luzon; Sams's diary deals with life in Santo Tomás and Los Baños, and Crouter describes her life at both Baguio camps; Vaughan's diary deals with Bacolod camp, then Santo Tomás, as does her later sociological study. Only Van Waterford's work attempts to deal in a comprehensive or representative manner with the whole American civilian internment experience in the Philippines, but it is a part of a larger history of *all* the prisoners of the Japanese—American, British, Dutch, Indonesian, Malayan, Chinese, Javanese, and others; POWs, civilian internees, native conscripts, and slave laborers. His treatment of the civilians, while authoritative and rich with statistics, is relatively brief and nondiscursive.

As well done as these works are, none attempts to provide a picture of the common American civilian internment experience or day-to-day life in camp in general (rather than in a particular camp); and none presents any attempted synthesis of accounts in the form of social history. Such a history should include not only the most famous camps—Santo Tomás Internment Camp (STIC), Baguio/Holmes, and Los Baños—but also less well-known (but recorded) camps such as Bacolod (on Negros), Cebu City (Cebu), and Davao (Mindanao) to get a more complete sense of what experiences were common to all camps, as well as to identify the significant differences in treatment or facilities on various islands and in the several camps that modified common experience.

One work that does attempt to do this is A. V. H. Hartendorp's two-volume "hidden history," *The Japanese Occupation of the Philippines* (1967), a study written secretly in Santo Tomás during the internment and then later revised. In this seminal work, Hartendorp not only records the events that happened in Santo Tomás itself but describes to a limited extent life in other camps, based on the reports of internees transferred to Santo Tomás. (Santo Tomás eventually became the central camp for all the internees from other islands, at least prior to the 1943 transfer of some internees to Los Baños from STIC.) Hartendorp also includes alternating sections in his work discussing living conditions under Japanese military control outside the sawali-covered gates of Santo Tomás and on the rest of Luzon among the Philippine population. Hartendorp solidly grounds that part of his account of camp life inside the wire by including verbatim orders and proclamations from various camp commandants, propaganda pieces from the Japanese-controlled *Manila Tribune*, as well as all the notes and correspondence of the camp's Executive Committee(s) when possible.

To understand what most civilians experienced during internment, the first and most vital place to start is unquestionably with *The Japanese Occupation of the Philippines*. Even Hartendorp, however, primarily discusses Santo Tomás and only briefly touches on life in the other camps. Here, too, in light of his mission to record everything thoroughly, his history tends to be studded with footnotes, statistics, dates, committee names, and administrative machinery, as well as descriptions of events. He is so thorough his original draft was used in the war crimes trials as documentary evidence. Though this is highly useful to settling questions of chronology and establishing fully detailed charges, other readers and researchers may find the book not very accessible, overly thorny with minutiae, and not representative enough of common camp life.

I must also mention other vital works already in print that describe camp life in great detail—these are the diaries, retrospectives, and memoirs written by former internees. These accounts have provided most of the details and flavor of my work; they are, however, limited by the time and space of each captivity to the camps in which the writer lived. Fern Miles, R. Renton Hind, James Halsema, Mary Ogle, and Judy Hyland lived in both Baguio camps, then for just over a month in Bilibid Prison with the rest of their camp population. Denny Williams, the Hills, and Eva Nixon, among others, lived entirely in Santo Tomás. Grace Nash, Margaret Sams, and Imogene Carlson primarily lived in Santo Tomás, then transferred to Los Baños. Elizabeth Vaughan, James and Ethel Chapman, and Alice Bryant all experienced internment on Negros (Bryant and Vaughan in Bacolod, the Chapmans briefly in Dumaguete and San Carlos, before their transfer), though all eventually went to Santo Tomás, as did Imogene Carlson (originally interned on Cebu) and Frank Cary (from Davao). Even though these personal narratives provide warmth and details for my work, they still are restricted by being personal experiences, which physically were limited. My goals here are to avoid the first-person narrative limitations (for more discussion of this, see "A Note on Sources" at the end of this work) and to try to find overarching similarities in all of these accounts, to note significant differences between camps (and also in personal reactions to events), and then to corroborate these accounts with other sources, putting the entire experience in a larger picture of war and imprisonment.

I have one other important goal, which is only possible because I am writing so long after the events. Using the resources of government documents, modern historiography, a variety of accounts now published, access to a number of unpublished manuscripts and diaries, discussions with people such as James Halsema who coordinate and keep up-to-date information on the Philippine internment, along with information gained from private correspondence, interviews, and questionnaires, I want to resolve any central discrepancies among various accounts and to address squarely the hovering historical controversies surrounding the subject of American civilian internment.

A number of controversial questions I intend to answer throughout my work include the following: Why civilians, having heard rumors about imminent war and having seen military dependents leave, chose to stay, risking them-selves and their families; why the Japanese only allowed limited repatriation for the internees; whether the Japanese applied international agreements such as Geneva, the Hague, and the International Red Cross to the internees and if not, why, and with what result; how the Japanese military and civilian chain of command operated, and who held the real responsibility for determining camp conditions, especially in terms of food; what the "soldier's ration" meant exactly in terms of portions and variety, and if the Japanese actually gave that kind of ration to the prisoners and if not, why not; what kinds of camp illnesses were present, as well as both the true morbidity and mortality rates, and how many actually succumbed to deficiency diseases; and finally, whether a gen-eral order of any kind existed from the Japanese Central Command detailing what to do with prisoners in the event of a Japanese surrender.

To find the answers to such emotionally loaded and controversial questions, I have tried to avoid bias from any single kind of source and to include as many applicable sources, both primary and secondary, as possible. To this end I have included a number of peripheral yet useful works. Obviously, military history and histories of prison camps and internment in general play a large part in determining such things. On the other hand, particular questions might re-quire more specialized knowledge. For example, one claim often made to explain prisoner starvation from mid-1944 to rescue was that the Philippines was a large rice importer *before* the war, and that during the war an American naval blockade continued to sink Japanese supply ships bringing rice and other grains. To consider this question carefully, it is necessary to consult a professional agricultural study of the Philippines before the war and one that also discusses the effects of the Japanese occupation on crops in the middle of the war. Another specialized source would be a contemporary ac-count (November 1941, for example) discussing crop conditions and kinds of rice grown in the Philippines and Southeast Asia just prior to the war, as well as a source that discusses the differences between varieties of rice, including how well each keeps and for how long. These then need to be coordinated with both U.S. and Japanese naval information to receive an accurate idea of the availability of rice stores in the Philippines.

Because I needed to bring a number of expert sources to bear on the contro-versies, along with primary accounts, I have used a number of more specialized peripheral studies, including those in nutrition and health; human parasi-tology; Japanese customs, attitudes, and military culture, especially from 1930 to 1945; Japanese histories of the Pacific War and their evaluation of it; histo-ries of the Philippines and American/Filipino relations between 1920 and

1945; studies of beriberi, hypoproteinosis, and other deficiency diseases in both POW and civilian internee populations (for comparative purposes); military history and studies of specific tactics; biographies of Douglas MacArthur; official transcripts and exhibits from the Tokyo War Crimes Trials; guerrilla histories; and studies describing the operations of the Japanese Imperial Army and Navy in the Philippines.

In terms of *kinds* of sources, as I explain in "A Note on Sources," I have tried to prevent any bias sneaking in because of the rhetorical or narrative form of a source. For this reason, in addition to primary accounts (by both internees and Japanese military personnel), secondary histories, specialized articles and works, and trial transcripts, I have also included newspaper and magazine accounts appearing in the popular press during and after the war, letters from participants, personal and telephone interviews of mine and questionnaires from former internees, and oral history collections.

I have also included as many points of view as possible in primary accounts. To this end I have deliberately included both men and women diarists and retrospective writers, accounts by those captured in Manila as well as those who hid out in the hills on either Luzon or other islands; missionaries and atheists; corporate employers and employees; writers who were college educated and those who only went through public high school or elementary school; military and civilian nurses; ordinary Japanese soldiers' accounts as well as those by internees tortured by the *kempei tai*; single people and married people with families; those over age sixty and those under age twenty; spies and collaborators; and administrative officers and work party participants.

Given this variety of sources, I have had to simplify my organization to keep both the focus clear and confusion to a minimum. Rather than do a separate history of each camp from 1941 to 1945, along with all the probable repetition of common details that would incur, I have organized "horizontally" — that is, by topic, not by camp. Also, I have set up Chapters Four through Nine (the heart of the work dealing with the details of camp life) to discuss a variety of camps simultaneously while investigating particular subjects (administration, food and health, shelter and work, rescue). I explore the prelude to camp life in Chapter One (one month before the Pearl Harbor attack) and in Chapter Two (December 8–January 2 on Luzon, including Baguio City, Manila, Rizal province, and first internments). Chapter Three deals with those American civilians hiding out and later captured on islands other than Luzon.

In all cases, I have indicated if the time period was significant — for example, a drop in food supplies was very marked in all camps following February 1944. By June true starvation began to appear, and health deteriorated accordingly, though nutrition had only been minimal before that date.

Another specific time is Christmas of 1943, when several shipments of American Red Cross kits filled with food and medicine arrived. This was the one and only delivery of them to arrive in camp to supplement what was fast becoming a starvation ration from the camp kitchen for those without outside aid or money. Such demarcations must be accurate when speaking of conditions. To say that the internees starved prior to 1944, for example, is not entirely accurate; the camps *started* with a less than adequate camp diet, and internees grew gradually weaker as time passed and outside food sources dried up. To say then that they were on the verge of starvation when the Red Cross parcels arrived *is* accurate. To state further, when the last of the food in the kits ran out (for most, almost a year later), that internees starved and some died is all too true. Obviously, generalizations that ignore these differences in time periods inadvertently make accounts of the internment either overblown or understated in terms of what life in camp was like and open the entire subject up to criticism. If this book accomplishes any purpose, I want it to offer a solidly researched, carefully written, and reasonably comprehensive account of what life in internment meant for ordinary men, women, and children during World War II in the Philippine Islands. I also intend it to be an account written without hysteria or hatred but without overlooking the truly terrible either.

To learn about events in this manner, it is important to begin at the beginning—with a short discussion of life for American middle-class citizens in the Philippine Islands when Manila was still the Pearl of the Orient and houseboys and amahs and laundresses were available even to the most modestly paid Americans.

1

Pearl of the Orient
Manila and the Prewar Philippines

Beginning with the Philippines' acquisition at the end of the Spanish-American War, America's attitude toward its new colony seemed a muddled mixture of entrepreneurship and paternalism. Throughout the years up to World War II, benevolence wound itself around both geopolitical advantage and the profit motive. As Karnow points out,

America's ultimate goal for the Philippines, a sideshow to the main Cuban arena, was left undefined. . . . McKinley pondered the problem of what to do with the archipelago—which he could not find on the map. . . . Eventually he later revealed to a group of clergymen, God told him to annex the islands and "do the best we could for them." (11)

But of what did "the best we could [do]" consist? Were the Philippines a colony to be used as an investment opportunity and an imperialistic source of raw lumber, sugar, copra, and precious metals? The presence of prospering large and medium-sized corporations throughout the islands, as well as a variety of small companies, seemed to suggest this was true. For eager others, the islands became a grand cause to throw themselves behind. Here, some thought, was a backward country needing help to advance successfully into the modern age as an independent power. Dedicated teachers, eager missionaries, doctors in tropical medicine, American government bureaucrats, and civil engineers arrived in waves to make this vision a reality. That such a cause also met other unstated desires for adventure, further medical knowledge, religious enthusiasm, employment, and nation building does not diminish the eventual result. Certainly, the quintupled literacy rate during the American control of the islands (Arthur, 11), a ten-year plan for eventual independence, the eradication of smallpox and cholera, and a network of new roads, bridges, and buildings testify to the energy expended.

Early ideas of the Philippines' strategic importance should not be overlooked, however. Manila Bay was, as both Arthur MacArthur (a general with experience in the Philippines) and later his son Douglas would point out, a large, well-fortified port in the Pacific. Unlike poorly fortified Pearl Harbor in Hawaii, Manila Bay also offered a handy surveillance post from which to keep an eye on a growing and militaristic Japan (Falk, 3).

The use of the Philippines as the home of strategic military bases seems odd, however, given the strategy evoked repeatedly in the various War College "Plans Orange" and ultimately "Rainbow" scenarios in the 1930s and in early 1940. In these plans drawn up to deal with the (then) hypothetical Japanese attack on Pearl Harbor, and afterwards on the Philippines, the planners wrote the Philippines off as indefensible, expecting the military forces there at best to provide a holding action of only six months (Pomeroy, 203; Miller, 54). Once again, American aims seem confused. Given the various versions of Plan Orange, why did the U.S. government first send a retired general, Douglas MacArthur, to serve as adviser, field marshal, and builder of a Philippine army—and then keep him in place? Did he "mesmerize both the War Department and the President" as Miller suggests (56)? After all, on only two occasions had the ability to defend the Philippines successfully ever been accepted even theoretically. The first occurred in 1923. Leonard Wood, former governor-general of the Philippines, made a successful plea to the War Department to revise Plan Orange. He based his argument on the belief that the islands could be defended, given sufficient weaponry and materiel. The second plea came from Wood's protégé, Douglas MacArthur, who repeatedly argued against the "defeatism" of the Orange plans and the defensibility of the Philippines; this resulted ultimately in the Rainbow-5 Plan but with MacArthur's revisions (Miller, 56).

Perhaps the individualistic MacArthur merely served as a widely publicized symbol of American support for, and belief in, the Philippines' importance. If so, why did the U.S. Joint Chiefs of Staff then let stand MacArthur's modification to the Orange (and then Rainbow-5) War Plan so that the latter now suggested a complete defense of *all* the Philippine Islands, not merely Manila Bay—the former something the war planners still considered impossible? Policy crossed and recrossed policy.

The contradictions are striking, yet the reasons behind them—and their visible results—seem all to have existed at least at certain times to a certain degree. Despite criticism of American exploitation from such historians as William Pomeroy (117–124), the United States did not act like an ordinary tyrannical power. Unlike Great Britain or the Netherlands with Malaya or Java, America's treatment of her colony seemed hesitant, reflecting a strangely reluctant and morally insecure imperialism.

During this political and military confusion, for the next forty years American citizens in the Philippines went about their business, enjoying the relative wealth all colonials experienced in such places. The missionaries set up schools, hospitals, churches, and youth clubs in terms of their own ideals, rather than those of the populace, and the populace comfortingly appeared (and frequently were) grateful for their efforts, ignoring their stateside parochialism. Miners and lumbermen, performing as foremen and owners, directed Filipino workers and paid what, at the time, were high wages. Most middle-class Americans continued this tranquil life generally undisturbed through the decades until the first bombs dropped on Camp John Hay in northern Luzon in December 1941. As one internee, Karen Lewis, remembers, "In the twinkling of an eye, we had left behind a life of privilege and possessions, a life filled with parties, clubs, and servants. We were pampered, isolated American colonials abroad. Things were about to change" (76).

To gain some perspective on the radical changes in lifestyle for the future internees, as well as their eventual survival, we need to understand the texture of the lives of Americans before December 8, 1941, when the first bombs fell. We need to explore the curious nature of Filipino-American relations, especially as these had an impact on internees' ability to receive food and help from former servants. Finally, we must also understand the attitude that "Society" held about the validity of a Japanese threat, because that attitude, along with soothing words from officialdom, seems to have influenced the future internees to stay, rather than leave the islands. According to the 1939 census (the last one taken before the war), there were 3,191 Americans living in Manila, and 612 in Baguio to the north (qtd in Halsema, personal communication, May 7, 1997). Between December 25, 1942, and February 23, 1945, allowing for population influx, as well as the number of Americans on other islands, Onorato estimates "over 5,000" Americans were still in the Philippines ready to be interned, though as I have indicated earlier, the number given for civilians varies (ix).

Initially, why did so many Americans flock over several decades to islands as remote from the United States as the Philippines — and in such numbers, especially with their families? More to the point, why did they stay, once rumors of a coming war circulated? One suspects that the reluctance to leave good jobs and excellent homes clearly played a part. Perhaps the higher standard of living, as well as the fact of having a job in the Great Depression, also had an influence. Many of the Americans in the Philippines had never lived so luxuriously. Most of those whose accounts I use were hardly originally from the leisure class, despite their lifestyle in the Philippines. Money and leisured living complete with servants were easily had in the Philippines on a relatively small salary. Oil company managers, export shipping executives (like Chet Magnuson), sugar refinery officials, mine owners, civil engineers (like Ralph Nash), and lawyers (like Alva Hill) all found a comfortable living on beautiful islands with gracious housing, and usually at least a lavandera and an amah, for what would be a moderate income in the States. A selected few others, such as Alice Bryant's husband, the former governor of Mindanao, had even become wealthy planters (in his case, of coconuts) and had plantations to protect.

The Great Depression also enticed a number of families to come to the Philippines where blue-collar or skilled labor jobs were more available. Some, such as Bessie Sneed's husband, came because there was a mining boom at the time (Alva Hill, 185). Others, among them educators and missionaries including Esther Hamilton and her friends, came under the auspices of various churches to work to increase all levels of education in the Philippines. Hamilton herself arrived on the islands in 1933 as an employee of the Association of Baptists for World Evangelism; she subsequently taught math for three years at Iloilo, Panay, at the Bible Institute before being reassigned to Manila (Hamilton, 14–15).

Other families came to exploit the Philippines' natural resources in timber, sugar, rice, minerals, and metals. Elmer Harold and his wife Ethel were one example. He worked as a manager for Benguet Consolidated Mining Company's lumber operations in northern Luzon (Bloom, "Death," 78). Others came to sell equipment to those doing the harvesting or processing.

Alice Morton Hill, for example, later an internee at Santo Tomás, came to the Philippines with her husband Harry Morton, who worked for International Harvester (Alice Hill, interview). Alva Hill and other lawyers benefited from such mining, processing, exporting, and harvesting operations by serving as the American law firms for these companies. Hill's law firm, Powell and Hill, was one of two American firms on Panay, and it served as the firm for two banks, three sugar centrals, and a variety of American companies selling automobiles, mining supplies, and farm machinery to American planters and mine owners. They also served as legal counsel for a number of wealthy Chinese merchant-exporters (Alva Hill, 185).

The American community that ultimately faced the Japanese would include not only entrepreneurs in sugar and cattle, mining and textiles, missionaries and teachers, and doctors and nurses but also groups of retired teachers, discharged soldiers (especially from the Spanish-American War and Philippine "Insurrections") who had chosen to stay in the Philippines, as well as junior executives of large American corporations and their families, along with "native" Philippine-born Americans whose parents had settled there years earlier (Onorato, ix).

Americans were local, social, and financial leaders of the community on all islands, but nowhere more clearly than in Manila, on the island of Luzon. Being an American in the Far East conveyed a host of privileges, some of which young Americans such as Chet and Frieda Magnuson were not quite ready to absorb with a clear head. An American working woman prior to her marriage, Frieda had managed, despite the Great Depression in the United States, to land a job as a secretary for Victory Washing Machine Company, and then later, one in the same capacity at Connell Brothers, a major exporting firm with Manila offices. There she met and later married Chet, and they were assigned to the Manila office where Chet was an executive. The "ordinary" social whirl proved a bit rich for their blood, as Frieda relates:

> Earl Anderson was the Manila Connell manager. He and his wife, Kay, and their friends entertained us lavishly and introduced us to the Polo Club, the Army and Navy Club, the historic Manila Hotel, and the practice of signing "chits." Long before plastic credit cards, transactions were handled by merely signing the chit. Any foreigner had instant credit and only a few abused the privilege. We sublet a house complete with cook, houseboy, lavandera and gardener. . . . The house was on about two acres of beautiful lawn and gardens with huge mango trees. (Magnuson, 29)

The young Magnusons discovered that their $185 a month salary was comfortable but did not cover quite such high living; they abandoned chits and moved into a much smaller house — one actually located in the garden of their first house (Magnuson, 30).

H. A. Burgers, another former resident of this American paradise, describes a typical evening at Luneta Park on Manila Bay, the notes of a band concert hanging in the air above the park and a cooling breeze coming in across the bay: "Twilight fades rapidly in the Tropics, and by the time the last strains of the national anthem floated over the bared heads of the crowd standing at attention, the clear sky would fill with brilliant stars. The Southern Cross would be plainly visible" (31).

For many Americans, then, daily life was frequently leisurely and pleasing. The schedule Stanley Karnow offers for the average male American Manileño, based on the model given by both the British and Americans in the early part of the century, appears largely unchanged even in memoirs and retrospectives of later periods, though increasingly less British as time passed. The Americans rose early and went to their offices in the morning, had lunch, and afterward took a siesta during the heat of the day. After siesta, men returned to work briefly, quitting at 4:00 or 5:00 P.M. A mixed social crowd of such men, their wives, friends, and acquaintances would probably go then to one of the clubs in town, especially the Polo Club or the Army and Navy Club. After drinks at the club (usually at sunset), the Americans would go to dinner at someone's house and then amuse themselves with bridge, opera, movies, theater, or a cabaret. Following these entertainments, favorite places, including Tom Prichard's "Dixie Kitchen," open night and day and home of the best southern-style American dishes, might host the après-play or concert goers (Karnow, 211; Gleeck, 233–234).

Another future internee, Martha Hill, Alva Hill's wife, also describes the leisurely, bucolic, and richly beautiful life of a colonial middle-class American in the prewar Philippines. Such a life of comfort and ease was not restricted to life in the big city or the island of Luzon. Prior to living in Manila, the Hills had lived for a long time in Iloilo on Panay. Martha Hill describes the tranquil tenor of life there with their two sons in a poem, "Iloilo Garden," commemorating an Edenic existence. She speaks of her

> Green-gold garden
> Shut in by a glowing wall
> Of wine-plumed bougainvillea
> And gay hibiscus tall

The garden yields a peaceful and richly abundant splendor with "sun-flecked paths" and "great, cool trees" and "lawns gold-washed with light" (Martha Hill, 5). Other poems speak of watching her sons, browned and healthy, swimming in rock pools and sliding down rock slide falls. This was the graceful life of country gentry or what passed for that class on the islands. As Alva Hill describes it, life for middle-class American couples on most of the islands was primarily characterized by elaborate social gatherings:

> Dinner parties are a favorite indoor sport, with cocktail parties a close second. The women invariably wear long dresses, and the men, white jackets. Bridge, poker, and mahjong parties are also popular. Ladies' afternoon bridge usually begins with an elaborate tea at 4:00 P.M., and continues until 7:00 P.M. Many of the men go to their clubs for tennis, or handball, or swimming after office hours. In many homes dinner is not served before 8:00. (Alva Hill, 126)

Baguio, in northern Luzon at the 4,291-foot level and nearly 200 miles from Manila, was not only a wonderful place to escape the draining summer heat but a truly American town — one built early in the century, according to Karnow, to *be* an American town. In keeping with the generalized American model for "summer houses" back in the United States, Baguio offered a series of large gabled houses whose huge front lawns "might have been [part of] a resort in the Berkshires or upstate New York" (Karnow, 215).

Chartered in 1909 and designed by the famous architect and city planner William Cameron Forbes and his uncle Malcolm, Baguio had originally been intended to serve as the government's "summer capital." This concept was soon crushed, however, by the Filipino legislature in 1913, which refused to consider a site so far from Manila and so extravagant as any kind of capital and cut off support (Halsema, "E. J.," 166; 169). Stripped of its quasi-official function, Baguio still remained for Manileños and guests the fashionable place to go — enough so that there was even a minor social "season" during April and May. Teachers, civil servants and their families, invalids (especially with tuberculosis), and occasional government officials and their families enjoyed this small town's climate and amenities (Halsema, "E. J.," 172–174).

Baguio sported a number of amusements for its residents and their Filipino associates. Saturday night formal dances and Sunday "lunches" vied with golf at the country club — and in Baguio, unlike in Manila, wealthy Filipinos were club members as early as 1910 (Karnow, 215).

The town itself boasted more amenities than did many small towns in America at the same time. Due in many cases to the creative and unrelenting efforts of Baguio's long-time mayor and city engineer, E. J. Halsema, Baguio featured sturdy, well-designed paved roads, running water from a gravity-fed reservoir, sewage disposal, cheap electricity, street lighting, a wide public market square, an ice plant (and hence refrigeration), a public school open to both American and Filipino children, telegraph service and mail delivery, and by the beginning of the war, telephone service and a small airfield (Halsema, "E. J.," 179–185; 201–202).

In both Baguio and Manila middle-class American wives had a leisured routine of dinner dances, bridge games, and elaborate children's birthday parties. The more usual slings and arrows of ordinary life—pregnancies, unwelcome visitors, meal planning, child-rearing, volunteer work with the Red Cross, and boorish dinner guests—also punctuated the year. With a staff consisting usually of at least a houseboy and a cook to keep meals prepared, the floors waxed, the airy houses cleaned, and the mess under control, with Filipina nannies to look after and amuse the very youngest children, and with the older children often boarding at a school such as Brent in Baguio, many of these American women had time to fill as they chose, often recreationally. Tennis, swimming, and boating are mentioned in several diaries, as is shopping in downtown Manila. This leisurely life spelled trouble to some men, as Margaret Sams records amusingly about her husband-to-be's Uncle Pat, a Philippine old-timer who believed: "The Philippine Islands were no place for a white woman. . . . They all took to bridge tables, drink and amahs" (Sams, 32).

Natalie Crouter is an excellent example of the life led by an ordinary American woman. A former Bostonian, she was the wife of a Shell station lessee who eventually hired a manager so he could run his highly profitable insurance business in Baguio. Natalie Crouter's household staff consisted of Ishmael and Nida Bacani, the Filipino cook and amah, respectively, who did all the domestic work and cooking, as well as the laundry and gardening. The Crouter children "like other American children in Baguio attended the Episcopalian-run Brent school" and were therefore not underfoot. Natalie, in Bloom's words, had a "busy social life" and enjoyed activities as varied as bridge, mahjong, little theater, and parties, as well as spending time preparing the socially obligatory Red Cross parcels of old clothes, baby garments, and towels—many of which Nida Bacani helped sew and hem (Bloom, "Introduction," xvii; xv).

Many Baguio and Manila resident Americans were not originally reared in wealth. As Alva Hill explains, many of the Americans suddenly sporting houseboys, cooks, and lavanderas "[were] often people who never had hired-help at home, and perhaps did their own washing, ate in the kitchen, and never heard of a *siesta* or a canape" (Alva Hill, 122).

Margaret Sams, like Frieda Magnuson and Grace Nash, is an example of this. Sams grew up in the small California town of Beaumont and worked to put herself through two years of college at Riverside Junior College before the war (Sams, 25; 29–30); she, like Bessie Sneed, came to the Philippines because of her husband Bob Sherk's job in mining — Sherk was a mine-shifter in a gold mine in Suyoc, northern Luzon (Sams, 32; 39–40).

Nor was Grace Nash wealthy, though she served on occasion as assistant concertmistress for the Manila Symphony or as a featured soloist. Grace Nash grew up on a small farm in Ohio, with a father who ran an insurance office and a mother who raised four children on a farm. Nash herself graduated from a small college with a B.A. in music and taught music in the Cleveland public schools briefly. Then she began studying for (and received) an M.A. in violin and composition at Chicago Musical College while putting herself through graduate school partly by scholarship and by working as a strolling violinist in the Chicago Bar and Grille (Nash, 1–3). She came to the Philippines to be married. Her husband, Ralph, worked as an engineer for a company with a large branch office in Manila (Nash, 6; 9).

None of the three women had lived a life characterized by servants before coming to the Phillipines, though Magnuson, Sams, and Nash were generally well educated (each had some college or a degree) and reared as members of the middle class. These women, as were hundreds of other Americans in the Philippines, were only temporarily "leisured" due to a geographical accident. Most of them knew how to cook and had done their own housework at some point in their lives, and all had been working women for a time. They also could perform such mundane activities as sewing, childcare, and cleaning — and indeed did not find it demeaning to do so. This background and the flexibility to switch back to a more laborious life are among the main reasons Lynn Bloom believes the women — and men too — survived life in internment. As Bloom points out, this adaptability and the American "do-it-yourself" pioneer spirit helped determine the Americans' response to harsh conditions and their ability to survive those conditions (Bloom, "Death," 77).

It would be too easy to see what happened to these "comfortable" Americans as a kind of morality play judgment on those with too many of life's resources suddenly forced to cope with life the way the "other half" lived — especially their servants. Some critics, especially those writing about the British internments following the fall of Singapore, have in fact struck this note about the British colonials. The American colonial situation was even more complex than that of the British, however, and harder to symbolize or judge.

Despite the earlier insurrection at the turn of the century and the Philippine Scout Mutiny in the 1920s, relations between the Philippines and the United States remained relatively harmonious, especially after the Tydings-McDuffie Bill formalized the Philippines Commonwealth status in 1934 (Petillo, 167–168). Because of a general uneasiness with imperialism, Americans in the Philippines tended to be less overtly racist than the British or the Dutch. For example, though clubs in Manila, such as the Elks, the Army-Navy Club, the Manila Club and golf course, as well as the Polo Club "were largely or entirely segregated," other clubs were not so restricted. Among the more liberal clubs were the Wack Wack Country Club in Mandaluyong, the Masons (established in 1898; both Filipino and American lodges combined in 1917), the Rotary Club, and all the women's charitable organizations. Some, like the Wack Wack Country Club, were established to provide "a specific expression of anti-segregationist sentiment" and to serve as "a pre-war symbol of Filipino-American socializing" (Karnow, 72–73; 239–240). Even the Polo Club dropped its overt color barrier in 1936 when it admitted President Manuel Quezon to honorary membership (213).

The Manila Rotary Club, with its approximately 200 members, is a strong example of the kind of clubs in Manila and elsewhere that continue to have open — and cosmopolitan — membership. H. A. Burgers, a former member, remembers that

> No other club in the city even remotely resembled Rotary membership. Perhaps half the members were Filipinos, leaders of their people in the professional and business world. The remaining were Americans, Spaniards, Englishmen, Scots, Chinese, Japanese, Germans, Frenchmen, Indians, and many other nationalities. Behind the President's table was a stand containing the flags of countries represented in the Club. I once counted 15 there. (32)

Alva Hill, both a Rotarian and a Mason, concurs with Burgers, explaining that as late as 1941, even Japanese members continued to be admitted to the Rotary (Alva Hill, 241).

In Baguio some institutions were integrated but not all. Brent School, for example, restricted its membership to Caucasians — excluding even mestizos (Karnow, 215); thanks to Mayor E. J. Halsema, however, an unrestricted public elementary school (Baguio Central School) was built in 1923. He also supported the city's decision in 1926 not only to subsidize but also to hire four more teachers to improve the faltering Mountain Province High School (Halsema, "E. J.," 202).

On the island of Negros, however, Filipino and American social groups had limited but integrated contact. Vaughan explains, "At frequent intervals afternoon teas brought together white and Filipino women who played mahjong and enjoyed refreshments without self-consciousness. Filipino and American women exchanged courtesy calls, but the intimacy stopped there" (Vaughan, "Community," 16). Vaughan also points out that Filipino men, along with American men and some British, played golf together at the integrated Bacolod

eventually and naturally waltzed into an easy collaboration with the Japanese, because their cooperation would, it seemed, continue to maintain this elite's powerful status—one that literally fostered corruption (Pomeroy, 117; Karnow, 13; 20–22). This in turn led to a certain well-placed cynicism on the part of both reformers and agitators about the "democratic" experiment, though Karnow strikes perhaps the proper note: "Ultimately, the American experiment in the Philippines was neither as brilliant as their publicists claimed nor as bleak as their critics contended. They never quite fulfilled their hope of transforming the Filipinos into facsimile Americans. But in contrast to the Europeans, they were uniquely benign, almost sentimental imperialists" (Karnow, 13).

Glenn May concurs to some extent. In his highly critical discussion of Philippine "nationalist" history as practiced in the past and currently by Renato Constantino, May rejects the automatic standard vilification of U.S. policy in the Philippines. Although he does not suggest a blindly favorable review of colonial policy, he deplores the Constantino strategy of denouncing anything colonial, whether Spanish or American, without regard to the effects of more complex economic, political, and especially social issues (May, 20–21). He explains both his own and Karnow's point again in a 1990 review of the latter's book; May praises Karnow's interpretative skill and his scholarship, noting the book caught the essence of the American attempt to recast the Philippines into mock-American form, as well as that attempt's sometimes laudable aims but disappointing results (May, "Review," 326)

Ultimately, perhaps, at least the attempt to transition some Filipinos into self-rule—this earnest effort, as McKinley said, to "do what we could" for the Filipinos in the form of engineering projects, health, education, and representative government, as well as trying to provide a more liberal racial atmosphere—was partly responsible for later Filipino attitudes toward captured Americans. Filipino guerrillas, spies, ex-servants, and ordinary citizens smuggled the prisoners food, medicine, possessions, and hard currency, though Pomeroy suggests that this was simply a function of Filipino anti-Fascism, not pro-Americanism (124).

Pomeroy cites the PKP *Partido Komunista ng Pilipinas* and the "12 point memo" they sent December 8, 1941, to President Quezon and U.S. High Commissioner Francis B. Sayre as support for this contention. In the memo the PKP called for "all-out support to national unity around an Anti-Japanese United front" and urged "all people and all strata of the population" to "organize, secretly if necessary, to assist the Philippine and American government to resist Japan." Pomeroy thereby tries to account for the obviously sympathetic attitudes of all social classes of Filipinos toward Americans by suggesting the former are merely responding to an indigenous call to arms ironically made by the communists, rather than by the *ilustrados* (Pomeroy, 124).

However the paternalistic and exploitative relations may have seemed to Marxist historians and modern eyes, it is obvious that the majority of Filipinos did not regard the American presence in that light, or the kind of spontaneous (and dangerous) help offered to prisoners would never have existed. Filipino civilians were frequently beaten or even shot for throwing food to American as well as Filipino prisoners, for example, during the notorious Bataan Death March; Filipinos were cuffed, kicked, and sometimes arrested for bringing food to slip through the gates illegally at Santo Tomás. Such acts of bravery and self-sacrifice suggest a much more complex relationship between servants and their former employers, locals, and colonials than many revisionist historians (Constantino and Pomeroy especially) have suggested, especially in light of possible *compadre* complications of feeling.

Confirmation of the generally strong regard throughout the war between American and Philippine citizens comes from an even more unlikely source. Tetsuro Ogawa, a civilian Japanese teacher attached during the war to the Imperial Japanese Army in the Philippines in northern Luzon, points out in his memoirs that, unlike the Burmese and Indonesians, the Filipinos "had been satisfied with American democracy and the civilization which huge American capital had introduced." He also points out, with some pain, that the Japanese, unlike the Spanish, who brought religion, or the Americans, who brought education, brought nothing and "the newcomer [the Japanese] . . . was all for taking what little the people had or could produce" (Ogawa, 32).

The previously mentioned American educational effort in the islands seems to be the most prominent reason given repeatedly for the relatively more successful American colonial experience in the Philippines. With both lay teachers and religious teachers arriving almost daily for the two decades before the war, the most remote villages had resonated to the ABCs chanted aloud and had seen arithmetic problems drawn and solved in the dust, if no blackboards presented themselves. As Bloom points out, the general friendliness of the population toward American residents was certainly buoyed by the continuing establishment of a variety of schools—from primary through university level. Various American organizations founded many colleges, including the University of the Philippines (Bloom, "Introduction," xv–xvi). Such groups also established the Central Philippine University, a Baptist college on Panay, Silliman University, and a Presbyterian college on Negros, among others (Alva Hill, 207).

Schooling for Filipino children—especially higher education—was a favorite charitable project for Americans who had lived in the islands for many years, according to both Hill and Esther Hamilton. Residents of the Philippines for thirty or forty years, men such as Mike Ryan and Col. Von Schaick regularly paid the private school expenses of a variety of Philippine children. Hill notes, "The sincerity and cordiality of such 'old-timers' are so genuine that there is little wonder that so many Filipinos took their *bolos* to the hills and became fighting guerrillas to help win World War II" (Alva Hill, 281).

But schools were not the only visible improvement Americans attempted to bring with them to the Philippines. Anthony Arthur explains that

> Benefits that the United States had conferred . . . were also considerable. Except for those remote areas in the South where only Stone Age tribes and head-hunters lived, public health officers had cleansed the islands of typhoid and cholera. Teams of civil engineers had built commercial docks, railroads, highways, and sewer systems. . . . A middle class of Filipino managers who would eventually run the country had been created [also] as a deliberate matter of United States policy. (Arthur, 11)

The growing racial tensions existed not between the majority of Philippine citizens and Americans so much as between both of those groups and the Japanese present on the islands. Immediately after the December 8, 1941 (Philippines time), bombing, American and Philippine authorities placed all Japanese inhabitants on those islands with sizable Japanese populations in internment camps (Halsema, "Oral," 18, n5).[1] The Japanese on Luzon were placed in the Philippine Scouts' barracks in Baguio or on the outskirts of Manila. On Cebu 250 Japanese internees spent almost two weeks in the provincial jail in Cebu City and then were re-interned in a school three kilometers away (Corbett, 50–52). On Mindanao at Davao, Japanese internees were placed in what Frank Cary, an American living in town and soon to be interned himself, called "improvised concentration camps" (2).

In the latter case, treatment was atrocious—but this apparently was primarily the fault of the Philippine Constabulary in charge of the Davao internees. After two Japanese air raids the Filipino policemen fired on the internment camp point-blank, killing five internees. The first day of the actual invasion of the island, Filipino guards stabbed another five. In all cases the worst incidents with the Japanese interned in the Philippines were perpetrated by the local constabulary (Corbett, 52). Ultimately, American internees would be interned at Camp John Hay in the same cells in which they had previously locked up local civilian Japanese. Natalie Crouter confirms this when she mentions that one of the first invasion sounds she and her husband heard in Baguio was the roar of "Banzai!" as Japanese soldiers released their interned fellow nationals on December 27, 1941 (Hamilton, 37; Crouter, 11).

Others, including Alva Hill, discuss the general distrust of the Japanese as spies even earlier than the Baguio internment. Hill explains that "for many years prior to our internment, the intention of the Japanese eventually to seize the Philippines was obvious . . . practically every inlet and gulf, every seashore, every mountain and mine, every forest and natural resource" was explored and reported to the "Japanese warlords" back in Japan (Alva Hill, 296).

Hill cites a specific suspicious incident that confirmed to him this silent conspiracy on the part of the Japanese government. Hill was requested as a lawyer by a local timber owner, Mrs. McQuaid, who wanted her timber contract with Sisi Matsui, a Japanese businessman, enforced. After some verbal jousting, Matsui agreed to advance the funds to pay for the government's accumulated internal revenue forest charges and all other charges for past labor (as he had agreed to earlier) but only on the condition that he be permitted to keep one Japanese national at the sawmill. Matsui, however, ultimately refused to advance the necessary money and sent "several" Japanese nationals to the woods after he signed the contract. Hill eventually made a trip to Matsui's office to try to get him to comply with the agreement. Whether he did or not, Hill's narrative highlights the suspicious activity in which Hill found Matsui engaged: "I noticed him working over a large roll of coast and geodetic maps which at the time were for sale to anyone wishing to buy them. When I entered the room, he called me to the table where the maps were spread out, and urged me to show the locations of various manganese mines of my clients [a key ingredient in armaments]. I did not give him the correct information" (Alva Hill, 291–292).

The American guerrilla leader Iliff David Richardson told war correspondent Ira Wolfert that it was very likely that such fears as Hill's were justified. According to Richardson, the Japanese who served as clerks and minor functionaries at many large offices and plants were often fifth columnists of a sort once the war started. Whether this was planned by Tokyo, Richardson doesn't speculate. He does mention that several Japanese officers he encountered, such as Captain Gidoka, were formerly employees of American companies; he also discusses what he calls their "pathological hatred" for whites in general and Americans in particular (Wolfert, 94). Other scholars such as Gavin Daws would support his notion, pointing out the racism of the Japanese toward all other races (179).

The flamboyant Carlos Romulo, however, is more specific in his accusations about spies. He discusses "massive Japanese espionage activity" in the Philippines prior to the war and cites bars around military bases as prime hangouts for picking up useful information from relaxed and intoxicated American soldiers. He also claims that many of the finest propagandists in the Far East and especially in the Philippines either were, or traveled as, Buddhist monks.

He discusses as well growing patterns of huts being built immediately outside the gates of American military bases and communications stations that served quick food and drink; a brewery, he claims, actually concealed a radio station that ultimately guided in Japanese war planes (Romulo, 20; 34–35).

Was a huge, almost invisible network of potential Japanese fifth columnists in place throughout the Philippines? Certainly, there was a strong Japanese presence on all the major islands just before December 8, especially around Davao, which had the largest immigrant Japanese population. Despite this — and Romulo's fears — given the ferocity of Philippine resistance to Japanese control during the war, this placement of hostile nationals was perhaps less substantial or their position less influential than both Wolfert and Romulo suggest, though ordinary professional people such as Hill and Romulo considered seriously the possibility that the Japanese were mapping out and spying on the Philippines for a possible invasion.

Before the war Americans in the Philippines seemed of two minds about any Japanese threat, however. One of the many internee complaints against the government after the war was the seeming lack of official interest or warning prior to December 8, 1941, even when civilians asked officials point-blank whether there was any danger. Official agencies (such as the high commissioner's office) and military authorities (including MacArthur's staff) appeared to ignore the immediate possibility of an invasion or hostile Japanese action of any kind. When concerned citizens (such as the newly formed American Coordinating Committee) tried to voice their suspicions and worries about a possible Japanese invasion, their fears were brushed off and their worries dismissed. For example, Hill and his friends were suspicious about sales of Philippine ore to Japanese clients. Hill contacted military authorities on behalf of his clients "to ascertain whether or not sales of manganese, copper, and iron ore should be made to the Japanese." His worries were dismissed somewhat scornfully, and he was told repeatedly that the United States was at peace with Japan — certainly the sales should be finalized (Alva Hill, 292).

Carlos Romulo's discussion of the officials' — and Douglas MacArthur's — perceptions of a coming war seems remarkably inconsistent, even given the wartime publication date of (and censored sentences in) Romulo's book. Indeed, in his use of telling detail, Romulo seems to be covertly criticizing both MacArthur and the U.S. government. For example, Romulo insists that two months prior to December 8, it was "evident" that the United States intended to "show a firm hand to Japan" by appointing MacArthur as commander in chief of the U.S. Armed Forces in the Far East. He also speaks indirectly of the "evacuation of American women" from the Philippines (by which he seems to mean the military dependents, given the hundreds of civilian women that were interned) and of an "arms embargo and the cessation of the sale of oil to Japan" (Romulo, 2–3). How curious, yet damning, it is for him to note two weeks prior to Pearl Harbor that no camouflage preparations had been taken in Manila, unlike extensive ones in Batavia, even though MacArthur believed a war was coming; vividly, Romulo gives a view from the air of a vulnerable Manila: "Our churches, our legislative building, our post office, our new city hall stood out like targets in the city below" (Romulo, 27). He goes on to mourn the fact that "only a few anti-aircraft guns" were deployed around the city—and those had been put up solely at the personal order of Colonel William Marquet (Romulo, 68). In his book, Romulo lauds the foresight and acuity of Douglas MacArthur repeatedly but then continues to slip in details that suggest a very different assessment. Despite his plaudits to MacArthur's resolution, for example, Romulo elegizes the so-called "Pearl of the Orient," Manila, left "unprotected and unprepared" on December 9, 1941, waiting later for wave after wave of enemy planes to bomb it beyond recognition (Romulo, 30). One wonders why Manila was so unprepared and why better military defensive measures hadn't been taken. Romulo's book seems intended to raise such questions, just as it helps explain, perhaps, at least one reason why so many American women and children were still in the Philippines when the war broke out. If even a "field marshal" and commander in chief, paid, as Lawrence Taylor reports, the highest professional soldier's salary in the world at the time ($33,000 per annum) for "his services as a military advisor" to the Philippine government (Taylor, 21–22), can misjudge a situation, how much more likely are ordinary men and women to do so?

Claire Phillips, for example, returned to Manila from the United States with her infant daughter in September 1941 to stay, even though American authorities were urging American military wives and children to leave only a month after her arrival (Corbett, 15). Though the American high commissioner and the State Department both made provisions for military dependents, according to Corbett, as far as American civilian women and children were concerned, the authorities "kept [their] warnings low key so as not to give the Japanese government reason to believe that the United States was clearing the decks for war" (16). Other factions at the State Department also wanted the civilians to remain to prevent the Philippine government from regarding a mass civilian evacuation as both a betrayal by the United States and a negative statement about the army's ability to protect the populace, as well as to avoid lowering morale (Keats, 12; Corbett, 10–20).

Another problem, which indirectly affected the civilian dependents, resulted from a bureaucratic power struggle going on inside the State Department itself. The "Special Division" had been set up in September 1939 specifically "to deal with the problems of Americans abroad in troubled areas," including attempting to formulate specific procedures and policies to help them if they were stranded in a foreign country when war broke out (Corbett, 9–10). Two obstacles to removing American civilians from the Philippines immediately presented themselves: First, the competing Far East Division of the State Department was opposed to the early warning and removal of American civilians; and second, Breckenridge Long of the State Department's Special Division had an obsession with thriftiness in regard to his department's expenditures.

The Far East Division showed its muscle early on in the squabble with the Special Division by blocking the latter's attempts to warn civilians to relocate as soon as possible. In fact, thanks to the Far East Division, what few warnings the State Department sent out for Americans to leave even Japan itself in February 1941 were "quieted down" and made into mere "advice." Other Americans in Asia during the spring of 1941 received only "suggestions" and "advice" as well. Americans in both Singapore and Batavia, as well as those in the Philippines, were not urged to leave, because, again, the move might be awkward from a public relations perspective and the presence of many American civilians "had a calming effect" on the local people (Corbett, 14–19). The Far East Division triumphantly trumped the Special Division's plans repeatedly with the result that High Commissioner Francis B. Sayre found it necessary to play down and even deny the danger when Americans directly questioned him about the wisdom of leaving the islands (Bloom, "Introduction," xvii).

Their worries about "appearances," however, were somewhat inconsistent, especially regarding the missionaries. In early fall of 1941 the State Department did approach "several religious denominations and [asked] them to furlough their missionaries back home or at least encourage them to send families back" (Corbett, 20). The State Department never made clear why it chose to warn the clergy and not the others. Indeed, at least according to one missionary, Mary Ogle, she received no warning from anyone; instead, she was told to relocate in Baguio, because "it would be the safest place in the whole Far East"—and the U.S. Army gave her this advice, not any member of the State Department, nor did Seventh Day Adventist officials call her back to the United States (128). Given the number of missionaries in the Philippines whom the Japanese eventually interned, the warning either didn't reach its intended religious audience or the people chose not to listen to it.

Long's stinginess with the State Department (and especially his division's) money was another reason many civilians may have been unable to leave. He flatly refused (generally speaking) to pay the passage back for those who were stranded without funds. As he explained, "it was not the State Department's responsibility to bail out stranded Americans financially"; rather, these unfortunates would *only* be loaned money *if* they could prove that family, friends, and employers in the United States "refused" to loan them the passage money; furthermore, this refusal had to be filed in writing with the Special Division through official channels so that the Special Division could "verify" the need for the loan (Corbett, 12). Corbett explains that this "cumbersome process would later handcuff efforts to extricate Americans from Asia" during the war itself (12). Elizabeth Vaughan claims that this practice *did* continue even after the war, noting that she was forced by the U.S. government to pay for her own and her two children's passage back from internment to the continental United States (March 10, 1945, 303).

The way in which the American civilians in the Philippines viewed the reality of a Japanese threat was another part of the reason, it seems, that the civilians were not overtly alarmed.

Phillips, as did many others, saw that corporate wives and children were staying, as were government officials' wives, and decided that the talk of war with Japan was "newspaper talk." All appearances to the contrary were mere "bluff," because the Japanese had more sense than to consider going to war with the mighty U.S. military (Phillips, 1–2).

Frieda Magnuson records much the same evaluation of the situation. Though originally scheduled to take her daughter and depart on the *President Hoover* in April 1941 (leaving her husband, Chet, behind), Frieda canceled the trip, pointing out that the High Commissioner's staff was staying, as were wives from Standard Oil, Chartered City Bank, and other companies. Besides, she records, "The Japanese wouldn't *dare* attack U.S. territory!" (Magnuson, 32–33).

A gold miner in northern Luzon, William Moule, concurs generally. Asking an American Army Air Corps officer about the "threat" of the Japanese, Moule reports that the officer jauntily dismissed such fears: "Well, confidentially . . . we have twenty-seven bombers and PBYs and personally I believe it's more than we need. The Japs have no first-class planes and no pilots" (Moule, 38). Another officer was equally vehement and told Moule that the Japanese army had "nothing" and he'd seen them in China. "They can't fight. They're crazy," he said (38).

Small wonder then that common speculation prior to the war generally regarded the threat of Japanese bombing as highly unlikely. Thanks to common earlier knowledge of the *initial* problems lining up targets that the Japanese experienced in Chunking because of defective bombing sights, Romulo notes, "We all agreed that the Japanese aviators were poor marksmen," and discounted their aggressive abilities because of this supposed technological impairment, when placed in conflict with a "modern" Western nation.

After all he'd heard, Moule himself ceased being particularly worried about the Japanese:

> I firmly believed Japan wouldn't, couldn't and dared not ever go to war with such a country as the U.S.A. So help me, when the news came, I actually felt sorry for Japan — a small nation, her air force falling apart in the sky, her navy being run down and sunk, those Japanese soldiers fighting with obsolete guns and swords, about to be slaughtered without a chance. I thought if the U.S. wanted to be chivalrous, she could put just an equal amount of men and material against Japan and make it more of a fight. (38)

His pity for the Japanese is particularly ironic, because these were the same "ineffective" Japanese who interned him as early as December 1941 and later quite efficiently tortured him. For those at Pearl Harbor earlier and at Cavite, Nichols Field, and Davao later, the soothing stereotype of a myopic Japanese pilot with buckteeth and Coke-bottle glasses, staring hopelessly down un-aligned bombsights, proved blisteringly false.

All of these reasons — the State Department squabbles, the duplicity of U.S. officials, the lack of resources to leave, misjudgment of the Japanese threat, and the desire to stay with family — became intertwined in most civilian decisions. Grace Nash's case is something of an exemplar for the others, though she was clearly more aware than other civilians that the Japanese posed a threat. Similar to Frieda Magnuson, who refused to leave on the *President Hoover,* Nash also didn't want to leave her husband alone to face whatever tragedy might occur — and her husband, too, refused to leave his work. Nash records her struggle with her apprehensions; unlike her friends, she believed that Japan might very well attack, and there was a good chance it would survive the effort. She did not fit well with her more optimistic and jingoistic comrades who didn't want to admit to such a possibility:

> I was in the minority; almost an outcast in the conversations. I had a gut feeling, without any facts, figures, geographical knowledge to back it up. I just felt that war was coming; that the islands were defenseless. Like most Americans in business in Manila, Ralph's company was doing very well. He was involved with new engineering projects for the government. This was not the time to pick up and leave, he said. (Nash, 15)

Grace couldn't bear to leave him alone and take the boys back to the United States. She is remarkably honest about her reasons, noting that she refused to face the "truth" that "Ralph was more married to his work and his company than to me!" and that, despite the dangerous times, he seemed more dedicated to his career advancement than to his family's safety. Also, she notes, she felt guilty "over the thought of leaving him to face destruction and even death without us. I couldn't bring myself to leave" (Nash, 15–16). After all, no one else seemed concerned, especially neither officialdom nor the military. As a navy captain told her at a cocktail party on the evening of December 5 (three days, Philippines time, before the raid on Pearl Harbor), the Japanese would never bomb an American installation: "Why we could finish off their navy over the weekend!" he blustered (Nash, 16).

And why should Phillips, Magnuson, Moule, and Nash have believed otherwise really? Certainly, the handful of women and children urged to leave earlier were a highly selected group; civilians observing military wives leaving may well have not taken alarm because they were used to them being transferred and moved regularly. The military, after all, had its own logic, its own rules that civilians never understood. Additionally, Douglas MacArthur had regularly written pieces for both prominent publications and radio broadcast that were distinctly upbeat about how small a threat war would be to the Philippines. In the late 1930s, for example, he wrote a strong article for the *Christian Science Monitor* explaining how easily and successfully the islands themselves could be defended. After all, the job for which MacArthur was hired in 1935 was as military adviser to the Commonwealth government, one who would help establish a Philippine National Defense and train an army (Taylor, 17–19; Falk, 2–3). As of July 26, 1941, the Philippine army, such as it was (more name than substance), was "inducted into" the U.S. Army by presidential order, raising the number of troops officially to 100,000 (Schaller, 48). The majority of these troops were raw and barely trained, as well as generally illiterate; many did not even speak a common language. Further, they were armed (if at all) with mostly obsolete weapons. Despite this, MacArthur "expressed only confidence in his command." Falk adds, "Although most of the Philippine Army was barely capable of minimal operations, let alone defeating a seasoned foe, his [MacArthur's] reports to Washington spoke only of progress and increasing strength" (3).

And so the public—or large sections of it—watched the high commissioner's office and its personnel in the calm belief that nothing seriously could imperil the Philippines. Even after the news of Pearl Harbor and the bombing of Baguio itself, Romulo notes that MacArthur tried to continue this public confidence by issuing optimistic communiqués such as his first one, directly after the Baguio bombing on December 27, 1941: "The military is on the alert and every possible defensive measure is being taken. My message is one of serenity and confidence" (Romulo, 38). That the Japanese Imperial Army would be marching into Manila less than a week following this piece of august nonsense was something his "confidence" and "serenity" obviously hadn't foreseen. An egocentric MacArthur would issue 142 communiqués for radio broadcast between December and March 1942 — the last ones from Australia. As Daws points out, this is more than one a day, and of that number, "in 109 [of 142] the only man in uniform identified by name was MacArthur" (66).

Most civilians were fortunate — or unfortunate — enough not to know the extent of the bombing's devastation of the U.S. Pacific Fleet. Alice Morton Hill, however, had a husband who was a reserve officer in Naval Intelligence. In a phone interview she recalled vividly that her husband, Harry, had come home grimly from the office and told her that "everything" had been lost at Pearl Harbor. He also informed her that the war was going to be very long and that eighty Japanese transport vessels were currently riding at anchor off Luzon. As he threw together a package of clothes and ammunition, he told her that the two of them would probably not see each other for a long time. She listened, she said, crying silently and cutting up a navy blue party dress to make shields to cover and help black out his car headlights. Harry was right. After she waved to him driving away, she never saw him again. After holding out on Bataan and making the Death March, he died in Cabanatuan Prison Camp, leaving Alice a widow with a small child in Santo Tomás Internment Camp (Alice Morton Hill, interview). As Alice Hill explained to me with great sadness, she and others believed prior to the war that, if one came, it would not touch them but would be "somewhere else": "We believe these [great] navies were going to do their fighting out there in the ocean somewhere" (interview).

After all, the Philippine Islands themselves supposedly were, in the words of MacArthur, "eminently defensible," and there was a commander in chief in charge of the islands' defenses who had, according to both the president and army authorities, "demonstrated brilliance in strategic planning" (Taylor, 22).

That in his brilliance MacArthur did not agree with the rest of the War Department about the meaning of a modified "Rainbow-5" plan was not well known. Earlier, the War Department (along with the State Department) had gingerly allowed MacArthur's interpretation to pass through and even seemed to approve it. As Cook points out, what were they going to do? They could not remove him — though obviously they should have, given his high-handedness with accepted strategic planning and military preparedness in the Philippines. MacArthur was a publicist's nightmare, given his extraordinarily positive relations with the American press gained early on from his appointment in 1912 as military assistant to the Bureau of Information. This appointment provided the basis for the press contacts he would use for the rest of his life (Petillo, 115–116). Such a man could have easily become a potential political blackmailer. He was in a position publicly to embarrass the U.S. government over Rainbow-5's dismissal of, even expectation of, the loss of the Philippines — that is, in the *unaltered* Rainbow-5 plan. He could have easily called a press conference and pointed out to both the Filipinos and the American people that the government was deliberately deceiving them about its intentions toward the Philippines, that even what reinforcements arrived were "a sham." The result would have been a public uproar and pressure to switch the objectives, materiel, and strength (too early, in the government's eyes) to the Pacific rather than to increase the aid to Britain. Additionally, such an announcement would have caused a loss of respect and tested the loyalty of the Philippine people whom, for moral and strategic reasons, the government needed to retain to maintain a strong holding action against the Japanese until Americans could reorganize (Cook, 72).

Therefore, MacArthur was neither restrained in his strategic plans nor removed from command, thereby inadvertently underlining his firm belief that "even an institution as all powerful as the Army might bend to his will" (Petillo, 80). Apparently, the War Department and the Department of State hoped that, when war came, the "impossibility of pursuing [his] grandiose scheme would become universally evident. The retreat into Bataan [a standard part of Rainbow-5, we remember] would appear, however, not as having been planned but as having been dictated by the fortunes of war" (Cook, 71). MacArthur's maladroit planning and his failure to cache medical stores, equipment, weapons, and food all the way down the Bataan peninsula as stipulated in both the last War Plan Orange and the unrevised Rainbow-5 more than adequately proves how resistant he would have been to the idea of the "impossibility" of his schemes.

According to some military historians, the defeat in the Philippines was the "greatest in the history of American foreign wars," and the swiftest to boot (Long, 226). More than anything else, it showed how much the "defense" of the Philippines (in *any* version) was a terrible sham. Civilians left in the Philippines would realize this fact forcefully and personally during the next three to four years of internment.

2

First Dark Days

With the bombing of Pearl Harbor, American civilians in the Philippines began the journey that would lead eventually into internment — for many in less than a month (as early as December 9, 1941, on Vigan Island, for example [Halsema ltr, May 21, 1997]). Disbelief in any kind of American defeat was soon followed by the growing realization during that month that captivity was no longer a possibility but a probability. As Japanese bombing became more frequent, especially on Luzon, Americans saw with their own eyes — the first time in history for this large an American civilian population — the face of modern world war.

A. V. H. Hartendorp, the Manila newspaperman and former editor of the

Philippine Bulletin who was appointed the "official historian" of Santo Tomás Internment Camp by an early internee committee, kept a monthly record of all events and incidents in the life of the camp, as well as of any news or details he could discover about other camps. He kept this history by secretly typing it in his room while his roommates stood guard to warn him of approaching Japanese sentries, as keeping a written wartime record of any kind was an offense punishable by death. He stored the growing typescript in two galvanized iron boxes, which he then hid in a hole that had fortuitously appeared in the mortar of the wall in an Executive Committee member's office. This history ultimately ran to 4,000 typed pages, and to two volumes when published. It contained not only Hartendorp's recording of incidents at Santo Tomás (and other camps he could verify) but copies of important documents in the life of the camps he collected such as internee petitions, replies from the camp commandant, official Japanese proclamations, and selections from official camp reports on sanitation, illness, deaths, housing, and other matters. Hartendorp's account was "official." Hartendorp even testified personally at Yamashita's Manila trial and in Tokyo (Hartendorp, *Santo Tomás*, xiii–xv; IMTFE, *IPS*, Order No. 112, RG 331, Roll 42).

Although Hartendorp gives a sense of the rocketing speed of the Japanese advance from the first bombings on December 8, 1941, to the victorious march up Dewey Boulevard on January 2, 1942, he does not provide any real idea of the sights, the sounds, the confusion, and the shock on the part of civilian, and even some military, observers in the Philippines. As Martha Hill recalls, on December 8, "The news of Pearl Harbor stunned us. Then we heard that all the planes at Clark Field had been destroyed, Camp John Hay in Baguio had been bombed, all the ships in Manila Bay sunk. We couldn't believe it" (M. Hill, 27).

Other future internees such as Quaker missionary Eva Nixon were caught in transit from one place to another — in Nixon's case, from Singapore to India. She and others heard the news of the attack while they were aboard ship just before sailing. Nixon, onboard the *President Grant* in Manila Harbor, was eating her breakfast when the news came: "I had a spoon in my breakfast grapefruit . . . stunned I looked around the room. Everything looked the same, but suddenly, everything was different. The world was aflame with blazes of war uncontrolled, and we were at the very center of the conflict" (1).

That same night Nixon and the other five missionaries with her were jolted out of bed and ordered into the hold as an air raid hit: "The hold was stifling and dirty. We waited anxiously for the clear steady signal of the siren indicating the raid was over. 'I think I hear planes! Listen!' 'What's wrong with you? Your head is buzzing, that's all.' 'No, really, wasn't that the all clear signal?'

'You're still dreaming! Didn't you hear that bomb fall? I hope it doesn't get any nearer'" (Nixon, 2). The raids continued during that night; according to Nixon, the *President Grant*'s crew woke the passengers and had them rush down into the hold, "dizzy with sleep," three times that night (2), though whether the hold would be any safer than anywhere else is questionable.

The missionaries, like many other people, were stranded in the Philippines in the middle of a war. They did not, however, want to alarm their friends and family back home—especially because the official news seemed relatively good. After all, MacArthur kept providing bulletins for broadcast telling of huge Japanese losses thanks to the preparedness of his troops (Long, 118; Schaller, 56). Buoyed by a certain optimism, then, Nixon and her friends, now lodged in the Orientale Hotel inside Manila's walled city, cabled friends and family this soon-to-be ironic statement: "DELAYED, MANILA" (Nixon, 4).

The terrible speed of events—less than a month from the first bombing in Baguio to the raising of the Japanese flag over Manila—continued to paralyze many in the city and elsewhere. How could this be happening? And why wasn't America doing something about it?

According to official communiqués from USAFFE (United States Armed Forces, Far East, under MacArthur's command), from the first bombings even to the fall of Bataan, despite the dastardly attack both in Hawaii and shortly thereafter in the Philippines, the Americans were "doing something about it"; according to the bulletins, Japanese troops were being killed at an enormous rate and stores of Japanese materiel burned to ashes. As one historian points out, MacArthur took measures even to expunge any negative information from the historical record (Long, 118).

The truth was much harsher. As Koichi Shimada, a Japanese officer on the scene, explained, in the first days of the war in the Philippines, the Japanese lost seven Zero fighters and one bomber, but the United States had 102 planes heavily damaged or totally destroyed (94). Along with the planes, the American forces also lost their hangars on Nichols Field to the Zeros' fury, as well as their supply of submarine torpedoes, two small transports, three surface ships, and a pair of submarines (95–96).

To some commentators, these sorts of losses were not simply the result of the superior strength of the Zero when compared with the American P-40 but in large part were due to MacArthur's dithering and lack of action immediately after hearing about the Pearl Harbor attack. Both Gavin Daws and Stanley Falk point out that, despite the nine hours that MacArthur had to prepare his forces after news of Pearl Harbor reached him, he did nothing strategic or even understandable. Falk blames this inaction on MacArthur's unwillingness to deal with reverses in his plans, explaining that "MacArthur's inability to face reality on the morning of December 8 illustrates the sort of self-delusion that frequently marred his career" (4). Daws is equally critical, noting harshly that during MacArthur's inaction, "planes of the Army's Far East Air Force were still on the ground at Clark Field, sitting ducks." He adds that "in a few minutes" of Japanese bombing, the United States lost half its bombers and two thirds of its fighters. Indeed, "in those minutes, after those nine hours, on that first day of the war in the Pacific, MacArthur lost control of the air" (60).

Even the attacking Japanese pilots were surprised at the lack of opposition as they approached the Philippines and initially suspected a trick: "Clambering down from their planes they [the returning air crew] said in great bewilderment, 'Are we really at war?' 'We met no opposition.' 'What is the matter with the enemy?'" (Shimada, 93).

The returning pilots did notice "some light reaction from anti-aircraft guns" but were astounded by the lack of enemy fighter interception. Shimada continues, confirming Daws's picture of the situation: "Even more astonishing was the fact that our fliers had found the enemy's [airplanes] lined up on the target fields as if in peacetime. Small wonder that the crews were bewildered. . . . It seemed as if the enemy did not know that war had started. Could it be that no warnings from Pearl Harbor had yet gotten through to the Philippines?" (Shimada, 93).

The news had gotten through, but its import had not. Thanks to security precautions, not only civilians but even Philippine president Manuel Quezon didn't know how extensive the damage was from the bombing raid at Pearl Harbor. As Jim Halsema reports, he and Yay Panlilio (both newspaper correspondents at the time, Halsema soon to become an internee and Panlilio, a guerrilla leader) interviewed President Quezon the morning of the bombing, December 8. It was so early that Quezon was still in bed when they came by. Quezon was "relatively calm" when they talked to him, and he informed them about a conference at Mansion House, the Philippine president's residence in Baguio, the day before the bombing, with General Richard K. Sutherland (representing MacArthur) and all the members of the Philippine cabinet including Jorge Vargas. The members at this meeting judged the situation between the United States and Japan to be so serious that they made the decision to close all the schools in the islands the next day. As Jim Halsema reported, Quezon did not seem so much surprised by the news of Pearl Harbor as "resigned" (Halsema, "Oral," 2–3).

Rumors about the nature of the conflict and the degree of destruction in Hawaii spread around the islands. As William Moule relates, there were claims that the Japanese emperor himself hadn't known about the war and was even then suing for peace. The radio aided in this delusion by relaying the soothing news that there was "very little damage" at Pearl Harbor (Moule, 54).

This was nonsense, as most of the Pacific Fleet had been wiped out at Pearl Harbor. Despite official lies transmitted from Washington D.C., to the contrary, for the civilians soon waiting to be interned and the army held up and fighting for its life on Bataan and Corregidor, help was *not* "on the way." [1] Even had the fleet been fully intact, we know now, given the 1938 version of War Plan Orange and the October 1941 Rainbow-5 plan, such help would never have come (Schaller, 44–49). Carlos Romulo, who during the fight for Bataan managed to keep up radio contact with the mainland, speaks poignantly of the infamous promises: "The men who were in command asked the same questions the boys would ask me: 'When is help coming from America?' My answer to them was, and would be through four months of questioning: 'Soon! President Roosevelt has sent word help is coming. Ships and planes must be on the way now'" (Romulo, 142).

Anthony Arthur confirms Romulo's angry charge, pointing out that it would gradually dawn on those on Bataan and even those later in the internment camps that

> their plight was not Washington's primary concern. . . . The primary enemy
> for America was not Japan, but Nazi Germany. The primary immediate military
> goal was the capture of North Africa in order to take the pressure off Great
> Britain. . . . Not until much later would it become common knowledge that
> the Pacific theater was scheduled to receive only *fifteen percent* [italics mine]
> of available money, men, and materiel until after Hitler had been crushed.
> (Arthur, 35)

Romulo discusses the bitterness on Corregidor when troops heard on a radio program picked up from the United States that Americans intended to produce 65,000 planes in 1942; many of these bombers, the news reported, would go to England. The men in the Philippines, running out of food, fuel, ammunition, weapons, and planes, could desperately have used such supplies (Romulo, 116). The War Plans Division's previous agreement to the precedence of the European war, even as far back as 1938, was not something MacArthur told his aide, though as USAFFE commander, he obviously would have known about it (Schaller, 62–64).

Claire Phillips, also in Manila, regarded the bombing more realistically than most other civilians, stung into doing so by her then-fiancé, Army Sgt. John Phillips, who insisted that Claire take certain practical steps in light of what he was sure would be a coming invasion and internment. Claire did so, taking her money out of the bank and getting Philippine currency exchanged for U.S. dollars. She then bought supplies, referring to the list John had written that noted items vital to survival: aspirin, quinine, sulfa, iodine, gauze, tape, corned beef, canned salmon, sardines, beans, fruit, and a ten-pound can of dry milk for the baby—all of which proved useful months later in her life as a guerrilla and a spy (Philipps, 9–10).

John also had Claire gas up the car and fill it with oil and stow away the army blanket and mosquito netting he had given her. He had her pack everything she had purchased into suitcases, including the canned goods. On an impulse, Phillips adds, she threw in her new "midnight blue cocktail dress studded with gold nailheads" with the more sensible slacks, shoes, and shirts John had suggested. The midnight blue dress was to serve her well later as a hostess in a bar run for Japanese officers, where Claire, posing as an Italian, along with her bilingual (Japanese and English) staff of hostesses, collected strategic information bandied about by drunken officers (Phillips, 10; 39).

She, John, her baby from a previous marriage (Dian), and the baby-sitter, Lolita, left Manila the night of December 9 by car, as did others. Despite several stops because of the snarled traffic (caused by others also fleeing), the group ended up in the hills outside Manila in a hunter's cabin. From there Claire was eventually to join the guerrillas, who were led by men such as John Boone and Colonel Straughan, but not before marrying John Phillips on December 24 in the jungle near Batangas. Relieved of patrol duty for the night, John convinced Claire to meet him; he brought Father Gonzales, a Filipino priest, with him, and the priest married them in a jungle clearing in the moonlight (Phillips, 23–24).

For others such as Martha Hill, the early days and nights of the war were punctuated by a kind of stunned wonder and a flurry of desperate activity. She describes the bombing itself:

> During the night, the Japanese bombers were busy. From our home at the edge of town we heard them going over, and the ear-splitting explosions echoed about us as the bombs found their targets. We watched the fiery streams of tracer bullets pouring up from nearby Nichols Airfield, saw the star shells with intense brilliance illuminating every detail of the surrounding countryside. As the planes left and once again all was still, we watched the fires blazing in the blackness. The war, then, became real. It was suddenly there inside our home. (M. Hill, 28)

Hill continued to work administering anesthesia at Sternberg Army Hospital even though she was a civilian. The hospital was filled with a steady stream of "badly-maimed and burned soldiers and sailors and civilians" who had come in "from Clark Field, Cavite, Camp Murphy and from the city streets. Cañacoa, the Navy hospital, had been heavily bombed during the night and put out of commission" (M. Hill, 29).

Nixon, too, watched with horror as fires and devastation spread through Manila itself. Feelings of frightened uselessness almost overwhelmed her; though she had no actual medical training, she started working at a Red Cross emergency station with three of her missionary friends — Evelyn Whittoff, a doctor, and Marion Childress and Geraldine Chappell, both nurses. Here even Nixon could clean the area, roll bandages, help cut away burned clothing, bring swabs, and generally provide the medical people with an extra set of hands. They were needed. Their emergency station was in an extremely dangerous area where bombings were so severe many were seriously injured or killed (Nixon, 6).

Natalie Crouter, closer personally to the earlier bombings in the north of Luzon, had seen the bombers in formation as they came over her house on December 8. Crouter's and her husband's astonishment was profound when what they supposed were American planes began to bomb Camp John Hay:

> As they passed almost opposite the house, we heard a long ripping sound like the tearing of a giant sheet and saw an enormous burst of smoke and earth near officers' quarters at Camp John Hay — the first bombing of the Philippines before our eyes. Huge billows of smoke and dust covered the Post as we looked. No one said a word. We turned to each other, speechless. At last Jerry said hoarsely, "My God, those are Japanese planes." The smoke rolled up and the smell of powder reached us. (Crouter, 3)

Closer to Manila, Alva Hill describes the war zone that Luzon had become, especially after the Cavite Naval Station was bombed:

> At night, the street lights of Cavite [had] always shown distinctly the curve of Manila Bay on which Cavite [was] located. The pounding of Cavite by the Japanese air forces was terrific. . . . For several days and nights, the people of Manila helplessly watched the flames and destruction, and worried over the fate of their friends in that terrible conflagration. (Alva Hill, 311)

Americans in Manila helplessly observed as one military landmark after another exploded and was lost: Clark Field, Cavite Naval Station, Nichols Field. General MacArthur's army was visibly in retreat on its way down the Bataan peninsula; it was obviously not going to protect American civilians in Manila or elsewhere. Even civilians recognized that the army was fighting for its own survival, rather than successfully attacking the Japanese and driving them out of the Philippines. Civilians watched and wondered as they heard that field hospitals were being moved farther south again and again as the army retreated; the wounded, no matter how dangerously ill, continued to be moved down the peninsula. Lt. Juanita Redmond, an army nurse, said that she and others started nursing casualties in Manila, then evacuated them to Limay (Hospital #1). Next, patients were evacuated either to the interim health station "Little Baguio," or to Cabcaben (Hospital #2) even farther down the peninsula.

As Mary Condon-Rall notes, conditions grew increasingly critical medically and militarily as the retreat down Bataan continued. Historically, the peninsula had proved itself "highly malarial"; originally, various Orange and Rainbow Plans called for medical supplies (especially antimalaria drugs) and food to be cached down the length of Bataan. Plans also called for temporarily detached medical personnel to maintain "mosquito control measures." With MacArthur's shift to his version of Rainbow-5, which envisioned a successful repulse of Japanese troops on the beaches, Bataan remained devoid of either food or medical caches of any size since both had been taken to the coast or stored in Manila (Falk, 5). However, even before the war, officials had deemed the mosquito problem "economically unfeasible to control" on the peninsula because of the double vector for malaria — not only mosquitoes but also other parasites. With both food and medicine in short supply, both malaria and malnutrition soon lowered combat readiness among the 80,000 American and Filipino troops by several percentage points a day (Condon-Rall, 38; Baldwin, 123).

The food situation was particularly precarious. Any single War Plan Orange had planned for only 43,000 troops to hold Bataan; now, 80,000 troops and 26,000 civilians fleeing with the army put a tremendous strain on what few resources there were. Had MacArthur cached food as the plans called for, however, it still would have been inadequate. No one had counted on civilian evacuees. With the food shortage aggravated, by January 5, 1942, troop rations dropped to half rations; by March, they were down to one-third rations. Not surprisingly, malaria and nutritional diseases increased the number of ill and reduced combat effectiveness by 75 percent, with front lines experiencing a malaria rate of 80 percent. This was hardly an army that would turn and rend the enemy, thereby saving citizens of Manila or Baguio. They fought for their own lives (Condon-Rall, 52–53), though many southern islands other than Luzon or Mindanao stayed free of Japanese occupation until the fall of Bataan.

The nurses with the army faced overflowing beds and overcrowded "wards" (from 2,500 patients in Hospital #1 to 6,000 in Hospital #2) (Condon-Rall, 52). They also faced increased shelling no matter how far south they traveled. The desperation of such moves, in light of the critical physical status of many of the patients, was only matched by their "new" medical accommodations. Another army nurse (and future internee) at the scene, Lt. Denny Williams, describes Hospital #2 and its crude design:

> I hitched a ride on a truck, and finally arrived at the hospital which was three miles west of Cabcaben in the bamboo thickets and jungles along the Red River.
>   What a surprise when I saw it! Earlier, bulldozers had pushed through several miles of tangled brush, knocking trees out of their path, while the engineers built roads, and storehouses, and installed electric plants and water chlorinators. Under the bamboo trees as far as I could see were beds already set up and many had pa-

tients in them. This was truly a jungle hospital, with seven wards or rooms cut out of the bamboo and already functioning. (48)

During this time MacArthur's reports from the front continued to exaggerate Japanese losses: Supposedly 22 enemy ships had been sunk and 12,000 enemy troops destroyed. Falk suggests that MacArthur's "unseemly paranoia" and his "reckless desire for success" were in part responsible for some "questionable strategic judgments." This last might include, for example, the attempt to meet and defeat the Japanese on the beaches or MacArthur's appraisal of the "fighting strength" of his command. His tendency to make "unfortunate tactical decisions" appears as well in switching war plans several times without prior preparation for any single one of them.

MacArthur's biographer, Carol Petillo, also suggests that the general was driven by the example of his swashbuckling hero-father, who, as a mere lieutenant, won a Congressional Medal of Honor during the Civil War. This "icon" always before him, his son sought to be worthy of the family name and to win glory for himself. The method by which to win such honor was also clear to Douglas MacArthur from his father's example: "Sometimes one had to decide for oneself the relevancy of orders" (Petillo, 2–4).

Despite publicity photographs of gallant nurses in fatigues, pictures of the general looking suitably determined, and Filipino children wearing army helmets, the war was obviously being lost. The fighting crept closer, and the patients, doctors, orderlies, and nurses had to leave Hospital #2 and join MacArthur on Corregidor in its sheltering tunnels (Redmond, 1–30; Williams 62; Hartendorp, I, 174–186). The U.S. Army, unprepared, undertrained, and strategically in disarray, was on the run, a sight many Americans, with MacArthur's jingoistic earlier promises still ringing in their ears, found hard to believe.

Civilians huddled in their homes and tried to prepare for what they could see was the inevitable invasion. To "save" Manila from further destruction, MacArthur and Quezon declared Manila an "open city" on December 24— that is, a city that does not intend to mount an offensive or even defend itself militarily. As Romulo explains, everyone, military and civilian alike, upon hearing this "relaxed in Manila," because "even the most savage army recognizes the immunity due an open city" (Romulo, 72). Alva Hill describes what happened next, following the declaration: "But even after we had withdrawn our forces and declared Manila an 'open city,' the Japanese continued to bomb it, especially the harbor, up and down the Pasig River, Fort Santiago and the piers" (Alva Hill, 302). Eva Nixon also remembers the scene of devastation following the announcement of "open city" status and subsequent bombing:

> In awe we stood gazing through arched Church windows where the terribly beautiful transparent golden flames leaped and danced around the statue of the Virgin

Mary, giving the illusion of her being burned at the stake. In the streets, cars were turned over, shot through with shrapnel, tires burned off or charred. Tin from roofs lay crumpled in the streets. Windows were shattered and walls smashed. A horse lay dead near a heavy, crumpled iron fence. Huge bomb craters made the streets impassable. (10–11)

Hill goes on to describe the growing sense of defeat and panic sweeping Manila itself, explaining that "everyone was hurriedly digging air-raid shelters and burying their treasures." His wife Martha buried her jewelry in a tin can in the backyard (which she actually recovered after the war) and hid her sterling silver golf trophies under and between the floorboards of the house. Alva hid his sword and Knights Templar uniform in a locker at the Scottish Rite Temple, and his sons hid their Boy Scout manuals and, Alva explains, "their telegraph instruments," because neither he nor his sons wanted anything available "which might cause trouble with the invading Japanese Army" (Alva Hill, 299; 301).

Manila shuddered under repeated bombings as vital services were interrupted, then abandoned. The cityscape became one of a nightmare, as Alva Hill describes: "The streets were filled with shell holes. Live electrical wires were dangling and wriggling in the streets, and water was gushing from the broken mains" (Alva Hill, 307).

Earlier, Esther Hamilton, another American in Manila on December 8, didn't stay to watch for any future destruction. She left for the highlands that day, following President Quezon's address in which he told those who could to leave the city. The men in Hamilton's missionary group of fifteen decided that the wisest course of action would be "to leave Manila [for] Baguio at the first sign of danger." They did leave soon after the news of Pearl Harbor appeared in the paper, ironically heading straight into the earliest area to be bombed on Luzon.

The trip to Baguio among the surging crowds after the Manila and environs bombing was both sporadic and nightmarish. The blackout caused terrible traffic accidents and added to the panic and war casualties (Condon-Rall, 45). After packing the car for Baguio at daybreak, Esther and her missionary colleagues held off until 7:30 A.M. to leave, because several more missionaries had yet to arrive. Even after they left, Hamilton claims they could only get through five city "squares" before they had to take cover in a church because of an air raid. After the raid, the roads were choked: "Traffic was bad. People with all their earthly possessions were taking flight in every usable conveyance. Near Tarlac, about one-third of the way up, we saw a huge, silver enemy bomber swooping low just ahead of us and a little later saw the train that had just been bombed" (Hamilton, 22–25).

Christmas Day 1941, just before which MacArthur would declare Manila an open city, was particularly distressing, as a host of pleasant memories contrasted sharply with the present misery. A stench of burning oil, for example, hung in the air from the storage and refinery fires the American troops had set by blowing up the tanks when they left Manila, hoping to keep valuable resources away from the Japanese military. The result was what the Filipinos called the "Black Christmas" season of 1941. Martha Hill describes the destruction of the refinery storage tanks: "Thunderous explosions and sky-high fountains of flame added to the taut sense of approaching disaster. Heavy black clouds formed a ceiling over the city which spotted the drying laundry and left a black, greasy film over everything" (M. Hill, 31–32).

Meals were eaten cold and hurriedly, often in stairwells or under tables to avoid the worst of the flying debris and rubble resulting from repeated bombings. The peculiar juxtaposition of holding Christmas in a war zone comes out as well in the flippant comments of a future short-term internee, Frances Long, who notes in a later magazine article that on "Christmas Day I got flowers, a compact, and three air raids"; she adds, "I was stunned. It never occurred to me the Japs would ever get as far as Manila" (Long, "Yankee Girl," 84).

Frieda Magnuson, also in Manila with her family during the "Black Christmas," remembers even more strongly the fantastic clash of observable reality and the "official truth" heard over the radio based on MacArthur's communiqués and in subsequent deluded reports from San Francisco. She, too, reflects the sense of American civilian dismay and disbelief so common during the early days when "Where were *our* bombers?" was a frequent question:

> It couldn't be happening, but it was. Clark Field was wiped out with our planes on the ground waiting for orders from Washington. We watched the systematic bombing of Cavite, the American navy base across Manila Bay. A Marine barracks was hit and hundreds killed. The Cavite Naval installation was completely destroyed in several hours. We would first hear the planes, then hear the bombs land, then see pillars of smoke rise from the ground. There seemed [to be] no resistance at all from the U.S. Armed Forces. Trucks drove down Dewey Boulevard loaded with dead bodies while we heard on the radio from the States, "Cavite Naval Base was hit but there was little damage and no loss of life." (Magnuson, 37)

She also spent Christmas dodging into the improvised home air raid shelter under the stairs, and she ended up eating her Christmas dinner on the safety of the floor (Magnuson, 38).

For Bessie Sneed, Christmas on an unnamed island in the Visayans was also harrowing. With a growing panic about the coming Japanese invasions and the scarcity of food on their island, Sneed, her husband, and several other miners' families decided to move to a nearby island where there was more food to be had. Fourteen people set sail on Christmas Day in a "small outrigger native boat" but were caught in a sudden squall around midnight, which swamped their boat 300 feet offshore. They struggled, paddling it for some twenty hours until they were rescued and dragged ashore by natives from the island that was their destination. The natives even salvaged their waterlogged baggage. The early morning of the day after Christmas found them shivering, but alive, onshore, surrounded by piles of soggy suitcases and footlockers (Sneed, 3–4).

Back in Manila, a "group of prominent American citizens" regrouped to discuss earlier-made plans for dealing with the Japanese invasion they believed was soon coming (Arthur, 19). This committee seems to have been the previously mentioned "American Emergency Committee" (formerly the "American Coordinating Committee").

A history of this committee reflects not only the issue of preparedness but helps explain indirectly why the internees initially did so well in the camps. At the beginning of 1941, this group of Manila businessmen and professional people were suspicious regarding the possibility of a Japanese invasion in the near future. This is significant, because it further buttresses the accounts that we have, such as Alva Hill's, which indicate unofficial worry on the part of some citizens and the way that concern was contradicted by "official" attitudes. Fredric H. Stevens, the first elected chairman of the American Coordinating Committee, explains that this committee was formed *eleven months* before the Baguio bombing because of the apparent complacency on the part of U.S. government officials: "As a result of the general lack of activity on the part of our government, a number of Americans [in Manila] deemed it advisable that some civilian organization be formed with a view to taking care of the interests of the Americans in the Islands" (Stevens, 2).

Worried about a possible Japanese threat, the committee sent out questionnaires to "all classes of American residents in the Philippines, with a view to ascertaining their views on forming a permanent committee for both the welfare and protection of Americans in Manila" (Stevens, 2). A fairly strong response followed, and in January 1941 the first public meeting of those interested was called in the Manila Elks Club, a notice of time and place having already been published in the Manila newspapers as well as having been broadcast over the radio. The meeting place — an Elks Club — accurately reflects, both symbolically and literally, the powerful influence fraternal organizations had on future membership. Three hundred people were present, including a handful of non-Americans. These people then elected the officers of the new committee and declared a purpose: to coordinate with the U.S. Army, Navy, and high commissioner's office, as well as the Philippine Commonwealth and the civilian population in case of emergency. The committee met once a week and attempted to arrive at solutions for matters of concern, many involving preparedness, civil defense, and national defense (Stevens, 2–3). The committee drew up plans for air raid shelter construction, designated evacuation centers in the event of Manila bombings, and advised residents to stock up on food, clothing, and medicine. The Red Cross even provided housing, sanitation, and water facilities for an evacuation center sixty miles from Manila in Pasanjan, Laguna.

Unfortunately, despite patronizing words, officials did not take the committee or its recommendations seriously, nor did they act upon them. From January to March 1941 the Coordinating Committee repeatedly begged the high commissioner to order nonmilitary American women and children home. The high commissioner's office told the committee that such an evacuation plan was "impossible" because of the lack of ships—which, though it is highly probable, overlooks the then-converted hospital ship *Mactan*, which had some space onboard and sailed December 31, 1941, for Port Darwin (Hartendorp, I, 4, n2), not to mention ships such as the *President Hoover*, which had come in that fall. As noted earlier, the commissioner, for geopolitical (and possibly career) reasons, refused to release any public recommendation for evacuation.

Despite officialdom's disregard, the (now) American Emergency Committee (which had been invited to incorporate with, and become, a special unit of the American Red Cross) decided that it would see if it could prepare for what would surely be capture and internment. Where, for example, would civilians be imprisoned? Would it be in a stockyard? In an existing prison such as Fort Santiago? In an open field outside the city? With retributive measures in mind, perhaps, given the conditions in which the then-interned Japanese were living, committee members decided to try in advance to find an acceptable site before harsh captors hurriedly chose a place hazardous to the eventual health of internees. If the *committee* chose a site, perhaps it could locate one that would allow future internees a solid chance at survival, a site that could support, for example, the necessary sewage and water demands of a large interned population, as well as provide adequate housing and shelter from the seasonal elements. To this end, Fredric Stevens, chairman, along with another member of the committee, Christian Rosenstock, "approached the authorities of the University of Santo Tomás, with a view to obtaining authority to use the University and its campus as a place of internment. The University authorities readily agreed to the proposal." Also identified as possible alternative sites were Holy Ghost convent and Ateno di Manila (Stevens, 6). Claude Buss, executive assistant to the Philippine high commissioner, was more sensible than his superior, and agreed to try to gain control of Santo

Tomás, though he added that the Polo Club might also be adequate (Harten-dorp, I, 4).

Santo Tomás was a sensible choice and, as it turned out, did allow a maximum number of internees to survive wartime internment conditions because of its sanitation facilities and their potential to be expanded. Reputedly one of the oldest universities under the American flag, it was founded in 1611, twenty-five years before Harvard, by the Spanish Dominicans (Petillo ed., 202n). By 1941, under U.S. control for approximately forty-one years, it consisted of several large buildings on approximately sixty acres of grounds in the center of Manila; it was bounded on three sides by high masonry walls and faced España Boulevard on the fourth side (Hartendorp, *Santo Tomás*, 7). With buildings already standing, sixty classrooms were soon turned into dormitory rooms, and the surrounding grounds were used for both recreation and gardening. It was much preferable to a "new" camp that would have to be built — an alternative some supposed was around the corner, if no more sensible plan were already in place. Camps that had to be built tended to provide inadequate shelter for internees during the building process; they also provided few sanitary facilities — a requirement vital to continued camp health during the rainy season, as a "built" camp (to some degree) such as Los Baños would later demonstrate.

Stevens's committee wrote up its plan, including the rationale for the choice and the permission given by Santo Tomás's authorities. This package was then forwarded to Claude Buss; the high commissioner made no comment, but eventually his office turned this plan over to the Japanese commanding officer when the Imperial Army troops entered Manila (Stevens, 6).

The American Emergency Committee was not the only group to take steps in advance to accrue a maximum benefit from early planning. As Natalie Crouter points out, some Americans gathered early at Brent School in Baguio on December 26 rather than risk being hunted down by the Japanese when the army inevitably came. This group volunteered to be concentrated in the school and indeed slept there; says Crouter, "We spent the night on mattresses on the floor of the school, devoured by mosquitoes, children crying and adults wondering in wakeful hours how soon the enemy would arrive." Earlier, Crouter explains, "It was a terrible day. There was panic in the air, in the trees, and in the ground" (Crouter, 9; 10).

Another recent Baguio refugee, missionary Esther Hamilton (who did not go to Brent School, incidentally), reflects something of the panic and the accompanying inability to believe the worst, so characteristic of many Americans at the time: "For a week we were told the Japanese were coming. Edna [a friend] and I could not believe it. Why? What did they want here? Why climb five thousand feet? Could our Army not keep them back? We did not realize that our Army had been ordered elsewhere" (Hamilton, 27). With only a small American and Filipino garrison at Camp John Hay and some units of the Seventy-first Philippine Division coming in as they retreated from the coast, there was no real defense possible (Halsema, "Oral," 4).

On December 27, 1941, the Japanese army entered Baguio. By this time, the Baguio city government had fled. Only E. J. Halsema, the former mayor (and Jim Halsema's father), and a ragged contingent made up of two or three American residents, several Filipino employees of the city, and the chief of police (J. J. Keith) were available to preserve order, to prevent looting, and, ultimately, to represent the town and meet the Japanese. Keith had actually talked with the Japanese commander on the phone and made some arrangements via a translator (a Japanese internee in Baguio) prior to the Japanese entrance (Halsema, "Oral," 4–5). After the Japanese arrived that morning, they occupied City Hall, lowering both the Filipino and American flags and hoisting the Rising Sun emblem. Noon saw the victorious Imperial troops freeing the Japanese internees held in Baguio. By dark, the entire battalion of the Imperial Japanese Ninth Infantry was in place (Halsema, "E. J.," 296).

Missionary Esther Hamilton's description of the Japanese entrance is particularly graphic:

> But they came! I'll never forget it. Our houses in Baguio are right next to a large Japanese school where all the local Japanese, about three hundred, were concentrated. That Saturday, about noon, they all marched out with Japanese flags to meet the victorious Imperial Japanese Army. Soon we heard shouts of triumph and ran to the windows to watch. Down the winding road they came, first the tiniest children, waving flags and shouting. Behind them walked the men, followed by several truck loads of dirty, tired looking soldiers in full battle regalia. (Hamilton, 27)

The Japanese army officially took possession of the town, according to Natalie Crouter, that night at 11:30 P.M. Their first act was to put all Americans back in the second story of Brent School with orders to sleep. Crouter points out indignantly: "Many did not have blankets, and it [the school] was a fire trap. [The Japanese soldiers] came about every half hour with heavy clumping boots and sharp staccato talk, [and they] would look in, stare at us like zoo animals, then go away. A machine gun was trained on us at the front door."

She goes on to explain that the whole night was disturbed by "stamping feet, clanking bayonets and guttural orders" (Crouter, 11).

In both accounts the Americans seem strangely quiescent about events; this may be due to the self-selection of those providing diaries and retrospectives:

obviously, few internees became actual members of a guerrilla unit (Claire Phillips, Yay Panlilio, and Mabel Robinson, whose texts I use in this study, are exceptions). In most cases, future internees saw the wisdom of coming down and turning themselves in with their families, hoping to make the best of a bad situation for their children.

Perhaps as well what the diaries reflect is also just plain shock. As Hartendorp points out, "Never before was such a large body of American citizens . . . held in so cruel a captivity or has an American community been compelled to maintain itself under such difficult . . . conditions" (Hartendorp, *Santo Tomás*, xiii). This just didn't happen to Americans — certainly not to white, middle-class civilians who only months earlier had been playing golf, attending cocktail parties, or, like Frieda Magnuson on December 7, enjoying a lavish garden party featuring a whole pig roasting on a spit, exotic drinks, servers in white coats (one to every five guests), and music (Magnuson, 34). Grace Nash could hardly have expected to be soon on her way to internment camp, not when on December 5 she too was enjoying a festive evening following the "usual custom" of attending a Friday night symphony concert, then meeting with friends in the Palm Garden of the Manila Hotel for drinks and discussion (Nash, 16). At least initially, there was no real concept of what was going to happen — and then, when internment began, no idea of what exactly to do. There was no cultural model to follow. The closest parallel was camping, backpacking, or pioneer homesteading — none particularly apt for what was to come but more useful than one would suppose, if only in terms of the attitude spawned by such analogies.

This unique problem seems, along with the curiously formal English of some of their captors, to have lent a quality of surrealism in many ways to the proceedings — a surrealism compounded by a sometimes weird politeness under the circumstances, mixed with simultaneous death threats. Esther Hamilton experienced the first aspect. She was one of those who elected to stay, along with other missionaries, in a house in Baguio itself, rather than turn themselves in early at Brent School. Again, the same missionary males who had advised the ill-fated flight to Baguio in the first place impressed on the group that they should not make things easy for the Japanese by turning themselves in. At midnight on December 27, troops at the door of the missionaries' house demanded entrance, and "a number of soldiers and local [previously interned] Japanese came in." One asked a missionary for all his money, and the missionary, Harry, explained that he couldn't give him any money because he (Harry) needed it to pay for his wife's hospital bill. Hamilton notes, "Strange as it seems, he was allowed to keep the money." A shot, however, did ring out, frightening everyone, but "then there was a moment of profuse apologies in broken English assuring us it was just an accident" (Hamilton,

30). Hamilton and her friends were then ordered to pack one bag and troop to Brent School to join the other Americans. Hamilton was told quietly by one of the local, formerly interned Japanese to pack a second bag, and she comments, "I guess he knew from experience, for he had just been interned for three weeks himself." She also says that after their bags were packed, the troops searched and then looted them, taking anything they wanted. She specifically mentions knives, scissors, fountain pens, and flashlights being taken (Hamilton, 30–31).

Crouter also notes the Japanese's seeming obsession with scissors. She gives, however, another disquieting yet fascinating detail: The officer-in-charge, Mukibo, claimed to be "a Harvard graduate" who spoke to them in "perfect English"[2]; Hamilton further adds that this polite, smiling Japanese officer was also a Methodist minister! (Crouter, 12; Hamilton, 37)[3] The mixture of the known and the alien must have been particularly piquant. Crouter and Hamilton substantially agree about what was said to the assembled prisoners next. Crouter records in her diary that, on December 29, "They called us all onto the tennis court and told us that if we did what we were told that the Japanese soldier was kind. We must give up all guns or tell where any were hidden. They had already taken all scissors, nail files and pointed objects the night before" (Crouter, 12).

Hamilton's account adds again the disjunctive sense of superficial politeness and deadly danger that seemed to characterize the early days of captivity for many American civilians. She explains that Mukibo

> made a very, very polite speech, smiling all the while. First of all he made it very
> plain that if anyone had firearms of any kind and did not surrender them at that
> very moment, he would be shot. . . . Several machine guns had been set up on the
> grounds round us and plenty of guards with fixed bayonets on their guns kept a
> sharp lookout. Then he announced that we were now in the hands of the Japanese
> Imperial Army whose orders we must obey and that we would be held by them
> until the war was over. (Hamilton, 34)

Brent School was not, however, to be their final place of internment. Prisoners were told to be packed and ready to leave in forty minutes to go to "another place, not far away" carrying their own baggage and bedding, as Hamilton recalls. The destination was the earlier Japanese-damaged Camp John Hay, specifically the section called "Scout Hill," where male Japanese civilians had been interned earlier. American and British internees now took their place. Young and old, men and women, teenagers and preschoolers picked up their baggage, bedding, and bundles and began the trek to the camp, approximately one mile away (Hamilton, 37–39; Crouter, 3; Halsema, "E. J.," 298). The Japanese eventually relented somewhat and let a truck transport the truly ill and those too infirm or old to walk the distance, but the majority of internees straggled after the truck on foot, shifting mattresses and baggage, pocketbooks, hats, and babies, as they led smaller children by the hand along Baguio's main highway, the Session Road (Halsema, "E. J.," 195; 297).

The battered camp presented few comforts to the weary and dispirited group as internees stumbled in and were sent to live in "huge, dirty, dark barracks" where they argued over personal floor space and then swept with crude twig brooms what spaces they had claimed. There was no running water, nor were there any toilets due to the bombing. Five hundred people had to get their water from containers and use pit latrines as soon as the male internees dug them (Hamilton, 39; Crouter, 12). For Hamilton, Crouter, and others in Camp John Hay, full control over their personal lives was over — they were now imprisoned for the duration. (They were to endure Camp John Hay, however, only until mid-April when they were moved to Camp Holmes for most of their internment.)

In Manila, several weeks passed before the actual invasion of the Japanese army. These intervening days were filled with frightened attempts by civilians either to flee or to pack what might be necessities for some unimaginable future. Douglas MacArthur went on the radio December 29; according to Frieda Magnuson, he offered little useful information and no hope to his terrified American listeners. The instructions from the man who had told them only weeks earlier that he was "confident" and "serene" seem particularly callous to modern ears:

> Do not follow the army to Bataan or Corregidor. Get together in groups rather than be taken as individual families. Destroy any papers showing a connection with the U.S. Military Reserves. Pour all intoxicating beverages down the sink. May God be with you — I shall return. (MacArthur, in Magnuson, 36)

Warned away from their only possible protection (the American Army), ordered to offer no resistance but simply to wait quietly to be picked up, and then abandoned to God's mercy, it is no wonder so few made any plans beyond internment. In the following days, many did what the general had ordered; they destroyed their private liquor supplies, having also heard rumors circulating about the behavior of Japanese troops in China when they reputedly went "berserk with alcohol and the fever of victory" (Arthur, 20). Huddling together in groups, many future internees poured hoarded bottles of scotch and gin down kitchen sinks. Some, however, including Chet Magnuson, rebelliously decided against the general's oracular warning and, instead, buried the contents of the liquor cabinet in the garden (Magnuson, 38).

The liquor question — and the different responses to it — reflect the contradictory ideas about the degree of personal danger that an invading Japanese army might mean for each person. On one hand, anyone with current affairs knowledge at the time had heard of the rape of Nanking and had seen bits of smuggled newsreel footage showing the destruction (and executions) in China carried out by what truly seemed a berserk army. Even earlier, in Baguio, Halsema points out that many were "concerned by the 1937 Rape of Nanking" as well as with the precedent such atrocities may have set with the Japanese army in terms of what constituted acceptable treatment of civilians (Halsema, "Oral," 6). On the other hand, many Americans (especially on Luzon, rather than on Mindanao) had known only a few Japanese, and those either smiling Rotarian businessmen or isolated individuals in service positions such as clerk, carpenter, or gardener — hardly a threatening stereotype consistent with war crimes. Captivity would surely be uncomfortable, many reasoned, accepting the fact that they would be interned for an indefinite period of time, but few probably visualized rape, mayhem, or sudden death as an immediate threat to them personally. So many ignored Douglas MacArthur's sermonizing and drank during the hours they waited. Still, as Magnuson notes, on New Year's Eve, no matter how much she, Chet, and her friends drank, "the situation was so serious that we remained sober as the proverbial judges. After a series of explosions, dense clouds of black smoke rose. It was a New Year's Eve to end all New Year's Eves" (Magnuson, 38).

On New Year's Day, when local officials opened warehouses, the commissary, and some retail stores to the public to let people carry away whatever they could, the scene, as Alva Hill describes it, was stygian and festive, simultaneously: "Not only were the doors of the commissary and the piers open to the public, but piles of merchandise were being burned in the open spaces near the piers. There was an excited crowd milling around. . . . People were carrying loads of things away on their backs until they became tired" (Alva Hill, 312).

Magnuson adds another gloomy detail with her description of the same event, noting that the opening of the warehouses "caused mob scenes but [were] helpful in hard times to come. They burned gasoline, tires, and army vehicles which they could not take, causing rain that fell to be black drops" (Magnuson, 38).

Alva Hill's son Jay managed to struggle through the crowd and nab an unopened roll of wrapping paper — hardly a prize in the normal sense, but, as his father explains, that paper eventually became a "prized possession" in the Camp Holmes internment camp school. There an ordinary student notebook eventually would cost $10 in gold — assuming that such a notebook could even be found! (Alva Hill, 313).

Another soon-to-be internee, missionary Carol Terry, remembers one particularly cruel misapprehension on New Year's Day:

> We could not, we would not believe the truth — the Japanese were about to enter the city. We grasped at every straw of hope. One day, truck loads of soldiers passed on an obscure road just back of our house [in the San Juan district]. We waved gaily at them, cheering wildly and showing the "V" for victory sign. Reinforcements had come! We were saved! The next day the Japanese walked into the city. Those soldiers we had hailed so joyously were our retreating army! (12)

January 2 saw the end of freedom for both Manila and ultimately any American citizen found on Luzon. Hartendorp recalls the ominous ambiance of that day; it was "dark and chilly": "The sun could not break through the heavy, smoky atmosphere, and looked like a pale moon. Pet canaries drooped and died in their cages, gassed. In the afternoon it drizzled a little, unseasonably. . . . The whole aspect of the silent metropolis was tragic and foreboding" (I, 5–6).

The Japanese Imperial Army entered a bombed and smoking Manila at eight o'clock that evening. From her hotel room Frances Long watched the troops enter the city:

> Jessie, standing by the window, screamed excitedly. We rushed to see. Here it was at last — the dreaded hour. Out of the dark came many lights, one following the other down Dewey Boulevard. As the lights came nearer, there was no mistaking the tinny sound of the motors of the Jap motorcycles. In they came, flooded the town and began [positioning?] guards at hotels, clubs, and apartment houses. (Long, "Yankee Girl," 84)

Somewhat earlier, Alva and Martha Hill recall events somewhat differently. Watching from a quiet residential side street, the Hills saw a curious celebration of sorts and a threatening number of paper enemy flags emerging out of the dusk:

> We were not far from the Japanese Embassy and Club and could hear the shouts and cheering, and see children running about waving the little white paper flags with their red circle in the middle. . . . The first Japs to appear were riding bicycles with guns strapped to their backs. They were followed by motor vehicles from which two or three Japs would dismount every few hundred yards, set up the machineguns [*sic*] and hurriedly point them around in every direction. . . . (Alva Hill, 318)

Martha Hill adds her own vivid recollection of the event as "screened by blossoming poinsettias and hibiscus, we watched the first trucks roll by filled with Japanese soldiers, all facing outward with rifles ready" (Martha Hill, 34).

Frieda Magnuson's memories of that day share something with the Hills' in that she remembers bicycles, though her attitude more clearly represents the continuing air of disbelief and unreality shared by many of the Americans about to be interned: "On January 2 we saw our first Japanese soldiers. From an upper window we could watch them marching down Dewey Boulevard. It seemed unbelievable that these small men in their ill-fitting uniforms (many riding bicycles for goodness sake!) could have brought the United States to its knees so quickly" (Magnuson, 38).

The next day, January 3, British and American citizens awoke to find that Manila was now officially Japanese. As Hartendorp relates, Americans opened their eyes to find

> the Japanese flag flying from the tall mast in front of the High Commissioner's residence on Dewey Boulevard, over Fort Santiago, U.S. Army headquarters at the mouth of the Pasig River, and over Malacañan Palace, the official home of the President of the Philippines, as it had been of the American and many of the Spanish governor-generals of the past. The Japanese flag—a red sun on a white field—was also flying over the Army and Navy Club and the adjoining Elks Club, the large government-owned Manila Hotel, and numerous other public and private buildings. Japanese sentries were posted by twos at all the main street intersections and in front of clubs, hotels, and apartment houses. (I, 6)

American and other Allied residents of the captured city were informed by radio and by loudspeakers to stay indoors and have the following stocked and ready to transport: food for three days, a blanket, a mosquito net, and a change of clothing. The radio informed soon-to-be internees that they would be picked up at their homes and in their hotels by troops and then would be taken to be registered. Three days later, according to Martha Hill, she and her family were taken (35).

For Eva Nixon, waiting for the inevitable Japanese patrol to come to her house was nerve-wracking. She sat on the floor in her hotel room, keeping busy by typing: "I was about halfway through [the page] when I heard the heavy tread of military boots. . . . My fingers froze on the typewriter keys. There stood a live Japanese soldier in full uniform with his bayoneted gun pointed directly at me" (13).

What happened next is amusing, yet rife with deadly possibilities. The soldier gestured at Nixon, making a sharp downward motion with his hand. Nixon obediently remained sitting. Frustrated, the soldier and some companions who had joined him then shouted furiously at Nixon in Japanese and motioned downward repeatedly. Again, Nixon remained sitting. Just as the original soldier started to advance on her threateningly, Nixon spotted some friends in a group being held out in the street and got up to join them. The soldier barked another order, and she and the rest of the group proceeded under guard down the street. Some days later in internment camp, someone explained to Nixon that, in Japan, the sharp, downward motion always meant "Come," not "Sit down." Nixon was very lucky; as the internees found out in 1944, soldiers normally punished internees for disobeying in that manner (Nixon, 13–14).

The future internees could look nowhere for help. By January 3, 1942, according to Celia Lucas, the following was accomplished by the Japanese in what seemed a juggernaut advance:

> Pearl Harbor had been bombed; most of the Pacific Fleet was sunk (though aircraft carriers, luckily, were at sea at the time and escaped destruction).
> Manila was held by the Japanese.
> The U.S. Army had retreated to and was bottled up on the Bataan peninsula.
> Guam and Wake Islands had fallen to the Japanese.
> The British battleships *Prince of Wales* and *Repulse* had been sunk.
> Kowbon on the Chinese mainland had been captured.
> Hong Kong had surrendered.
> All U.S. planes in the Philippines had been destroyed.
> Brunei in Borneo was Japanese occupied. (Lucas, 7)

Americans waiting in their households for the Japanese military to come and collect them had very little recourse but to go with their captors and hope for a livable situation in the camps.

Some may wonder why prior to the invasion more American civilians had not tried to leave Manila and melt into the hills, perhaps to join the guerrillas. A few actually did — but with mixed results. American housewife and eventual spy Claire Phillips took her baby with her into the hills to join the guerrillas, though ultimately the baby made it impossible to stay there. An English teacher at the University of the Philippines and her novelist husband, Doris and Ron Rubens, unencumbered by children and carrying only several books of Shelley and a volume of philosophy, did take themselves into Luzon's Sierra Madre Mountains slightly north of Manila near Montalban; ultimately, they felt compelled morally to surrender in mid-1943 to save the life of their guide Fabian and his family. Other families initially tried to hide out as well.

Karen Lewis (then age nine) and her parents in the Balatoc mining community of northern Luzon practiced slipping off at the first alarm "to a cave stocked with medicines, food, water and . . . cotton swabs and bandages." Late in December, near Christmas, the army told those at Balatoc to evacuate the women and children (ironically) "to the safety of Manila" by bus because of the proximity of the Japanese landings at Lingayen Bay; at this point Karen and her mother stopped planning on cave dwelling and dutifully boarded the bus to Manila (Lewis, 74).

William Moule's children, Billy and Eileen, and his pregnant wife, Marg, like the Lewises, initially went farther into the mountains of northern Luzon near Lusod lumber camp. Unlike the Lewises, Moule decided not to send his family on the bus to Manila. Some time later, having discovered that the Japanese were much closer than he had previously thought, Moule and his family attempted to make their way down the backside of the mountains to Manila *on foot* with a very pregnant (but game) Marg in tow. Halfway down, news came that Manila would not hold out for long, so Moule changed his mind and reversed course, taking his family (and weary Marg) back up the mountain toward the Lusod lumber camp (Moule, 53–56; 71–74; 87–89). Eventually, they ended up with the Japanese (but not before Marg had her baby by the side of the trail) and were put in the Baguio (Hays) camp (104–110).

The Moules refused to take the bus, but those who did were told to leave immediately and to take only one suitcase apiece. Karen Lewis took two of her Christmas presents—one of which was a silver framed photograph of her favorite dolls. She explains with remembered sadness that she was unable to take all the dolls and accessories "for the beautiful doll house my mother had designed and I was never to see." Lewis's mother apparently hadn't heard of the problems in Manila, given what she took as she evacuated. Explains Lewis, "Since we were going to Manila, Mother packed an evening gown and a tennis racket" (Lewis, 74–75).

Most civilians, at least on Luzon where the main military action was taking place and which held the largest number of Japanese soldiers, recognized that a life hiding out in the mountains was probably too dangerous and too filled with privation for children or elderly parents. Most of my sources had families, usually children, and had to take what they saw as a sensible course of action. It is easier to be a hunter-killer member of a guerrilla band if a person is in his or her early twenties, has no back problems, and is not saddled with three children, than if the person in question is in his or her midforties with a family and a widowed mother to consider. Few modern readers, faced with such circumstances, would have the nerve to risk taking such an entourage into a jungle. No one could have had the foresight to know that in the camps all would eventually face starvation without the ability to forage as could someone in the hills. Additionally, as Grace Nash explains, for some, resources probably would not have permitted flight: "The idea of fleeing to the hills was out. No gasoline was available, and little chance of escape. Were there any hills *not* infested with Japanese? They were invading our island, Luzon, from all sides, it was reported" (Nash, 30).

Beyond the question of resources, it was a matter of ignorance. No one knew what to expect by late December 1941 or early January 1942. That the army left civilians behind to fend for themselves and, as Grace Nash and others have reported, officials urged civilians to wait quietly to be picked up (Nash, 30) seemed to suggest the civilians' fate in camp would not be terrible but rather uncomfortable and inconvenient — a brief period of inconvenience before the inevitable repatriation that would surely follow soon. After all, as Magnuson points out, those working for the U.S. high commissioner's office, which refused to tell civilian women and children to leave earlier, were repatriated in 1943.

The first repatriation, six months after the initial internment, was limited to a specific number of internees (only around 2,500 "non-official" Allied personnel out of 7,800 possible; Frances Long was lucky enough to be among them [Corbett, 67; Waterford, 261]). Further repatriation seemed a cruel joke; a year and a half after their initial internment, internees were beginning bitterly to refer to the hypothetical ship that would supposedly repatriate them as the *Phantom Maru* (Lucas, 39). The second exchange (on the *Teia Maru*) took a mere 151 people, only 131 of them Americans, and 24 of these were consular staff who weren't picked up at Santo Tomás but elsewhere. Among those leaving from STIC were some caught in transit to points beyond Manila (Dr. Leach, for example, and Cronin of the Associated Press), businessmen and their families in transit from Shanghai and Hong Kong, and five or six urgent medical-surgical cases, along with one internee coming in from Baguio. The second group left for their ship on September 26, 1943 (Hartendorp, II, 9–11).

Indeed, beyond the second exchange, there was no other. As Corbett explains, the long delay of the second repatriation ship was due at least as much to bureaucratic, governmental in-fighting (and J. Edgar Hoover's paranoia) as it was to Japanese perfidy. By the time the second exchange was in the planning stages (September 1943), at least eighteen U.S. government agencies and subagencies were involved, among them Customs, Immigration and Naturalization, the Coast Guard, the Office of Naval Intelligence, the Air Transport Command, the Provost-Marshall's Office, the Office of Censorship, the Special Division, the Justice Department, and the FBI (Corbett, 70–75).

Back in the Philippines the actual initial contact and final arrest of civilian families seem to have followed a general pattern with odd individual touches. In the Hills' case, two Japanese officers (one of them English speaking) and three soldiers "pound[ed] on our front gate" (Alva Hill, 320) several days after the army entered Manila. Somehow, the Japanese had a list of all British and American homes — lending some credence to Hill's and Romulo's earlier spy theories. The Japanese came to each door on the list and demanded entrance, then proceeded to make an inventory on the spot of all household and personal possessions. They posted notices on the front of the house or gate or apartment building stating in both English and Japanese, "This is Property of the Imperial Japanese Government. Do Not Remove." After completing the inventory, the soldiers left the Hills in their home under guard for three days before finally coming back to take them away. During those three days, the Hills learned to use caution with members of the Japanese army, as Alva Hill explains:

> We were very cautious every time we ventured outside our gates. Failure to stop and properly bow down to each of the numerous Jap sentries caused many Filipinos, Americans, Spaniards, and others to be slapped in the face. Ladies, old and young, were cuffed by ordinary private soldiers. As time passed, their cruelty increased. (Alva Hill, 320)

Frieda and Chet Magnuson and their daughter Susan as well as visitors and friends were waiting with packed suitcases in a compound for the Japanese to come. On January 5 a car drove up to the compound. All the Japanese wanted, however, was to confiscate the Americans' cars, and they ordered each of the men to drive his own car and follow in a convoy to Japanese Headquarters. The women quite sensibly thought they would never see their husbands again, but several hours later two Japanese cars drove back into the compound and all the men got out. Notes Magnuson, "They had delivered their cars, been given grape juice by the Japanese officers, and returned intact" (Magnuson, 39). Until some ten days later, when the group was finally picked up, the Americans slept in their own houses, quietly arranging a nightly dig for liquor in the Magnuson backyard. Chet and his friend Tom dug up a bottle a night, and stoically everyone had a cocktail, keeping an eye out for block guards who roved around in front of the houses (Magnuson, 39).

Women with small children were initially allowed to stay outside camp, as was the case with the Jensen family, which consisted of the mother, her three-month-old son, a three-year-old daughter, and an eight-year-old daughter, Sascha, who wore heavy leg braces; the father, however, went immediately to Santo Tomás. Those Allied women and children allowed to live in town were given armbands "to show that it was OK for us to go out and get food at the store" (Jensen, 37–38). The armbands, at least according to Sascha Jensen, didn't always protect them from Japanese anger:

> Presumably we wouldn't get picked up, but they [the Japanese] were very aggressive, and they would scream and yell at any of us in the street. My mother was worried and told all of the children not to ever answer the door. One day, I opened

the door when someone was knocking and a gruff Japanese soldier marched in. He reached over and tweaked one of my breasts and laughed—I felt terribly humiliated and cried for hours. (38)

Mrs. Jensen and the children lived outside for almost a year and then voluntarily joined Mr. Jensen in camp. As Sascha Jensen explains, "We felt we'd be safer inside since many atrocities were still being committed and many women were being beaten and raped; others were brutally murdered" (39).

Claire Phillips's account, written about Manila a year later under Japanese occupation, suggests what those staying in the city faced each time they left the house, even in those early days of captivity:

> We never knew when we saw Nips walking down the street, whether they would turn into our house. They came in any time they felt like it, asked for food and drink, and we dared not refuse them. They even made us mend and wash their clothes without pay. If they took a fancy to any article in our homes, they picked it up and walked out. We could not telephone the police and complain that it had been stolen. That would ear-mark us for undue attention, and they would not believe our story. It was plain, unadulterated open looting, but we were helpless. (Phillips, 116)

Frieda Magnuson confirms that Japanese soldiers often demanded that captive women do domestic chores for them. She remembers that a soldier came to the amah who was staying with her (Magnuson was pregnant and therefore not yet in the camp) and waved a shirt at her. The soldier demanded in sign language that the two of them iron his shirt—which they did (Magnuson, 44).

Not many Americans stayed outside the internment camps, however, though women with ill children, pregnant women, and missionaries who agreed to support the laws of the newly imposed Japanese government were allowed to live outside the camps. Most civilians ended up being transported (in the Hills' case, in their own car) to Rizal Stadium or to Villamore Hall to be registered and interned in Santo Tomás. At the stadium, everyone stood in line to report to a Japanese clerk who spoke English regarding such matters as citizenship, family names, personal circumstances, marital status, and former jobs. It was a process that took all afternoon. Comments Martha Hill, it was "a long and tiresome process among crowds of people and crying children"; at its conclusion, around six o'clock in the evening, the Americans and the British in Rizal were packed aboard trucks and taken to Santo Tomás Internment Camp (Alva Hill, 327; M. Hill, 36).

Though the registration process had been tiring and tedious, many were glad that there *was* a registration; at least their names would be somewhere on a list, and maybe their families would know where they were—and in what circumstances. This proved to be a futile hope for many stateside families, however, until late in 1943, as selected Red Cross bulletins show and Daws confirms (273). The American National Red Cross's *Prisoner of War Bulletin* ("For the Relatives of American Prisoners of War and Civilian Internees") in its first issue (June 1943), for example, talks of "difficulties which at times have appeared overwhelming" in opening relief channels and getting accurate registration numbers and names of both POWs and civilian internees in the Far East (1–3). The summer of 1943, approximately a year and a half after the civilian internment in Luzon began, still saw no completely accurate list of internee names compiled nor camps identified except by numbers. Information, especially via neutral observers, was nearly impossible to get. The Japanese refused to let neutral observers or even Red Cross officials into the camps. As Daws explains sarcastically, the Imperial Army refused to allow anyone to enter camps in a war zone, "and they defined most of their Co-Prosperity Sphere as a War Zone" (273–274).

A series of telegrams between the Swiss Embassy and the Japanese Foreign Ministry illustrate this point very clearly. Between June 4, 1943, and May 10, 1944, a cat and mouse game played itself out, as the Swiss (the chosen "protecting power" for the United States) requested the right to inspect both POW and internee camps and collect accurate numbers, and the Japanese Foreign Ministry refused:

June 4, 1943: The Swiss request the right to talk to prisoners without guards or witnesses present.

June 24, 1943: Shigemitsu (foreign minister) tells the Swiss that regulations prohibit talks without a guard; therefore, the request cannot be granted.

July 29, 1943: The Swiss repeat an earlier request of July 10 to visit the camps in the Philippines and get an accurate census.

March 30, 1944: The Swiss state that from February 1, 1942, to March 15, 1944, they have intervened in writing 134 times regarding visits to, and information about, the camps of prisoners. There have been only twenty-four replies, and in the last nine months, only three. Most of the replies have been negative.

November 10, 1944: The Swiss ask for confirmation of a promise made by Shigemitsu that permission to visit camps in occupied territories would be given on condition of reciprocity.

November 13, 1944: The Japanese say that visits to Manila, Shonan [Singapore], and Bangkok may commence.

December 8, 1944: Foreign Minister Shigemitsu tells the Swiss that the Japanese government will allow visits to camps in occupied territories provided that these visits do not interfere with military operations and on conditions of reciprocity. They will commence after negotiations with the International Red Cross and involve visits to the Philippines, Shonan, and Thailand (IMTFE, *Record*, Reel 11, 14,742–14,745).

As late as May 1945 the Swiss were still asking fruitlessly to visit all camps. Earlier requests were at first agreed to (for example, that acknowledged from Suzuki to the Swiss on November 13, to visit Bangkok and Manila) but then retracted a month later when the ministry suggested that such visits would, unfortunately, interfere with military operations. Reciprocity had never been an issue, because U.S. camps of interned Japanese and Japanese-American citizens such as Manzinar were regularly inspected both by our own Red Cross and by groups such as the American Friends (IMTFE, Reel 11, 14,740 [telegram of 10 May 1944]). There had already been objective visitation by both the Spanish (Japan's "protecting power") and Swedish representatives as well as by the International Red Cross, who visited every place in the United States where Japanese or Japanese-Americans were being held (IMTFE, Reel 11, 14,899–14,900; Corbett, 41–47).

The openness of U.S. internment camps and their operations is perhaps most dramatically illustrated by an incident at Lordsburg Internment Camp in New Mexico and the consequences to those involved. In the predawn hours of July 27, 1942, a group of 127 Issei (Japanese born) internees were brought to the U.S. Army Internment Camp at Lordsburg. Earlier identified and interned through an "Enemy Alien" roundup by the Justice Department, these were selected individuals who had been ordered into internment after individual hearings before the Enemy Alien Hearing Board (Culley, 225–226).

The incident began when Private First Class Clarence A. Burleson shot two Issei for "trying to escape" when they lagged some distance behind the rest of the column coming in from the transport. The attempted cover-up of this homicide as well as Japanese internee complaints about being worked long hours in the sun and forced to clean officers' latrines (both against the Geneva Convention) eventually resulted in a telegram sent by the internees to the Spanish Embassy. Following the delivery of Spanish Memorandum No. 352, along with the Provost-Marshall's Office comments, the camp commandant, Lundy, found himself summarily removed from office to face court-martial along with the shooter, Burleson, not only for graft and corruption but for "gross administrative mishandling" of the shooting incident. During the time of complaint, an independent inspection committee of the American Friends also visited Lordsburg camp (Culley, 238–243).

Certainly, the deliberate shooting of two internees and theft of recreational funds, band instruments, and letters, as well as inappropriate work assignments — all eventual charges against the camp commandant — showed our record toward prisoners to be blotted here and there, as it was overseas in the Pacific War after Guadalcanal, when captured Japanese were frequently shot rather than taken to holding areas (Dower, 35–37; Linderman, 178–179).

However, it is important to note that even though the United States was not clearly winning (and to some obviously losing) the war in July 1942, the government did not condone abuses of internees and abided by international agreements and the mechanisms for adjudication when such incidents occurred. This did not prove true of Japan.

The nature and texture of the next three years for the American internees in the Philippines — invisible years from January 1942 to February 1945 when they remained uninspected by any neutral organization or protecting power — would be only partially foretold by the internees' first impressions after entering Santo Tomás that January. Margaret Sams remembers it vividly:

> Words fail me when I try to picture the scene that met our eyes as we entered the large front door of the university. I hadn't seen Macy's during a Christmas rush at that time, but as I look back at it the crowds are similar . . . with a subtle difference. There were people, thousands of them, all ages, types, colors, descriptions. They were all worried to death, and they all dragged, pushed, hauled, and carried everything that was left to them in the world. (Sams, 60)

As Stevens explains, the so-called "Manila Internment Camp #1" (Santo Tomás) began filling with prisoners on January 4 when 300 internees arrived by truck from the South Malate District of Manila. Other groups soon followed (Stevens, 12).

Martha Hill describes their first night after being dumped unceremoniously, bag and baggage, in the center of Santo Tomás. Already the campus was crowded when the Hills arrived on the sixth. Assigned to the Main Building, the family discovered that the rules demanded that men and women have sexually segregated living quarters. Martha Hill absorbed this blow, only to receive another shock when she went to Room 25, her assigned sleeping space. Room 25 had fifty women in it and only enough floor space remaining for a single bed — though there was no bed, only a blanket. Hill notes, "What a night that was! January nights in Manila can be damp and cold. One blanket on chilly cement is not conducive to sleep. New people kept arriving. Young mothers with crying babies they weren't used to caring for, were disturbing Japanese guards [who] clumped in and out and flashed lights in our faces" (M. Hill, 37; Alva Hill, 329).

Eva Nixon also recalls her first night at Santo Tomás vividly. Her bed and those of her three friends were nothing more than "simply a place on the cement floor" where they shared "a bit of the same steamer rug with housecoats used as covering" and without any mosquito netting. Nixon reported twenty-seven mosquito bites on one hand the next morning (20).

Nor did things improve in those first days. There was no food, for example, except what the prisoners had carried in with them. Prisoners had to rely on friends (of neutral nations), on other internees, or on former Filipino servants to bring them food and necessities, as well as on hard currency derived from selling their jewelry and valuables. As Martha Hill explains, "A few old people who had no regular outside contacts and were too proud to ask for food from their neighbor's small supplies, nearly starved before the first camp meal was served" (M. Hill, 37–38).

This first meal occurred, incidentally, on January 31. For many people in Santo Tomás this was twenty-five or twenty-six days after their initial internment, and even so, this was food pooled by the prisoners and supplemented by supplies bought with money collected by the Executive Committee from the internees, not food provided by the Japanese (Hartendorp, I, 12). Alva Hill speaks for the majority of American prisoners when he praises the Philippine people for the part they played in those early days—indeed months—when the Japanese were not supplying the internees with food:

> The Philippine people came to our rescue. Houseboys, cooks, lavanderas, neighbors, friends, and peddlers flocked around the walls of Santo Tomás and peeked through the iron bars. They handed us bundles of every description containing bread, fruit, clothing, canned goods, toilet articles, candy, and every conceivable sort of native delicacies. Part of that supply was goods ordered and paid for by the internees, but much of it was given freely by friends and neighbors. (Alva Hill, 331)

James McCall, an internee in Santo Tomás, gives a vivid, final picture of the entering internees and of the difference three years of captivity would make:

> Entering STIC healthy, well-groomed, defiant and arrogant, we left it three years later undernourished—many to the point of emaciation—ill, humiliated, silent. What few clothes we still possessed were in tatters and patches. Many of us for the first time in our lives understood the meaning of filth, unfit food, crowding, regimentation, and misery. Business executives and [the] social *élite* picked "butts" to smoke and searched the commandant's garbage can for bones and rinds. (McCall, 1–2)

3 Meanwhile, on Several Islands Not Far Away

The unfortunate Americans on Luzon almost immediately faced capture and internment by the Japanese in what seemed a Pacific Blitzkrieg, as we have seen. By December 31, the island had been invaded in two different locations, and a full-scale army was settling in. Americans on the other islands had perhaps a harder choice to make, because they *were* on other islands and thus had more time to mull over the choice of hiding out or preparing to go to camp voluntarily. On islands such as Cebu, Panay, the Visayan Chain, and especially Negros, the lead time between the December 8 bombings and the actual invasion of any one of the islands was a matter more of months than of weeks, as it was on Luzon, with the exception of Mindanao, which Japan had long considered an outpost due to the large Japanese pre-war population in Davao (Agoncillo, I, 49–50). Davao was one of the first places bombed and one of the earliest to be invaded, finally taken on December 20, 1941 (Brown, 74).

With the extra time available on most islands outside Luzon, Americans, some with strong prior civil defense plans in place, could and did prepare hideouts in the mountains and a plan of evacuation. With an eye on the occasional Japanese patrol boat or plane going by, civilians loaded up heirlooms, canned food, baby blankets, the family silver, pots and pans, bedding, mosquito netting, native stoves, mattresses, bolas, and sacks of sugar, flour, rice, and powdered milk, and headed for the hills. Frequently the hideouts were well stocked and remote. Assuming erroneously that help from the United States would come to relieve Bataan, Corregidor, and the rest of the Philippine Islands, the people believed that they would be hiding six or eight months at most, not for years. As events became progressively more bitter, the decision to stay hidden or to follow Japanese orders to surrender voluntarily loomed as a harder choice.

By late May and early June, most islands had been invaded, and the Japanese were offering food, shelter, and no reprisals to those who turned themselves in; they threatened severe punishment or death, however, to those who continued to hide out, explaining that holdouts would be considered guerrillas and spies and treated accordingly if captured (Onorato, x; Clarke, "Army," 177). Some, including Mabel Robertson, an American and a second lieutenant in the Army Nurse Corps on Mindanao, joined her English engineer husband, Bill, and refused to go in. Instead, they joined forces with the guerrillas (Clarke, "Army," 177), as did Roy and Edna Bell on Negros Oriental until they were finally evacuated by submarine to Australia in 1944 (Bell, 13–14). Others — such as Elizabeth Vaughan and her two small children on Negros Occidental; James and Ethel Chapman, the Lowrys, Charles and Hettie Glunz, and Alice Bryant and her husband on Negros Oriental; Bessie Sneed and her husband on Masbate Island in the Visayan Chain; Maurice and Virginia Chapman, along with Ray and Imogene Carlson on Cebu — all went to internment camp eventually. They went for two reasons: either because they voluntarily surrendered or because they were ultimately betrayed to a roving patrol. This chapter focuses upon the American reaction on islands other than Luzon to the first news of the Japanese attack on Pearl Harbor and Manila, the coming months of preparation, the period of hiding out, and the eventual decision of the concealed islanders either to turn themselves in or to attempt to stay hidden until the end of the war.

The Unbelievable Happens

James and Ethel Chapman, both professors at Silliman University at Dumaguete on Negros Oriental, turned on their radio Monday morning, December 8, to hear that Pearl Harbor had been bombed, followed hours later by the bombing of Davao. Ethel Chapman, whose voice narrates the diary account, describes the shock: "We left our breakfast to sit by the radio and gaze blankly into each other's faces as one awful detail followed another and our peaceful academic world crashed about us" (13).

It was the beginning of another school week, and the university's 1,600 or so students milled around the campus, the resolution of a worried university administration being to hold classes "as usual" (Chapman, 13). The word to close down all schools (what Halsema heard from Quezon in Baguio) had not yet been received from Luzon. Closing or not closing the school was really moot. Nothing was ever, it seemed, going to be "as usual" again. Because most of Silliman University's students were boarders, the telephone lines were soon tied up with calls from anxious parents: "When Manila and Davao had been bombed and invasion was imminent in the north, a general exodus began. Frantic parents wrote or wired or came for their children; autos, buses, trucks, boats — all were filled to overflowing as boys and girls head[ed] for home" (Chapman, 14).

By Wednesday, not even a token attempt existed to hold classes at the university, and, as the news sank in, the ROTC units still on the island were told to stand by. At the chapel service at the university's assembly hall, the governor of Negros Oriental told remaining students and staff that they would begin following the National Emergency Act of 1941. Roy Bell, professor of physics at Silliman, was put in charge of all civilian affairs; Ethel Chapman's husband James, professor of zoology and entomology at Silliman, was made food administrator for the province; and Major Robert H. Vessy, commander of the Seventy-third Infantry Regiment, took over all military and ROTC matters under USAFFE (Chapman, 14).

Despite the plan, certain nagging problems remained at the outset. Siamese students, for example, could not return home because of both the bombing and the Japanese attacks on trans-Pacific shipping. Even Filipino students from Mindanao were afraid to go home not only because of the bombing on their home island but also because of the dangers of even interisland sailing (Chapman, 14). Obviously, these students and others still waiting to be picked up by parents would have to be provided for. Bell assigned these unfortunates to the care of Silliman professors and other adults on the island. Things in the province of Negros Oriental were at least proceeding according to the Emergency Act.

Across Negros, over the mountain ranges and into the Occidental province, Elizabeth Vaughan's diary recorded less attention to the Emergency Act's civil defense plan and more confusion. It seemed that no one in Negros Occidental had even heard of the Emergency Act and its contingency plans. At 6:15 A.M. the radio reported, "The U.S. is at war with Japan." Vaughan's diary entry notes that this strangely calm announcement was followed at noon by the much more threatening information that several major Philippine cities on two islands had been bombed as well: Davao (on Mindanao) and Manila and Baguio (on Luzon). Following these reports, telegraph and telephone lines were abruptly closed to civilians (Vaughan, 3–4). Vaughan, cut off from her husband, who was away from Negros on a business trip to Manila, was terrified and tried repeatedly to get a message through to his home office. She eventually received one message back from him, but she never saw him again. He was to die, ultimately, in Cabanatuan Prison Camp.

The civilians on Negros Occidental, like those in shattered Manila on Luzon, however, were still in disbelief about events. On Negros Occidental, too, Americans failed to make simple preparations for flight. Vaughan noted the next day (Tuesday, December 9) that "there was a bridge and mahjongg party at the Hawaiian-Philippine Sugar Central at the manager's house." The invitations had, after all, been posted days earlier, and it seemed somehow improper, despite war, to call off a cherished social event. Vaughan noted cryptically "only one-half of invited guests were there" (4). In itself that is an interesting comment either on American blind optimism or on the need to continue with some sort of "normal" structure in an increasingly threatening environment.

Even this fragile attempt at normalcy foundered, however, by Thursday, December 11. As Vaughan explained, there was then a false alarm about Japanese troops landing at Bancigo pier:

> At 11:00 A.M. Mr. Serobe called excitedly saying Japanese had landed . . . and were now marching on Bacolod—that roads were blocked, and to leave the house at once with one suitcase. Frantic packing of one case for children with diapers and Carnation milk principally, also blankets (weather cool). Second suitcase with bandages, gauze, iodine, mercurochrome, many bottles of cod liver oil. (Children catch cold easily if not given concentrated cod liver oil daily). Servants running wildly, children screaming because of noise and excitement around them, my heart missing every other beat with fear for children—thinking of horror stories of torture administered by Japanese soldiers and my lips repeating, "Jim, oh Jim, come home." (5)

With no car and no way to obtain a taxi, Vaughan ultimately stayed home, because she simply couldn't carry two young children *and* the luggage. A second telephone call informed her somewhat later that *this time* it was a false alarm. The ship spotted was an American naval vessel patrolling the straits (Vaughan, 5).

Several differences existed in terms of reaction to possible invasion between Vaughan's group on Negros Occidental and people such as the Chapmans on Negros Oriental. The Occidental side of Negros had ignored the Emergency Act and had, consequently, no clear plan to follow — no Coast Guard, no coast watch, no preplanned evacuation centers or vehicles, and no rationing or immediate provision for unattended mothers, small children, the elderly, or Filipino friends and servants. Everything, as Vaughan records, was clearly haphazard, jury-rigged, and temporary in nature initially, and only somewhat more thoughtfully planned weeks later.

As Ethel Chapman's account explains, Negros Oriental, on the other hand, had taken the threat of a possible invasion much more seriously and had done its best to follow the provisions of the Emergency Act. This showed in their reaction to the news of possible invasion and the subsequent steps they took (15). James Chapman, the emergency food administrator, made organized lists of necessary supplies and started a steady, logical packing operation that bundled up tinned, dry, and bulk food, medicines, and other necessities for the move to the mountains above Dumaguete. As Ethel explains,

> The possibility of evacuation had been thoroughly discussed at faculty meetings for days and Filipinos as well as Americans had made plans of a general "it can't happen here" optimism. The many excellent places for hide-outs, and several general locations had been suggested for the fifty or sixty faculty families. One of these was Camp Lookout [the Chapmans' own summer home], only eight miles from Dumaguete . . . but sixteen hundred feet in elevation. (15)

The Silliman University president, Dr. Arthur Carson, had previously been subjected to Japanese bombing and had seen the invasion of China; perhaps this experience was largely responsible for his urging the faculty to have an evacuation plan for women and children ready. Camp Lookout became the first choice of the evacuation committee because of its amenities and its elevation. Three female faculty members, in addition to Ethel Chapman, and some female students (among them, the Siamese who could not go home), went to prepare and open the house (Chapman, 15–16).

Though Ethel does not directly speak of it in this passage, it is obvious in later chapters that key Filipino families who either worked at the university or were supporters of it, as well as any household staff who so desired, were included in both the evacuation and later housing and rationing plans. Ultimately, James Chapman's sensible choices, the centralized rationing plan, and strategically organized food caches in five-gallon steel containers prevented actual starvation for all evacuees or even severe hunger for the next year, allowing many to hide out almost until the end of the war. The Chapmans and the Glunzes, for example, were not captured until November 1943—almost two years after the war started.

Such calm rationing and planning were absent in Vaughan's province. She speaks on December 11, for example, of servants "refusing to work" and running away (5). She relates subsequent furious attempts to use credit with the local Chinese grocer to get supplies. Unable to convince him to extend her credit, Vaughan purchased (from her dwindling cash hoard) "a few groceries, powdered milk, canned vegetables, canned meat, matches, flashlight batteries, cigarettes" (6); others were not so fortunate, because earlier "one customer . . . bought $700 worth of groceries including almost *all* the powdered milk" (Vaughan, 6). Very shortly, the shelves got increasingly bare, even for those with cash. Something as sensible as central rationing had obviously not been planned.

Nor were things much more organized, it seemed, on the island of Cebu where two other couples, Ray and Imogene Carlson and Maurice and Virginia Chapman, were ensconced. Preparations for evacuation and life on the run existed early on Cebu, though some did not take advantage of them. Imogene Carlson, however, did hide from the expected Japanese in a number of locations, along with her sons. Her husband Ray, though a civilian and a minister, agreed to accompany and help the USAFFE troops with codes, leaving Imogene in what he believed to be a safe location. Because of an early alert, ultimately, Imogene had to leave with other civilians before Ray returned. For the Carlsons this resulted in an unexpected separation for several months in early 1942. During this time Imogene and her sons lived in a number of different "hide-outs" on Cebu, ranging from a cave to a rather decent hut, even though the Japanese did not land at Talisay until April 10 and did not begin to intern Allied civilians until mid-May 1942 (Hartendorp, I, 315).

Life in the rough presented Imogene with a regular series of unexpected problems and hardships to overcome. In the first hideout at Sudlon, she worked hard to wash her family's clothes (including diapers) under primitive conditions; however, she had to learn the facts of life in the bush where nature seemed to conspire with the Japanese to make her life difficult: "We soon learned that we couldn't hang our clothes out to dry. The monkeys tore them to shreds at night" (Carlson, 63).

Later, in the hut higher up in the mountains, she settled in fairly well, except for a phobia about rats. The cabin was the favorite commodities trading floor, it seemed, for a large number of pack rats. Imogene's fear of rats became a problem to other civilians in hiding. She concludes, "I'm ashamed to admit it now, but I did a lot of screaming. Those pack rats frightened me so much. They'd run all around our [mosquito] net. We were sleeping on the floor." (64). Carlson says that her houseboy Domingo tried to be sympathetic to her fears, telling her over and over, "The pack rats won't hurt you." She did not believe him, however, given their size and huge teeth. She explains, "I was sure they'd bite holes in the net, and then bite us too" (64).

As it turned out, they didn't actually bite—and Carlson eventually conquered her phobic terror of them—but they did steal! One of the other Americans, for example, loaned Imogene a magazine to read—a rare treat. Unwisely, Imogene, after only partially skimming it, put it away in what she thought was a safe place: the top of the partition separating rooms in the cabin. As she explains, it was not a prudent action: "One of those pack rats got up there and literally tore it to shreds. They'd pick up all the small things they could find and fill their cheek pockets like gophers. Then they'd run outside with their loot and bury it. In return, they'd bring small stones to replace the stolen articles" (64–65).

As we will see later, this would not be the first time that Imogene had to deal with regular theft, though perhaps none was ever again so innocent. Theft would be a continuing problem in internment for many others. Unlike the pack rats, thieves in camp (both Japanese and civilian) didn't bother replacing the goods with rocks or anything else. In a camp in which survival ultimately depended on both food and those personal possessions that could be traded for food, theft was not only antisocial but deadly.

Some of the other Allied civilians on Cebu had another plan. Virginia Chapman, an American and the niece of Admiral Dewey, was willing to go to the hills, and so was her British husband, Maurice, a junior "sub-accountant" for the Cebu branch of the British Chartered Bank of India, Australia, and China in the Philippines (M. Chapman, 7). Though American forces had indeed built a camp in the mountains for those on the island wishing to hide out (the first one in which Imogene Carlson and her sons lived), only a handful ultimately elected to consider the proposition. Some of these reversed their decision later, perhaps, because the danger had not yet materialized. As Maurice Chapman explains,

> We were asked the question [who wanted to hide] and twenty-five of us — only five British—voted to take a shot at it and go up there. The rest of the people said, "No, we'll go to our consulates and stop in our bungalows and wait for the Japs to come

in, and just surrender as being civilians." The night before, those who were going to evacuate went up to the hills behind and spent the night. At dawn we looked out to sea and we could see the ships coming in, and we heard the blowings up in Cebu [City]. (M. Chapman, 11)

In deciding whether to put up with the dirt and rigors of hiding in the hills, Maurice and Virginia Chapman, along with many others, were forced to try to forecast the reactions of a completely alien group of invaders. As civilians, according to the known "rules" of warfare, they were supposed to be safe from deprivation, torture, lengthy confinement (after all, repatriation was the obvious choice), and death. Prudence then seemed to dictate that to be treated as a civilian, one should *resemble* a civilian — that is, make it a point not to hide out in the hills where one might be confused with guerrillas or guerrilla sympathizers.

The fall of Manila helped solve the dilemma for many non-Filipinos on Cebu. As Maurice Chapman related to Michael Onorato forty years later, "It was the end, anyway. All there was to do was to wait for the Japanese to come down . . . [Hearing an enemy task force was on the way] we were not surprised. We were ready and made accommodations to set the city on fire as soon as they were sighted." (Maurice Chapman, 10).

On the other hand, a number were not so willing to wait passively or even to turn themselves or the city over, as they agreed with Virginia Chapman, who points out caustically that such prudence might not have been of much use. Being clear noncombatants hadn't saved the Chinese elderly, the women, or children in Nanking from torture or death, and declaring Manila an open city hadn't stopped it from being bombed repeatedly. Rules of either logic or war didn't seem to be applicable (M. Chapman, 8–10).

The reaction of those Americans and British electing to hide or to stay reflected a certain confusion about aims and a proper course of action on Cebu. Between December 25, 1941, and April 10, 1942, Maurice opened his bank branch every day from 8:00 A.M. to noon, to cash military officers' checks so that "American authorities could buy up everything they could find — medical supplies, army supplies, anything" (M. Chapman, 8). The bank itself issued its own money, authorized peculiarly by Washington D.C., even though it was a British bank. Despite this semblance of normalcy, authorities initially evacuated the British and American women and children back into the hills the day after Christmas because of a rumor of an imminent invasion. A tense month passed, but nothing happened. No Japanese fleet appeared on the horizon. The women and children, tired of their forced primitive living and separation from husbands and fathers, returned to their homes where they stayed until surprised by the actual invasion in early April (M. Chapman, 9). Imogene

Carlson and her sons were eventually reunited with her husband during this period, though well after Christmas.

Davao, though it was the first of the islands (other than Luzon) to be invaded, still held at least a small population of Americans hiding out, though obviously not for long. Just after December 9, 1941 (and the first Davao bombing), USAFFE officer Lt. Colonel Hillsman arrived and appointed all Americans and British to civilian defense committees, not unlike those on Negros Oriental though not so thoroughly planned or organized in advance (Brown, 73). Between December 14 and 19, 1941, most American women and their children went to one of two "safe" locations," Bukidnon or Madaum.

Jane Wills, wife of a mine operator at the Davao Gold Mine, her husband, Hugh, and their daughter Trudi (who was less than a year old) trekked into the center of the island, because it seemed the safest place to go.

As in so many other cases, the Japanese sent word into the Mindanao interior for the civilians in hiding to come out and report to the authorities, promising that they would receive good treatment. In this case, a German, Waldo Neveling, whom the Americans had interned right after December 8 as an enemy alien, was to take the message. After freeing him, the Japanese sent him into the backcountry to "persuade all American civilians in hiding, all miner, all missionary, all school teacher [sic] to come to Japan Army headquarters." If they did not, and they were later found, they would be killed (qtd in Keats, 5).

As it was, the point soon became moot. Interned honorary British vice consul Alex Brown recounts the Japanese landings at Talomo and Sasa on December 20, 1941, which overwhelmed even the hopes of the limited defense force that soon took to the hills. Some of the civilians joined them at Malaybalay, but soon the Japanese captured those; others voluntarily came out to be interned. In any event, by late December some civilian internment began in Davao, though it occurred initially in the quiet elegance of the "Foreigners' Club" (Brown, 74) on a limited basis. From December 20 until January 3 (the day civilians were first interned in Manila), a small number of internees (both British and American) were held exclusively in the club library (Brown, 74), while more civilians straggled out of hiding to join them, in twos and threes, and the struggling USAFFE forces continued to fight hopelessly. Finally, on May 10, 1941, the American forces surrendered, as did most other units on other islands — these last were the neglected remnants of MacArthur's earlier master plan to fortify all the islands for a total defense of the Philippines (Schaller, 66).

Christmas Day loomed dark for all the various families mentioned so far, though in the case of Elizabeth Vaughan, the Sugar Central people on Negros

Occidental had finally come up with a flimsy evacuation plan. The extant authority in the area de facto was the Hawaiian-Philippine Sugar Central located at Silay, a port town on Guimaras Strait on the northwest coast of Negros, nine miles north of Bacolod (Petillo, ed., 12n). As the largest employer, and with the major concentration, of Americans, the Sugar Central took over the duties of looking after Americans in the vicinity on an ad hoc basis, doing whatever planning managed to get done. Though not a member of the Sugar Central "family," Vaughan knew the manager's wife socially, as well as others connected with the Central; because Vaughan was without her husband and had two small children, in addition to being the only visible American in Bacolod, the Wileys invited her and her family to come stay with them in Silay. Vaughan relates the last hours of Christmas Eve in Bacolod prior to her evacuation to Silay:

> No Christmas tree, toys for the children, decorations, or other signs of the season. On the radio a few scattered out-of-place Christmas songs, but most stations broadcasting of the extreme suffering in Hong Kong where the civilian population as well as the army were fighting Japanese in the streets, of cut water supply, but valiant efforts to hold out, of reinforcements to Japanese in Philippine Islands, of bombing attacks, Manila to be declared an "open city." (Vaughan, 11)

Furthermore, Vaughan expresses anguish about her husband's whereabouts, noting that a morning broadcast earlier on Christmas Eve described the massive destruction of Manila's port area—the section that contained Jim Vaughan's office. Vaughan notes there was "no thought of Christmas" after this news.

Christmas Day, though gloomy with war news and the continuing absence of her husband, did prove cheerier than Vaughan had originally supposed. After moving her to Silay, the kindly Wileys provided Vaughan, four other Americans, and one British family with a house and even supplied small gifts for Vaughan's children (Vaughan, 12). Servants at the Silay's Central were, however, expensive; wages for a cook, for example, were $15.00 per month with "chow"[1]; for an extraordinarily faithful houseboy, Seijo, the cost was $6.00 per month and chow (13). Judiciously, Vaughan fired the cook (who was too expensive) but kept Seijo, the amah, and the lavandera. Food, too, was cheaper at Silay. The Central had a garden that provided vegetables at cost and even "white leghorn eggs for sale," and, for $7.00 a month, the company even provided lights, water, and all the ice a person could use. In addition to this, the Central also maintained, weeded, and harvested the garden produce for those Americans living there (13).

There is an eerie sense throughout much of Vaughan's early account that the Japanese invasion, indeed the war itself, was a bad dream, soon to be awoken from. Vaughan's assumptions seem out of keeping with those of other evacuees and appear almost disassociated in their lack of apparent understanding of the events surrounding her, similar to Karen Lewis's mother going into internment in Manila with her tennis racquet and evening gown. Even as Vaughan watched air raid shelters, lined with blocks of pressed sugar cane residue, finally being completed December 28 at Silay; even after simple gas masks had been distributed to all men, women, and children; even, finally, after both Vaughan and her children had been inoculated for cholera, typhoid, and dysentery, she was still able to talk happily two days later about a dinner party (Vaughan, 14–18). "Dinner at McMaster's," she details, featured "a real rolled roast, drinks before dinner, and Christmas pudding with whipped cream," as well as a bridge game following. She notes that there was an effort to forget the war, but it was only partially successful; conversation "invariably" returned "to fighting in Manila" (14).

But the war refused to go away. By December 30, Manila had been repeatedly bombed, which destroyed even the ancient Santo Domingo Church in Intramuros, and the Japanese were announcing over the radio that Baguio was also taken. As Vaughan notes, "At news hour broadcasts, there is only 15 minutes of music and then silence. This silence of radio stations and obvious avoidance of local news is ominous" (13–14).

Some other islands fared better, but only initially. As Grace Savary notes, the Japanese were "deathly afraid" of lepers, and so they left Culion Island Leper Colony in the Palawan chain in peace for the length of the war. They kept traffic away from it, and eventually most of the lepers starved to death because the island was only marginally self-sufficient and depended on the outside world for most of its food (Savary, 9).

Back in Negros Oriental, by early January 1942, the last preparations for evacuation were being completed. As Ethel Chapman explains, "In the province, committees had been appointed to handle money, food, fuel, transportation, sanitation and health, local defense, and evacuation of citizens. Doctors and nurses worked under the Red Cross, and the provincial and municipal teachers helped in any department to which they were assigned" (28–29).

Despite the turmoil during the early months of the war, business on Negros Oriental proceeded unsteadily along a preplanned path. Food stocks especially were of concern because of the number of children. The committee (headed by Jim Chapman) set local retail ceiling prices for almost all commodities, and each local group of evacuees was asked to send in a list of food requirements. These lists were then forwarded to local merchants and those on neighboring islands to see if the requests could be filled. Often (somewhat surprisingly) they were. For several weeks in mid-January and early February, for example, the committee ordered, paid for, and received milk from large storehouses on Cebu (which had not yet been invaded). Additionally, several thousand kilos of corn and rice, ordered and paid for earlier, finally arrived from Mindanao at approximately the same time.

This system of relayed requests and central procurement prevented hundreds of private requests from irregular channels either stripping the warehouses or starting the cutthroat practices of a black market in which seemingly dwindling supplies are sold for more and more exorbitant prices.

Other planning involved sanitation and the capability of shifting production from one commodity to another before the islands were overtaken. Soap, for example, was absolutely vital to sanitation in the tropics, if only as a basic antiseptic against tropical ulcers and the nearly immediate infections that occurred in that climate with untended or open wounds and scrapes, as Frank Cary would illustrate at a later date on Mindanao. As Ethel Chapman explains, Negros Oriental's Bais Sugar Central on the coast twenty-five miles from Dumaguete "stopped making sugar and made soap out of soda (byproduct of paper mill) and coconut oil (from unexportable copra)." This soap eventually sold both in Negros Occidental and on the black market in Mindanao for three times the price as in Dumaguete. Valuable stocks of the soap were stored for future use in caches on Negros Oriental well before the province was occupied (Chapman, 30–31). That Hawaii-Philippine Sugar Central on Vaughan's side of Negros didn't think to convert its plant is strange, especially because it had the same raw materials and technology available that Bais Central did. The proof that it didn't do so is the exorbitant prices it paid for Bais's soap. This is one more example of a lack of preparation that continued to plague Negros Occidental's evacuees.

Though preparation continued for their hideouts in the hills in January 1942, civilian evacuees on Negros Oriental were still making trips into Dumaguete to their old homes to pick up items to take with them because the bombing had not touched Dumaguete at this point. The trips into town, however, were eerie, much in the way that a visit to the house in which someone has died is unnerving. Ethel Chapman notes, "We went through our strangely quiet houses, listened once more to the radio, and took what care we could of our favorite plants" (27). The life they had led before the war was gone, but the empty shell of it remained behind, tugging at them with plants, radios, and other routines. The province held its breath, knowing that invasion and the end even to these visits was only a matter of time.

To all those on islands other than Luzon listening to whatever news they could find on the radio, the Japanese advance seemed inexorable: "All the while the conquering Japs marched on! Hong-Kong, Singapore, the Dutch

East Indies—only heroic Bataan still stemmed the tide. But while Bataan held, we pinned our hopes on that" (Chapman, 33).

The bitter knowledge of possible invasion finally percolated through Negros Occidental's encampment and to Elizabeth Vaughan as well; in her January 7, 1942, entry she tells of the strange, yet touchingly impractical, preparations people took in light of a coming invasion. At Sugar Central women did not cache food in five-gallon tins; they destroyed personal effects: "The things that people throw away when they think everything may be taken by aliens—old letters, souvenirs, pictures. There was a general burning of old love letters on Central" (Vaughan, 19).

Vaughan questioned an elderly woman about why she was burning love letters that she and her husband of thirty-two years had written. The woman said that she would rather burn all her husband's love letters than let the Japanese either besmirch them or "scatter them if they could not read them" (Vaughan, 19). This ceremonial burning apparently followed both the breaking up and dispersal of stores of whiskey and the decision of some, including Vaughan, to take the strangely legal step of making up a will. In Vaughan's case, she left her two children to her mother in Mississippi, though how this will was to be read, understood, mailed, probated, and carried out from occupied territory was somewhat problematic, though mail could be sent out of Cebu City on the neighboring island to the United States until the fall of Bataan. While Vaughan makes no specific mention of using this avenue, it was theoretically possible at the time (Halsema ltr, May 19, 1997).

By late January American evacuees across the island in Negros Oriental had finally moved into the hills, ignoring for the time being the need for wills. Ethel and James Chapman, with their children safely in the United States at school, were perhaps less terrified and more calm than Vaughan with two children under age seven. In any event both Chapmans were among the last to leave for hiding. James, in addition to his other duties, supervised the evacuation. The Americans realized that they needed to spread out, rather than live in tight groups. For this reason Ethel Chapman tells us the Lindholms and their four children went with the Winn family and the Scaffs to the Northern Mountains near the Old Mission Hospital. A single evacuee, a woman from a mission station, joined Alice Bryant and her husband at their Pamplona Coconut Plantation in the hills. The Bells and the Carsons, with the last of the dormitory girls who could not get home, settled at Malabo. The Chapmans and the Sillimans went to Camp Lookout six miles above Dumaguete (Chapman, 23–24), with the Glunzes settling nearby. Even amid these preparations, however, some evacuees were more pessimistic than others. Most, including Ethel Chapman and her husband, claimed that "From the very beginning we had no idea of ever surrendering to the Japanese; we thought we could surely evade them for the first few months they [would] stay in Negros!" (24). As friends were splitting up to hide on various mountain chains and ridges, Mr. Winn's final salute to a departing convoy of friends and neighbors seemed grim, but realistic: "'See you all in concentration camp!' We thought that an utterly absurd idea, but two years later there he was to welcome us on our arrival at Santo Tomás!" (Chapman, 24).

Internment

Internment camps came earlier for those on some islands than on others. Obviously, despite the desperate fighting on Bataan and Corregidor, American civilians on Luzon were already in camps by the end of January, or at the very least by the fall of Singapore in February. Luzon had become a major military base, supply port, and stepping stone for the continuing Japanese invasion of the South Pacific and Australia. For those trapped in the path of invasion on Cebu, capture came relatively early in April. Maurice Chapman, on Cebu, discussed what happened in early April 1942. Those few who insisted on staying hidden in the hills were literally "sent for" after Corregidor fell. Two Japanese officials and an American medical officer sought out the handful of evacuees in the hills and told them there would be "no reprisals" if the evacuees surrendered immediately and went in. The evacuees, fearing ill treatment because the Japanese already knew their position, complied. On April 6, 1942, the Japanese came and collected the evacuees in trucks and took them to a temporary internment camp in Cebu City, where they were decently treated before being shipped to either Bacolod on Negros or Santo Tomás on Luzon (M. Chapman, 12–13).

On Negros Occidental Vaughan heard horrific rumors about the Cebu surrender. Her entry for Sunday, April 19, is a vivid account of the fears spawned by tales from Luzon and, earlier, from China under the hands of the Japanese. Though Vaughan never faced what she described here, it is worth noting that many Filipina women *did* suffer exactly this sort of treatment, as did some American women, both in 1942 and 1945 — the Bayview Hotel incident being one of the most infamous, as depositions from the Tokyo War Crimes trials attest (IMTFE, *IPS* Document No. 2844, Exhibit #1421, RG 331, Reel 42; IMTFE, *IPS* Document No. 2848, Exhibit #1426, RG 331, Reel 42). Vaughan's worries, though they may sound racist, were actually a preview of the treatment experienced by a variety of women at the hands of the occupying troops:

I am drunk today, as drunk as one can be and still be aware of the world about me. Beth and Clay need their faces washed and I don't care. . . . The news is that the Japs are ten minutes away by plane, having occupied Iloilo airport, or one and a half hours away by boat. Our American friends on Cebu have suffered the cruelest torture at the hands of Japanese soldiers who are turned loose on small islands with no one to check their sadistic pleasures.

White women are a prize. The army advises us that if a message comes to regis-ter, to pay no attention to the summons—though there is a threat of death if we do not come. A handful of women who answered the summons in Hong Kong and in our neighbor city, Cebu, were put in a brothel for use of Japanese soldiers. So the U.S. Army advises white women not to be captured alive. There are two or three guns in camp for hunting. How we are to end our lives was not explained. We giddily took a second and a third drink.

I would kill Beth and Clay before destroying myself. (Vaughan, 47)

Nothing in my notes about Cebu (though possibly on Palawan) indicates at this time this was the case, though there were several famous atrocities to-ward both men and women on Cebu in 1944 (IMTFE, *IPS*, Doc. No. 2807, Exhibit #1386, RG 331, Reel 42). Fortunately, Vaughan had rethought the army's draconian advice when she actually had to surrender in 1942. One wonders about the Wild West attitude of "Save-One-Bullet-for-Yourself" that the army, bottled up on the Bataan peninsula and (to some) shamefully un-able to protect its citizens, apparently supported. On the other hand, the Japa-nese practice in conquered territory to arrange involuntary "comfort women" drawn from the subdued population to service the troops was widely known. No one knew if this included "colonial" women, as well as the scores of Ko-rean, Filipina, and Chinese women, but given the very real racial hatred the Japanese preached against colonial masters through the propaganda of the "Asian Co-Prosperity Sphere," this sort of obvious degradation probably seemed likely.

Vaughan's dark thoughts were perhaps logically justified by the news from Bataan and Corregidor that reached Negros in mid-May. On May 7, 1942, Corregidor fell. The shock waves reverberated through the islands, despite a general sense that Corregidor could not hold out indefinitely. Vaughan, as did many others, directed her anger not at General MacArthur for his army's shocking lack of preparation or his unsuccessful tactics but at Roosevelt and the Congress because they had not sent help in time to the Philippines. They *had* found time, it seemed, to send bombers to Britain:

It is difficult to understand—repeated [radio?] reports of our efforts to save English homes and English lives—but American lives in the P.I.—What is the U.S. atti-tude? . . . Jim, I now know is either dead or a Jap prisoner, which is worse than

death. As long as Corregidor stood I could ease my aching heart with hope, however distant, that he had escaped with a handful of soldiers who arrived safely on
Corregidor before Bataan fell. It must be necessary and good military strategy to
let the Philippines go to the Japanese without assistance to American civilians
while the aid we feel a right to expect goes to other, to non-American parts of the
world. We wonder if people at home know that there is an American civilian population, like themselves in every respect, living in the P.I., Americans who were
never warned of impending danger from the war and who have been seemingly
forgotten. (Vaughan, 57)

As we now know, relinquishing the Philippines and throwing the main weight
of the United States into the war with Hitler was a foregone conclusion in
prewar strategic plans. Vaughan's rage at the lack of warning that put civilians
in the Philippines and kept them there is, however, more justified.

For Ethel Chapman on the other side of Negros, Corregidor had been a
"feeble ray of hope"; while Corregidor held out, orders came from USAFFE
headquarters in Dumaguete to "prepare lights for the landing field and camouflaged stalls for forty bombers." USAFFE believed that bombers, probably
soon to be on their way to Australia, were actually coming to help relieve
Corregidor. Ethel Chapman explains, "Men worked frantically to carry out
orders. Day by day we waited for the bombers to appear. The fields were ready,
but nothing happened!" (43).

Finally, Corregidor surrendered. The blow was so great that Ethel Chapman barely remembered MacArthur's famous promise: "General MacArthur's
promise, 'I shall return,' was almost overlooked in the disaster of General
Wainwright's surrender and radioed order to the USAFFE commanders to
cease resistance" (47–48).

Vaughan, on the other side of Negros, noted in her May 20 entry that "[the]
white flag still flies on Negros" and that the invasion is expected any day by
those at the Central (74). Her reaction to Wainwright's surrender speech, the
latter broadcast over Japanese-controlled radio, was typical of many Americans' first reaction: the denial of an unpleasant reality that had seemed to
be impossible just months before. Huddled around the radio, Vaughan and
her friends listened as Wainwright proceeded to announce the particulars
of surrender. Vaughan refused to believe it: "Replayed before audiences in
America who knew Gen. Wainwright's speech phraseology and pronunciation
of Philippine names, it has been proved conclusively that the surrender
speech . . . was a forgery of the Japanese" (Vaughan, 74).

Hidden in that pathetic passive construction is the kind of hopeless refusal
to face facts that continually paralyzed Sugar Central's thinking. Wainwright
(the argument seemed to proceed) would never mispronounce the names of

Philippine towns; he would never surrender Corregidor; therefore, he hadn't surrendered it. This was merely a propaganda trick by the enemy to dishearten resisters and disarm American guerrilla groups.

Alas for patriotic daydreams. Wainwright, with his troops facing starvation and disease, did surrender, and more to the point, surrendered on behalf of all the American troops in the Philippines. Though MacArthur (we note, from Australia) condemned Wainwright's actions loudly, he either didn't know or didn't care about the condition of his former soldiers on Corregidor, nor did he know that the Japanese, in light of their inevitable victory, threatened to massacre all the troops if the Americans did not surrender (Schaller, 66).

As Carol Petillo points out, logical constructions and linguistic secret signs aside, "There is no reason to believe that the surrender speech of May 7 was a forgery" (Vaughan, 74n). News of earlier events — including the horrors of the Bataan Death March — finally established the terrible truth: American forces had been defeated utterly, and the islands were now controlled by the Japanese. Capture, it seemed to many, was now only a matter of time. Both news and rumors from other islands suggested that the trap was even closing on Negros itself. As Michael Onorato points out, Americans on Panay, Cebu, the Zamboanga peninsula, and smaller islands were being rounded up and sent to prison camp throughout May 1942 (Onorato, xi).

Vaughan, on Negros Occidental, heard on May 20 about the capture of civilians on Cebu and Iloilo:

> All the American and European evacuees to the hills above Cebu City were ordered by the Japanese to return to Cebu City. A few came from their hiding places to the Japanese headquarters to register as ordered. These were put into [a] concentration camp in Cebu City and are now being given a daily ration of rice and an edible but not palatable variety of seaweed. No other food. White women have been assaulted. We plan to stay here until forced to leave. (Vaughan, 75)

Though she makes one statement about reported rape near the end of the entry, Vaughan does acknowledge that, generally speaking, the particulars passed along suggest decent treatment for prisoners, though raw seaweed served for dinner might have been a "cruel and unusual punishment."

Later, however, she heard rumors from Iloilo of the price of surrender, once again frightening Vaughan and others who would soon be forced to make that decision. As Vaughan's May 21 entry reports, Col. McCelland of Iloilo "was standing on the bridge of the first transport [to prison camp], a prisoner-of-war put in a conspicuous place to insure no resistance. Surrender terms had been discussed in Iloilo and no resistance and *no sabotage* were agreed to by the American officers" (Vaughan, 77–78).

Despite these terms, Vaughan heard of the death of British civilians and other acquaintances who were apparently not covered by the surrender agreement. The British president of the Hong-Kong Shanghai Banking Company, for example, and four of his friends were taken out by the Japanese and shot. Captain Paul Ming, a former interisland pilot whom the Vaughans knew well and whose plane they had often used, was another shot by the occupying forces (Vaughan, 66). This was the Iloilo experience to Vaughan.

The question of whether to surrender if Negros were occupied was a difficult one in light of two sets of rumors — some of humane treatment and some of horrors. According to one set, the Japanese merely rounded up civilians and interned them; this squares with the account given by Maurice Chapman about Cebu; other reports, such as those Vaughan heard, suggested executions, indignities to women, and cruelty, such as in Iloilo. Here for the first time we see the frightening uncertainty that internees faced daily with their Japanese guards. Would the internees encounter cruelty or kindness? It varied by guard, by hour, by day, by season, and by immediate context. The same guards could show cruelty, even sadism, one day, and then altruism, kindness, and even sensitivity on the next. This unpredictable behavior prevented the internees from relying on any routine behavior to protect themselves. Becoming sensitive to the moods of the guards and commandant became a matter of survival for both the internee committee members and their fellow countrymen for whom they petitioned, in addition to their individual everyday concerns when passing a guard on the way to the toilet or the water faucet.

Others beside Vaughan considered the varying reports and, like Vaughan, decided initially to continue hiding rather than risk death by firing squad or by other means. With the news of the Bataan march and the cruelty and starvation afforded the prisoners, the balance tipped and many were not anxious to put themselves in the hands of conquerors who acted in such a manner to helpless prisoners. The Robertsons on Mindanao, after the shelling of the island began in May, knew the odds and chose survival in the hills with the guerrillas. Explains Mabel:

> There we lived in fear of capture, a new sensation to us, while the Japanese overran the island. We were frightened — afraid of what might happen to us if we were discovered. Our life was not one of hardship for we had plenty of supplies and our health was good. In this group of refugees I was the only white woman but I had the companionship of Filipino women who accompanied their men into hiding. (Robertson, qtd in Clarke, "Army," 177)

Alice Bryant and her husband, the former provisional governor of Mindanao, now living on Negros Oriental, decided by May 13 that it was time to evacuate to the hills. Quietly, in the early morning they and their "houseguests" (other refugees) left for "Camp 1" in the interior of southern Negros. This hideout, as was typical of so many others on Negros Oriental, had been prepared in advance and stocked with food. Although the accommodations were not palatial, they were realistically capable of housing those who arrived. The camp itself was handily and deliberately located by a mountain stream (the Magsusunod) to manage a steady supply of clean water. The camp consisted of one-room huts with bark slab floors, no walls, and overhanging roofs of palm fronds (Bryant, 66). This, as we shall see from the more detailed descriptions of jungle camps given by both Vaughan and especially Ethel Chapman, was a typically practical hideout, making use of easy native materials for the building. Nipa or even sawali (woven bamboo), bark, and rattan were used in some cases for additional walls, and bamboo always for housing frames as well as for crude plumbing pipes, stoppered containers, and even, when split, for flooring (Bryant, 66–70). These huts were quick to build, easy to replace, close to water, and camouflaged both by the natural materials used to construct them and by the flora surrounding them with which they blended. Each camp could be assembled in a matter of days, even in one day, and so evacuees tended to have more than one camp to which to retreat.

Bryant, like Chapman, moved farther and farther into the hills as she perceived danger pressing closer. On May 28, only a little over two weeks from the Bryants' initial evacuation, she and her group set out for "Camp #2" built, again, near a water source — the Magalai River. Bryant describes this second sanctuary, and especially the main camp block: "It was a long, one-roomed building without walls and constructed without a nail. . . . The floor was made of the split trunks of a small palm lashed with rattan to the poles that supported it" (72–73).

Supplies placed earlier in caches or carried in on the trip provided adequate meals, even with the extra mouths of the "houseguests." Bryant provides an example of a typical day's menu at "Camp #2" in early June 1942:

Breakfast: flapjacks or cornmeal mush
Noon meal: rice, toasted dried beef and vegetables or rice with vegetable stew
Night: rice or corn, canned fish, vegetables. (82–83)

Bryant tried to have canned fruit or fresh fruit from the jungle at least once a day and insisted for the sake of nutrition that each day also feature a salad made from the buds of the forest palm trees (83).

Vaughan's accommodations in her hidden camp on the other side of Negros were much less primitive but, unfortunately, were less well camouflaged. In early April 1942 Central ordered several buildings made of local materials to be built in a clearing. A number of Central's employees and their families moved in, with the general intention of inhabiting the houses only briefly following the Japanese occupation of Negros. Unlike Chapman's or Bryant's camps, however, Central made one with amenities. Each house was six or seven feet off the ground (allowing the inevitable servants to be housed underneath); there was an open native kitchen with a five-gallon gasoline tin of water that had to be refilled regularly since the camp was two kilometers away from the nearest water supply. Sewage was provided for by tiny outhouses attached to each house and, according to Vaughan, looking like exact versions of the houses. The houses were also equipped with kerosene lamps (45) and white-painted, rock-rimmed paths.

Medical help centered in the single person of a Miss Ganahan, a registered nurse "formerly with Dr. Jardelega"; she also was an evacuee at the camp. Her skill in cleaning infected cuts (undoubtedly with soap purchased from Negros Oriental), tending deep wounds, and caring for the ill made her a valuable addition to the camp, according to Vaughan (46).

In addition to providing houses, water, kerosene fuel, and a nurse, Sugar Central also sent fresh vegetables to be divided among the eight households. These loads of vegetables were abundant and grown by Central itself. The variety Vaughan lists here refutes later Japanese claims that a wide variety of "Western" vegetables would not grow in the Philippines. One typical shipment to Vaughan's camp in 1942 consisted of beets, bananas, lima beans, parsley, white turnips, asparagus, green peppers, cucumbers, and spinach, as well as onions and avocados. Many of these items could easily have been fed to the prisoners later in concentration camps, to prevent scurvy or beriberi, because the food could be grown locally.

During all this discussion of vegetables sent to the camp, however, Vaughan makes no mention of onion sets, cucumber seeds, tomato plants, or any other method of actually growing these vegetables at the hideout. Whether this was a detail Vaughan neglected to include or, more likely, was typical of the absence of foresight on the part of the Occidental Negros evacuees, is unclear; certainly, this carelessness about future self-sufficiency was reflected in other ways, and it is important to note that Vaughan and her group were forced into surrender much earlier than were the Chapmans or the Glunzes on the other side of Negros. Conversely, Ethel Chapman's detailed account of the preparations she and her fellow evacuees made for self-sufficiency gives readers the same satisfying, cozy feeling that many found as children when they read *Swiss Family Robinson* and watched "Mother" Robinson produce all the necessities of life, seemingly, from her personal bag. It seems apparent that those, like Vaughan, who denied reality enough to believe Wainwright's speech was a hoax were also spiritually part of an insular community on Luzon that re-fused earlier to look realistically at world events and plan for ugly eventualities.

Vaughan's account in the early days of the Negros occupation continues to create an air of fantasy; her April 17 entry, for example, explains that servants could be obtained at the camp and would accept lower wages (six pesos monthly, no chow) and still do housework and washing as well as iron clothes and look after children (Vaughan, 45). In a May 2 entry Vaughan's sewing machine had been sent up "tied to a long bamboo pole carried by two men." (It remained useful, because it was an old-fashioned treadle machine requir-ing no electricity [Vaughan, 54].) That the sight of a cumbersome, black treadle sewing machine slung on a pole and carried up a mountain trail might be a giveaway to any hostile eyes searching for signs of European or American evacuees in the hills is something on which Vaughan never remarks.

Vaughan is not unusual in her seeming lack of concern. While Central personnel sent cases of food, built storage sheds, and practiced jerking beef, the assumption in the air seemed again to be that this was only a brief delay in a normal routine, that normalcy would be restored by fresh American troops. Certainly Vaughan's entry of May 13 (the same day Bryant, on Negros Oriental, went into hiding at Camp #2) suggests less concern than pique and irritation. Her description of the early days of invasion in Silay is particularly hard to understand, in light of events such as Wainwright's surrender, the fall of Corregidor, MacArthur's evacuation, and the loss of the American Army, which had already happened. Vaughan's discussion of the "servant problem" is as revealing as it is odd:

> The other servants [excluding Seijo] fled when war fear swept the Islands. I begged them not to become panicky and told them each day of the news. When I realized Jim could not get back and I should have to see things through without him, I still prided myself in the girls [amah, lavandera], in their neat white dresses which I had designed and made for them. These had button openings down the side in-stead of in the front, as front buttons might hurt the children. But the girls left without a word. Only Seijo remained. (May 13, 1942, 67–68)

That same day Vaughan gave details of the meal at the Binagsukan hideout: "midget peas, tenderloin roast, spiced pears, canned Irish potatoes, avocado salad, Jacob's cookies (biscuits), prune whip, and coffee with cream. The peas, pears, and potatoes were being hoarded as gold. Now that we've surrendered [referring to Wainwright] they are not going into Japanese stomachs." She then asks with playful curiosity, "Is this the way a death-sentenced prisoner feels when a sumptuous meal is laid before him after months of prison fare?" (Vaughan, May 13, 65).

Even at this late hour, there was obviously some concern that food might not last, as Vaughan duly, if offhandedly, records:

> That we shall soon be without fresh meat is a known fact. Whether our last fresh roast will be this week or next is uncertain. . . . We buy [meat] by the kilo [not the cut] and get a hunk of flesh, bone, skin, and hair from the part of the carcass adjoining the last piece severed. Each household is taking all that's available and putting it, covered with coarse-grained salt, in direct sun each day (May 19, 1942, 73).

No one at camp, however, knew exactly how to jerk the meat, nor had anyone brought any books to refer to for instruction. Vaughan notes that meat was wasted repeatedly when the supply they experimented on simply spoiled: "Camp reeked with decaying meat scent," she notes (73), before, finally, there was even a partial success in relearning "a process known to our forefathers in the wilderness" (73).

Meanwhile, Vaughan and her party continued eating out of the cases of commissary goods still left from the initial Central supply. In April, households had been allowed to buy individual cases of food, sight unseen and goods inside unfortunately unlisted. Vaughan bought Case 51, which contained the following: seventeen cans of fruit cocktail, five cans of cherries, one can of niblet corn, three cans of pineapple juice, four cans of sliced peaches, and one can missing an identifying label. Vaughan's suppers made use of these supplies and any fresh meat or vegetables that arrived in camp; in Vaughan's case this was even more challenging than normal: when she left her children to go to the outhouse, they merrily removed the labels from all the cans while she was gone.

The Central evacuees in camp with Vaughan now included six women, five children, and three men, not to mention (as Vaughan does using a separate category) six dogs, four cats, seventy-five chickens, twelve servants, forty porters, and thirty carpenters and helpers who arrived earlier to get the camp ready and then stayed. The families of Woods, Conant, Brown, Gibbs, McMaster, and Vaughan made up the party, with Mr. White, Mr. Conant, and Mr. Brown in charge of the camp's supplies, housing, and movement (Vaughan, April 14, 1942, 44).

On May 21, 1942, the trap finally closed on Negros, as the Japanese invaded and occupied Bacolod on Vaughan's side of the island. At 2:00 P.M., Mr. Woods, the former Central manager, announced the news and by 6:00 P.M. received a message that "two Japanese transports" had tied up to the main pier at Bacolod, accompanied by a torpedo boat, a cruiser, and six "Q" boats. The message ended with the news that the Banigo pier and oil storage tanks were in flames (Vaughan, 77). Rumors flew that the Japanese had chosen Thursday,

May 21, to land, because they considered Thursday an auspicious day. The Japanese had succeeded twice before on a Thursday landing, which led them to choose the day for the advance (Vaughan, May 22, 1942, 77). To complete their occupation, at 9:20 the next morning nine truckloads of Japanese soldiers took over Central at Silay. To the evacuees in the hills, this meant the end of any food, supplies, gasoline, sugar, medicine, or canned milk; above Silay at Binagsukan camp, Vaughan and her friends were now on their own. They had to find food, ration what the camp had collected, and deal with medical emergencies with the few supplies on hand (Vaughan, 78).

Across the island, the Chapmans, the Glunzes, the Bryants, the Bells, and the others from Silliman University and environs were watching their own town being taken. There would, however, be little for the invading army to find. Not wanting the Japanese to capture any of their equipment, the Chapmans, as others did, hid their valuables in *bukogs* (storage sheds) cached all over the mountainside. The Chapmans cleared out their first hiding place, Camp Lookout, when they left to go farther up the mountain, packing *bukogs* with kitchen utensils and throwing those they couldn't cache down the ravine. Food — canned meat, cases of milk, cans, and jars — they buried in a hole their Filipino caretaker dug behind the camp where the goods could be found again and dug up in the dark, if necessary. This the Chapmans did under the noses of occupying Japanese soldiers three months later (Chapman, 37).

The Chapmans' other preparations were equally sensible. Knowing that, as they continued to hide, they would need to be less, not more, burdened with possessions, Ethel packed up "a few of our most necessary belongings, enough to begin . . . when the war was over" (38). This included their linen and silver, aluminum kitchen pots and pans, a box of dishes, two trunks of clothing, heavy clothing for a return to the States, a small, painfully selected box of both Ethel's and Jim's college lecture notes from Silliman, reference books, and finally Jim's scientific equipment and his thirty-year collection of mounted insects in their glass cases. These items were moved after dark to a secretly made *piyag* (native hut) unknown to anyone except Jim and his caretaker's (Simplicio's) two sons (Chapman, 38–39).

The occupation of Negros Oriental was not long in coming. As Edna Bell recorded, the Japanese occupied Dumaguete on May 26, only five days after Bacolod (Bell, 6). Despite this "official" presence, Ethel Chapman pointed out that the Japanese spent most of their time making swift raids into the small communities and farms near the coast, rather than up in the mountains, where guerrillas and straggling U.S. military groups owned the trails. In the mountain town of Malabo, for example, guerrillas and other Allied military roamed the streets, and the town was the center of a "flourishing civilian government" that called itself "Free Negros" well into June 1943 (Chapman, 141).

Despite their relative freedom in the mountains, Chapman and her friends watched the actual invasion of their side of the island with heavy hearts; Ethel recorded in her diary the way it looked to those in hiding:

> Before daylight on May 26, Miro, who had been watching all night, came to call *"Daghan mga vapor sa Dumaguete"* ("Many boats in the bay at Dumaguete"). The invasion! We all scrambled into our clothes shaking with cold and excitement, and gathered in a little open space with field glasses and telescope. We looked and looked, and looked again at the boats and shore. The sun broke through the clouds above. Siquijor and the rosy dawn gave promise of a bright day, but to us the future looked dark and uncertain, and our hearts were full of gloomy foreboding. The end had come. We were fugitives! (49)

Not long after this, Simplicio's son, Catalino, brought in a Japanese poster that ordered all Americans north of a certain point to report to Fabrica in Occidental Negros and those living south to go to Dumaguete. Needless to say, the Chapmans ignored the poster (Chapman, 54).

News filtered in over the coming weeks of the discovery of other Americans on Negros — and their capture. The Chapmans and their friends had, for example, spread out and avoided building their hideouts in the same areas. This way, Silliman and Chapman both earlier argued, if one family were captured, others "up the line" could be warned and escape. Some of the families voluntarily turned themselves in, however, fearing reprisals if they did not, and others *were* turned in by collaborators.

Such was the case with Chapman's friends, the Bryants, originally from Pamplona Plantation. The Bryants, along with eighteen others, were turned over to the Japanese authorities by a collaborator, Pepe Martinez, who secretly instructed a laborer to follow some of the party to the hidden "Camp #2"; after the laborer's report, Martinez took Filipino soldiers with him to get the Bryant party to surrender, rather than making them deal directly with the Japanese. Explains Bryant, "He [Pepe] thought we should be well treated, but he made no promises. The Japanese were very strict, very stern; indeed, they had slapped his brother, but they were not at that time exercising a great deal of brutality in our province. Yes they had tortured Caballero, and he [Pepe] had seen it" (Bryant, 87). Bryant's husband, the "Guv'nor," accompanied Pepe down the mountain to meet the Japanese and try to negotiate decent terms, one of which (though their captors refused later) was that the party be allowed to be interned under house arrest at Dumaguete (Bryant, 121). Five days after Mr. Bryant's trip, Alice and the other eighteen evacuees descended to surrender formally. Bryant explains the curious relief that, after five months of hiding out, she and the others felt upon capture:

> Now we would not have to hold our breath for fear of discovery. We would not have to worry about Pedro's being caught and tortured to reveal our hiding place — although he had resolved never to be captured alive. Now we would not have to build another camp and transport all our supplies to it. All that was finished. (Bryant, 93)

The Bryants, like the Chapmans, the Bells, the Glunzes, the Sillimans, and others from Negros Oriental, had begun hiding out in January 1942, and so the Bryants' surrender was after a considerable time spent stocking hideouts and moving between them. The Chapmans, approximately a mountain away, had also moved several times. First they stocked up and hid away at Camp Lookout, their summer home, which was several miles above Dumaguete. It was painful for them when they had to leave Camp Lookout because it was the most palatial of their hidden houses. It was built originally in the late teens and sported a sawed-frame wooden structure, floors of split bamboo, a roof of nipa shingles, a summer kitchen connected to the main house by a screened breezeway, a dining area, a large bedroom on the breeziest corner of the house, and two porches (both with spectacular views, one of the mountains behind, the other of Dumaguete and the ocean in front). Camp Lookout also featured a second bedroom for dressing with sawali walls, and a shower, flush toilet, and running water in the kitchen piped in from two reservoirs fed by a mountain spring (Chapman, 17–18).

Camp Lookout was also the center of a fairly large community on the mountain. Because it was much cooler than Dumaguete, with a sea view of other islands, several Americans and the more prosperous Filipino families had built homes there before the war. Bob and Metta Silliman and their sister, Abby Jacobs, all professors with the Chapmans at the university, had houses next to one another, and there were 150 Filipino families with homes on the same ridge within a radius of a mile. This particular colony of integrated nationalities was very supportive; explains Ethel Chapman,

> We knew each of them [the Filipino families] by name, even the children; many had been friends for more than twenty-five years, as ready and willing to do things for us as we were to help them. They were accustomed to bring eggs and vegetables and fruit to our camp . . . we were sure that in a crisis we could depend on these friends to bring us food and we were sure too of their loyalty to all Americans. (16–17)

Chapman's faith in her Filipino neighbors was not violated; for the next year and a half, the Chapmans and their American colleagues concealed themselves in the hills, and their Filipino neighbors never turned them in, despite the posting of large rewards and threats from the authorities to the Filipinos' families. The Chapmans and the others succumbed to capture only because a Japanese patrol stumbled across them.

Part of the Chapmans' and the Bells' successes were certainly due to their adaptability. All of the Chapmans' friends, for example, soon managed to do for themselves without the help of servants. Camp Lookout was the place Ethel and Jim Chapman learned and first practiced the mechanics of survival. Like their neighbors, Ethel and Jim soon mastered the art of building and cooking on native stoves. These stoves were simply wooden boxes approximately 18 inches deep, and 3 by 4 feet square, set on legs to bring the box up to an acceptable height. The box on its stilt legs was filled with hard-packed dirt; the cook then built a fire on top of the dirt, one bracketed by "carefully placed stones" or the ring of an iron tripod (Chapman, 35). The cook then set pots or pans over the fire, resting them on the tripod (or between the stones). Because lighting the fire normally required a match, and the supply was limited, the Chapmans allotted only one match per day for emergencies and used instead a homemade kerosene lamp, with a hand-cut brown beer-bottle chimney, which burned all day but used very little fuel. No slouch, Ethel eventually "learned to strike sparks from a flint-like stone with a small iron hammer and, even more difficult, to catch the spark in the fuzz from a patican tree . . . and then in fine shreds of coconut husk" (35).

The Chapmans' self-sufficiency at Camp Lookout also required their knowing how to plant, weed, and make the best use of food. Chapman talks about the acre and a half behind the house that grew several varieties of banana in season, avocados, and pineapples, as well as several coffee trees. These were augmented with a full garden of string beans, corn, mung beans, and peanuts — all of which had to be hand watered during the dry season as well as carefully freed of insects by hand (Chapman, 17; 34). In addition to her garden, Ethel Chapman also learned to use native vegetables, as well as produce from the jungle, such as palm hearts.

Camp Lookout, however, had to be abandoned in March 1942; though this was still two months before the actual invasion of the island, it was close enough to it so that prescient Americans could extrapolate a warning from the ominous activities they observed. Early in March, for example, the Chapmans and Sillimans saw Japanese destroyers cruising Tañon Strait, just off Dumaguete, then zigzagging over to nearby Cebu across the strait. The destroyers were apparently looking for a U.S. plane that had ditched earlier, though they did not find it (Chapman, 36). Using this as an impetus to stock up a second mountain hideout built several months earlier, the Chapmans planned their move. Feeling that they would probably personally need to carry whatever stock or supplies they required, they had Graciano make both of them personal native carrying baskets with shoulder straps made of hemp. Black oilcloth lined the baskets and provided a covering flap on the outside to protect the contents from rain. Each emergency basket (made for a sudden escape in the middle of the night, with only a moment's warning) contained a number of necessities: a complete change of clothing, a passport (and other valuable papers), an emergency medical kit, a sewing kit, a writing case, and (in Ethel's) a diary, as well as toilet articles, some food, and matches wrapped in oiled paper kept in a tin box. Not only the Chapmans but most of their friends at Camp Lookout kept such a bag on hand, in addition to clothes, just as a common precaution (Chapman, 37; Glunz, 6).

The Chapmans were not the only family to decide to move away from Camp Lookout. The Glunzes (living at Camp Lookout with the Chapmans) and the Lowrys did as well. The Glunzes and the Lowrys both moved up to a new camp they had just had built at Dalasag (elevation 3,000 feet), along with the Chapmans (Glunz, 4). The Chapmans originally went to Dalasag because water would not be easily available if one went too high in the mountains. For example, at the 6,000 foot level, on the twin peaks, the "Horns of Negros," there was no water at all. Dalasag was near Camp Lookout but about 800 feet higher and with more difficult access from the mountain village of Luzuriaga. Though safer as a hideout, Dalasag was not on a stream and drinking water had to be carried in by five-gallon tins, until the evacuees could catch and store enough rainwater from the roofs. Ethel Chapman adds poignantly that they planned to collect rainwater: "If (we were still optimistic) it should be necessary to live there any length of time" (Chapman, 25). Despite her hopes, the Americans were there for the beginning of the rainy season, though happily the amount of rainwater was adequate to most of their needs. As Henrietta Glunz explains, the huts had 6-inch split bamboo gutters around the room and could supply almost "a week's supply of water in five minutes." She adds, "The sibit roof tended to color the water, but with heavy rains the water soon came off clear as crystal and was good for drinking without boiling. Only once did we have to send a man down into the steep main canyon, a three hours round trip, to get water from the stream there" (6).

Dalasag did, however, have some interesting hiding and caching places, as well as vantage points on activities down below. Henrietta and Charles Glunz, for example, soon discovered a huge overhanging ledge that both could reach in only five minutes from their new house. Not only was it a magnificent place to dig a cache for canned goods, but it soon became an informal reading room, napping area, and unofficial observation post, as Henrietta explains,

It kept dry during rains, and by closing the trail with brush after reaching the ledge, it would have been difficult to find.

For a period of nearly two months, while the Japs were roaming about the region below us, stealing cattle, killing people and burning houses, we stayed on the ledge during the day leaving our Dalasag house about 8:00 A.M., after breakfast, and returning about 4:00 P.M. by which time the Dalasag region seemed comparatively safe. We heated food for our lunch on a [portable] alcohol stove and read or slept most of the time. This ledge was about 8 feet wide and 30 feet long. (Glunz, 4–5)

One thing that both Ethel Chapman and Charles Glunz both noticed was how conspicuous their clothing was on the trails. No matter how grimy or tattered, the Americans were all in tropical white clothes easily seen against the green foliage. Ethel and the other women soon dyed everything dark green or brown. Ethel noted wryly the transformation of her sporting wear from the old leisured life before the war into something more suited for survival: "My knickerbockers, made from a discarded Palm Beach golf outfit, became a chestnut brown that made my trips along the trail less dangerous" (25).

The changes not only in the clothing, but also in the former eminent professors' appearances, were startling. As Henrietta Glunz recalls, one day Charles met a former student of his, Honorato Solis ("Lis"), on the trail below Dalasag:

[Lis] had heard of our whereabouts and was coming up to see us. Charles and Lis were both much surprised to meet on the trail, but Lis more than Charles. Lis was dumbfounded and Charles wondered why. Then Charles realized that he presented a very unusual picture. Clad in old torn clothes, wearing a shirt once white but dyed brown to avoid its being so conspicuous on the trails, with a canvas knap sack also dyed and leaning on two sticks (home made Alpine-stocks) and having lost 40 pounds in weight, the ensemble was probably enough to shock anyone at first sight, especially a former student beholding his teacher. (8)

The Dalasag camp consisted of three houses that, Chapman notes, "squatted" on the edge of a ravine. They were only one and a half feet above the ground, unlike the native huts, which usually stood seven feet above the ground. The huts, built by the evacuees so that they were camouflaged by the trees, lacked the spectacular view and many of the amenities of Camp Lookout. At first, each hut simply consisted of one large 12- by 16-foot room, though Jim Chapman immediately began working on a lean-to kitchen addition, located near the side of the house, for his hut. Ethel Chapman did not waste her time bemoaning the loss of running water or a view. She points out that "if we could see nothing from the house . . . neither could we be seen and even a minute's warning would enable us to drop over the edge of the cliff and disappear in the jungle" (46–47).

Curiously, the optimism of Ethel and her friends about the length of time they would spend at Dalasag—that they would not be there long enough for more than a single rainy season—was justified. By May (and the beginning of the 1942 dry season), with the news from Dumaguete and the occupation, the families once again decided to move—spurred on by the information that their friends, the Bryants, had been captured and another friend near Dalasag, Dr. Ruperto, had also been arrested (Chapman, 63). Other news filtered in from Bill Lowry, who operated a gasoline-powered radio in a cave near the camp. Though it was pleasant for Charles Glunz and others to listen to KGEI, San Francisco, every afternoon (Glunz, 7), it presented an unnecessary risk of possible detection, and the rest of the evacuees soon moved to a third camp, in the Chapmans' case, Ta-as Tubig, and in the Glunzes', Fernview. Both were at the 4,000-foot level, so high that strong winds blew and other families warned that the region was so damp that rheumatism and colds would drive the families back down to Dalasag in a matter of months (Chapman, 66; Glunz, 8).

The group lived there for a year and a half in increasing relative comfort as they built, adapted, and figured out remedies to current ills. There is an odd bucolic quality about Chapman's description of Ta-as Tubig, almost as if the war were far, far away and not really pressing on them. Each refugee couple soon constructed means to make their stay more comfortable. For example, a fireplace in the house soon took care of the cold and the damp, and the forest in which the house stood provided not only building materials but stabilizers for the house, which was tied at each corner to a large tree (Chapman, 57–58). The Glunzes' house also sported stabilizers and a fireplace (Glunz, 8). The Chapman house consisted initially of a 14- by 16-foot room with a second room eight feet wide tacked on for additional inhabitants. The framework was made entirely out of bamboo poles with a floor of split bamboo a full five feet off the ground (unlike the earlier Dalasag huts). Abaca shingles covered the roof, and a combination of poles and shingles made the walls. Inhabitants entered by means of a pole ladder—on the side facing the deep woods (Chapman, 57–58).

Jim once more built a lean-to kitchen open at both ends, and made Ethel two "stoves"—one for the kitchen (native design) and a fireplace to heat the house (Chapman, 63). Water was within walking distance and came from a small stream with both waterfalls and a rock pool.

Weather during the time the Chapmans hid away at Ta-as Tubig averaged a low of only 55° F and a high of 72° F; the mean temperature remained at

65° F (Chapman, 122). While the two dry seasons were two and six weeks long, the first in August, the second in May, mostly the days were an even mixture of sun, rain, and overcast (121–122). Obviously, this was a climate that was cool, but not cold; it was also a climate discouraging to the dreaded malarial mosquitoes—another benefit to life in the mountains. As Ethel pointed out, with two or three woolen blankets on the bed, a fireplace, and long sleeves against nonmalarial mosquitoes, they were reasonably comfortable and certainly healthy.

Jim later improved the original design of the house, building yet another kitchen with a dirt floor and a living room "downstairs" (under the hut) and then converting the large room above into several bedrooms. In these he built shelves along the walls and extra bunks. In addition, he divided a separate space which served as a bedroom for him and Grace.

Continuing flexibility and adaptability marked the Chapmans' successful time at Ta-as Tubig. A neighbor, Maria, for example, convinced the Chapmans to plant a native starch tuber, *gabi*, because it grew well in the mountains—in addition to squash, pechay, onions, and even flowers, all of which grew well at higher elevations. The abundant and flourishing *gabi* crop soon amazed Ethel. Jim also improved the swimming hole, widening it into a bathing pool by moving rocks away and then increasing the force of the extant waterfall by supplementing it with extra water piped in from above by means of a system of split bamboo pipes. Once again, similar bamboo pipes soon brought water down from the tin gutters of the house and took it directly into a tank in the kitchen. Again the Chapmans had running water.

Some additions proved to be just a little dangerous, however. The wooden fireplace Jim had originally built in the living area caught fire in a frightening accident and scorched through the side wall. Jim and his Filipino neighbors then built a new fireplace of river rocks chinked with mud, which worked beautifully and drew even better (Chapman 78–80).

A peaceful, even Eden-like feel emerges from Ethel Chapman's account, especially when she describes Ta-as Tubig's bathing pool, now a place of luxury given Jim's further modifications:

> A hollow in one of the rocks formed a soapdish. The branches of near-by trees or poles stuck in the ground made convenient pegs for our clothes, and we made a rustic bench to sit on. The dense foliage gave a feeling of privacy; ferns, orchids, even Jack-in-the-pulpits grew there; birds called to each other from the treetops; the sun at times came peeping through the leaves. (71)

Moreover, as part of a deliberate self-imposed program of "health," "exercise," and "developing a fresh mental outlook" which they practiced vigorously, Ethel and Jim made regular trips down the trail to see a hidden patch of lavender and white orchids blanketing the ground (70) and in other months took excursions to observe the midair mating of colorful butterflies (71).

Part of the natural beauty of life in the mountains was augmented by the personal warmth of close friendships. Every Sunday, for example, one or the other of the Americans in the area would host both American and Filipino families and provide ecumenical church services. Notes Ethel Chapman, "It helped to make this day of the week different from the others, and we enjoyed the fellowship of worship" (81). In addition to the fellowship provided by the church services, many of the families were often able to enjoy each other's company because they lived within rough proximity of one another. The Glunzes' house "Fernview," for example, was about halfway down the mountain from the Chapmans' Ta-as Tubig. Lieutenant Ben Viloria, his wife, Flora, and their children were even closer, living as they did at Dalasag in a house formerly owned by the Glunzes (Chapman, 83).

For the first wartime Thanksgiving (1942) the Chapmans invited Charles and Hettie Glunz and the Solis family to dine with them. The entrée was easily provided by the hosts. Earlier, the Chapmans and their caretaker Cataliano had gone in together financially and purchased a pig. Cataliano raised it and, after it was slaughtered, kept one half as payment. The rest of the pig became the roast pork of the Chapmans' Thanksgiving Day dinner (Chapman, 90).

The evacuee families during their time in the mountains (1942–1943) celebrated a variety of holidays, each family taking turns playing host. Christmas, for example, featured a "program" at Fernview. Guests included the Chapmans, Mrs. Lowry and her son Billy, and "some mountain families"; there were festivities and a meal, along with a gift exchange. In the latter case, some presents were in keeping with evacuee and mountain needs, not convention. The mountain people gave the Glunzes fruit, and the Glunzes gave them salt ("this seemed to be their greatest need"); all the children received homemade candy (Glunz, 10).

During 1942 and most of 1943, food was plentiful, thanks in part to both the ingenuity and the flexibility of the Chapmans, the Glunzes, and their friends. Ethel Chapman pointed out that the evacuees were in better circumstances in terms of food than they believed their friends to be in the internment camps (97) — which, as we will see, was frequently true, depending on which internment camp Chapman would choose to use for comparison. Certainly, they were much better off than Alice Bryant and the others already captured and put in Bacolod; their food was scarce, portions were small, and no one had any money to buy more, nor could they hunt, scavenge, or even trade for food, because they were restricted to the camp and forbidden contact with the Filipinos after a point.

The other reason the evacuees did so well was, ironically, the war itself.

With the Americans cleared from the lower parts of Negros, evacuated Americans (and any other Allied personnel in hiding) immediately became the only profitable market for all the food the Filipinos had previously sold in Dumaguete or even at Camp Lookout. The occupying Japanese did not "buy" so much as they simply took. To make money, Filipinos had to sell to Americans. Another factor also entered into the equation. In addition to the regular lowland farmers selling to the Americans, the highland Filipino farmers preferred staying in the mountains rather than risking their lives and crops in Japanese-controlled territory. They began bringing salable fruits, vegetables, rice, and meat to the Chapmans and the others to supplement the evacuees' own gardens (Chapman, 108). "This was not without risk," as Hettie Glunz points out. "We were never sure whether those who came to sell food were friends or spies or when the Japs might make a raid. There were constant Jap patrols, raids, burned houses and killings down below. Often we could see the burning and hear the shooting" (6).

Despite these qualms, those in hiding continued to supplement their garden produce on occasion. The evacuee gardens featured a sensible mixture of American and native vegetables. Potatoes grew, as did *ubi*, a lavender, yam-like tuber that tasted (according to the more adaptable evacuees) like a potato. They also grew *gabi* (as previously mentioned), which they boiled and sliced or mashed, as well as camotes, squash, green beans, eggplant, mung beans, white radishes, lima beans, green onions, tomatoes, and some corn and peppers in season (Chapman, 112; Glunz, 6). Such a variety of fresh vegetables and fruit, as well as occasional large portions of meat, helped to prevent the deficiency diseases that the majority of Americans in civilian internment camps, especially on Luzon, were starting to develop by late 1943.

According to some internees in the camps, deficiency diseases started as early as late 1942. Natalie Crouter in Baguio talks of seeing the "beriberi" signs (edema especially) (44), though these particular symptoms might well have been due to insufficient protein as well. Both vitamins and protein were insufficient at the Baguio camp. With deficiency diseases lurking in camp, perhaps buying sufficient food from possible Japanese spies was worth the risk. Ethel Chapman, Henrietta Glunz, Mrs. Lowry, and the others, eating a generally balanced diet of fruit, vegetables, rice, potato, and meat every day, were in an enviable position, compared to Natalie Crouter at Baguio, or Martha Hill at Santo Tomás, or the hundreds of others who were starting to feel the pinch caused by a lack of fresh and sufficient food by the beginning of 1943.

A quick review of one of Ethel Chapman's ordinary daily menus during this period shows the variety and quantity of food for those who, as Chapman did, kept chickens, grew a garden, brought home game, raised pigs, or traded regu-

larly with the Filipinos for coconut meat, oil, milk, native sugar, and sometimes beef. The menu here is even richer than that of Mrs. Bryant, who lived
only a mountain away prior to her capture:

> *Breakfast:* sliced papayas, cornmeal mush with sliced bananas, coconut milk,
> brown sugar (native), coffee, 3 eggs for Jim
> *Dinner* (at noon): orange juice, beef pot roast with peppers, onions, tomatoes,
> squash vine tips (boiled with meat), mashed camotes, avocados, and chocolate
> pudding (made with cocoa, cornstarch, coconut milk)
> *Supper* (5:30 P.M.): Mung bean soup with tomatoes, fried eggplant, rice, and
> "three-in-one" (pineapple, banana, grapefruit ambrosia). (Chapman, 109–110)

When we consider that the Chapmans also pressed the bananas, fermented
them, and made vinegar, and had all the citrus fruit they could eat—all of
which was native, such as pomelos, grapefruit, oranges, green lemoncitos,
pineapples, and tangerines—we can understand why scurvy (a Vitamin c deficiency disease) was not a problem, though it soon proved to be one for interned civilians from 1943 until their release in February 1945.

Chapman herself understood how fortunate she and her friends really were.
She saw their sojourn as a time to prepare mentally and nutritionally for whatever they would face when they were finally captured. She explains: "Certainly we were a long way from starving in the mountains! Indeed, we were
well prepared for the ordeal ahead and undoubtedly one of the reasons we
came safely through it was our well-balanced diet during our months as fugitives" (117).

With a U.S. Army Medical Report officially listing a total of 115 deaths from
1942 to February 1945 for internees from malnutrition, deficiency diseases,
and related heart problems (Hartendorp, II, 613), Chapman's evaluation of
the reasons for her ultimate survival seems accurate.

From January 1943 through June 1943, the Chapmans continued to live at
Ta-as Tubig, a period that Ethel called the "least alarming" of their entire time
spent hiding out (97–98). Sunrise each day saw them out of bed after nine or
ten hours of sleep, eating breakfast, and then beginning the daily chores.
There was always the need to collect firewood, and both Jim and Ethel, each
armed with a bolo, went outside camp and hacked up dry branches or pulled
logs from a pile they had collected earlier and then cut them up. Jim split, and
Ethel carried and stacked. Chickens also had to be fed and the garden had to
be watered; both were Ethel's responsibility. Ethel and Jim weeded the garden
together. After the noon meal and, perhaps, a nap, the Chapmans worked at
odd jobs around the camp, such as building a stronger fence around the garden to keep wild pigs from rooting up and eating their produce during the

night. Afternoons sometimes were spent at the swimming pool Jim made, or gathering flowers, sewing, or mending clothes. Jim often followed his profession and happily observed insects (Chapman, 98–104).

At other times, when the area seemed relatively safe, Ethel and Jim, as well as other evacuee couples, took trips to each other's houses or to Malabo. The Chapmans, for example, tried every two or three months to visit the Carsons in their "lake" home. This consisted of a lakeside house in the mountains with a thatched roof, hand-sawed lumber walls, and a hidden trail leading to it. The building housed four Carsons, four Bells (the hunted guerrilla leader Roy Bell, his wife, Edna, and family), two "stranded dormitory girls from Davao," four Norwegian sailors who escaped from Cebu earlier in the war, and a fugitive American officer waiting to join the guerrillas on Mindanao (Chapman, 150).

Ethel points out that going to the Carson hideout was no light undertaking: "It was a four-hour trip [from Malabo] at my rate of speed, over bare rocky fields, through patches of tall cogon grass, along narrow sloping paths dug out of the mountain side, up and over the wooded ridge of thirty-six hundred feet, and down the last long winding trail to the lake" (Chapman, 149).

Trips back were not only tiring but unappealing as well; even minimal rain not only made the trail itself slippery but "brought out numerous leeches, which were waiting all along the way, reaching out from every twig and leaf to grab hold as we went by" (Chapman, 150). Mrs. Glunz concurs, noting that not only did the trips require "hours of difficult climbing over steep mountain trails, frequently bare footed" (shoes were too precious to wear out for frivolous reasons, according to her), but travelers soon inadvertently hosted not only leeches but chiggers and ticks as well (Glunz, 10).

Despite four-hour trips fighting insects and other pests to see friends, the Chapmans, the Glunzes, the Lowrys, and others lived a much more pleasant life than one might suppose would be the case in an occupied country during a war. Malabo considered itself the center of "Free Negros" and prided itself on having an attorney who administered food reserves, a school of sorts, a rough army hospital, and the guerrilla headquarters of Major Placido Ausijo, coincidentally a former Silliman alumnus and friend of many of the American fugitives (Chapman, 148). Contact with the guerrillas and General Wendell Fertig (based close by on Mindanao), who trained guerrillas under orders from MacArthur, allowed the Chapmans to send out one letter a month by submarine to their children in the United States. Another guerrilla, the famous Major Villamor, also had a radio set up at the southern end of Negros; he allowed the Chapmans to talk with their children by radio in early April 1942 (Chapman, 143). Guerrilla involvement had its dangers but also its unexpected benefits. Their university colleagues, the Bells, were not only friends with the guerrillas but, as I mentioned earlier, guerrilla leaders themselves; ultimately, American forces evacuated the Bells and others from the Philippines to Australia late in the war, rather than allow them to be captured and put in internment camp or in a prison like Fort Santiago as the Japanese began to close in (Bell, 1; 13).

Malabo was a settlement with the feverish party atmosphere of a community that knew it was living on borrowed time. Despite the fact that the Japanese had not raided far into the interior at this time, there was always the chance that they would — especially with a flourishing (and notorious) guerrilla camp there. Meanwhile, parties flourished night after night, oiled by native fermentations from coconuts. Fruit and even meat dishes were plentiful to go along with the drinks; friends could meet to talk and exchange news as well as give handy hints to one another about how to "make do" when manufactured goods ran out, rusted, or simply fell apart. Ethel Chapman talks nostalgically about this state of mind, explaining, "We . . . took pleasure in finding substitutes for supplies which began to run low." She cites the use of long abaca fibers for "excellent" thread, betal nuts' fibrous outer covering to substitute for a toothbrush, and yet another clever find to replace lost or broken buttons: carved bits of coconut shell (Chapman, 133).

The Glunzes, too, participated in this substitution and make-it-yourself fad. As Hettie explains,

> In the forest we learned of the location of several Almaciga trees (Mastic Gum). Almaciga dissolved in alcohol makes a clear white varnish used on oil paintings and is used in book varnish etc. We had a supply of alcohol that Bob Silliman had brought . . . for use in alcohol stoves. We found the varnish very useful in water proofing paper, cloth, suit cases, and even in making adhesive tape. It was excellent in making cans, etc., more rust proof. Rust was one of our mountain enemies. (8)

Nor did the Glunzes stop with such useful but inedible inventions. They also found that whole corn, when put in a frying pan and then ground, made "an excellent cereal" and that "coconut tree sap," when fermented, made *tuba*, an intoxicating local drink (Glunz, 8).

Malabo's fun lasted only until June 19, 1943, when a 700 man Japanese mobile unit destroyed the guerrilla headquarters and burned the settlement (Chapman, 154). Ethel Chapman describes events graphically, explaining that "this was to be the last big party at Malabo . . . Japanese soldiers were swarming over that very plaza, burning and pillaging and shooting, and both the unarmed guerrillas and civilians were fleeing to the mountains for safety" (149).

The Japanese did not stop with Malabo and continued to torch any nearby settlements, including Chapman's Camp Lookout home (already bombed in December 1942, six months earlier). Chapman's account is poignant; alerted at their Ta-as Tubig camp by a Filipino friend, Ethel and Jim viewed the damage: "Jim and I dressed in a hurry and followed [Miro] down the dark trail to his house, where we stood until daylight, watching the fires below. We could hear the crackle of the flames and the loud popping of the bamboo as the hollow tubes exploded in the heated air. The Silliman house was burning also, and there were several more fires farther down the road" (154).

Disasters followed quickly. A month later, the evacuees in the hills heard that Bill Lowry (who had hidden out with them before joining the guerrillas) had been killed on Mindanao. The Chapmans' latest (and most elaborate) secret hideout, Woods Hollow house, had also fallen down in a windstorm (Chapman, 156; 159).

An evil wind did seem to be blowing. Evacuees started finding new (and more remote) hideouts. The Glunzes concocted another hideout—simply referred to as a "jungle house." It consisted of the "top of a large rock" on a flat space on a steep canyon wall with enough room to build something similar to their Fernview house. Hidden by two steep banks on two sides and the jungle on the other two, it was invisible until someone came within ten feet of it. But even this was not enough to calm Charles Glunz's fears. Farther away, but reasonably close to the "jungle house," he also found a hollow under an overhanging rock and, with one of his friends, built a small *piyag* in it, which would shelter two people and hold a few emergency supplies. As Hettie explains, "this was to be a sort of final retreat," along with yet another one Charles threw together near the Chapmans' Ta-as Tubig. Neither was used; the Glunzes surrendered soon after Jim and Ethel Chapman were captured (Glunz, 11).

It was five months later when the Chapmans, despite rebuilding their secret hideout, ran out of luck. On November 25, 1943, the Chapmans went down to the Glunzes' for Thanksgiving. All along the way they saw posted signs warning evacuees who were hiding out that "they must return to Dumaguete before December 8" (Chapman, 159). By now, following the Malabo raid, the Japanese had become bolder, setting up and extending zones around each coastal town. They then announced that anyone who lived outside those zones after December 8 would be "shot on sight." The Chapmans were still mulling this over as they returned the next night to Ta-as Tubig from the Glunzes' hideout, (apparently) preparatory to moving permanently to the more remote Woods Hollow hideout. Early on the morning of November 27, the Chapmans were warned by Filipino neighbors that a Japanese patrol had arrived in Dalasag (one hour away) and was headed up the trail. The Chapmans cleared out of the Ta-as Tubig house, grabbed their emergency packs, hid their guns and papers, and slipped through the woods to their secret piyag to pick up food supplies. Deciding to wait before proceeding to the next hideout, they waited over an hour, listening for sounds or any indication of an imminent Japanese patrol. Another hour passed. Jim Chapman decided to check Ta-as Tubig. He did so and, seeing nothing, called an "all clear" to Ethel, who returned to the house. Together they laughed over their alarm and unpacked their bags. Jim then sauntered down to look over the damage done at Dalasag and to see if their friends had gotten away. Jim promised he would "be careful," so Ethel stayed behind, despite her misgivings. When she went outside some time later to check her vegetable garden, Ethel was startled to see Jim emerging from the trees—followed closely by two Japanese soldiers holding him at bayonet point. Ethel, frightened that they would kill him, decided not to run even though he urged her to do just that. She was not only worried about Jim's safety, but, as she explained, she was frozen by the shock of disbelief:

> Even then I could not realize what had happened. These could not be Japanese. It just couldn't be that we were captured! When I started back toward the house, three soldiers with fixed bayonets appeared in front of me, but I only looked wonderingly from one to another until the commanding officer, a pleasant-looking young fellow, reached out to pat me on the shoulder with a reassuring "No afraid, no hurt"—in English too! (159–160)

Soon Jim and Ethel Chapman stood side by side and were told by that same officer, "Prepare everything, food, clothes. You go Dumaguete" (Chapman, 160).

Altogether, the Chapmans had lasted twenty months as fugitives. So had the Glunzes and Lowry families. Only the Bells, the Sillimans, and the Carsons, eventually evacuated by submarine, lasted three months longer in the bush. And thereby hangs a tale—or at least a murmur—of civilized but definite resentment. Hettie Glunz explains that she and Charles had discussed surrendering as an option rather than continuing to hide out. Even though their Filipino friends Henio and Maria urged them to go to another ridge and begin their fugitive life again, even offering to bring them food once a week, the Glunzes knew that this kind of regular aid would become increasingly dangerous for Henio and Maria and for them too, given the Japanese penetration into the area. They thanked their friends and considered their options:

> We debated two possibilities. One was that if the Japs would leave us alone for three months or be driven from our neighborhood in that time, we could stick it

out. The other was that if we could reach Tolon on the south west coast of our Island we might be picked up by a submarine and be taken to Australia. The first we rejected. There was no information upon which to base such a hope. The second seemed fantastic. It seemed impossible for us to undertake a 50 mile journey across mountain ridges and canyons. As we found out later, this was just what Bells and Carsons did three months later, but they had received information (*which we did not*) [italics mine] that a submarine would be at Tolon at a given time. They were safely in America by the middle of 1944, six or seven months after we surrendered. But they were much younger than we, and had done much more mountain climbing. (Glunz, 12)

The Glunzes started down the mountain toward surrender on Monday, November 27, 1943, after hearing that the Chapmans had been taken. This apparent neglect to tell the Glunzes and others about the possibility of submarine rescue acquires a darker import when we realize that Charles and Hettie Glunz ended up in Los Baños Internment Camp—the last camp to be liberated and one that suffered longest with severe starvation (Glunz, 13).

On the other side of Negros, Elizabeth Vaughan's party experienced surrender, rather than capture, having remained free only until early June 1942, shortly after the actual invasion of the island. Terrified by the possibility of being considered guerrillas, trusting the Japanese posters that there would no reprisals, and lacking both the skills and the necessary time or preparation to go into hiding higher and deeper into the interior, the group decided to surrender. Vaughan's diary discusses the group's frail hopes for life in internment. The May 30 entry explains,

> The end is near at hand . . . Mr. Woods [the *de facto* leader] had a summons to report to Japanese in Bacolod for instruction for our entering concentration camp. We think and hope that we will be put in schoolhouses. This means we will have no beds and no chairs—but what are they compared to food for hungry children? (83)

Though Vaughan talks of hungry children, it seems apparent that this is perhaps a projection into the future or a touch of melodrama. It was, after all, only a day earlier when neither Beth nor Clay would eat scrambled eggs because they "tasted like smoke" from being cooked over a wood fire (82); a few weeks before (May 13, 1942) her entries discuss a meal consisting of "midget peas, tenderloin roast, and spiced pears" complete with dessert—prune whip and coffee with cream (65). The starving children would not truly appear until mid-1944, and then it would be no metaphor.

After returning from a meeting with the Japanese the next day, Mr. Woods and Mr. Robinson set a system of Filipino lookouts on the mountain peaks to

give warning to those about to surrender so that they could bury their valua-
bles before any Japanese troops came to take them to camp—a prudent pre-
caution, given internee experiences in Manila and Baguio in December 1941.
The lookouts were also there, notes Vaughan, "to give time to [*sic*] for the
Filipino lavanderas, amahs, and housegirls to leave camp as they all fear rape"
(May 31, 1942, 84).

After these precautions, Woods told the group about the three different
camps located on Negros for Allied and other nationals of enemy powers on
the island (probably Bacolod, Dumaguete, and possibly Fabrica). Woods's information came from the interpreters working at Japanese headquarters—
both of whom Woods had known before. One of the two, Ishawata, was a local
Bacolod contractor and scrap-iron dealer; the other, Yasamori, had actually
been employed as a carpenter by Woods's own Central. Apparently because of
Woods's familiarity with the interpreters, the Japanese allowed him to choose
a camp for the men, women, and children of his group from Central—a camp
in which all of them could be together. This was supposedly quite a conces-
sion. Woods chose Fabrica (Vaughan, 85). Evacuees had ten days to report to
Fabrica, and the authorities allowed them to send clothing and food stocks
ahead to the camp. Understanding the future internees' reluctance, the Japanese authorities promised that the supplies would not be "molested," restricted only firearms and whiskey (85), and did not bother with the searches
practiced on the prisoners at Baguio and Santo Tomás in which all sorts of
things—especially scissors, cigarettes, and jewelry—were regularly taken by
the soldiers.

As it turned out, Vaughan and her party were not sent to Fabrica, but to
Bacolod, and not before they were given time to make as many preparations
as possible. This surreal courtesy on the way to concentration camp is only
matched by Vaughan's partly rational comments in her diary as she readies
herself and the children. Her June 2 entry is a whirlwind of things she feels
she must do to prepare for leaving Camp Binagsukan and heading into
internment:

> Must retuft Clay's [her toddler's] mattress, wash bedroll covers, put in aprons for
> children, oil the children's shoes (leather is stiff from repeated wettings), don't for-
> get tea and a pan for heating water, leave a recipe for fudge with Seijo so he can
> make some and bring to camp if he can secure Japanese pass. (88)

Vaughan's preparations were not shortsighted. Two days later, on June 4,
she muses in her diary about whether to take currency with her to camp. The
Japanese officer in charge of Negros, Colonel Ohta, has informed the soon-to-
be internees to "bring all our money in concentration camp and *if it is accept-*

able we will be given yen in exchange" (Vaughan, 92). She explains sensibly that prisoners will probably need cash in camp, if only to buy fresh fruit and vegetables, but then she again veers off into obvious misunderstanding of the nature of her coming internment. She explains that she will probably need money not only for foodstuffs but for "tips, tips, tips" for servants or possibly for the guards so that, if, for example, the water goes off, or the lights fail, or "other necessities need attention," she will have some money to get these things done.

Another early captive was Bessie Sneed, who as we recall sailed with her husband from one island in the Visayan chain to another, Masbate, where they were captured, according to Michael Onorato (Onorato, xviii). The Sneeds did not surrender, nor were they betrayed or hunted down—rather, ironically enough, they literally crashed *into* the enemy while attempting to escape from them. After sailing to a different island on Christmas 1941, Sneed, her miner-husband, and several other families and stray American officers decided to stay where the food was plentiful with the chances seemingly remote that the Japanese would come. Months passed, and finally, on April 16, 1942, the Japanese landed on Masbate. By April, however, other women in her party had elected to separate from their husbands and take their children into the interior of the island for safety's sake. Bessie Sneed, without children, elected to stay with her husband in town (Sneed, 4–6). Filipino associates earlier reported the Japanese unit landing on the islands; Sneed, her husband, and others still living in the highly vulnerable coastal town decided it was time to head into the interior themselves. Trying to take back roads, Bessie and her husband careened around a corner in their truck and literally ran into the head of a Japanese army mobile column. They had somehow driven unknowingly past the "short range of machine guns set up on the roads," Sneed notes (6–7). After the dust and radiator vapor cleared, Sneed and her husband "climbed out of the car into the arms of a Jap officer who had the biggest, shiniest pistol I ever saw. We were herded off the road and placed with Filipinos who had just been captured, keeping me separate from the others. I was the first white woman captured on the island" (7).

The Japanese then marched Sneed and the others to a vacant house where another male American and two English men were already in custody. The scene was grim; notes Sneed, "All three of these men were accused of being soldiers and were taken out and shot" (7–8). The single, frail reason that Sneed's husband did not join them in their fate was, according to Sneed, because the Japanese believed all military wives had been sent home (as indeed they had, at least on Luzon), so Sneed's presence with her husband convinced the authorities he was civilian (which he was). This apparent status initially prevented a snap execution; a quick check of his passport also showed him to be civilian (8).

That day the Japanese captured approximately fourteen British and American civilians (including the three who were shot) and about sixty Chinese. The soldiers next moved the group for safekeeping to the front hall of Japanese headquarters. Conditions there were cramped; only a third of the prisoners at any one time had space to lie down, knees drawn up, on the hard concrete floor. The prisoners quickly arranged shifts: two hours up, two hours down (except for the two women, of which Sneed was one, whom the men chivalrously allowed to stretch out for longer periods of time). This arrangement continued for three days and two nights, accompanied by small rations of water but not food (Sneed, 8–9).

Sneed and her fellow captives' imprisonment is important here, because it serves as an early example of the typical Japanese treatment of American and other Allied prisoners. Rather than being deliberately cruel, the Japanese seem to have been only offhandedly negligent, which was generally the case elsewhere in the first month or two of the Japanese occupation of the islands. Though internees found conditions uncomfortable or possibly even animalistic, they were not unbearable or clearly sadistic in intent. Floor space on which to sleep was limited, the floor itself was hard, and food was scarce; prisoners, however, were not forbidden (as others were later) to lie down, sit down, talk, or change positions. The Japanese did not force them to sit or sleep on sewage-drenched mud (like the POWs), nor did they deny the prisoners water. The authorities only denied them food for three days, and this may well have been due more to incompetent logistics than to army discipline or deliberate punishment, though the absence of *any* food (not just the wrong number of portions) suggests that the Japanese might have seen its lack as a possible enforcement weapon. Sneed articulates a pattern that others in all of the camps were to notice and mark repeatedly over the early years:

> During the early part of the war, when the Japs were still marching South, they were far more lenient with us than they were months later, after the tide began to turn against them. During these early months, the Japs allowed the American and British women who had a child two years or younger to go outside [camp] to her home or hospital, or any other place where she had been living. (18)

Although this describes life at Santo Tomás camp on Luzon in particular (where Sneed was soon transferred), this pattern of whimsical attitudes and actions characterizes the first weeks of capture for others as well. We remember, for example, the small, polite speech the commanding officer at Camp John Hay made, alternately soothing the captives' worries on one hand and then threatening to shoot them in the next sentence. Other island captures or surrenders reflect a similar peculiar mixture of neglect, benevolence, and cruelty.

Sneed, for example, spent the first three weeks of confinement in jail, in an 8 by 14 foot cell with six other women and four children. Their "European" cell was palatial, compared to that of the forty Filipino POWs captured on Bataan, many of whom lay wounded or blinded and who were never allowed out of the cell, though minuscule amounts of rice and water were put through the bars daily (Sneed, 25). The Japanese did not subject the white civilian prisoners to the same brutality they meted out to fellow Asians. At Sneed's camp both civilian and military Filipinos and Chinese prisoners were routinely beaten for information or shot. The result was a nightmare of guilt for Sneed and the others in adjoining cells: "We could go into our cells where we would not have to see this [the beatings or executions], but we could not get away from the groans and screams" (Sneed, 25). That fellow Asians ("inferior racially" because they were not Japanese [Dower, 277]) were treated with more contempt and cruelty than were white civilian prisoners was an irony not lost on the Filipinos to whom the Japanese had preached the racial unity and benefits of the "Greater Asian Co-Prosperity Sphere."

We should note, however, that the Japanese did not treat white American, British, and other Allied POWs as well as they did the civilian internees. They regularly beat, starved, tortured, experimented upon, shot, or beheaded white Allied POWs. However, with the exception of the occurrences at the Puerto Princesa camp and the medical experiments in Unit 731, Manchuria, the Japanese did not execute masses of white POWs, unlike the massacre of the Philippine Scouts they committed after the fall of Bataan.

The civilian experience in the early days, either on Luzon at Hay/Holmes (Baguio) and Santo Tomás, or on Negros (Bacolod), on Mindanao (Davao), or on Cebu (Cebu City) was hardly of the same monstrous nature as that lived by the POWs; granting this, it is important to point out that internment was not easy or pleasant, especially for untrained civilians of all ages and health conditions; internees had to perform the hard labor or chores that were required daily to make all the camps habitable and continually healthy. Sneed, for example, watched male civilian labor detachments go out to build a new camp for the internees. This kind of labor among other tasks involved digging post holes, nailing up cross-pieces, stringing barbed wire, and attaching sheet iron; notes Sneed, "businessmen . . . not accustomed to manual labor found it rather strenuous" (26) — a point particularly worth making given the ages of many involved.

Alice Bryant's early experiences with captivity and the attitude the Japanese evinced toward Europeans, Americans, white women, and work are what I described initially, and I will explore these issues more fully in later chapters. Initially, the Japanese promised Bryant's party that they would be interned at Dumaguete; "orders," however, negated this promise. Their Japanese interpreter and officer in charge of them explained that the prisoners were going to be interned on the other side of Negros, at Bacolod. The interpreter seemed apologetic: "It's orders . . . . They are from above. Maybe not so bad in Bacolod" (Bryant, 123).

Despite their initial disappointment that they were not going to be in camp closer to home (and near Filipino friends, servants, and associates), Bryant's party speculated that life in an "official" internment camp might provide more benefits than an "unofficial" camp loosely arranged in Dumaguete. Bryant explains their reasoning:

> The Japanese burnt everything that they thought the guerrillas might use; the guerrillas burnt everything they thought the Japanese might use. It is quite possible that some fires were started without any thought at all . . . there was such violence and lawlessness. In the camp we were much more secure than were the people outside, and, since the group was larger, we felt safer here than we had in Dumaguete, where we feared the Japanese might hide behind us if guerrillas attacked. (138)

Soon the drawbacks to life in camp became evident—including the inability of the inhabitants to search, glean, or shop for food, and the lack of medical attention. Barbed wire, crowded conditions, and the behavior of the guards imprisoned people more cruelly, time would show, than the Japanese officials had led the internees to expect initially.

Ethel Chapman and Elizabeth Vaughan both, though at different times, saw a blasted landscape through which they traveled on their different ways to concentration camp. Vaughan describes leaving Camp Binagsukan at 7:00 A.M., with *pacqueros* (porters) carrying bedrolls, food boxes, and her children's beds. The children themselves also "had great fun riding astride the backs of the pacqueros and walking for a rest in a few level places" (Vaughan, June 6, 1942, 93). The reality of her plight touches her as the prisoners pass the ruins of the old Hawaiian-Pacific Sugar Central:

> Fifteen or so looted boxcars stood amidst rubbish scattered by robbers at the end of the line. Half-empty food cans—anchovies, olives, asparagus which had been opened, tasted, and discarded with part of the contents still in cans—littered the ground. Hawaiian-Pacific Co. Papers (office records) blowing in the wind had been discarded in order to empty drums, and empty house (former house for guards at end of line) told the story of theft and destruction. (93)

But Vaughan's heart was fortified by, again, an unusually elaborate "care package" put together by the faithful Seijo; Vaughan and her children drowned their sorrows on the trip to camp by digging into the picnic hamper Seijo had stocked with "peanut butter sandwiches, hard-boiled eggs, bananas, scones, fudge, and filled waterbottles." When the group finally arrived at the train tracks (from which they left by handcar for Bacolod-Muria Central, where they then took a truck to Bacolod), Seijo came to see the Vaughans off. At this point he also received Vaughan's last instructions: "Said goodby [*sic*] at track line, gave him $16.00 to keep for me, or use for food for me — paid him salary to the 15th and told him to charge my account rice, fish, sugar, mangoes, and salt and other supplies needed at camp. Left $10.00 with Mr. Diaz for meat" (Vaughan, June 6, 1942, 93). Then Vaughan and her children, along with the rest of the party, vanished down the line, in a clackety-clack of teeth as the handcar took them, well-fed, to internment.

Over eighteen months later, the Chapmans were taken into captivity with their friends. The capturing officers treated the prisoners reasonably well. One of the hardest things Ethel Chapman endured was watching Ta-as Tubig's destruction. Just as the Chapmans were about to leave, however, Ethel was allowed to go upstairs to retrieve a few final items. The last moments of freedom passed, and then the captured Chapmans were taken down the mountain: "At Luzuriaga, trucks were waiting, and quite a crowd had assembled to watch the prisoners come in. Many gloomy faces indicated the consternation our capture had caused, but the Filipino mayor, he who had escaped the guerrillas some time before, grinned in triumph so evident I pretended not to see him" (Chapman, 165).

Grimly, Chapman and her husband and her friends (including the Lowrys and the Glunzes) clambered aboard the trucks taking them to Dumaguete (and Silliman University, now a Japanese command post). Despite months of hiding out, Ethel and Jim Chapman, Hettie and Charles Glunz, and Jean Lowry and her son Billy were now in the hands of the Japanese. For Bessie Sneed in Masbate camp in the Visayan chain; Vaughan and her children and Alice Bryant's party already at Bacolod; Natalie Crouter, Esther Hamilton, Mary Ogle, and James Halsema at Baguio (Camp Holmes); and the Hills, the Nashes, and the Magnusons at Santo Tomás, the ordeal begun would not end until February 1945, with the deliverance of Bilibid Prison and the main internee camps of Los Baños and Santo Tomás by MacArthur's troops. This was an ordeal that would demand not only strength, cleverness, and perseverance to survive but courage as well. Ethel Chapman's last defiant gesture as the truck carrying her rolled into Dumaguete before a silent crowd of Filipinos was typical of the small, courageous, but seemingly trivial, acts that prisoners tended to perform to keep up their hope and their spirits: As the crowd looked on, Ethel Chapman forced herself to her feet, and despite the truck's lurching she held tightly to the swaying side and stood tall. She did this not only so that news of her capture and survival could be relayed to her friends but, more important, so that the Japanese would know she was not afraid (Chapman, 165). Eventually, after arriving at the Silliman campus, the driver screeched the truck to a halt in front of Guy Hall (currently the Japanese military headquarters), and the guards ordered Chapman and the others out of the truck. Internment had started.

4

Inside the Gate

The Nature of the Japanese Administration
of the Civilian Internment Camps

When Ethel Chapman got down from the truck at Silliman, when Alice Bryant and her husband heard the gates shut behind them at Bacolod, or when Jay Hill, Grace Nash, and others found themselves dumped unceremoniously in the dusty center of Santo Tomás, where was it exactly that they found themselves—and more important, in *what?* Neither a POW nor a temporary transit camp, the internment camps almost defied official classification. Even today, if one tries to locate documents relating to civilian internees in the Philippines during World War II, the researcher usually finds records indexed with those of prisoners at Camp O'Donnell or Cabanatuan, as if the civilian internees were some form of honorary

POW (see, for example, Paul S. Dull's *The Tokyo Trials: A Functional Index*).[1]

Although it may seem a niggling point to arrive at a sound classification for the kind of internment civilians suffered, such legalism can have tremendous ramifications. Depending on its title, under which rules or international conventions would the camp supposedly operate? Did, for example, the Hague Convention or provisions of the International Red Cross or even Geneva apply to those who were clearly not combatants? Did the requirement that prisoners receive an Imperial Japanese "soldier's ration" seem adequate for nursing mothers, children under twelve, Spanish-American War veterans in their seventies, or teenagers? Should middle-aged couples be forced to do field labor, exist in jail cells, or suffer interrogation? Obviously, ordinary standards of military reciprocity wouldn't suffice. Neither would ordinary rules of administration.

Administration on its surface seems a dusty, tedious subject filled with, perhaps, management techniques, accounting procedures, and chains of command. Examined more closely, however, administration assumes a vital importance, because it ordinarily outlines the procedures any captor uses to decide such things as food allotments per person, personal square footage, rules affecting movement in and out of camp, and punishment for offenses. The nature of the civilian internment camps' administration, then, becomes a transitional but important subject in this work—somewhat similar to a gate that leads from the early chapters dealing with civilian life before and at the beginning of the war to the later chapters that describe life in the internment camps and, ultimately, rescue. Only by understanding the rules, regulations, and orders (or specific lack of any or all of these) can anyone begin to understand the reasons for the necessity of repeatedly bowing at a correct angle on every occasion to guards, for having only camote tops, fish heads, and rough rice for a meal, or indeed why over 7,000 people of various ages found themselves languishing in camp at all (Waterford, 146). Administration guided and limited, allowed or disallowed, and shaped and changed every concrete aspect of the internees' lives, and it helped to shape their hope as well.

As there is difficulty defining an internment camp, it is obviously even more difficult to define the nature of that camp's proper administration. What can be said tends initially in the broadest classification to be a negative definition. Civilian internment camps were *not* set up or administered like the POW camps in the Philippines, nor were they equivalent in nature or administration to the infamous Nazi concentration camps. Ultimately, they even differed significantly from the civilian internment camps for the Japanese in the United States, especially in terms of the way they were run.

As noted earlier, the first misapprehension comes, perhaps, by confusing the civilian internment experience in the Philippines with that of the POWs there. Though POWs and internees were both generally badly fed, the degree of suffering differed markedly *in the Philippines* in terms of medicines available, physical torture, slave labor, and punishment. (A much more likely comparison would be with those civilian internment camps of mostly British and Dutch in Sumatra, Malaya, and Java, where treatment and conditions were brutal enough to resemble the conditions of the POWs [Waterford, 32–45; Russell, 205; 209]. The farther south the camp was, the worse the conditions.)

Unlike Cabanatuan or O'Donnell or Davao Penal Colony (the largest POW camps in the Philippines), Santo Tomás and the other civilian camps were partially administered by the civilian internees themselves to a much greater degree than was true at the POW camps. Perhaps this was because, measured by that Japanese national yardstick, the code of Bushido, any military prisoner who disgraced himself by surrendering rather than seeking an honorable end in suicide was worthy only of contempt and did not deserve to administer himself in any significant way (Nitobe, 116; Linderman, 145–147).

The Japanese administration of civilian camps also tended to be more lenient toward civilian prisoners than toward POWs, perhaps because middle-aged men and women, children, and elderly people did not present much of a threat if they ran wild, compared to even weakened but battle-wise soldiers. As the war progressed, however, what started as comparative laxity on the part of the administration grew increasingly severe as the Japanese began to lose the war. Where once a violation had warranted a beating, later in the war it might result in execution. Still, despite growing rules, regulations, and restrictions as the tide of battle changed, the civilian camps never, at their worst, fully resembled POW camps in terms of death rates or lethal treatment, though by the end they were closely approaching them.

In this same light, civilian internment camps in the Philippines were also run nothing like the death camps in German-held Europe and in Germany itself, where millions eventually went to an automated death in the showers, died by the bullet or were slowly killed by work. Some civilian camps, according to Lord Russell, were very similar to the Nazi camps, with everything "minus the gas chambers" (209), but this was not the case in the camps on Luzon, Negros, Cebu, or even Mindanao. An internee from Baguio, recently arrived from Germany and therefore more able to make such a comparison, disagreed with Lord Russell. Of the Hay camp (Baguio), the internee noted that "the camps in Europe were far worse than this one. Many members would be taken out at night, and after horrible sounds of torture, they would never be seen again nor would any one know what happened to them" (Crouter, 24).

Though a critic might easily point out that Baguio (especially in its Camp Holmes incarnation) was not comparable to the European camps because it was, perhaps, the most physically comfortable civilian camp in the Philippines, even so Baguio, Santo Tomás, Los Baños, Bacolod, Davao, and Cebu City camps were clearly different from those under Nazi control. The biggest difference was that the administrative intention and goals of the camps in the Phillipines and of those in Europe diverged wildly; in Treblinka or Auschwitz, unlike in Santo Tomás or Baguio, the camp commandant and his directives intended for all the camp inmates to die sooner or later, depending on their need for slave labor. The commandants of the civilian internment camps, especially in the Philippines, as far as anyone can tell, apparently intended for the internees to live—though not well, of course, and primarily by their own means, with minimal help from the Japanese. There was at least *initially* no intention of making any of the camps for civilians in the Philippines into death camps, though there is some argument now among both former internees and historians about what the Japanese intentions toward civilians were near the end of the war as MacArthur retook the islands.

Nor did the Philippine civilian internment camps duplicate either in administration or nature camps such as Manzinar or Topaz in the United States, which imprisoned over 100,000 Japanese and Japanese-Americans (Corbett, 36). The comparison is a natural one—especially because the Japanese, as mentioned earlier, used the supposed treatment of Japanese civilians in the United States as a justification for the kind of treatment meted out to American civilians in the Philippines. However illegally—by our own Constitution—the American government founded, filled, or maintained such camps, it differed significantly from the Japanese captors in administrative aims and practices, especially in terms of using the Geneva and Hague accords as guidelines as soon as the camps were fully in place. Though on February 24, 1942, the Japanese agreed to apply the Geneva Convention to all their civilian internees (Corbett, 50; IMTFE, *IPS* Doc. No. 10-E, Exhibit #1470, RG 331, Reel 42), they rarely did, as prisoner testimony proved before the International Military Tribunal for the Far East. This failure became a point of bitter dispute, especially in the civilian internment camps in the Philippines during the war itself, as internee committees besieged Japanese commandants on almost a weekly basis with petitions for more food, greater living space, and a cessation to physical punishments. All these petitions justified themselves by written references to the Geneva Convention especially.

In accordance with the Geneva Convention, the United States allowed international and neutral inspections of camp conditions and internee complaints in all of its camps, as I discussed in the Lordsburg incident. Additionally, there is no record of deficiency diseases on a mass scale, of camp deaths by starvation, or of lack of adequate medical treatment in the camps in the United States (see Appendix A for a list of internee rations in the United States). As the rest of this study will show, this was not something the Japanese could claim in the Philippine camps.

As Lordsburg indicates, the United States' record was hardly spotless (for instance, the government's use of county jails and local prisons violated the Geneva convention). However, the United States generally tried to guide its administrative policy by the tenets of international law (IMTFE, Reel 11, 14,728; Corbett, 37).

What, then, did the administration of a Philippine civilian internment camp resemble? To answer that fully, it is important to understand that there were not any completely "typical" internment camps or "typical" stated official guidelines for camp administration (Waterford, 31). Although many accounts discuss Santo Tomás especially, it was only one camp, even if the largest. This does not make it "typical." Instead, several factors caused the camps to differ markedly, especially the personality of the commandant and the location of the camp.

The personality and nature of the camp commandant were all-important. As Hartendorp explains, "It appeared that the Japanese did not have a standard plan for the organization and management of internment camps. What type of organization was developed probably depended on the character and attitude of the officer in command, the situation and size of the camp, and the strength, efficiency, and diplomacy of whatever internee organization evolved" (I, 174).

Individual commandants could (and did) allow different liberties, punishments, and degrees of self-government and were obviously the most important factor in camp life. Though internees governed themselves partially and promulgated some rules, they did so only as much as, and to the degree that, the Japanese commandant allowed them to do so. As internee Frederic Stevens explained, the commandant was at the "head of camp organization." This meant he was responsible for the camp's "orderly operation"; for making and issuing most regulations; for "receiving and releasing inmates"; and, generally speaking, for "the government of the internees" (21). This was true in all internment camps, especially those covered in this study. Because authority was "vested in the person" of the Japanese commandant (Whitesides, 14), the commandant's "person" and his personality resulted in tremendous leeway when making the rules and enforcing them too.

The attitude toward internee personal freedoms not only varied but did so dramatically among commandants, as did the rights of internees to amenities and necessities: to play music, to buy "outside" from food vendors, to go on sick call, and to travel outside. Some commandants, such as Rukuro Tomibe (Holmes/Baguio), Majors Tanaka and Urabe (Los Baños), and even, according to some reports, Commandants Kuroda and Kato of Santo Tomás, were humane and decent men who administered as fairly and reasonably as they could, given military restrictions.

Tomibe, for example, was very popular with the internees; according to interviews of Baguio internees taken over thirty years later in 1977, 83 percent of those interviewed said Tomibe was "humane" and "an officer and a gentleman" under whose aegis the camp experienced "a period of peace and calm" (Bloom, "Death," 81). Under Tomibe's civil hand, internees were allowed to picnic outside the camp on the surrounding hills, to take walks in and around the compound, and to hold Easter egg hunts, Christmas celebrations, and even a wedding (Tomibe, 41–43). Internees from other camps heard stories and soon envied those 500 or so at Baguio: "[Baguio inmates] had a rather placid existence. The Japanese gave them wide latitude in order to make prison life bearable under the circumstances" (Onorato, x).

Tomibe also attended church services with the internees, respected their religious beliefs, gave extra food to the children, and made sure the camp residents received their Red Cross parcels without the supplies being pilfered by guards or the omnipresent *kempei tai* (Japanese secret police), who were often guilty of using the slightest excuse to hold back or ransack parcels (Bloom, "Death," 81). In this case, the message reportedly stamped on each cigarette pack, "I Shall Return," was enough "enemy propaganda" to give guards and police alike a reason to tear apart parcels. Despite this, Tomibe ultimately convinced the guards and police simply to restore the vital Red Cross parcels (Tomibe, 42).

The reasonably pleasant reign of Tomibe ended abruptly with the escape of two prisoners, Swick and Green. Not only were several bunkmates (including James Halsema) subsequently tortured for information about the escape by the *kempei tai*, but a unit of ninety Japanese troops "were assigned to the camp, barbed wire fences were erected and walks to the mountains behind the camp forbidden" (Tomibe, 44). Despite this, the Baguio inmates remembered Tomibe so fondly and with such affection that they made him the guest of honor at the 1977 reunion in San Francisco at the Presidio; Tomibe and the 135 former internees present had, apparently, a marvelous time. Notes critic Lynn Bloom, in conclusion, "As far as can be determined, this was the only prison camp of World War II (perhaps of any war) to maintain such affectionate relations with their former captor" ("Death," 81).

Los Baños camp also fared well in the early days under one of the first commandants, Major Tanaka. Later, after the second decent commandant,

Major Urabe, the camp would become one of the worst administered and most cruelly punitive of all the civilian camps. Under Tanaka, however, conditions were as fair as possible, despite the immediate hardships involved in living and working in a camp still under construction. Tanaka, a veteran of the China campaign, had been removed from the Infantry because his left arm had been shattered by a Chinese grenade. The arm continued to pain him intensely, but this never manifested itself in any arbitrary or cruel administrative policies, despite his service in China earlier. First, Tanaka went out of his way to *support* the internee objections lodged by the Internee Committee at Los Baños with Santo Tomás's commandant, Kuroda, over the policy of continuing transfers to Los Baños camp—a camp half the size of Santo Tomás, but expected, it seemed, to house the entire population eventually (Hartendorp, I, 525). Major Tanaka added his warning to that of A. D. Calhoun, head of the Los Baños Administrative (Executive) Committee (Arthur, 54).

Beyond this, Tanaka made it official camp policy that internees could trade for food with native vendors who were allowed inside camp to sell their meat, eggs, and produce. This meant that meager camp rations could be supplemented daily by fresh fruits and vegetables or occasionally meat. Santo Tomás, by contrast, had a commandant's directive that closed down the "package line" and forbade this kind of trading by early 1944. Tanaka also showed his humanity by allowing the Philippine Red Cross to deliver comfort kits, by refusing to require a grueling extra roll call (a Santo Tomás procedure), and by encouraging the Internee Committee to run as many of the camp's affairs as possible (Arthur, 55).

Major Urabe, Los Baños's second commandant, was a man for whom many internees felt some fondness, because his efforts on their behalf "seemed real" (Nash interview). When he was reassigned in July 1944 (because the Japanese authorities thought him too lenient, according to rumors), the internees lined the road and bowed voluntarily (Arthur, 140–141). These kindnesses were allowed by a loose, poorly defined state of administrative regulation that made, in essence, every commandant his own rule book. Kindness might be the result; cruelty, unfortunately, resulted more often, especially in the latter half of 1944 and early 1945 at both Santo Tomás and Los Baños.

Finally, an odd anecdote from a former teenage internee, Martin Meadows, helps show that commandants could be understanding if they chose—even about customs completely outside their experience. Meadows's thirteenth birthday occurred in December of 1943 in Santo Tomás. His parents decided to try to observe religious tradition:

My parents, being Jewish, decided to ask the commandant [probably Kato] to permit us to leave camp for my *bar mitzvah* (I think my parents used the term "confirmation" to enhance ambiguity) at Manila's synagogue. Remarkably, the reply was that my father and I—though not my mother—could have one-day passes for the occasion. My father sent out word to some of his non-interned (non-"enemy-alien") friends, and when the day arrived I had my *bar mitzvah*. (Perhaps the only instance in World War II that an Axis captive was allowed to leave a concentration camp for such a ceremony.) (Meadows ltr, December 6, 1997)

Meadows suspects his mother was denied a pass "possibly because the Japanese did not want an entire family (I am an only child) outside at the same time, and/or they considered a woman's position to be unimportant" (Meadows). In any event, it is a startling anecdote for the times.

Whether under military or supposedly "civilian" administration (as the camps were in 1944), Jim Halsema explains, it didn't really matter: "Japanese or any other civilians never had any real authority during the Japanese occupation from the initial December 1941 landings, but technically the Japanese Military Administration ended with the establishment of the [Philippine] republic" (personal communication with author, March 1, 1997).

Indeed, as one staff member, Ohdaira, explained the prejudices of the Japanese hierarchy: "Military Number One. Then dogs. Then Civilians" (qtd by Halsema, personal communication with author, March 1, 1997).

Camps, under both military and "civilian" commandants, were run by rules established by those same commandants. They were the "authority" and had the ability to "prescribe the rules and regulations for the administration of the camp." The commandant could "delegate authority" to others, such as the internee committees, but then their generated rules would still have to be subject to the guidelines and regulations he himself decided on (Hartendorp, II, 168). In essence, the commandant ran the game at the behest of the military and decided how cruelly or how kindly he would force the internees to play; the internee meetings were only effective so long as the commandant didn't notice or didn't care, nor did the Imperial Army.

Despite internee protests, for example, if a commandant decided to use the rice ration as a tool of discipline (despite the fact that this was forbidden by both the Geneva and Hague Conventions), then that became an administrative tool, despite fervent objections by the internees who appealed to the various international agreements, specifically, Articles 42 and 43 of the Geneva Convention, especially as these pertained to the transmission of complaints to "protecting Powers." As one memorandum by internee Pond explained glumly, however, to the Executive Committee, if the internees followed the convention and chose members of the Executive Committee to serve as their "representatives" to the international agencies, the situation would not only not be made better but could even be significantly worsened. As Pond explained, by Japanese rules the commandant was the "head" of the Executive Committee and, according to the Japanese, served as the internees' "true representative" outside the command. This made any idea of real "internee representation" to a neutral outside authority a cruel joke. Obviously, any use of the Geneva Convention as an administrative guideline was moot or at least hopelessly circular (Pond ltr, quoted in Hartendorp, II, 168–169, n5).

Despite seeming access to "higher authority" (at least Japanese authority), the so-called chain of command *always ultimately had to get its information from the camp commandant.* As Hideki Tojo, former prime minister and minister of war, testified at the Tokyo Trials, "heads of various prison camps had to make a monthly report to the Military Affairs bureau with respect to the prisoners under their care in connection with food, health, labor, and so forth" (IMTFE, Reel 27, 36,425).

Additionally, as Tojo goes on to explain, any deaths in either the POW or civilian camps due to malnutrition, execution, or disease were to be reported to the army commanders *in the field.* These commanders, as we will see later, were administratively the source of most information about prisoner conditions (36,435), thanks to their reports from camp commandants, despite the presence of the Geneva-required "Prisoner-of-War Information Bureaus."

The army commanders of the area then reported to the Military Affairs Bureau and eventually to the War Ministry itself, who then might or might not inform the Foreign Ministry so that it could provide answers to any queries from international agencies. More often than not, as with the case of the protests filed (or attempted to be filed) by the POWs, the protest went through a number of bureaus but ultimately was sent back down to the commandant to answer; the fox, in effect, was asked to testify about the health, welfare, and condition of the chickens (IMTFE, Reel 11, 14,284–14,287). Unfortunately, complaints about internees followed the same route. Though the internees were not in the same category as POWs, procedures were highly similar and illustrative of the obstacles the internees faced, especially late in the war.

Perhaps part of the problem in accepting this circular reporting system comes from an American misunderstanding of Japanese culture and its significant differences with cultures in the West. As Ryuzo Sato, a distinguished professor at Brown University and an expert on Japanese and Western cultural differences, explains in his landmark work, *The Chrysanthemum and the Eagle,*

Japan is a country without an explicit set of rules or, perhaps more accurately, a country that does not need such rules. In a homogeneous society, where complete understanding can be achieved through monosyllables, the rules governing communication and other ordinary activities do not need to be set down in writing or even explicitly articulated. Someone who submits a contract to be signed or proposes a set of rules to be followed runs the risk of being frowned upon for "alien" or "unsociable" behavior. In general, Japanese feel strongly that it is not a virtue to prescribe rules. This is a major difference between the United States and Japan. (75–76)

Although this is a fascinating discussion of basic cultural differences, Sato's implicit argument—that the Japanese authorities did not "believe in" or "value" international contracts and agreements (such as those of Geneva, the Hague, or even the International Red Cross)—is ultimately somewhat ingenuous. Whether that is true culturally or not, the Japanese publicly signed international (not merely American) agreements such as the Hague Agreement (1907), and even the Geneva Convention of 1929. This allowed diplomats from many other countries to believe that the Japanese, with their strong sense of personal honor, understood and intended to fulfill these international treaties. Initially, at the beginning of the war, Japan's compliance with international conventions of war seemed historically assured. After all, Japan had made an international name for itself as a compassionate captor during the Russo-Japanese War (1904–1905). The Western powers had even commended Japan for its treatment of prisoners (Linderman, 144–145).

Japan had signed both the Hague and Geneva treaties, for example, both of which provided for humane treatment of prisoners and sufficient medical attention and food for them. Though Japan signed the Geneva Convention, the Diet refused to ratify it, so the Japanese were not "legally" bound to follow its provisions (Corbett, 3–4). If, as Sato points out, the Japanese had a distaste for legalisms, then one can assume that they did not feel bound by their "legal" position as a result of signing the treaties. This seems especially true since the Japanese government informed the International Red Cross that it would "abide by the provisions of the Geneva Convention regarding the treatment of war-prisoners although Japan is not bound by the Convention" (*Manila Tribune*, February 17, 1942, qtd in Hartendorp, I, 55).

International agreements, in this war, did not modify Japanese administrative rules, nor did the administrative rules receive very careful scrutiny by the Japanese authorities themselves, especially judging by the cursory, sporadic inspections listed in both the IMTFE transcripts and in works such as Hartendorp's.

Perhaps in answer to growing protests, for example, Los Baños received an "inspection" from General Hamada, supposedly the officer in charge of all internment camps in the Far East (Hartendorp, I, 544). To say that the inspection was cursory is not to do it justice; Hamada came June 23, 1943, to visit, "but only stayed about an hour. During this period he conferred with the Colonel [Narusawa — transitional camp commandant] and motored through the camp, including the new section under construction" (Hartendorp, I, 547). According to some, the "motoring" was fairly speedy. Never during the "inspection" did Hamada get out of the car to examine the camp, its buildings, or its sanitary facilities, nor did he meet with any of the Los Baños Internee Committee either singly or together. As Commandant Narusawa explained to the disgruntled internees later, "time did not permit" Hamada to speak with them (Hartendorp, I, 547, n10). Once again it is obvious that the only authority questioned was the officer in charge — possibly the same officer responsible for the very conditions that may have sparked the protest.

The same was true at Santo Tomás, over a year later and during the time of the titular "civilian" administration. Santo Tomás, for example, received a June 29, 1944, inspection by General Kuo, director-general of the war-prisoners camps. His visit, from 10:20 A.M. to 11:40 P.M., passed "without incident," though it appears he asked questions of no one but the commandant and did not see conditions inside the buildings or talk to the prisoners at any length (Hartendorp, II, 296).

Any attempt to pin down a chain of command whose edicts *really* governed the administration of civilian internment camps is doomed, as both the Allied prosecutors in Tokyo and even Japanese experts, such as Saburo Hayashi in his book *Kogan*, suggest. Despite testimony during the Tokyo Trials by Tadashi Odajima (formerly a senior official in the POW Information Office, as well as a senior member of the POW Supervision Department in the War Ministry) that the "duty of the War Minister is administration and the duty of the various bureaus in the War Ministry is to assist that work . . . no particular bureau in the War Ministry is directly connected to the work—with prisoner of war camps" (IMTFE, Reel 21, 27,805–27,806; 27,865). There is a slippery vagueness here that influenced the civilian camps as well.

The vagueness of Japanese authorities may have been deliberate, thereby allowing much greater administrative leeway for the commandant in the internee (and POW) camps. Such imprecision also suggests the confusion present in the higher echelons of the Japanese Imperial Army. Col. Hayashi, though in the Russian section most of the war, was transferred to Imperial General Staff Headquarters, Operations Organization and Mobilization Section in 1944 and then became the military secretary to the minister of war,

General Anami, in 1945 (Hayashi, x). Hayashi explains that the Japanese Imperial Army had undergone a tremendous revolution earlier in the 1930s, because the Japanese had been "dazzled by" and modeled themselves after the army of Nazi Germany. Because of the German model, the Japanese Imperial Army began to meddle in domestic politics and the setting of policy (8; 18). Just prior to World War II, Hayashi explains, "the tendency toward insubordination became even more conspicuous with the Army. For example, headquarters staff officers, whose essential function is to labor in the background, pushed forward into domestic politics. Some of them actually acted as if they were themselves Prime Ministers or high commanders. This state of affairs often led to hushing-up of culpability or responsibility" (6).

He goes on to explain that areas of military responsibility and accountability were "exceedingly ill defined," because, for example, a field general might make a public statement completely "unrelated to the true will of the War Minister" and go unpunished or uncorrected. He suggests that on-the-spot commanders "always exerted a more powerful local influence than did the High Command itself" (6; 11). Weak and foggy administrative guidelines then were the result of several factors, including the incompetence of superior officers "to guide the key officers and troops," the presence of departmental and factional quarrels determining who was in power, and, most of all, a "style of leadership" that Hayashi calls "broad-minded"—one in which superior officers, in an effort to appear Olympian and calm, "blindly swallowed whatever the young officers had to say" (6). As Hayashi himself points out, "An Olympian 'general-like' attitude tended to imply at least superficial encouragement of each subordinate opinion, but without commitment" (195, n9). Given the penchant for the camp commandant to be the sole judge of both administrative regulations and protests about regulations, confusion about which ministry or bureau the commandants should report to, and the tendency of superior officers to be "Olympian" and ignore unenforced orders take on a darker, more lethal light.

This problem is especially evident in the treatment of the citizens of Manila at the end of the Japanese occupation. Here, despite an order from Lieutenant General Yamashita *to retreat* from the city, Admiral Sanji Iwabuci, the local commander, ordered 20,000 Japanese sailors and naval troops, along with 1,600 rear guard army infantry, *back into* Manila. The result, over a period of approximately two weeks (February 17 to March 3, 1945), was a killing spree carried out in a fury against the citizens of the city by drunken soldiers under the direct auspices of Iwabuci. The combined Japanese forces killed over 60,000 Filipinos, and the incident became known as the "Rape of Manila" (Linderman, 176). It was considered a war crime, and despite his earlier order and on the basis of his greater command authority, Yamashita found the ordeal placed at his doorstep during his trial in Manila.

Because of the vagueness of the Japanese command, higher military authority could not be appealed to, and the internees had to learn to bend to the wind of each commandant's temper and to follow whatever rules existed. No superior officer was going to swoop down on the camp and discipline or arrest a cruel or vicious commandant. Commandants could and did, even in civilian camps, turn over those they thought suspicious or "willful" to the secret police for questioning. Nor were camp commandants able to stop the *kempei tai* from taking whomever they wanted, even assuming the commandant did want to prevent it. As Russell Brines, a former newspaper correspondent in Manila, stated, civilian internees from a number of camps, including Santo Tomás and Baguio, found themselves questioned under torture (Brines, 42–47).

Civilians in the Philippines were not exempt from the attentions of the *kempei tai* or the guards. Several civilians, for a number of reasons, were tortured. Frederick Stevens, at age 64, spent seven months at Fort Santiago for helping, while in Santo Tomás, to raise money for internee food or aid for the POWs (Waterford, 261). Stevens's membership in the Masons and his prominence in that organization caused him to receive severe treatment; his interrogators repeatedly demanded that Stevens expose the Jewish and Masonic combined international conspiracy to rule the world and ruin Japan. To Stevens's incredulity, his interrogators pointed out that Roosevelt and MacArthur were, they had on good authority, Masons, and this was why the United States had declared war on Japan (Hartendorp, II, 577).

Obviously unable to divulge details of this phantasmagoric plan, Stevens faced severe and sustained torture: the *kempei tai* inserted bamboo splinters under his fingernails, held his bare feet to a hot stove, and cut off flesh from the back of his hand and then made him eat it (Hartendorp, II, 577).

Nor did even relatively peaceful Baguio, under the gentlemanly Tomibe, avoid having some of its people tortured, though none for so long as Stevens. The three male internees who shared a sleeping space with Swick and Green —the two escapees from the camp—were taken by the *kempei tai* for questioning. Though Tomibe protested, he could do nothing to countermand the powerful secret police. Kept for four to seven days, E. J. Kneebone, William Moule, and J. J. Halsema (the latter two, authors whose works I use in this book) were routinely tortured by being hung up by the thumbs and lashed or beaten as they were hanging. No one knew anything—though, as Halsema explains, "Obviously, we were going to answer anything they asked us, but they didn't ask me the right questions" (Halsema, "Oral," 11). All three were released, but two had to be hospitalized on their return (Hartendorp, II, 299, n1).

Santo Tomás, some two months later in May 1944, also saw the use of torture—this time by the camp guards. Frank Cary, a camp translator who got along well with the Japanese, describes what happened on May 13 to several Santo Tomás male internees engaged in "over the wall transactions" with Filipinos outside the camp. The Japanese guards grabbed the men's Filipino contact and coerced signed evidence out of him against the internee prisoners. Cary was asked to translate during the guards' interrogation of the internees; he refused, and another of the camp translators served during the torture session: "In the investigation there was very rough treatment given the men and one was operated on yesterday for broken face bones, and another may go to the hospital today for injuries to the sciatic nerve. Had no share in the interpreting while the beating up was in progress" (Cary ltr, May 13, 1944, 60).

Neither international protest, nor military inspection, nor the displeasure of superior officers had any real influence or provided any meaningful check on the ways in which individual commandants ran their camps or on the measures they chose to use to ensure discipline or to carry out punishment.

In sum, the only set "rule" that the Japanese higher-ups seemed to recognize as valid and unchanging was the unstated but understood rule of "no escapes from camp"—one that commandants were actually expected to enforce. When they didn't do so, there were severe repercussions. Though earlier no higher authority had stopped Baguio's commandant, Tomibe, from treating prisoners in accordance with a freely translated Golden Rule (he said his policies were "based on what I thought I would want if I were in their place"), the escape of Swick and Green was another matter altogether. Tomibe was transferred to a post supervising rice harvests and later placed as an infantry officer in the rugged uplands of Nueva Vizcaya—some believed because of leniency toward the prisoners and a successful prisoner escape (Tomibe, 39; 44; Halsema ltr, May 13, 1997).

Certainly, the experiences in both Baguio and Santo Tomás seem surrealistic and ironic when measured against the standards Hideiki Tojo claimed were the regulations regarding the treatment of prisoners: "In regard to prisoners of war as well as civilian internees and inhabitants in occupied territories, I gave orders in accordance with the POW Treatment regulations [exhibit 1965, 3] and POW Service Regulations [exhibit 1965, 4] prohibiting maltreatment and imposition of forced labor, and directed that they be treated according to the principles of international law and the regulations" (IMTFE, Reel 27, 26,414–26,415). But then, as we know from Sato's study cited earlier, legal documents and agreements had no real meaning for the Japanese. Scholars probably should keep this in mind when considering Tojo's statement—or those of any other Imperial Army authority during the war.

Perhaps in reaction to the Japanese generalized confusion of administrative aims (other than preventing escapes), the internees in all camps made a point of delegating responsibility clearly, appointing subcommittees to deal with specific camp problems and requirements, and often electing a governing (or "executive") committee that coordinated the others. A camp such as Los Baños or Santo Tomás, for example, had subcommittees committed to dealing with problems of sanitation, health, recreation, work assignments, food, shelter, and safety (Arthur, 27). Each of these committees had its own contingent of internees to deal with the implementation of committee decisions (Whitesides, 15). The subcommittees in Santo Tomás were responsible for setting up the "package line" (which allowed in and regulated food brought in from outside the camp by purchase or by friends); establishing a regular garbage collection and burial; providing for the allotment, supply, and planting of camp vegetable gardens; staffing, running, and maintaining the camp health facilities, as well as authorizing passes for internees with serious illness to go to hospitals outside the camp (Grace Nash's child with diphtheria is one example); establishing, staffing, and supplying materials for K–12 classes for the camp children, and setting up college classes for adults and late teens; organizing intermural sports (especially baseball) and selecting teams and leagues; providing entertainment including musical evenings, live shows, and records played over the loudspeaker — most of which were cut off, punitively, in 1944; planning, building, and maintaining laundry, shower, and toilet facilities for the camp of over 5,000 people; and finally, assigning work to all camp members except those in the hospital or under age six. Children not only went to school but had chores to perform as well. The Japanese use of an indiscriminate net for hauling in "enemy aliens" after Manila was occupied inadvertently gave the camps a gift of survival by incarcerating some of the most highly trained professionals and mechanics in the city.

Other camp committees to a greater or lesser extent (in terms of number of committees) mirrored Santo Tomás and strove as well to "provide for the common good," to keep the internees and their children engaged in useful work or schooling, and to discipline their members for camp rules infractions (such as liquor consumption or sale, and sexual contact, which most commandants forbade), rather than have the Japanese deal with it (Whitesides, 15).

Even the Japanese noticed the almost-immediate organization and purposeful activity of the internees. Rukuro Tomibe, of Baguio, for example, said that he was "impressed" with the American and British prisoners and with their "common sense, wisdom, organizational skills, and will to carry out [the commandant's] decisions" (39).

The committees promulgated their *own* administrative rules within whatever framework the camp commandants defined. Though, for example, a pyrophobic Kato in Santo Tomás would forbid the use of cooking fires in the shanties (and to avoid Japanese punishment, the internee "police" would check to make sure the ban was obeyed), the committees still generated regulations regarding who was or was not able to build a shanty, how internees could "pass on" this housing to other families, what materials internees would use to build the shanties (and their prices), and even the size of the "lots" on which the shanties would stand. Even with shanties, internees exercised a rude, but necessary form of urban planning and zoning.

Internee committees also chose the work details and the number and kinds of meals for those doing heavy manual labor. At Bacolod, for example, each man, woman, and teenager had approximately two hours a day to do camp work. Every able body was assigned some sort of duty, which included garden tending, garbage disposal, outhouse sanitation and maintenance, picking and cleaning rice of weevils and debris, preparing vegetables and cooking meals, washing dishes, boiling drinking water, tending the sick, serving food, cutting or collecting firewood, or hauling stones (Bryant, 124–126). Men who hoed, cut firewood, hauled stones, or performed similar jobs were "paid" with extra rations at a number of camps not only to make the jobs more appealing, but also to provide the workers with the necessary energy to complete their tasks.

In Los Baños camp, internees had a choice of two hours a day of "heavy work" or three hours a day of "lighter work." "Heavy work" at Los Baños involved chopping wood, digging post holes, and stretching and stringing barbed wire around the camp; "lighter work" meant nursing the sick, cooking, cleaning rice, providing day care, teaching school, handing out and monitoring toilet paper use (it was rationed), mending clothes, and cleaning (Read, questionnaire, 1990; Hartendorp, II, 41). Those too feeble to do much work (those in their late seventies) were given light chores commensurate with their strength.

Though there is not a great deal of information in personal narratives about Cebu (or Davao) camp, there is an indication that they chose representatives from among themselves to deal with the Japanese commandant. In Cebu internee administration of its own people was rudimentary. The Japanese allowed the internees to choose two representatives, one American and one British; they were Father William McCarthy (American) and Hector Mac-Lean (British). As with other camps, loosely organized groups were responsible for various camp tasks such as hauling water, finding firewood, cooking, gardening, and so forth. Imogene Carlson does mention that, unlike the women with children under six in other internment camps, those women at Cebu did not have to spend two hours a day cleaning vegetables, though the other women in Cebu camp did. Mothers of small children had the dubious advantage of shorter working hours, but more noisome duty: cleaning the camp latrines (Carlson, 103).

Unlike the larger camps on Luzon, however, in Cebu camp two Filipino houseboys were allowed to go with their former employers into camp; the advantage to this arrangement from the Japanese point of view was having several Filipinos available to go shopping and do the marketing in town, rather than risking internees on the "outside" or showing the locals in what condition the internees were as time passed (Hartendorp, I, 316–317). Also, in comparison to Bacolod on Negros, Cebu had a Filipino doctor, Dr. Ramos, who was allowed to visit the internees on a semiregular basis. Eventually, after the camp was moved several times, the Americans and the British prisoners were separated; the twenty-three British internees were taken to Lahug Primary School, while over one hundred Americans (along with Dutch and Norwegian internees) were finally interned and settled at Cebu Junior College, a branch of the University of the Philippines (317).

What information we have on the administrative mechanisms of Davao camp is based on the limited information provided by Frank Cary and Jane Wills, and on some early observations by Alex Brown, who, as British vice consul, left in June 1942 to be repatriated. Cary's observations about camp life come from a perspective somewhat tinted by his lifetime experience in Japan, his fluency in Japanese, and his abilities in translation. Because of these, he became the de facto "speaker" for the internees to some extent. As he himself explains it, thanks to his own earlier compassion for, and acts of kindness toward, the Japanese civilians from Mindanao interned by the Americans at the beginning of the war, Cary believed he had a strong position with the Japanese from which he could try to steer orders and effect changes:

> I have won the confidence and respect of the officer who threw me into jail and since he prefers to use Japanese rather than English as a medium of communication—I see him on most of the important as well as unimportant occasions. As I have taken the initiative a couple of times to see that justice was done—I have his respect, I am convinced. (ltr of April 14, 1942, 5)

Brown, however, points out that by April 1942 the feeding situation changed for the worse and that the former cornmeal and canned fish the Japanese had been regularly giving the internees were now to be paid for *retroactively* (76). Even though the Japanese had allowed internees to keep a chicken run early on (Wills, 20), once again it seems the result of whim rather than rule.

It isn't clear how duties got assigned at Davao. Perhaps internees chose their own, based on their former occupations or tastes. In Davao the use of a central executive committee to assign work doesn't appear to have applied, though obviously each internee did perform some sort of work. Cary discusses his own duties, including performing worship services for the internees in rotatation with the other clergymen in camp, making coconut "milk" every morning for the internees' breakfasts, and working in the vegetable garden. Other internees apparently did other jobs such as cooking, cleaning, and latrine duty.

In all cases, internees soon learned to do the work assigned. Indeed, dereliction of camp duties was punished regularly in most camps by the internees themselves with fines, "jail" time (in an internee space), confinement to quarters, or extra duties, in addition to the severe social censure that came with slacking off (Lucas, 40).

To some, this private policing presented a philosophical administrative problem. If internees made sure, for example, that those who were drinking (banned by most commandants) were taken into custody and punished by an internee court, did this make the internee court "collaborationist"? Weren't they then working with the Japanese? Wasn't enforcement of this kind merely doing the Japanese's work for them and furthering their aims? To this the internee committees answered with a resounding "no." As chairmen such as A. D. Calhoun, Harry Fonger, Carl Eschbach, and Carroll Grinnell pointed out, if the internees policed themselves, then the Japanese would not have to — and the policing was done not for such idiosyncratic Japanese violations as "failure to bow correctly" but for offenses either that threatened the life of the camp or that would result in the loss of dear and hard-won privileges for fellow inmates and for the camp. Further, it was an obvious truism that internee punishment, while onerous, did not involve the kinds of typical beatings and often torture used by the Japanese themselves if they caught an offender; in fact, the personal safety of the offender dictated internee policing and fines rather than something worse.

Hartendorp advances another ingenious (and satisfying) argument on this issue. He points out that the camp government's necessity to "bow" to superior military might (which couldn't be avoided) did not invalidate control of the daily administration of most venues, because "[it] seemed to them [the internees] to be a government of Americans by Americans subject though it might be to limitation, interference and coercion on the part of the Japanese" (I, 60). Hartendorp carries this argument to its natural, metaphysical, and philosophical conclusion:

> Because . . . under the American Constitution, sovereignty lies with the people, Americans carry their sovereignty with them, and wherever they go where there is no government they recognize, such as in enemy-occupied territory, and where they are separated from regularly constituted American authority, they can set up

their own government and that government will be American. Foreign interference with and coercion of that government cannot affect its fundamental nature. Under such circumstances, wherever two or three Americans are gathered together in the name of America there can be an American government. (Hartendorp, I, 60–61, n6)

Even with a metaphysical sense of American democracy operating, most internees strove, as did their executive committees, to avoid angering the Japanese if at all possible. Sometimes, however, internees could not morally avoid risking their wrath. For example, toward the end of the internment, at least two camp doctors — Drs. Lloyd and Stevenson — refused to sign death warrants with a diagnosis of "heart failure" or "senility" as the Japanese commandant demanded when the actual cause was starvation, malnutrition, or beriberi. Dr. Nogi, the Japanese medical officer in charge of prison camps in the Philippines, said that such diagnoses as "malnutrition" and "starvation" "cast an unfair stigma on the Japanese administration" and that these problems were merely because of "world conditions" (Hartendorp, II, 508). (As I show in the next chapter, this excuse would prove very thin upon examination.)

All in all the committees worked as best they could to protect the internees from Japanese anger. Sometimes this had the look of pandering to their captors, especially when this sensitivity toward Japanese fixed beliefs and prejudices seemed initially to degrade the democratic election process. For example, women's participation in camp voting at Baguio (in this case, Camp Holmes) — especially for spaces on the Executive Committee — was temporarily forbidden by the internee committee. Natalie Crouter complains on August 13, 1942:

> It is election day for our men. It still surprises me that the chairman doesn't want the women to vote or have any kind of election. The General Committee appointed our group and will continue to appoint them but we can write in any ideas we may have for the Men's Suggestion Box. He [Eschbach] thinks any other way would end in a mess and the Japanese don't consider women people anyway so it is all one piece. Perhaps there never will be any official democracy in here except for men. (Crouter, 81)

The internee committee wanted the Japanese commandants to respect their committee members and decisions — something the presence of women on the committee might not allow. The Japanese had a long tradition of excluding women from politics, so much so that scholars have called it a "distinctive feature" of Imperial Japan (1895–1945). While general Japanese male suffrage came late (1926), a weak parliament limited the power the men could exert, and a series of necessary voting "qualifications" in talent, education, and "connections" lessened even that impact if only in terms of numbers. Conversely, even highly placed, educated, and well-connected women could not vote at all and were "prohibited from elementary political activities" of any kind, especially joining political organizations. Japanese authorities suspected female voting and political participation of "disturbing family harmony" as well as threatening the social hierarchy, because it was well known that voting led to "propagating pornography and socialism" (Nolte, 1; 7).

Calling the Executive Committee chairman's (Carl Eschbach's) exclusion of women based on Japanese attitudes merely an "excuse" that had grown "rather thin," Natalie Crouter does explain further on in her diary that this antidemocratic idea is eventually quashed by the members of the camp themselves. Her August 20 entry (a week later) rejoices that the Women's Committee elections are being held; this means, she says, that women "are considered people again" (Crouter, 84; Bloom, "Crouter," 536, n43). Crouter herself was elected to that committee. Despite the seeming "separate but equal" division of men's and women's committees, Crouter, Miles, and other Baguio internees seem fully satisfied with the arrangement, because "both men and women shared a number of . . . major responsibilities, including camp leadership" (Bloom, "Death," 78).

Bloom points out, however, that the Women's Committee, though they did "allocate jobs and supplies to all able-bodied women and teen-age girls," had direct control of little else. The Men's Committee (elected exclusively by men) controlled camp money, school curriculum, hospital policies, and organization as well as managed and stocked the camp store. Further, the Men's Committee could veto any decision of the Women's Committee ("Popular," 800). Though, administratively speaking, the inclusion of women in the committee structure did not present major problems, despite Japanese uneasiness, the commandants generally preferred (at Baguio and at other camps as well) to deal with the men in charge when internee rights were the subject. In any event, as Bloom points out, all decisions—even those reached by the Men's Committee—had to be approved by the Japanese commandant. How much a commandant followed the recommendations of the internee committees depended, as always, on the personality of the commandant.

Another occasion in which the democratic process seemed weighted down and distorted by Japanese opinion occurred initially at Santo Tomás during the first months. In the chaos of the first few days at camp, as truckloads of 200 and 300 people came in and were dumped in camp, the first commandant, Lt. Tomayasu, asked whether the Americans had a "leader." The question was not exactly simple to answer, because before the war broke out, the Americans had formed the "American Coordinating Committee" for protection in the event of invasion. On January 4, 1942, the day Commandant Tomayasu asked, only Earl Carroll (the leader of the South Malate branch of the ACC) seemed available, and other internees pointed him out as a "leader" (Hartendorp, I, 3; 8). Technically, Carroll was only a member of a committee largely elected by concerned Elks, Chamber of Commerce members, and Rotarian businessmen in Manila in 1940; this group was not really representative of the larger population of either Manila or of Santo Tomás itself. Despite this—and Carroll's attempts to explain—Lt. Tomayasu demanded that Carroll "become the 'general chairman' of an organization." Carroll himself was to set up the camp and gather "leaders" from each room and building in which people lived. He was then to bring them together for a meeting (Hartendorp, I, 8).

Beyond this, Tomayasu told Carroll to make Executive Committee, as well as building monitor, selections as soon as possible; though Carroll tried to arrive at a sensible basis for such selections, Tomayasu told him simply to "choose such persons as he knew." Quickly in the confusion Carroll chose those he recognized and whatever ACC members he could find. When he spotted Frederick Stevens, the former head of the ACC, in the next prisoner group to be dropped off in camp, Carroll offered to resign and let Stevens take over. Stevens refused, citing an odd, but perhaps pragmatic, reason: things were running smoothly and the commandant had already approved of the Executive Committee the way it now was; getting along with the commandant and being part of a committee with which he was willing to work was the primary consideration (Hartendorp, I, 12–13). Carroll agreed then to remain as head of the Executive Committee.

This lack of democratic selection did not go unnoticed by the internees, especially because the new Executive Committee seemed to be composed exclusively of the leading financial and social lights of Manila business and society. Indeed, some suggested that the committee operated by helping only "insiders" and buddies, to the disadvantage of those not in the inner circle— especially in terms of later work assignments in coveted areas such as the kitchen (Alice Hill, interview). To try to take the sting out of the fait accompli demanded by the commandant, Carroll and the others insisted that floor and room monitors (unlike building monitors) would still be elected (Hartendorp, I, 14). These elected officials would be chosen by a vote; each room and floor would, therefore, elect its own representatives to make sure that the camp regulations were followed, that space in sleeping quarters remained distributed fairly, that rooms remained "orderly," and that internee concerns were fairly represented among other monitors and within the Executive Committee (Stevens, 15–16).

This uneasy balancing act of election and appointment and the actual administrative posts that women could hold (none on the Executive Committee, for example) never did resolve itself completely at Santo Tomás. Los Baños, Baguio, and other, even smaller camps, such as Masbate, the one Sneed was sent to initially in the Visayans (Onorato, xviii), had "fair" elections to some degree, though that degree varied considerably. Sneed complains (along with others) about the rights of the camp minority not being preserved, citing the first semi–self-appointed committee, heavily weighted to the missionary majority in terms of representation, and who, Sneed claims, refused to take action against their missionary comrades when the latter hoarded food, camp medicine, and soap (16). Eventually, the unhappy internees not part of the missionary clique managed to stir up enough resentment with other non-aligned internees to stage a coup. Ultimately, the missionary clique was replaced with a fully democratic committee, though Sneed makes no mention of the degree of female enfranchisement. Los Baños's second committee also was an improvement and the result of a fully representative election, especially because the first executive committee in Los Baños had been appointed by the only quasi-legitimate Santo Tomás Executive Committee (Arthur, 61). Baguio and Bacolod both had regular elections from the first committee, and Cebu apparently chose representatives rather than forming a committee.

The manner of any internee committee selection was particularly important, because the democratic selection presupposed a general belief in the value of similar procedures in establishing rules and restrictions for camp internees, and became a useful tool for internee advocacy. A committee appointed by the Japanese rather than being elected found itself inevitably shaped by Japanese, not democratic, assumptions — and these were only weakly representative and generally strongly hierarchical. Even with a fully democratically elected committee, the brick wall that was the commandant's will often negated those principles. As a result, the tension between the rules the internees set and those of the various commandants became one of the distinguishing problems of camp life, as undemocratic means decided food rationing, transfers between camps, personal freedom, and punishment.

Los Baños camp — and the struggle between the internee executive committee(s) and Japanese officialdom over the move to it — provides a dramatically detailed example of the vulnerability of internees to the prejudices and whims of higher authority. In this case, the struggle occurred throughout the spring and summer of 1943 in the form of internee protest letters, petitions, and reports condemning the projected (and then continuing) transfer of the population of Santo Tomás to Los Baños camp. In brief, the Japanese had decided to shift the main internment camp from downtown Santo Tomás in

Manila to a "new" camp farther southeast on Luzon at the site of the University of the Philippines Agricultural College at Los Baños. Though Los Baños was less than half the size of Santo Tomás, the plan was originally for all 5,000 new and current internees to be transferred as soon as practically possible. The given rationale for this transfer was that "2,000 more enemy nationals" had applied to enter Santo Tomás (probably those who had been allowed earlier to live outside, such as the missionaries or mothers with small or sick children). Santo Tomás would, with this addition, outgrow its boundaries. As the official announcement forwarded from the Japanese commandant explained, Los Baños was "an ideal health resort noted for its hot springs," and in addition to the college's handful of standing buildings and gymnasium, new quarters were being erected. Internees, the proclamation explained, would "enjoy fresh air and find an easy access to fresh meat and vegetables" (Hartendorp, I, 522).

The internee committee, suspicious, understandably, of flying to evils they knew not of, immediately appointed a special inspection committee (on May 9, 1943) to travel down to the new site at Los Baños, accompanying the transition commandant of the new camp, Col. Naruzawa. The inspection committee's duty was to ascertain if the site could be made habitable for transferring internees and whether it would provide at least the same degree of food and comfort that Santo Tomás did (Hartendorp, I, 523). At this stage, the Santo Tomás commandant agreed that an inspection team might prove useful before transfer but only in making the event proceed more smoothly when the time to move came.

The brief two and a half hour inspection (all that Naruzawa allowed) horrified the internee inspection committee. The thought of a total of 7,000 persons (5,000 plus the new 2,000) — or even the first transfer of 800 — using the existing facilities was absurd. According to Calhoun, Duggleby, and Muckle (the inspectors), the space was too small for 7,000 people; what buildings existed were in critical need of repair, even for the first group. Sanitary facilities were in urgent need of extension and redesign, because the camp had only a small septic tank, and even 800 people a day would require a tank with a 150,000 cubic foot capacity merely to remain adequate. More than 800 internees would also require at least 20,000 gallons of water a day, with a 10,000 gallon reserve pumped through a supply line at least four inches in diameter (Hartendorp, I, 525).

Indeed, the available water supply was so inadequate that earlier American plans to use the area for a military base had been scrapped. No kitchen facilities existed; food had to be brought in from the outside (given the projected number of internees, the camp would be too small for suitable vegetable gardens); the camp lacked cooking equipment, and even then the only source of fuel was green wood, which had to be dried before it would burn well. Despite these concerns, the hospital there, as noted in a sarcastic internee inspection report, "is eminently suitable as a headquarters *provided* it is supplemented with a 100-bed Men's Ward on one side and a 100-bed Women's Ward on the other side, and is stocked with surgical instruments, dressings, beds, and linens" (italics mine) (Hartendorp, I, 526, n1).

The inspectors also grimly noted that internees would need full hospital facilities, given two other factors of Los Baños camp life: the presence of "malignant" malarial mosquitoes in the area (the Japanese had ceased using mosquito control measures earlier), and the incoming internees' low resistance to disease (Hartendorp, I, 525, n1).

With all these deficiencies in mind, the committee could visualize what would happen should the inevitable occur, and the whole of Santo Tomás be moved to Los Baños; indeed, even the lodging of 800, in a camp filled with half-finished nipa and bamboo "barracks" constructed by forced Filipino labor, with a lack of water, an overflowing septic tank, malarial mosquitoes, and no hospital facilities, was courting disaster. This made the issue of the transfer a matter of life and death to the committee.

Convinced that their report and recommendation forwarded to Commandant Kuroda would stop the transfers immediately, the Inspection Committee was astounded when the commandant turned down the report after meeting with the Executive Committee and Carroll Grinnell (the new head of the committee). Kuroda remained adamant that the transfer would take place and that the first 800 internees would leave in a matter of days. The commandant did agree to allow a ten-man team to go down several days before the first group to "try to get things in shape" for the 790 other internees and to report if conditions appeared "impractical"; if this proved to be the case, Kuroda explained, then those remarks and protests could be forwarded at that time to a higher military authority, while the move proceeded. The commandant stressed that military authorities were "fixed in their determination that all internees [would] be evacuated from Manila." Further, Kuroda warned, if Los Baños proved too "unsatisfactory," then there was a "definite possibility that internees [might] be sent to Camp O'Donnell [a POW camp] in Capas, Tarlac, which [was] not considered a desirable camp site" (Hartendorp, I, 526). This was something of an understatement at the time, because O'Donnell and Cabanatuan both experienced staggering death rates (Utinsky, 42–49).[2]

The internee committee and the inspectors frantically tried another tack, putting forward a protest by DeWitt and Gray (two ranking members of the U.S. high commissioner's staff interned in camp). In this "official" protest (which cited a faded official legitimacy no longer recognized by the Japanese), the two told the commanding general of the Imperial Army in the area, by way of the camp commandant, of the problems the Inspection Committee found, reiterating these in stronger, less tactful language than in the first report. The water supply, first called "limited," now was "utterly inadequate"; the food supply was not just "insufficient" but insufficient "even by stripping the countryside"; finally, due to the chance of malaria and the poor health of the internees being transferred, "there [could] be not the slightest doubt but that the proposed transfer [would] cause widespread disease and scores, if not hundreds, of deaths" (Hartendorp, I, 527, n1). DeWitt and Gray's appeal fell on deaf ears. The Japanese set the first transfer for May 15. Even Dr. Leach, asked by Kuroda to serve with the transferees as camp doctor and to accompany the first 800 down, refused and wrote a protest letter to Grinnell. In it Leach announced that he would not go without receiving a direct order — one he immediately received from the Japanese, along with a threat, on the day before the transfer (Hartendorp, I, 530; 527–528, n3). He went.

At this point it is obvious that duly elected inspectors, carefully documented reports, and officially filed protests with the Executive Committee, with the camp commandant, or with "higher" Japanese military authorities (via the same commandant) carried no real power. Democratic self-government simply could not change or abolish Japanese orders; self-government only existed so long as the Japanese allowed it to do so; its only power derived unhappily from the favor of the commandant. Even to those involved this came as something of a cruel surprise, because they believed that the Japanese simply weren't acquainted with all the facts and would, logically, relent once they knew them.

The transfer continued, oblivious to internee facts, fears, or complaints. Indeed, the Japanese commandant announced the procedures for the first transfers in an initially soothing, yet ultimately menacing message via the Executive Committee: "It is to be emphasized that this change of location is entirely based on your own welfare, and that fairness to the treatment to be accorded the internees shall always be maintained. In this connection you are warned not to make careless utterance which will distort the true intention of the Military Administration" (Hartendorp, I, 522–523).

The first 800 transfers, according to the commandant, were to be "composed of able-bodied men to expedite the establishment and expansion of the new camp"; he also preferred men without families — and he expected the first group of 800 to be made up entirely of *volunteers!* If that number were not filled by volunteers, then the Executive Committee would be forced arbitrarily to choose men to make up the balance. Only 280 internees ultimately volunteered, with those who held back probably having heard something of the nature of camp conditions, details of which had leaked out from the inspectors' report (Hartendorp, I, 523). As Hartendorp explains, it was not that Santo Tomás was an ideal camp or even a very healthy one; it was simply that Los Baños was so dangerous, and Santo Tomás at least had some hard-won amenities and a familiar daily routine to follow. Additionally, some of the internees had Filipino or mixed blood families not interned to whom they could send messages or even see occasionally so long as they were in Manila. Los Baños was 69 kilometers away to the southeast and isolated by bad roads and weather (I, 523).

Despite the Japanese-controlled *Manila Tribune*'s statement that "the Imperial Japanese Army Authorities [have] always been kind and impartial, in accordance with international law" and that Los Baños was "tranquil . . . with splendid scenery, and where there [was] ample space available for farming," and even after 275 more bachelors volunteered, the final 525 "volunteers" had to be chosen by lot by the Executive Committee from a list of all unattached and young married men. One internee, Isla Corfield, compared the night of the drawing to similar nights she had seen in the Welsh coal fields, noting that "during the drawing . . . the women looked just like they did at mine disasters, waiting to hear if their men were safe or not. The lots continued to be drawn into the early morning" (Corfield, qtd by Lucas, 83).

The dreaded day came and the first 800 left, accompanied by eleven navy nurses who volunteered to go (Hill, interview) to take care of the health of the first group; the army nurses, according to a navy author, declined (Evans, 462).

As things turned out, despite enormous hardships upon arrival—including among other things, merely broken ground instead of the full complement of constructed barracks, inadequate hospital facilities, a total of four working toilets, and an outbreak of "*B. Coli*" (*E. coli*?) in all the water because of storm contamination—the internees grimly set about making the place if not habitable, then at least less toxic. None died—though this was largely due to the internees' own efforts. By June 26 (a little over a month later), the rest of the dormitories-barracks were well under way (though with lime and clay floors, not concrete, due to a lack of materials), internees were regularly boiling huge cauldrons of drinking water, an ingenious homemade toilet system was in operation, and the nurses had finagled some medical supplies from the Los Baños College Hospital. Luckily, the first 800 transferred internees were strong and relatively healthy; by the time of the next transfer, the situation had improved even more, enough for less hearty internees (older adults and children) to come with at least a chance of surviving camp illnesses.

Throughout the continuing transfers (the number "7,000" still hung above

Los Baños Internee Committee's heads like the sword of Damocles), both the Santo Tomás Executive Committee and the Los Baños equivalent wrote protest letters, filed complaints, and tried to get an answer from the Japanese Military Authority. The transfers continued unabated (Hartendorp, I, 533). Finally, after the Japanese had completed over 1,500 transfers, on August 5, the Santo Tomás commandant announced casually just before the evening propaganda movie that further transfers would be postponed "not only in consideration of the bad weather . . . but also because of delays in the completion of the camp" (Hartendorp, I, 557). Postponed indefinitely? Many didn't dare to hope. So far, following the August 5 announcement, the Executive Committee had set a theoretical camp limit at a maximum of 3,000 internees (a terribly high number, but to the internees far preferable to 7,000). Finally, by August 30, 1943, Commandant Kuroda announced that, after his two-week stay at Los Baños, Santo Tomás would not be replaced by Los Baños (Hartendorp, I, 558). The later camp population ultimately swelled to over 2,100, but it never grew larger than 2,500.

Of what significance is this final act of seeming grace by the Japanese? Does it mean that internee protests ultimately proved powerful enough to end the transfers? Did it mean that Kuroda relented, after seeing the state of things with his own eyes? What does this sudden end to the transfers provide proof of?

Halsema suggests that the shift in policy arose because of several factors, none related directly to the *fact* of the internees' complaints: the lack of materials and water available on site; Japan's knowledge of its own growing military defeats; and storm damage that made building materials hard to acquire (ltr, May 13, 1997).

I suspect that Halsema is correct. I would argue that what the policy shift does not prove is internee strength with or without petitions and protests to higher authority; rather, a commandant's personal decision seems the reason. Later, when the matter for internee protest was far more critical and involved the deliberate destruction of food in front of malnourished internees and repeated punitive cuts in the rice ration down to 600 calories a day (Hartendorp, II, 444; Hill, interview), protests and petitions were completely impotent to save lives. Nor do I think this seeming partial victory over Los Baños was indicative necessarily of the powers of logic and observation to change a visiting officer's decision. After all, Kuroda knew at the beginning of the transfers, by logic if by nothing else, that 7,000 people were not going to fit in a space half the size of the current camp. Despite this, he ordered continuing transfers, even claiming that the move to Los Baños would be an "improvement" in internee circumstances.

As usual, personal whim and perhaps some professional pressure (through

Major Tanaka at Los Baños, who added his name and words to the protest letters) turned the tide. Certainly, 500 to 600 more internees beyond the 1,500 ultimately were transferred to Los Baños; that most survived was a credit to the ingenuity, hours of cooperative work, and sheer fortitude on the part of those in camp—it was not due to Japanese clemency.

Clemency grew to be an even scarcer commodity in the internment camps than it had been previously by February 1944; the Japanese began to realize with increasing swiftness that they were losing the war. Though administrative control earlier had not been particularly lenient per se, life definitely became more rule bound and strict. February 1944 to February 1945 (when the camps were liberated) is a period painted in the grimmest colors in the personal diaries and especially in the secret in-camp histories such as Hartendorp's.

Earlier warning notes had already sounded that the Japanese responded poorly to even equivocal American victories in the Pacific theater of the war. Lucas points out that in late 1942, a mere rumor of the victory at Midway in June was enough to invoke punitive searches for anti-Japanese propaganda in the camps by the "V. V." ("Visiting Vermin," as internees called them), as well as increased slapping and harassment (Lucas, 52). Even in Baguio (Holmes) camp, the end of 1942 saw a rather severe punishment after apparent news of American gains trickled in. Natalie Crouter's December 4, 1942, diary entry seems completely out of keeping with her earlier descriptions of life at Baguio. It was, after all, a camp in which the commandant before the noble Tomibe, Nakamura, came to see camp spoof shows during which he clapped loudly and distributed looted canned goods (Crouter, 32). It is surprising then when Crouter tells us unflinchingly of the fate of Mr. "Menzies" (a pseudonym later used for people Crouter disliked), an internee bootlegger caught with an illegal still. First, he was taken by the Japanese to the guardhouse, then,

> An hour later, from our window, we watched him standing at the guardhouse, taking it. About eight guards standing around him, before our eyes, two beat him with bamboo sticks—legs, back, head anywhere it fell. He tried to shield an infected swollen thumb and a boil on his head. Finally they closed in, made him lie on the ground, beat him with army belts, a golf club, baseball bats, anything at hand until he was unconscious. His screams at the last were horrible to hear. He was taken to the camp hospital, and no bones were broken. (Crouter, 111)

Though Crouter goes on to say that he had been "warned" two days earlier (whether by the Internee Committee, camp police, or Japanese guards, is not clear) and that he was "suspected" of carrying notes to the guerrillas, this incident occurred significantly post-Midway, and it was singularly brutal for Japanese soldiers, not *kempei tai*.

Certainly, by late fall 1944, with the Battle of Leyte Gulf won in October, along with the so-called "Marianas Turkey Shoot" earlier, the seas around the Philippines fell under a tightening blockade, and Americans began landing on the southern islands. The handwriting was on the wall—and it was in English, not Japanese.

Administrative rules inside the internee camps became stricter and more punitive as 1944 drew to a close. Eva Nixon records that a number of changes took place at Santo Tomás in terms of information, medicine, and food. The Japanese military, for example, did not allow even the Japanese-controlled *Tribune* in the camp, because it seemed to provide (primarily through internee speculation and reading between the lines) too much war information. This added yet another dour note to camp life, for the *Tribune* had regularly lightened the long days as internees tried to decipher the true state of affairs based on propagandistic nonsense; such interpretations were not unlike reading code or putting together a jigsaw puzzles and provided a form of recreation for many of the internees.

One of the worst aspects of the newly stern authority involved the changes in medical care inside the camp. In early February 1944, Filipino doctors and nurses helping at the camp hospital were also barred, along with all other Filipino personnel, including vendors. This draconian regulation was a heavy blow to the hospital, because it was already severely understaffed owing to the growing degree of malnutrition even among medical personnel and the number of related cases of illness in the camp. The Japanese also prohibited internee doctors from going in and out of civilian hospitals in Manila—thereby effectively cutting them off from outside equipment and surgical facilities. Surgery had to be performed in camp, then, with whatever instruments, antiseptic, and anesthesia the camp could scrape together out of the last Red Cross supplies—medical supplies that had been raided earlier by the Japanese army. As if this weren't enough, despite the lack of beds, the reduced level of the staff, and the lack of space, the Japanese now insisted that all chronically ill elderly, all women, children, and anyone else out of camp on a special pass had to return to camp permanently. Now the camp facilities were flooded with chicken pox, whooping cough, measles, and diphtheria, as well as a large population of ill geriatric patients, further overstraining the hospital's space and resources. As Nixon points out, eventually the camp maintained four "hospitals" in camp—and these facilities were still not adequate by the time that the American rescuers arrived (60).

The new Japanese regulations in Santo Tomás camp also crucially affected the food and supply system as well. The package line closed, along with access to Filipino vendors. Further, the Japanese authorities forbade the internee buyers to leave camp in search of food to purchase; now the Japanese themselves bought and measured out the food allowance. This meant for most people that the rations from the camp were all they received, except for what they could grow in their gardens or had saved from their personal Red Cross kits. Once having money had made it possible for some of the internees to eat better food; now there was a democracy of hunger and growing malnutrition. Even with diamond rings available for sale or trading, there was no place immediately convenient to buy more food (Nixon, 60).

Camp rules and routines also seemed to become more punitive. Instead of just one roll call a day at Santo Tomás, there were now both morning and evening ones and sometimes one in the middle of the night as well. Strict bowing demands resulted in many mandatory "practices" for the internees until they were able to bow using the correct etiquette (Nixon, 60–61).

Finally, in one last bitter blow, the Japanese authorities demanded that all personal internee money had to be turned in by August, 1, 1944, so that the camp authorities could "invest" in the Japanese-approved Bank of Taiwan, where the money would be converted into the official occupation currency (the infamous Mickey Mouse money). The internees could, of course, withdraw money from "their" accounts but only at the rate of $25 (new currency) per month per adult, along with $12.50 per child (Nixon, 62–64).

Los Baños Internment Camp was not spared after the reasonably decent reigns of Major Tanaka and his successor, Major Urabe, ended in July of 1944. The third commandant, Major Iwanaka, appeared to the internees to be senile, and he left the daily running of the camp to his second-in-command, the hated Lt. Sadaaki Konishi, previously from Santo Tomás. Now there were two roll calls a day, sometimes more; also, as in Santo Tomás, private garden produce metamorphosed into part of the "official Japanese ration"; further, the medical facilities, as rough hewn as they were, were the only ones allowed. The hospital soon witnessed Dr. Nance perform, despite lacking a decent supply of anesthetic, an emergency appendectomy that nevertheless saved an internee's life (Arthur, 140–142).

As Lynn Bloom explains, Baguio (Holmes) Internment Camp provided a paradox. For the first two years, the Japanese strictly forbade the internees to plant a communal garden "because they [the Japanese officials] expected to move out before harvest" ("Popular," 802). By the third year (1944), however, the Japanese military administration ordered the internees to plant a communal garden—though this meant backbreaking labor plowing the jungleland (sometimes without an animal's help) for the internees (Bloom, "Popular," 802).

Nor were they spared from the guards' indignities, despite generally more lenient treatment overall. As Hartendorp explains, the guards were rotated frequently so that they never got to know the prisoners too well. This allowed for little understanding to develop. The new guards, charged with enforcing "rules" that were never put in writing (and which were impossible for most internees to discover), in their zeal made it a point to leap on any "infraction" they found (Hartendorp, I, 173). Slapping the face was a favorite punishment. For example, a guard slapped a female internee for smoking without an ashtray with her, even though it was easily within reach. The blow was "hard enough to knock a man off his feet." A fourteen-year-old boy, son of a missionary, was "slapped down" inside the barracks for no apparent reason, and another woman "had her arms slapped down when she stood with her arms akimbo as an officer passed" (173). Lacking any standard organization or administrative guideline, camp discipline took whatever form the camp commandant desired—or what his subordinates desired. Given the brutal manner in which the Imperial Army disciplined its troops (which involved officers slapping their soldiers' faces so hard their noses bled or kicking them with boots or wooden clogs repeatedly), it was not so odd that the officer in charge consistently allowed his underlings to discipline prisoners in this manner without interference (Gilmore, 203).

The American military tempo increased as 1945 began. A further increase in brutality and severity also occurred. Driven by hunger, for example, one internee at Los Baños sneaked outside the camp wire to get some fruit in the village; as he was attempting to struggle back under the wire to re-enter camp, the guards shot him fatally, four times in the chest, even though he was returning, not escaping. This was on January 17, soon after the landing at Lingayen Gulf (January 9). January 28 saw the wounding of another internee—George Lewis—as he, too, returned from a foraging trip outside the wire to the nearby banana groves and perhaps the village. Caught coming back in, he was shot in the arm by guards; they then left him for an hour and a half lying bleeding and moaning by the gate where he fell. Camp doctors Nance and Gray struggled to go to him but were prevented by Commandant Ishawara; in answer to the doctors' protests and their citing of the Geneva Convention, Ishawara hesitated, then had the guards drag Lewis to one side. At Ishawara's signal, guards then shot Lewis in the head, before the doctors could move (Arthur, 143; 145–146).

During the Yamashita trial in Manila, this seeming connection between

American victories and cruelty to prisoners emerged obliquely during questioning of a witness, Ishikawa, supposedly charged by Yamashita with checking on complaints of prisoner abuse and questioned by the Allied prosecutor:

> *Q*: Did you at any time either during your trips to Santo Tomás, Bilibid, Fort Mc-Kinley or at any other time hear any reports of cruelty and ill-treatment of prisoners of war and internees?
> *A*: No. (IMTFE, Reel 21, 27,635)

Though this seems innocuous and hardly relevant to the connection between American victories and cruel treatment, it is important to understand that Ishikawa denied any knowledge of "cruelty" to the internees even though he had visited the Santo Tomás camp during the same months that the rice ration was being cut repeatedly, and at least one doctor was thrown in jail for refusing to write "heart attack" rather than "starvation" on death certificates. Indeed, Ishikawa even claimed to have inspected the Santo Tomás food warehouse in December 1944—the same month the internees were eating canna lily bulbs, pigweed, and grass (Cates, 232). The Allied prosecutor then asked Ishikawa about the contents of the Santo Tomás warehouse at that time (December):

> *Q*: What did you find at the warehouse with regard to supplies?
> *A*: They had food stored there similar to our standards.
> *Q*: What kind of food?
> *A*: Mostly rice. (Yamashita trial record, qtd in IMTFE, Reel 21, 27,635; 27,641)

There is, of course, no mention of angrily reduced rations or food being withheld by the Japanese for minor infractions of the camp rules. Because the warehouse held stored rice, the implication would seem to be that internees apparently preferred to eat pigweed and poisonous lily bulbs.

By the end of January 1945, as the full-scale invasion of Luzon itself grew, Col. Hayashi, the last Santo Tomás commandant, demanded the ultimate penalty for the continuing so-called stubbornness and infractions on the part of members of the Executive Committee. Grinnell, Calkins, Duggleby, and Johnson were taken from Santo Tomás and never seen again. In April of that year, after the liberation of the camp, the U.S. Army found the four men, their hands bound behind their backs, a bullet in the back of each head (IMTFE, Reel 11, 14,897–14,898).

An overview of the nature of Japanese administration as it was influenced by Japanese character should perhaps be left, finally, to two Japanese writers. The first of these, Professor Inazo Nitobe, a classics professor and internationalist, a man of peace, and later, a representative to the League of Nations, wrote the definitive study of the code of Bushido (the "code of the

Samurai") in 1905. In his book he discusses how Bushido represents the "soul of Japan" and explains the principles as "an exposition of Japanese thought." This text, despite its turn-of-the-century publication date, remained a central text in Japan, cited enthusiastically by militarists as late as 1941 (see as an example, Yasunosuke Fukukita's *Japan's Innate Virility*). Professor Nitobe discusses especially the value the code of the Samurai places on self-control and benevolent mercy—these along with "rectitude and stern justice." While "benevolence indulged beyond measure sinks into weakness," he warns, and "rectitude carried to excess hardens into stiffness" (41), Nitobe continues to stress the concept of "*bushi no nasake*," the so-called "tenderness of the warrior." The concept, according to him, was one that appealed "at once to what was noble in us . . . because it implied mercy where mercy was not a blind impulse, but where it recognized due regard to justice." Nitobe goes on to say that "benevolence to the weak, the down-trodden or the vanquished, was ever extolled" as peculiarly becoming to a "samurai" and that "tender feelings breed a considerate regard for the suffering of others" (43; 49).

The Bushido principles as previously outlined seem ironic, given the Bataan Death March, the POW camps, and the increasingly grim administration of the civilian camps, and yet it was *specifically* this code by which Rukuro Tomibe, the humane commandant of Baguio, said he conducted his administrative decisions (Tomibe, 42). Majors Tanaka and Urabe of Los Baños both tried as well to be as humane as possible to the "vanquished" and the "weak," so the code was not without practitioners, though these men seemed fewer than those who ignored the code or (possibly) thought it applied only to other Japanese, not outsiders.

Perhaps it takes a Japanese soldier such as Tetsuro Ogawa to explain the actions of the army men who violated the code—men including Konishi, Ishawara, and Hayashi. In his memoir, *Terraced Hell*, which described the last year of war on Luzon from a Japanese soldier's perspective, Ogawa explains mournfully: "We [Japanese] were notorious for our cruelty in dealing with a surrendering enemy and with the people in our occupied area. . . . Although these cruelties were committed by wartime Japanese made fanatics by mass psychology and by the heady wine of success, I have no intention of trying to defend them here. Words fail to express our shame and regret" (21). Though shame, according to Kawasaki (another critic), may not function far from home during a campaign, it apparently does function if one is losing the war. Kawasaki and Ogawa, Fakukita and Nitobe: Both contradictory pairs of commentators seem to describe the paradox of the Japanese character accurately, though it was the "innate virility" of the soldiers and their cruelty that seemed to predominate as the war drew to a close in the Philippines.

As the tempo of loss increased, so too did the Japanese tendency in the camps to falsify administrative records or lose them. "Per diem," which the Japanese claimed they were paying the internees for their subsistence (or "banking" for them), was actually given not in currency but "in kind." This was a radical change that worsened an already bad system. From July 1, 1942, to February 1944, the standard per diem support money the Japanese officials provided was from 35 cents to 75 cents per adult (and half that per child). This money the internees then "turned over to the Executive Committee for purchases for the common good," such as foodstuffs, medical and surgical supplies, and mosquito netting (Pearson, 990).

Food records were falsified as the war dragged on but were not the only records either tampered with or inherently inaccurate. As mentioned earlier, it is even now almost impossible to find undisputed mortality and morbidity figures (Pearson, 988) for the internee camps because of the Japanese habit of listing starvation or deaths due to malnutrition under a number of other diagnoses. As previously noted, courageous doctors did fight to list correct causes — beriberi, amebic dysentery, starvation — but they were not generally successful, and records were often rewritten for them if they would not rewrite the records themselves.

Finally, almost all the official Japanese records for the entire war are scattered and incomplete. After the surrender in August 1945, six weeks elapsed before the American forces actually occupied Japan; during that interval "a huge bonfire was fed the secret files of the Metropolitan Police Headquarters" (Mitchell, 14), and Japanese military officers "destroyed evidence of war criminality by the warehouseful" (Brackman, 40). One rumor suggested that a secret document dated August 21, 1945, from the high command ordered all records to be destroyed and "not a single sheet [to] be left behind" (Brackman, 40). Whether this is true is immaterial in the larger scheme; certainly, huge stacks of documents, files, orders, and account books were missing at the end of the war. Some files still remained, however, despite the best efforts of the Imperial forces.

What records remained, along with eyewitness accounts from both Allied POW and civilian prisoners, helped provide a corrected base of information for various trials, especially when it came to weeding out falsified "official records," such as the one based on the notorious disinterment and use of dead bodies on Wake Island or the causes of death at Fukoka POW camp (Brackman, 41–42).

For all these reasons, the paper view explaining the "official Japanese administration" of each camp — in terms of illnesses, death, food ration weights, and punishment — must be taken with more than a grain of salt. What few

Japanese administrative regulations existed do not reflect accurately the way in which the camps were run, nor does their War Crimes defense testimony suggest truthfully the nature of internee or POW experience. A closer and more personal (even if anecdotal) knowledge of camp life — from internees, secret camp historians, and others — is necessary to put the sketchy administrative guidelines in some sort of perspective, especially because Hartendorp, for example, kept as many "official pronouncements" and Japanese written orders for the camp as he could (Hartendorp, I, preface).

What can be said, then, finally about the Japanese administration of the civilian internment camps? Any truthful or accurate analogy must shift to match different realities as the years of internment passed.

Selective Japanese propaganda photographs continued wrongly to suggest to the outside world that each civilian internee camp was some sort of "resort," as publications such as the Japanese-controlled *Manila Sunday Tribune* splashed across their pictorial section photographs from the first few months in the internment camps. In the July 12, 1942, issue, under a headline reading in boldface type, "PEACE, CONTENTMENT PREVAIL AT INTERNMENT CAMP," apparently well-fed women are shown washing clothes at a laundry trough, lining up to eat in the mess hall, or happily listening to music over the camp loudspeakers in the cool of the evening (2–3). Not only do these pictures not show the guards stationed everywhere, the mandatory roll calls, or the preponderance of slapping and kicking administered by the guards, but the pictures were deliberately posed by Japanese photographers and taken mostly in the first two months of internment (though used several months later) — long before hunger, and then starvation, had a chance to set in. As Lucas explains, even as late as fall of 1942, the Japanese continued to take and pose propaganda photographs: "The rice that came into the kitchen was full of rat droppings and alive with worms and weevils. Isla [Corfield] was amazed when she heard the de-weeviling process had been the subject of one of many propaganda photographs the Japs were always making of the camp" (Lucas, 60). (One caption in the *Sunday Tribune* under a picture of this kind of activity reads like a demented commercial for Rubbermaid: "SOME [LADIES] USE GLOVES TO CONSERVE THE HAND BEAUTIFUL.") The idea that women in internment camp were worried primarily about their "hand[s] beautiful" is distinctly anachronistic, given the situation. That people on the outside thought such falsehoods reflected reality is tragic.

With internee cameras forbidden, generally only camp drawings and cartoons dispute these broadly distributed propaganda photographs — those and the pictures taken at liberation by the Signal Corps, by *Collier's* ("Nightmare at Santo Tomás," 34), and by *Life* photographer Carl Mydans, a former internee and one of the few repatriated. Having promised, like MacArthur, to return, Mydans was one of the first people to enter the Santo Tomás camp, and he took pictures even as he greeted old friends. Mydans's pictures of fathers with stick arms and legs, pinched-faced mothers, scrawny children, and skeletal old men exposed the propaganda photographs and disparaged the whole "resort" idea once and for all ("Santo Tomás Is Delivered!"). By the end of internment, Santo Tomás and Los Baños camps were beginning to resemble a POW camp more and more; the unfortunate internees from Baguio were, in fact, in a literal prison camp—they were interned in the dank confines of Bilibid Prison across a barrier from POWs (James Halsema, "Bilibid Diary," January 1, 1945; January 11, 1945).

The severity of camp life during the last year and a half of internment remains generally unknown or confused to those with spotty memories of early magazine articles. Magazine accounts by Frances Long and other fortunate repatriated internees, such as the September 7, 1942, article in *Life*, "Yankee Girl," dealt with the experiences of those who spent only the first five or six months in camp. These tended to paint a much more pleasant picture than the camps deserved and suggested, if only by default and a lack of other information, that the camps remained the same throughout the war. Other factors caused confusion as well; sometimes other historical events blocked out information, or later revisionist historical accounts of the Tokyo War Crimes Trials resurfaced and clouded the issue. Finally, the confusing and murky nature of the prosecution objectives in the Tokyo Trials discouraged finding facts to rebut the Japanese defense arguments and also contained their share of confusion.

Frances Long's flippant account of camp life in "Yankee Girl" is a good example of how a mistaken vision of camp life could evolve. In her account, Long suggests that captivity was a kind of "adventure" from which she, the plucky heroine, emerged relatively unscathed (82). Unfortunately, her "Girl Scout cookout" vision of internment seemed to stick in the public mind if anything did.

As it was, even that natural showcase for the historical facts—the Tokyo War Crimes Trials held in Japan—went almost unnoticed by the public. The earlier dispersed Far Eastern Allied War Crimes Trials, which were taken over by each country involved and then staged in Darwin, Manila, Singapore, and other places, including Jakarta and Peiping, garnered little publicity, despite the horrific nature of the testimony. The Tokyo Trials seemed a "mop-up" operation of sorts. Additionally, there is some sense that the nature of the atrocities testimony heard at the Nuremberg Trials diverted attention from the more cerebral Tokyo Trials, as did the weirdly focused prosecution case.

Arnold Brackman, a correspondent for United Press International who covered the trials, has suggested that the trials were not organized in a way interesting to the media, nor was the stated aim of the Tokyo prosecution as clear as its counterpart in Germany. Perhaps, too, the conditions under which the International Tribunal for the Far East (IMTFE) was held, following the earlier, more sensational jurisdictional trials in outlying areas and the slow movement of the judiciary, also contributed to this lack of public interest.

The true nature of Japanese POW and civilian internee camp administration soon became lost and overwhelmed by the intention of the IMTFE prosecutors to apportion blame by proving "conspiracy," charging that the Japanese actions throughout the South Pacific, Hawaii, China, Burma, and the Philippines were the result of "a reign of barbarism conducted as state policy from 1931–1945" (Brackman, 23). Court observers and transcripts recorded many hours of testimony exploring the Japanese-introduced opium trade in "Manchuko" (Manchuria under Japanese rule) and the pre–World War China campaign, military factions inside the Imperial Army, and other exotic bits of information only indirectly related to the crimes on hand, as well as private diaries of government ministers, and early texts supporting the militarist cadre in the government in the late twenties and early thirties. Days passed as prosecutors sought to establish—or even discern—a clear chain of command by which to assign responsibility and distinguish between Class A, B, and C war criminals. The Tokyo Trials were set up to do just this and punish Class A "mastermind" criminals, leaving those allowing or committing atrocities (Class B and C) to prosecutors in the various Allied countries where the crimes occurred. As I have shown, such an attempt to recognize Japanese lines of authority and chains of command was destined to fail, making the prosecution resemble the famous statue of Laocoön more than a portrait of Sherlock Holmes. The attention to the treatment of prisoners, seemingly at the forefront of the Nuremberg Trials, was only interspersed with, and buried under, the prosecution's grand design to prove that Japanese state policy was the source of the savagery, not merely individual guards or commanders. The question of the nature of administration of the camps, when it did come up, often fell victim to snarls of interrogation deciding which bureaus and commands "had responsibility" for prisoner sustenance and welfare. This approach begged to be neglected. It wasn't simple; it wasn't clear; it wasn't always interesting; and ultimately, by late 1946, with the slowness of the judiciary movement and defense obstructionism dragging things out, it wasn't "news." Information from the Tokyo Trials slipped to the back pages and then out of view altogether (Brackman, 23–24). The result was that the issue was not kept before the public eye, and the complex truth about both administration of and subsequent conditions in the camps—especially those in the comparatively rarer internee camps—faded from public knowledge.

Somewhat later, old Japanese defense arguments from Tokyo, stripped of the prosecution trial rebuttal and therefore using exactly the same supposedly "unbiased" facts and figures (grams of food given daily, amount of space per person, kinds of punishments, average weight loss), reappeared magically. This time, however, the account was streamlined, unlumbered by rebuttal and lacking the full context of diaries and camp histories; even more important, it was an account by the victors. Works of historical and political revisionism suggested the truth of the Japanese defense and the perfidy of subsequent Allied sentences. Books by Richard Minear and Robert Storey, as well as articles in and out of the law journals, argued the constitutional nature or appropriateness of military justice at all. In these cases, the Japanese defense posture, seemingly without demur, gained acceptance, and the Military Tribunal found itself accused of its own crimes (see, for example, George Blewett, "Victors' Injustice: The Tokyo War Crimes Trials" in *American Perspectives*, summer 1950).

The result of this sort of confusion, despite a review by the Supreme Court that upheld the War Crimes Trials' constitutionality (Piccigallo, 58), has been a snarled ball of historical fact and fiction, supposition, claim and counterclaim hard to untangle in a context of academic and public indifference, ignorance, and often hostile misunderstanding.

Primary sources would, as they do in so many cases, settle many of the arguments over facts, especially about Japanese administration of the Philippines. Unfortunately, the documents (in Japanese in particular), when they exist, are scattered among Japan, the Philippines, and the United States and often have only recently been partially catalogued for bibliographies or even indexed (Hayase, 7). Trial transcripts in English from Manila and other local earlier trials prior to Tokyo (the latter luckily available on microfilm) are difficult to locate or, as with the transcript of *The United States of America v. Lt. General Masaharu Homma* (commanding general, Philippines, from December 1941 to August 1942) appear to be not only uncatalogued but still in loose sheets of typescript in unindexed boxes, as opposed to being recorded on microfilm.

Both Japanese and Filipino scholars have continued trying to recover lost documents of the Japanese occupation of, and administration in, the Philippines (Halsema ltr, to author, April 21, 1994). Many of these, however (some found and published in Volume 2, "The Japanese Polity," in Saito's *The State of Retrospective Research Materials in Southeast Asia: The Philippines*, 1973), seem to deal more with the administration of conquered and occupied territories than with internee or POW camps. Until more primary sources can be located and translated, however, the actual nature of Japanese administrative policies for civilian internee camps will remain clouded and confused, especially in terms of assessing responsibility for what happened. This is particularly important to know, in regard to vital subjects such as food and medicine, which soon became a matter not of niggling administrative differences, but, as the next chapter will show, one of life and death.

Kitchen in Santo Tomás Internment Camp, February 1945.
SC 263634. All Signal Corps photos courtesy of Martin Meadows.

Santo Tomas Internment Camp

Manila, Philippines

CERTIFICATE OF AWARD FOR MERIT

Presented by The Internees' Sanitation and Health Department

Be it known by these presents that Room No. 43 under Monitor H.E. PILE was duly adjudged the cleanest and most sanitary room in Santo Tomas Internment Camp for the week-ending JULY 3, 1943 and this Certificate is hereby issued to the occupants, whose names appear on the reverse of this certificate in recognition of their outstanding contribution to the health and well being of this Internment Camp.

In Witness Thereto, we have this Fourth day of July, 1943. set our hands and Seals.

Chief of Examining Board

Department Head
Sanitation & Health Department

Chairman of the Executive Committee

Clean Room Award, 1943. Courtesy of Martin Meadows.

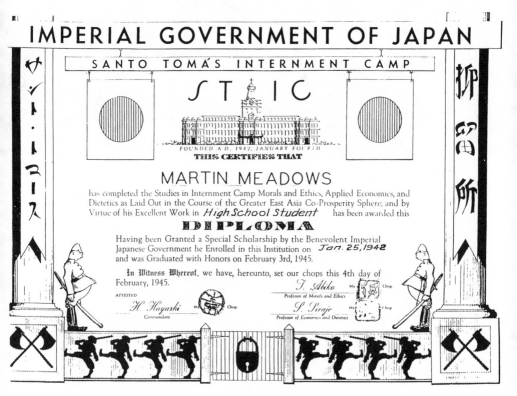

Internment diploma, 1945. Courtesy of Martin Meadows.

March 1945: One of the two patios upon which the "aristocracy" of the Santo Tomás camp built their private, personally financed shanties. They did not live in them until late in the occupation and then only to avoid overcrowding of the other buildings. Generally, shanties were simply places where families could have a meal in private, talk together, and rest. Signal Corps (SC) 202141

February 1945: American internees of Santo Tomás Internment Camp
raise the U.S. flag for the first time since the fall of the Philippines.
SC 202599

Internees released from Santo Tomás in front of the main building, February 1945.
SC 220298

Soldiers fire a 105-mm howitzer from the grounds of the Santo Tomás University in
Manila, February 1945. SC 203004

A photograph of internee Sam Schier taken by a friend with Schier's camera just as the evacuation by the U.S. Army and Filipino guerrillas began, February 23, 1945. Copy of this photo given to Wally and Pam Gillette and used with their permission.

Los Baños internees immediately following their rescue as they wait on Mamatid beach on the American-held side of Laguna de Bay. Photograph taken by internee Sam Schier and given to Wally and Pam Gillette; used with permission of the Gillettes.

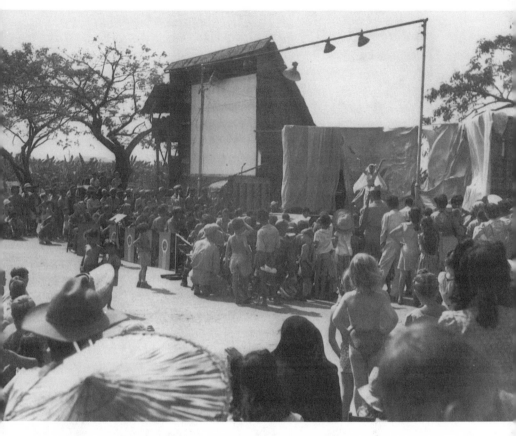

An audience of internees and GIs watch a dance act during the first show to be held after renewal of shows at Santo Tomás University, March 1945. SC 203050

Nash family arriving home to Sacramento, California, May 1945. In back: Grace, Roy, and Ralph Nash and Ralph's brother Clarence Nash. In front: Stan and Gale Nash. Courtesy of Grace Nash.

Martin Meadows in 1948, three years after his release from internment. Courtesy of Martin Meadows.

5

The Japanese Soldier's Ration

Food and Health in Civilian
Internment Camps

More than the crowded rooms, the whimsical restrictions on movement, or even the ultimate loss of home and money, food and its availability became for most internees the defining concern of their captivity. It is a rare account that does not list the grim details of calories, portions, and supplies on which the prisoners lived and, eventually, on which some died. Food became part of an equation for life or death. Unlike the POWs, civilian internees generally as a rule were neither worked as slave laborers nor shot or tortured. For most, malnutrition and related illnesses such as beriberi, dysentery, and hypoproteinosis were the acute threats to life. Indeed, the apparently deliberate use of food as an instrument of punishment, repression, and, ultimately, retribution made it one of the crimes against American civilian internees covered in depth in the Tokyo War Crimes Trials.

Such an important subject demands to be judged in a complete context. Obviously, the interrelationship of food to health in the camps cannot be overlooked. The rise in what the camp people called "wet beriberi" (hypoproteinosis) and various kinds of dysentery in late 1944, for example, followed directly on the heels of reduced rations, the previously mentioned package line closure in Santo Tomás, and the ban on native vendors in the other camps. Conversely, earlier, after the American Red Cross parcels of Christmas 1943, the vitamins, cans of Spam, milk, butter, cheese, and chocolate allowed internees to recover their health briefly. The rate of deficiency diseases and new cases of dysentery slowed, and thousands, though their lives were soon threatened again, managed to last until rescued in February 1945.

Additionally, the obvious chronological nature of the rise and fall of nutrition and the increase ultimately in mortality figures from the beginning to the end of captivity insist that any discussion must be organized by periods. The first, from January 1942 to April 1943, not only covers the so-called "good period" and the change in financial custodianship and responsibility for the camp but also saw the establishment of a new camp, Los Baños. The second period, from April 1943 to February 1945, is the last eighteen months of internment and the worst period of starvation; it is also during this time that Baguio (Holmes) closed and its internees were transferred to Bilibid Prison. This period also saw internees from Iloilo camp on Panay, Bacolod on Negros, and Davao camp on Mindanao transferred to Santo Tomás or Los Baños camps on Luzon (Waterford, 260). This chapter will deal with the first period.

As in the other chapters, clarity about the health situation and the food supply also demands that these subjects be tracked in a variety of camps. Food supplies and the availability and quality of health care varied widely among camps, as did the differences, mentioned in the last chapter, among commandants' dispositions as well as the physical environment. I will again be examining primarily the cases of Santo Tomás, Baguio (more precisely referred to as "Hay" or "Holmes" after the two consecutive army posts used), Bilibid Prison, Bacolod, and finally, Los Baños, because even internees from Davao and Cebu ended up in one of these camps. Throughout I provide an illustrative glimpse now and then of Cebu and Davao camps, especially in comparison with, and contrast to, the other four; unfortunately, the lack of substantial narrative or extensive information about other civilian camps on Panay (Iloilo) and Leyte (Tacoblan), composed of approximately fifty and twenty-three people, respectively (Waterford, 260), forbids any proper discussion of conditions in these camps, though, again, these internees eventually ended up in one of the main camps on Luzon.

One of the most important points to understand at the outset, because it influences all other considerations regarding both food and health as well as the "necessity" of aid, is the concept of the so-called "Japanese soldier's ration" and its true nature. This is the ration that both civilian and military Japanese authorities claimed civilian prisoners were receiving. In the last year of the war in the Philippines, for example, when internees were heavy with "hunger edema" and listlessly existing on 800 to 1,000 calories a day, Japanese camp commandants repeated to those Internee Committee members strong enough to demand more and better the same answer — that "the Japanese soldiers were not eating too well themselves" (Tomibe, 40). The internees were receiving, they were informed, the *same* ration as the Imperial Army soldiers (Pearson, 1000; IMTFE, Reel 11, 14,771–14,772; Reel 21, Ishikawa testimony, 27,631), though as has been pointed out earlier, simple internee observation of the guards and their meals refuted this claim.

The reason for this theoretical food measurement was a single reference in the 1929 Geneva Convention that specifically mentioned civilians caught in times of war. They were, the convention insisted, to be "treated as military prisoners of war, leaving the application of the convention to general noncombatant internees as a matter of national opinion" (Geneva Convention, qtd in Waterford, 48, n6).

The convention's insistence on equal rations for prisoners of war compared to those issued to the captor's troops was well known. Article 11 stated, among other provisions, that "The food rations of prisoners of war shall be equal in quantity and quality to that of the troops of the base camp." It also stated that "all collective disciplinary measures affecting the food are prohibited" (Geneva Convention, Art. 11, qtd in Waterford, Appendix A, 346). Though the Japanese authorities explained that they had not ratified the Geneva Convention, they also insisted that they practiced voluntary compliance with the ration provision, even officially noting that they treated internees (by way of assigned rank and ration) as noncommissioned officers (Waterford, 45).

Given its centrality as a vital unit of food measurement, it might be useful to discover the specific nature of the "Japanese soldier's ration" and then compare it to rations issued at various times to the prisoners. It is also important to understand how the link between rations and base camp occurred. The "base camp" policy was initially intended to ensure fairness: If any area in which the Japanese army was based lacked sufficient produce, then it was unlikely that internees would have — nor could they demand — more produce than the soldiers themselves got. This rationale depended on an accurate assessment of resources, obviously—something about which there is dispute, especially in the case of the "shortages" around both Manila and Los Baños from 1944 to 1945.

Although it might be instructive to trace the army ration size for the entire period, the greatest significance emerges, in contrast to prisoners' rations, between 1944 and 1945, though all years show a distinct disparity. In the beginning of February 1944, the official Imperial Army daily ration stood at 400 grams of rice, 100 grams of fish, 20 grams of sugar, and 10 grams of oil (coconut) (Pearson, 990). There is some evidence, however, that even Japanese soldiers were not actually receiving this much, although Tetsuro Ogawa does mention the plentiful rice to be obtained from the Cagayan Valley for the troops, as well as the meals of boiled rice and roast pork that he ate in camp as late as February 1945 (Ogawa, 33; 40–42). Obviously, Ogawa was not eating standard rations, but, as he explains, he and his fellows supplemented the rations with local food bought or simply taken by the army. As Ogawa again points out, though rice rations were "limited to 400 grams per day," soldiers regularly snatched chickens, eggs, coconut oil, pigs, papayas, carabaos, or anything else they fancied, only sometimes leaving worthless military scrip behind (Ogawa, 66; 56; 40–68).

The internees, on the other hand, were confined to camp and even forbidden at this date to supplement their diets with *any* food from outside the camp, even (as in the case of Los Baños) when it fell from banana trees just outside the barbed wire fence (Nash, interview). Just as they could not obtain more calories on their own, neither could they get their hands on any variety of foods. In the last fifteen months especially, a combination of *lugao* (watery rice gruel), camote top, and talnium green "stew" (sometimes with shreds of carabao or floating fish heads with the eyes intact in it) formed the standard basic diet of the chow line (Hartendorp, II, 443–444, n1; Chapman, 194).

The health problems associated with inadequate vitamins and minerals (as well as the lack of proper amino acids and protein in general) become clearer when we review the findings of medical personnel in the various camps that were turned over to researchers after the war. The poor health of internees at the time of rescue is attributed to these deficiencies.

In addition to simple starvation, then, the other problems that doctors identified in the camps as due to probable protein and vitamin deficiencies include "hunger edema" or "wet beriberi" (hypoproteinosis), night blindness (Vitamin A deficiency), burning feet and hands, as well as swollen arms, legs, and faces, "true beriberi" (thiamin deficiency), and several kinds of dysentery (from semistarvation, spoiled food, or garbage). However, Dr. Haughwout, the dysentery expert in Baguio, considered many of the so-called "amoebic" cases to have been misdiagnosed food poisoning (HEW Report, 35; Butler et al., 643; 651; Haughwout, 134). In conclusion, although the basic chow-line diets in all camps were generally inadequate from the beginning of internment, the acute avitaminosis, hypoproteinosis, and real starvation occurred from January 1944 to February 1945, especially after all sources of supplemental food were cut off (Butler et al., 643).

The real story of food and illness starts much earlier than the horrific last year of internment. To understand the problem—illness due to inadequate nutrition and deficiency—and, paradoxically, the reasons for ultimate survival, one must look at the crucial first year, in particular, of captivity, when, for six months, the internees supplied all of their own food and medical needs with almost no assistance from the Japanese civilian authorities. Because of this the groundwork was laid for the last eighteen months when the internees became increasingly malnourished and severely ill. During those earlier months, the internees, left to their own resources in all of the camps, forced to finance, find, beg, or sign IOUs for food to feed themselves and for medical supplies to tend the sick, started out their internment behind a health and nutritional eight ball and never really caught up during the rest of internment. Despite this, only 7.9 percent of the civilian internees died during internment—a low figure largely due to their own efforts (HEW Report, 2). Most of those who succumbed did so only during the harshest period, the last four months (2). That *any* died from disease or malnutrition, of course, is inexcusable. That a large number survived is something of a miracle. Pearson notes that the morbidity and mortality figures for the official thirty-seven months of internment are, "on the one hand, a high tribute to the internees themselves, and the medical care that they received [from their own people], and, on the other hand, an indictment of their Japanese captors" (988). Perhaps in no other civilian camp in the Philippines is this picture of initial self-reliance in supplying food and medicine better documented during this first year than in Santo Tomás Internment Camp (STIC). Hartendorp's precise and detailed secret notes of the internment provide the ideal template for understanding the experience. As explained earlier in Chapter Two, the first weeks of actual internment (as distinct from house arrest in Manila) in Santo Tomás were hectic, dusty, and improvisational, with only some internees arriving with food, bedding, or mosquito nets. Others had nothing. Very soon the camp became a tiny economic model of the "haves" and the "have-nots," a fact that some internees (especially Margaret Sams) note bitterly (Sams, 70, n16). As the Hills, the Magnusons, and other internees described, in emotional shock from the swift and terrible events, family groups and friends hunched together on the STIC grounds and made skimpy meals with what food they had brought with them. Ultimately, Earl Carroll and other early members of the first Executive Committee insisted that all food be pooled, as well as money, so that a central food fund could be established and a free chow line set up to feed all in camp, with or without money. Internees realized after a time that "there was no assurance of being provided for by the Japanese." They then set about finding more funds and making bulk purchases to feed the camp (Whitesides, 14). By January 25 the internees had put together a "central purchasing committee" whose main function was to acquire supplies for the camp through outside shopping for bulk foods and staples (by internees let out on passes), as well as for vital nonedible supplies (pipe, wood, electrical wire, and so forth).

Put together out of this fund and a food cache from individuals or from former Philippine Red Cross benevolence, the first kitchen opened for women and children on January 10; by late January and early February, Santo Tomás's central kitchen opened, following in the path of an earlier "restaurant" that had served coffee. At this time the central kitchen food distribution (the "Line") regularly fed between 2,500 and 3,000 people both breakfast and dinner without charge. (The kitchen for women and children in the annex fed almost 600 women and children three "light" meals a day.)

The menus were hardly appetizing, and the limited amount of food and lack of variety made constant low-level nutritional inadequacy predictable for many who had no supplementary funds during those first six months. Breakfast, for example, offered cracked wheat porridge, a small roll, and coffee with sugar (but no milk); dinner consisted of a stew (with small pieces of meat), a banana, a roll, and sometimes noodles or beans as well as chicken on occasion (Hartendorp, I, 17–19).

Four actual lines made up the figurative Line. These wound through the rear hallway of the main building and past several serving counters; people then trooped outside with their trays to eat at long, uncovered tables on the grounds (later given roofs) or in the case of rain, wherever they could find shelter. Inside the main building was off-limits for sanitary reasons, as were the sleeping areas, so internees huddled outside under overhanging eaves or ate beneath trees (Hartendorp, I, 19–20).

Though the basic diet served on the Line was meager, those with friends on the outside, either faithful Filipino servants or acquaintances willing to bring food or to hock the internees' jewelry for food or cash, were able to supplement their basic rations with extra food. This was the "Gate" (soon to become the famous Package Line), and from the first days of internment, friends and servants of those inside arrived with vital supplies and then crowded around the front gate and iron fence of Santo Tomás. Here in a dense shouting, shifting, surging crowd, friends or servants brandished the names of lucky internees on placards held high, while Filipino vendors sold food and sundries, and others outside reached through the ornamental iron pickets with bundles, notes, and messages for those inside the camp (Hartendorp, I, 19–20). This particular madhouse free-for-all atmosphere and camaraderie at the Gate distressed the Japanese administration, who saw it not only as unruly but possibly dangerous. Eventually, the administration screened off the fence with sawali (possibly at the internees' request, rather than lose the contact with the outside altogether), and allowed only notes, packages, or parcels of food to be delivered at the gate through a series of Japanese checkpoints, where they were searched for weapons, liquor, or current accurate war news (Whitesides, 15).

Between private supplementation and the camp food, the internees at Santo Tomás ate their own supplies for six months, receiving not one centavo from their captors for support. The Japanese authorities explained that the internees were not "prisoners" but rather were "in protective custody" (from whom was unclear). The Japanese therefore denied any responsibility for feeding them (Hartendorp, I, 12).

Part of this, Hartendorp suggests, may have been because of a disinclination on the part of the Japanese to commit themselves to any particular course of action regarding the internees. These civilians lacked a formal, international, or legal characterization and were not covered by either official expectations or procedures. These were not Americans or Allied civilian personnel inadvertently trapped inside Japan at the outbreak of war (i.e., aliens in a belligerent's country) nor people transported *into* Japan (aliens sent into a belligerent's country). This was unprecedented—they were civilians caught in a formerly friendly country or commonwealth thereafter *occupied* by a belligerent. Neither the one international convention the Japanese actually signed (the Hague Convention of 1904) nor the Tokyo Convention of the International Red Cross (1934), which they didn't sign but agreed informally to abide by, covered this situation; the lack of specificity therefore presented legal loopholes for those so inclined. The Hague only covered POWs, not civilian internees, and Tokyo didn't cover civilians caught in *occupied* countries. Despite this snarl, Claude Buss, the former executive assistant to the U.S. high commissioner to the Philippines, Francis B. Sayre, and at this point the sole representative of U.S. authority in the area (Buss, 227), said he had been "personally" reassured by two high-ranking Japanese officers who visited incognito on January 5 that the Japanese government would absolutely and punctiliously abide by international law in regard to civilians (Hartendorp, I, 97). Did Prince Tsuyenoshi Takeda (one of the two probable "incognito" visitors) mean *all* civilians or only those who fit legal definitions? Later treatment suggests the Japanese themselves weren't completely sure or willing to decide, given their curious off again/on again application of international rules over the next three years (Hartendorp, I, 97).

Once obtained, food in Santo Tomás camp was not only bland and portions slim through most of 1942, but internees themselves inadvertently may have destroyed many vitamins and nutrients during the preparation process. The primary requirement for assignment to the kitchen shift early on was not culinary experience or a degree in nutrition but physical strength. Camp food was cooked in huge iron cauldrons, and it took strong biceps and triceps to move, fill, and clean these. Nutritionally ignorant but muscular kitchen staff boiled the vegetables until they were mushy, threw out the leftover vegetable water, mixed vegetables that didn't belong together, and refused to use spices (even salt). Worse yet, beans and rice (camp staples) were only half cooked. Beyond these inadvertent outrages, the kitchen workers often assigned themselves extra servings of food because of the "hard physical labor" involved in being a cook! Not surprisingly, other internees objected strenuously to this thinking (Hartendorp, I, 243). Only after several months, however, did the Executive Committee put a professional dietitian in charge of the kitchen, and only then were the meals to some degree nutritious.

The bland diet, however, was supplemented eventually with produce grown in the camp by internees. In early February internees cleared an old site that had formerly been a dump on the northeast corner of the campus. They planted large beds of talnium, pechay, beans, camotes, Swiss chard, tomatoes, and kangkong. By March the internees had brought under cultivation over a hectare of ground; by April 2 the first harvest produced ten large baskets of talnium greens, which were then sent to the hospital (Hartendorp, I, 33–34).

Other camps, obviously, suffered because of the same problems of definition that Santo Tomás did, though the internees at Bacolod on Negros had less to work with by far in terms of physical buildings and supplies, while Baguio, and, to an extent, Davao had a more accommodating climate and commandant.

According to internee Alice Bryant, the Bacolod Internment Camp was uneasily situated in several buildings constituting an old private school compound outside the town of Bacolod, just in front of a large mangrove swamp (124–125). Initially, the first group of internees delivered there had been forced to clean, build, and repair the building and grounds, in disarray following the earlier confinement of both Germans and local Japanese civilians immediately following the Pearl Harbor bombing. By the time Bryant arrived about three months after the first group, a chow line was shakily in operation, though as in Santo Tomás camp, meals were "both insufficient and unbalanced, consisting mainly of rice" (128). With a camp size never more than 150 people at most, Bacolod camp was able to offer three of the usual rice-heavy "light" meals a day (although "dinner" was often only a piece of fruit). As Bryant summarizes and explains,

> The people of Bacolod were making the best of a bad situation. . . . The Japanese had never done anything for the camp except to guard it to see that we did not escape or communicate with outsiders. Some of the internees from western Negros had brought cases of food with them, and the manager of a lumber mill had entrusted quite a sum of money to a Swiss to expend for the general benefit. As soon as we [her husband, "The Guv'nor," and herself] arrived, [we] had to turn over to the camp one hundred pesos from the small amounts we had left. The Millers turned over a like amount, and we all had to sign an agreement to pay our share of camp expenses after the war. (127–128)

Another Bacolod internee, Elizabeth Vaughan, does mention, in addition to pooling resources, that a variety of package lines existed for those supplementing their meals, in which fresh produce and sometimes meat were sent in, "bought for us by our servants outside" (98). Here, if anywhere, internees with money or servants received necessary additional doses of vitamins and calories while those like the Bryants, who had no money available, simply went without.

The first Fourth of July celebration in Bacolod Internment Camp (an ironic Independence Day indeed) featured, through outside sources tapped by the camp committee, a full day of holiday fare, including scrambled eggs and red rice oatmeal for breakfast and, for dinner, boiled ham slices in biscuits (two per person) as well as potato salad, rice, iced tea (the ice from a captured Central plant), a salad with bits of chicken and sausage in it, spiced cake, and candy (Vaughan, July 4, 103–104). The Japanese authorities allowed this nationalistic extravaganza as long as the celebration could be done, the internees were told, "without violating the rules of camp"; it was perhaps evident later *why* the authorities had been so lenient. As the internees hungrily gulped down "real food" instead of the usual lugao, their captors took more propaganda photos—this time of the happy inmates eating a special holiday meal provided (the viewer was led to assume) by the Japanese (Vaughan, 104).

Cebu and Davao camps, respectively, on the nearby islands of Cebu and Mindanao, provide a brief, but interesting comparison to the hard conditions at Bacolod on Negros. According to Imogene Carlson at Cebu Internment

Camp, since in a rear-guard action the retreating U.S. Army had blown up the waterworks and the electrical plant, food had to be cooked in the "main" junior college camp using an old iron gate as a grill over an open fire. Internees such as Ray and Imogene Carlson were responsible for hand fanning the fire in the evening for meals. The internees collected rainwater when they could, fixed a pump in camp, and until the water system was restored, brought barrels of water to camp in a human-drawn pony cart (Carlson, 86–87; 90–91). Boiling and grilling seem to have been the main cooking styles, with wood or charcoal the only fuel. Despite these limitations, the ever-resourceful Ray Carlson managed to make pans of gingerbread as a special treat with nothing more than a piece of metal for a cooking surface and the serviceable gate. As his wife, Imogene, explains about Ray's amazing energy and inventive proclivities, "He was young and had much energy, even on our simple diet" (90). The "simple" diet apparently included flour, ginger, some form of shortening, brown sugar, and eggs, because they appeared in Ray's "gingerbread."

Not surprisingly, given the experiences in the other camps, on Cebu, even when under house arrest and later when interned on the junior college campus, the prisoners provided their own food. Initially, they lived on what friends brought them or on what was available in the houses in which they were confined. The internees later took a stockpile of six hundred cases of canned goods collected earlier by the Americans on the island before internment. The one hundred Americans and the twenty-three British internees eventually to be separated from them watched their captors raid the stockpile on a regular basis (Hartendorp, I, 316). Ultimately, out of the six hundred cases of canned goods, the internees were left with only 120 cases. As Hartendorp explains, "The Japanese kept what they liked, including most of the milk and fruit, and doled out [irregularly] what they didn't like, such as spaghetti in tomato-sauce, and sauerkraut" (I, 317).

One anecdote vividly illustrates the growing hunger in Cebu camp even in December 1942. On December 8, the Japanese sent twenty-eight small frosted cakes to celebrate and commemorate the Imperial victory at Pearl Harbor. The guards told everyone to be downstairs, to bow to a visiting general, and then to enjoy and eat the cakes. Given the occasion, which was being commemorated with cakes and frolic, it is no wonder most internees were angry and many refused to go downstairs. For some the cakes became a character test, one that Carlson in her own eyes failed, as she explained: "Many [internees] said that they would not conform. When the cakes arrived, there were no Japanese present. We waited and they didn't come. A few strong-charactered people remained upstairs, away from the sight, Ray among them. We waited some time and the Japanese still did not appear. Some of us weakened when we saw the cakes, and ate them" (98). Though the hunger was not at this point what it would become in all the camps by mid-1944, still there were enough hollow stomachs so that the cakes did disappear.

The civilians interned at Davao were moved several times, as they were at Cebu. The nature and quality of food changed with the internment facilities. During the period of December 20 to January 3, while the internees were living almost exclusively in the club library (though allowed to exercise by jogging or walking around the main room of the club for twenty minutes), the food was "almost entirely . . . rice and rolled oats," and not much of that, though the captors seemed to be providing *some* food. Sometimes, the Japanese allowed the prisoners "a meager portion of canned fish" in addition to the cereals (Brown, 74–75).

The prisoners, having swelled in number, moved again and then again, eventually landing in Davao Central School compound, from April 1942 to December 1943. During the intermediate time from February to April, the internees settled briefly at Rotaeche House. At this point there were approximately twenty-six internees. Food was unspectacular and limited. The Japanese now provided cornmeal instead of rice, but they did also allow the internees to use pooled camp money to purchase fresh vegetables, fruit, and some meat once a week from Filipino vendors. The internees did their own cooking, even though at Rotaeche House (the upper floor) they had no stove and, similar to Ray Carlson north of them on Cebu, "had to improvise one from pieces of galvanized iron we found lying around" (Brown, 75).

By the time the internees moved to internment quarters in Central School (April 1942), the Japanese changed food policy once more, bringing it more in line with that practiced at other camps. The authorities now insisted that the internees "be completely self-supporting" and pay for any supplies the Japanese gave them. As if this weren't harsh enough, the Japanese ordered the internees to pay *retroactively* for the cornmeal, rice, and fish the authorities had supplied since the beginning (76). No more were the internees to buy vegetables or fresh produce. Instead, internees were given, as Alex Brown notes, "a piece of land in the Central School grounds, where we were permitted to work a few hours a day, raising vegetables for our own use. . . . The gardening tools given to us were few and very decrepit, but Christensen [another Carlson-like internee inventor] showed great ingenuity in manufacturing tools out of odd pieces of wood and galvanized iron" (76).

Internees were apparently allowed to receive packages from friends, servants, or relatives outside the camp. Friends, for example, brought the Wills family laying hens (Wills, 20). A description of Jane Wills's morning routine, from mid-1942 to December, suggests skimpy but decent meals of a sort — at least for those internees with additional supplies: "In the morning the camp would have coconut milk on the lugao rice and the residue from the coconut we would feed to the chickens. With that we had a little supplement of eggs to our diet" (Wills, 20).

Whether the camp at large shared in this useful protein meal supplement is not clear, though another internee, Frank Cary, wrote in a letter of April 14, 1942, that they did, though the Willses are not named as the source. Cary mentions, for example, canned fish, vegetable stew, corn mush, and "something to set it off," such as fruit, bread, or (specifically) eggs (9).

Baguio camp (in both Hay and Holmes incarnations) back on Luzon was almost double the size of Davao camp, with a population of around 550 people at the largest. As at Santo Tomás, Davao, Cebu, and Bacolod camps, the Baguio internees themselves provided their own supplies. Initially, internees pooled money and food, as well as set aside ₱ 1,500 out of the pooled money for a secret hospital emergency fund. January 1942 saw the expenditure of ₱ 120 to ₱ 150 per day (approximately ₱ 2 a week per person). Until mid-February, five male internees were allowed to take this allotted money and go to the town of Baguio every day to purchase food and necessities. The men on the shopping detail brought back their purchases and then dumped their loads of food, especially vegetables such as cabbage, camotes, string beans, onions, and pechay, along with rice, on the ground floor of the men's barracks, the so-called "rice room," to await further processing, storage, and preparation (Ogle, 193–194).

By mid-March, the Japanese confiscated all money (but the hospital fund) and took over all the buying, as well as cut the daily internee food expenditure from the earlier ₱ 120 to ₱ 85, explaining that the internees were eating "too much" (Hartendorp, I, 171). As one internee, Natalie Crouter, notes in her diary on May 6, 1942, "Nakamura still says we waste too much; we don't eat the vegetable tops and many things that the Chinese and Japanese use" (45).

Though there was no actual Package Line at Baguio, friends or servants outside could, as at Bacolod and Davao, send in parcels of food, though no outside servant contacts were allowed (Hartendorp, I, 169). Such parcels were brought into the camp by truck after first being inspected in town and then again in camp. A second source of supplemental food came from the camp "store," a small concern that purchased items from the Baguio market and then resold them to those internees with money. Items ranged from eggs, tobacco, and muscovado sugar to bananas, papayas, limes, and the like (Halsema, "E. J.," 300). These products were subject to a stiff Japanese tax, which added to the price of the produce. As Crouter explains caustically in an

April 30, 1942, entry, "The Japanese wouldn't let us buy out here [in town]. It [food] must come from the market where they can tax, put the squeeze on the stalls as well as on us, catching it both ways. They say we must live on our 21¢ a day per person, not a 39¢ average [the earlier figure]. That is what a soldier is allowed per day. They won't listen to argument even though it is our own money from the bank" (43).

Yet another source of supplementary food came from the "extras" some of the camp women made privately out of hoarded materials on a pair of "wood-fired iron stoves and charcoal braziers" in camp. Women such as Jim Halsema's mother Marie, his sister Betty Foley, and some of their friends supplemented their families' meals by concocting and serving such delicacies as imitation bread and faux-cake made from cornmeal (Halsema, "1944 Diary," June 10; Halsema, "E. J.," 300).

Internees at one time could also, apparently, arrange purchases in town secretly on occasion, as Crouter's husband did on the couple's fifteenth wedding anniversary in February 1942, when he presented her with a box of candy that "he had secured with great difficulty from town"; this munificent gift Jerry supplemented with "sugar he had boiled down from dark and dirty cakes [of raw sugar]" (he was on the garbage detail) as well as (later) marrow he had dug out of bones "at great pains" (February 3, 10; 18; 19). Despite the more communal than capitalist ethos of the camp, Jerry also told Natalie in an understandably noncommunal moment that he would "knock [her] block off" if she shared these gifts or the "two infinitesimal tomatoes" he also gave her with the rest of the camp (18).

As an index of growing internee hunger even as early as April through June 1942, Crouter admits (April 17) that "All we think about is Freedom and Food" (38). By June 16, she records an extraordinary event after only six months of captivity: "Mrs. Estrich had handcuffs clipped on because she took a knife engaged in slicing bread and went after one who was eating a fried egg sandwich in front of people who have nothing" (59).

Baguio did, however, have something the other two camps did not—a professional chef, Alex Kaluzhny, formerly head chef at the Baguio Pines Hotel before the war (Ogle, 192). He and his kitchen crew "learned to use native ingredients for exotic-sounding but minuscule meals based on rice, vegetables, sugar, coconuts and bananas, flavored with a little meat or fish" (Halsema, "E. J.," 300). Chef Kaluzhny's crew was surprisingly professional— though not necessarily in the culinary arts. As Mary Ogle explains, a number of prominent businessmen, many of whom held high positions at International Harvester, Singer Sewing Machine, and General Electric, as well as an

Episcopal priest and a number of missionaries, traded cooking responsibilities (192–193).

By May 1942, internees were beginning to experience some weight loss (Butler et al., 650). At Santo Tomás, muscles were beginning to shrink, especially in the thighs and arms, as the lack of properly nutritious food continued. To illustrate, Hartendorp tells of "an unhappy circus strong-man, though he immediately got himself a job in the kitchen, [who] watched his bulging muscles shrinking with acute anxiety" (I, 112).

By July 1942, because the Philippine Red Cross funds from which the internees drew money were exhausted, the Japanese finally agreed to furnish the per diem required for the internees' food; this they agreed to do at the rate of one peso a day per adult and one half that per child (Whitesides, 15).

Life rolled on as 1942 progressed. Little by little, the internees worked to adjust to the dust, the crowded conditions, the bartering, and the crude sanitary facilities. In Santo Tomás, as in the other camps to a lesser extent, lines became the measurement of life itself: lines to wash dishes at the series of wooden troughs with multiple faucets the men had set up; lines to go to the bathroom; lines to receive medical attention; lines to return battered books to the "library"; and, of course, *the* Line. This most important of all lines was one in which internees waited twice (or, in some camps, three times) a day for several hours balancing crude cups and cans with bailing wire handles for the gift of lugao, beans, and vegetable stews with shreds of meat or fish. The Line was the initial great teacher to internees just becoming acquainted for the first time in most of their lives not with real hunger but with the hollowness that comes from eating unnaturally small portions with no second helpings.

The internment camps also taught all those unfortunates inside the walls to learn to depend on themselves. As with food, internees in all camps also provided their own medical facilities. Once again, the Japanese did almost nothing to provide for public health needs or medical care. And once again, the internees' drive, ingenuity, and work made the camps livable rather than pest holes during these first six months (and then thereafter). Not surprisingly, Santo Tomás had the most complete facilities among the camps, though Baguio had the largest proportion of doctors and the only dysentery specialist; Bacolod was in the worst shape, with only one doctor, no hospital to speak of, and not even disinfectant or bedpans.

In Santo Tomás, one of the first head nurses, Dorothy Davis, R.N., a civilian internee formerly at Sternberg Army Hospital in Manila, helped organize the first hospital. She was aided by Dr. Charles Leach, a former field director of a Chinese public health mission through the Rockefeller Foundation (Hartendorp, I, 28, n10). As Davis explained in a 1944 article in the *American*

Journal of Nursing (written after she was exchanged following twenty-one months in Santo Tomás), "We were moved into camp without provision for clinic or hospital" (29). Eventually, Leach and Davis set up a small hospital in a one-story mining school building. It had space for only eighty beds and four wards, but it did contain additional space for a combined examination room and doctor's office, a small laboratory, a physiotherapy room, and a kitchen (Hartendorp, I, 28). During this period, if the medical staff needed to isolate cases of acute infectious diseases, they used several large circus tents (loaned by E. Tait of the Tait Shows). Venereal disease and tuberculosis cases especially found themselves under the Big Top.

The Red Cross provided both the supplies and most of the equipment. Red Cross Emergency Unit #1 in Manila, for example, proved invaluable in this regard. Cast-iron beds, assorted chairs, boxes of medical supplies, and some medicines from the unit arrived by truck at the gates of Santo Tomás very shortly after the camp opened (Davis, 29; Hartendorp, I, 28).

Several other sources provided supplies as well. Some doctors, such as Dr. F. E. Whitacre, who was caught by the war on his way back to the United States, brought in their own instruments and a variety of medications; the University of Santo Tomás furnished a student microscope and a centrifuge for the tiny laboratory and loaned tables and benches. Even the local convents contributed additional beds and linen, and the camp itself provided extra rations and the more nutritious foods especially for the hospital.

Beyond actual physical facilities, Santo Tomás was also fortunate in having a variety of qualified doctors and nurses, as well as a laboratory technician, a physical therapist, a dietitian, and four dentists. These personnel eventually trained many interested female internees to be hospital volunteer aides (Hartendorp, I, 29; Davis, 29–30). With no facilities in camp for surgery, Japanese authorities permitted patients in need of it (or with extremely serious conditions) to be transferred to one of the outside hospitals in Manila—at least during the first eighteen months.

Despite these limitations, the camp hospital in Santo Tomás managed to function surprisingly smoothly by improvising. Davis and the others came up with a variety of homemade accommodations. Cleverly worked scrap metal became a bedpan; bottles cut off at the neck and sterilized by boiling metamorphosed into hospital tumblers. When part of the hospital therapeutic regimen required different diets for conditions such as dysentery or ulcers, nurses concocted diet "cards" out of strips of bed sheets to alert the crews serving food. These strips, dyed in various chemicals, were then tied to the foot of each bed in the hospital using the following code: white (undyed) stood for a regular hospital diet; purple (dyed with gentian violet) indicated a "soft" diet;

red (tinted with mercurochrome) signaled a liquid diet; and yellow (dipped in picric acid) meant a "special" diet to be discussed with the doctor or nurse on duty (Davis, 29).

Davis herself fell ill several times and had to enter St. Luke's Hospital in Manila; another former head nurse, this time from Peiping Medical College in China, Ethel E. Robinson, took Davis's place. Robinson also became sick and had to be released to an outside hospital in March 1942. Luckily, by this time a group of military nurses drawn variously from Cavite Naval Base (and other smaller navy installations) and from Sternberg Army Hospital, as well as captured army (and a handful of navy) nurses stranded on Corregidor by the surrender, had arrived. Navy Chief Nurse LCDR Laura Cobb took over Robinson's duties (Davis, 29–30).

Early doctors' reports are important, because they give some idea of the base-line health of the camp in the first six months of camp life. Even then, camp medical records show a gradual rise in a series of health complaints. From January 8 to February 4, 1942, for example, 1,185 patients (out of a camp population at that time of approximately 3,800) presented themselves for treatment. Of these 1,160 received actual diagnoses. The largest group of complaints were for respiratory infections and the second largest were for gastrointestinal problems (including diarrhea). A handful of other complaints, including earaches, venereal disease, hernia, and minor heart problems, made up the rest. These figures would change as the year wore on, with gastrointestinal problems—especially dysentery—becoming one of the main problems over the years. Even in the *first month* of internment at least a third of the internees had diagnosable health complaints (Hartendorp, I, 29).

Doctors worried as well about the eventual effects of crowded sleeping and living conditions. By March of 1942, for example, Dr. Leach reported that a "high percentage" (18 percent) of the camp children had reacted positively to the tuberculosis skin test (conducted, at Dr. Leach's request, by the Philippine Health Service). Leach insisted that exposed children needed to be segregated and provided with an improved diet. Soon afterward, the Executive Committee made provisions for the food and opened up a children's hospital in the separate Women and Children's Annex. The committee also urged mothers to send their uninfected or unexposed children under the age of ten to Holy Ghost College (a convent), which was functioning as a kind of boarding school, complete with three meals a day (Hartendorp, I, 96; Sams, 71, n17). Leach was also the first doctor to begin reserving camp milk for children and the sick.

By July cases of dysentery had increased dramatically. As it turned out, some of the kitchen workers were dysentery carriers as well as carriers of salmonella. Out of 164 internees working in the kitchen, six carried dysentery, and fifty, salmonella (Hartendorp, I, 156). The carriers were discharged, and Leach and the other doctors tried to set up regular screening tests for health and food care workers, though this was only spottily observed for a short time.

The final figures for illness by the end of the first six months (just before the Japanese military takeover of finances) are telling. Despite medical facilities, competent staffing, and even innovative public health programs, as well as regular individual camp duties such as room scrubbing weekly and toilet basin cleaning by hand with disinfectant after each user, "gastro-intestinal problems" (including dysentery) soon topped the charts as the most common illness in camp. By July there were 975 cases compared to only 197 in February (over four times the number, and now almost a fourth of the camp population) (Hartendorp, I, 153–154).

Despite the illnesses present, Santo Tomás's medical facilities were heaven itself compared to the crude medical accommodations of Bacolod camp on Negros at this same time. Lacking a hospital (except for a *completely* empty former manual training building in which "patients" could sleep undisturbed on the floor), all cases of serious or even moderate illness had to be sent to a hospital in either Bacolod (city) or Cadiz, *if* the Japanese authorities permitted transfers. Even basic medical supplies were scarce in camp. As Vaughan notes in her June 16, 1942, diary entry, by this date the camp had five serious cases of diarrhea accompanied by fever. The one internee doctor, Dr. Smith, had his personal supplies and medications confiscated by the authorities when he was interned in Bacolod camp. As of June 1942, the camp lacked even bismuth or a bedpan, not to mention anesthetic (Vaughan, 99).

Enterprising Elizabeth Vaughan had squirreled away calcium powder and some cod liver oil for her children as she was being sent to camp; beyond whatever personal supplies people might have kept secretly — and a bottle of camp iodine — medications did not exist, and health problems generally went untreated in Bacolod.

The case of a Bacolod internee, Mr. Williams, is an excellent example of the paucity of medical care, facilities, instruments, medication, or anesthetic in Bacolod, as well as the normal state of seeming Japanese indifference to prisoner needs. In June 1942, Dr. Smith diagnosed Williams as having a severely infected foot (possibly from having a toe amputated before coming to Bacolod). When Dr. Smith tried to obtain the tools and antiseptic to clean out the wound and drain the abscesses on the foot, the Japanese authorities refused to provide them. They also refused to send Williams to the town hospital to have his foot amputated to stop the spread of obvious infection (Vaughan, June 16, 1942, 99). When told sharply by Dr. Smith that Williams would surely die without medical attention, the Japanese guards said not to worry: "If man dies we will bury him." Dr. Smith swore at them angrily, which, as Vaughan notes in a coldly practical tone, "only angered the Japanese and got us no anesthetic." Smith then told the assembled internees that *even* when he served in Turkey during World War I, "no cruelty of the Turks equaled the smiling refusal of Japs to answer his humane requests" (Vaughan, 99). Incidentally, Smith was right; the infection spread from Williams's foot to his whole leg, which ultimately the Japanese doctors amputated at the hip. Williams died the following morning, despite this last-minute procedure (Vaughan, October 5, 1942, 132).

It was also during these first six months that more internees arrived in Bacolod after capture and brief internment on Cebu, Iloilo, and Zamboanga peninsula on Mindanao, though not from Davao camp; the internee refugees stayed in Bacolod until late 1943 when the camp population was transferred to Santo Tomás on Luzon (Onorato, xi). Bacolod internees suffered from scarce resources, as the wave of new internees entered camp — resources, incidentally, that were augmented neither by Japanese funds for food nor by Japanese medical supplies.

Unlike Bacolod, the Baguio camp (Camp Holmes instead of John Hay, from late April 1942 on) was not plagued by large groups of incoming new and hungry internees, though it did lack some medicines and, initially, roomy medical facilities. The camp, however, was fortunate to have a variety of specially qualified doctors (six), a pathologist, and eight nurses interned, as well as a renowned expert on dysentery, parasitology, and tropical diseases, Dr. F. G. Haughwout (Bloom, "Death," 79; Haughwout, 123, n3).

Dr. Haughwout was also fortunate to have qualified co-workers. Several of his associates had "broad experience" in medicine in the Far East. Doctors Beulah Ream Allen and Dorothy Kinney Chambers, both experienced in dealing with tropical illness, along with Dr. Haughwout, worked around the clock to stop Baguio's repeated epidemics of dysentery. In the first five months, for example, Baguio suffered three separate outbreaks (Hartendorp, I, 172); 80 percent of the camp eventually contracted diarrhea, dysentery, or "food intoxication" (food poisoning). Despite these numbers and a lack of proper medical supplies, Dr. Haughwout's measures, including his famous diet and drink, seem to have prevented any deaths (Haughwout, 134). The famous diet, as James J. Halsema explained it to Hartendorp, consisted of a large dose of castor oil and then an absolute fast with only strong tea to drink. This went on for twenty-four hours. The next day the patient received soft lugao and, finally, mashed bananas. The diet, by all accounts, was noxious, but it obviously worked (Halsema, qtd in Hartendorp, I, 134). An added future benefit to both science and history was that Haughwout's work with his fellow internees provided him and other researchers with accurate figures and laboratory studies of some 2,000 internees, including ultimately those in Santo Tomás; such a population suffering those kinds of deprivations usually cannot be documented clinically due to prison camp rules. The civilian internees, however, *were* documented, along with their gradually weakening health. Haughwout's figures show clearly "the *progressive* deterioration in function and resistance of the alimentary track that beset the greater number of internees [italics mine]" (Haughwout, 134). In Baguio (Holmes), as was the case later in Los Baños, at least one doctor (Dr. Welles) stubbornly documented this deterioration by sending a death certificate forward to the Japanese Headquarters in Manila, listing "malnutrition" as one of the main causes of the patient's death. As with Dr. Stevenson's similar rebellion in STIC, Halsema noted sardonically, "They didn't like it at all" ("1944 Diary," September 25, 1944).

It is remarkable that more deaths from a variety of causes did not occur, given the initial state of the John Hay camp and its lack of facilities when the internees were first interned. For example, because of earlier Japanese bombing raids, the pumping station that supplied water and the power plant were both damaged. There were no electric lights at first, no running (or potable) water for three days, and the very few toilets that were available were broken or "choked with feces and debris" (Halsema, "E. J.," 298; Haughwout, 125). Moreover, the Japanese refused to let the internees fix the pumping station until three days elapsed.

Because of these conditions, a major health threat existed; according to Jim Halsema,

> With no water to flush toilets, sanitation immediately became a major problem. [E. J.] Halsema tried to get the Japanese to provide a shovel so he could dig a privy. No, they replied. So he found a broken length of steel pipe and a shrapnel-severed piece of roofing iron and constructed a makeshift shovel which he and other volunteers used in shifts to dig a hole. After seeing them at work, the Japanese provided a shovel. ("E. J.," 298)

Ultimately, the internees themselves fashioned a crude privy, using a board over two wooden crates over a pit. This provided two "seats"; to assure privacy, an internee would yell out, one hour, "ladies' turn" and the next hour, "men's turn." Fortunately, when the water came back on, the privy holes could be filled in and covered with ashes (298). "The internees' sanitary efforts were not enough however. Despite the return of running water, the damage caused by inability to wash hands and dishes was done: bacillary dysentery had appeared, not to disappear during the entire internment period" (Halsema, "E. J.," 298). Nor was there a standing hospital building, though Dr. Allen was allowed to try to make an adjacent officers' quarters into one, but only after it had been cleaned of the masses of feces deposited by the former military occupants (298). Later, at Camp Holmes, other doctors, including Doctors Nance, Vincent, and Cunningham, as well as eight full-time qualified nurses and a pathologist, helped staff the small camp hospital eventually set up in the former Philippine Constabulary Headquarters after arriving in April 1942 (Bloom, "Death," 79; Halsema, "1944 Diary," December 26, 1944).

At first the staff had little to work with. The hospital lacked many instruments and even aspirin, as well as any kind of disinfectant for the toilets (Hartendorp, I, 172). Fortunately, in March 1942, Dr. Devenicia of the Philippine Red Cross brought supplies of cod liver oil, various medicines, milk, and fruit juice (Crouter, March 16, 30–31). Cases requiring surgery, as in other camps, were sent into town — in this case, it seems, to Baguio General Hospital.

As the years passed, Halsema's "1944 Diary" notes a growing number of internees being sent to Baguio General Hospital to recover from serious illness — including James Halsema himself:

> A month ago today I ate my breakfast of cornmeal mush and tea; soon after began to experience pains in my belly but went out with the garbage anyway [his camp job]. After, struggled down to the hospital [camp hospital] almost doubled up with pain, lay on the operating table groaning. Ensued fruitless enemas, hot water bottles, codeine, fever . . . castor oil, vomiting. Snap judgment of dysentery. (November 24, 1944)

After being taken on a stretcher by truck to Baguio General Hospital, another diagnosis revealed he had a swollen liver, possibly due to amebic dysentery, the treatment for which was a needle in the abdomen, doses of emetine, sulfathiazole, and more emetine, along with strengthening food such as liver and eggs. These were "bought at enormous prices" after Marie Halsema sold her bed sheets for cash (November 24, 1944).

In addition to (apparently) much more reliable health facilities and supplies at hand, part of the reason for the Baguio internees' fewer deaths — the smallest number among the camps throughout internment — may also have been due to demographics. As Lynn Bloom shows, the rate of death in Baguio was less than "actuarial rates would predict for a comparable civilian population" ("Death," 76). As Fern Miles, another Baguio internee, points out in her account, a May 1942 survey showed that "ninety percent of the internees were under sixty" and that the largest group of internees was between the ages of twenty and thirty-nine (Miles, 123). A camp with young members in their prime years of health inevitably did better than a camp which had older internees or more infants, such as Santo Tomás. The statistics concerning the deaths in Baguio support this theory. Of the fifteen people who died at Baguio, seven were over sixty and two were premature infants, thereby showing that those internees who were in the prime of their lives survived the conditions at the camp for the most part (Bloom, "Death," 76).

Baguio, Santo Tomás, and Bacolod camps struggled on through the rest of 1942. Apparently, the Japanese government did not subsidize the camp finances at Bacolod after the first six months as it did at Baguio and Santo Tomás. Neither Hartendorp nor Elizabeth Vaughan mentions the Japanese authorities supplying the internees with a per diem amount of either money or food; on the contrary, the internees were still purchasing all their necessities. Vaughan comments furiously in her diary on November 30, 1942, about a departing Japanese officer (Colonel Ohta) and his request that the internees "tell others how kind the Japanese have been to internees":

> They have done nothing at all for us, really and truly *nothing*. They have furnished no food and no aid to facilitate the preparation of food we have furnished. Even the large cisterns for catching rain water were bought and delivered to camp by Swiss and Filipino friends outside who used our money. The camp kitchen was built by our men with their own tools, of materials bought with our own funds. Had we not been able to afford transportation to bring our mattresses and mosquito nets, we would be sleeping on the floor (unswept without our own brooms) or on haystacks for all the Japanese cared. And now our fuel is giving out and so is food and the Japanese only smile and say, "Look out for yourselves and tell others of our kindness." (162)

In lacking Japanese financial support as late as November Bacolod seems unique; other camps (Davao, for example) had been taken on as a financial responsibility in July of that year.

Santo Tomás internees, thanks to the unique and unexplained efforts of a commandant, Tsurumi, who went to headquarters and "insisted on ₱ 70,000 minimum be[ing] given for [each] month" for food, eventually received the highest per diem allowance among the camps: ₱ 70 per person per day (Hartendorp, I, 150). Baguio, with its smaller and less noticeably hungry population (and no Commandant Tsurumi in the wings), received only ₱ 30 per person per day. As Crouter notes in a July 21, 1942, entry, this was based on ₱ 4,500 a month sum and was to cover "everything" (Hartendorp, I, 150; Crouter, 73).

After the Japanese took over administration and finances, food and necessity monies followed a fairly regular pattern in Santo Tomás and Baguio camps. The commandant would issue the Executive (or Central) Internee Committee the proper per diem amount per month, and the internees would then purchase materials for the camp, including not only food but also medical and surgical supplies (Pearson, 990). These supplies were then turned over and administered by the various units and subcommittees in camp—the hospital, the kitchen, the annex, and so on. Because of this, the chow lines in each camp continued to provide a very basic diet (generally insufficient in calories or vitamins but enough to sustain life above a starvation level).

Some perspective is in order here. To understand what the *usual* standards for "minimum requirements of nutrition" were among the Japanese and indeed the rest of Asia, it is useful to consult the November 1941 Wickizer and Bennett study, *The Rice Economy of Monsoon Asia.* The authors point out: "By Occidental standards of 'optimum' or even 'minimum' requirements for nutrition, surveys of food consumption or analyses of food supplies show that Oriental diets are deficient in both total calories, and in animal proteins, fats, and several of the vitamins and minerals" (128).

An earlier report in 1937 by a League of Nations–sponsored intergovernmental "Conference of Far East Countries on Rural Hygiene" held in Java reached this grim conclusion: "Undernourishment and malnutrition is widespread [in the Far East] and that much impairment of physical development and general health, low vitality, and actual disease result from insufficient and improper diet" (qtd in Wickizer and Bennett, 128). The report went on to discuss the Japanese diet specifically: "In Japan, malnutrition is responsible for eye diseases, beriberi, scurvy, Miller-Barlow's disease, rickets, 'Mehlnahrschaden' (Czerny-Keller) and underweight. The prevalence of beriberi is due to rice being the main item of food in [the] Japanese diet" (qtd in Wickizer and Bennett, 130).

By Japanese standards, then, the *initial* "insufficient" nutrition allowances the internees received were entirely sufficient, even "liberal" (Hartendorp, I, 241). We should remember that this determination was undoubtedly made by a captor who regarded semistarvation and deficiency diseases among its working class as an accepted fact in a part of the world that lived regularly with malnutrition. However, despite a certain familiarity with such a diet and its effects, Japanese authorities obviously did not regard it as either beneficial or a normal diet for even the lowliest private soldier or guard in their army—and certainly not for the officers. The meals internees observed being carried in and out of the guardhouse or to the officers' mess hardly matched the scurvy-rickets-hypoproteinosis-producing lugao or polished rice given prisoners. It was commonplace, in fact, for all internees in the camps later in the war to paw through the guards' garbage to try to find something of nutritional value to eat. Dr. Jay Hill, a sixteen-year-old in Los Baños camp at the time and care-taker for the commandant's chickens, remembers in the last year of the war being blessed with the half-eaten remains of a meal of tongue that the com-mandant gave him from his own plate (Hill, interview).

The contrast between the guards' meals and those of the annex mothers, the children, and the sick is particularly glaring, especially since the authori-ties provided no *extra* food for these groups. As Hartendorp points out: "The meals served to mothers and children at the annex and to patients at the camp hospital were strengthened at the expense of the meals served to the internees generally from the central kitchen. Actually, in spite of the improvement ef-fected by the Finance and Supplies Committee through the new appropri-ations from the Japanese Military, the diet remained a slow-starvation one" (I, 241). Margaret Sams would disagree that the rations were strengthened. Her experience was one of bitter poverty for the first six to nine months, despite Hartendorp's insistence that help was available to those without money. It may indeed have existed, but she certainly knew nothing about it (Sams, 89; 95).

Imogene Carlson, newly arrived at Santo Tomás early in 1943, remembers the special food given to the small children—delicacies out of the range of possibility back on Cebu or at Bacolod:

> The children received special food, prepared and supervised by U.S. Army women dietitians. Strained and mashed food for the babies, as well as milk, were served from the same diet kitchen. It seemed almost heavenly to me after the way I had had to struggle over a gate-stove in the open air [at Cebu] for an hour getting Larry's cereal ready. The baby bottles and nipples were boiled and filled with warm milk appropriate for every infant. All that was required was that the mothers wash and return the bottles and nipples. (102)

The operating rule of Santo Tomás and Baguio, even of Bacolod, camps, was both instinctive and instructive: "Women, children, and the sick first" in terms of food. As Butler concludes passionately, it is for this reason that chil-dren and the sick did as well as they did in camps: "Continually . . . evidence of chivalry of men to women and of self-sacrifice of men and women for the sick and the young was revealed that should be recorded in honor of these persons and as a tribute to a society whose code they adhered to under trying circumstances" (651).

To lessen these sacrifices some Santo Tomás internees did have (and could make use of) vendors, the camp canteen, and packages for supplemental food. For those with funds (or those such as Sams, ultimately, who earned money in camp doing extra work), the camp canteen offered a variety of supplementary foods. Using money obtained by the Executive Committee on short-term credit from banks and firms in Manila, the canteen bought and then sold such items as duck eggs, coconuts, bananas, raw peanuts, coffee beans, Filipino cigarettes, and tobacco, as well as raw sugar and fruit, to the internees. All of the profits went, after paying off loans, to the Santo Tomás Welfare Fund to provide an extra midday meal for those without supplemental food or contacts, as well as the regular breakfast and dinner (Whitesides, 19).

Though Hartendorp, Stevens, and Whitesides agree that a Welfare Fund which doled out money to the less fortunate existed in Santo Tomás, some internees do not remember it that way. Margaret Sams, for example, says that at the time she entered Santo Tomás she had never heard of any such fund, nor did she receive any benefits from it, despite the claims of such "official" historians as Hartendorp and Stevens. She explains angrily, "I was able to make very little use of the Filipino stalls that were eventually allowed in camp for awhile, for I never had more than a few pesos during the entire time we were interned except for the loans that I was able to make just before the birth of Gerry Ann" (72).

She adds that there may well have been a Relief and Welfare Department, but she never heard of it or saw any benefits from it (72–73, n18). She does mention later that with the money she had she bought fruit as well as vegetables through the gate and that David did get free oatmeal every morning, but it was only near the end of 1942 that she had enough money to buy a whole case of milk for David to supplement whatever milk he received regularly at the annex (Sams, 63; 69, n15).

However necessary the food was to sustain their lives, none of the internees could deny that the food served every day on the Line was dull and bland. At least at Santo Tomás camp, the arrival of South African and Canadian Red Cross kits in December 1942 enriched this diet enormously. The kits, Hartendorp suggests, were given to all prisoners, not simply to those nationalities only (I, 331). They contained a cornucopia of wonders: tinned pears, jam, sugar, tins of Nestlé's condensed milk, chocolate bars, cans of turkey and beef paté, and canned margarine (Lucas, 63). Not only did the kits add variety to the diets, but they also provided supplemental (and badly needed) vitamins and calories for everyone in camp. Butler calculates that total daily calories increased in the internees' diet since the supplies in the kits (especially the canned margarine) raised a sadly deficient Vitamin A level, supplied more calcium (with the milk) and Vitamin C (with the fruit), and raised the allotted milligrams of protein due to the paté (Butler, Table 3, 641).

Baguio camp was not so lucky. There seem to have been no South African or Canadian kits for them, and their diet remained substandard. For example, Baguio meals provided only about half as many daily calories as the Standard Daily Allowance (SDA) recommended, as well as only a fourth as much calcium (Butler, Table 1, 640). Even with the occasional addition of meat and more vegetables, Baguio camp's line diet lagged a bit nutritionally behind that of Santo Tomás by the end of 1942, despite an earlier addition of chickens and goat's milk from camp animals. Even privately owned chickens or goats ultimately became communal; camp policy demanded that all eggs and milk had to be shared with the camp kitchen if the animals were tended by camp personnel (Crouter, August 18, 1942, 79).

As usual, Bacolod camp not only didn't receive any South African or Canadian comfort kits, but the internees were *still* paying for all food and necessities themselves without any true Japanese aid.

Alice Bryant's account initially seems to contradict this until she explains the sort of sleight-of-hand being practiced in camp by the authorities. According to the Japanese, they *did* pay per diem to the internees—₱ 50 (25¢ day, American). However, "deductions would be made for the supplies he [the Japanese purchasing agent] bought—at a far higher price than the market price—and for light and water from the time the camp was opened" (Bryant, 138).

This is payment—and yet not. The electricity was, of course, from a recently (American) constructed plant, and the water was so foul it had to be boiled. In addition to the expensively procured per diem supplies, both Bryant and Vaughan note in their accounts that the "head" of the camp internees, Mr. Pope, would collect more money from the internees (or have them sign IOUs to redeem after the war for their share of the food if they were penniless). With these funds he would occasionally have the Swiss or friendly Filipino go-betweens purchase stock for the camp as a future supplemental food source. Vaughan remembers in an August 17, 1942, entry that the first purchase of this sort was a young carabao bull ("Ferdinand") and a variety of sheep, rabbits, ducks, and chickens. These additions of livestock, as well as pigs and more chickens purchased later, added to the growing barnyard. These, again, were purchased with internee, not Japanese per diem, money (Vaughan, 117; September 17, 126–128). Milk supplies were here, too, reserved for children under twelve, though they had ceased drinking Carnation milk and had switched to carabao milk brought in from outside the camp at a high price. The milk, for safety's sake, first had to be delivered to the hospital and boiled (Vaughan, 126).

Despite high hopes because of the stock, by October 1942, meals were still low in both calories and nutrition at Bacolod. For one thing, the food produced by the stock was very limited. Many animals had to be killed earlier "due to heavy toll from disease and death"; explains Vaughan: "Other pigs, sheep, chickens and rabbits have died. The goats have almost ceased giving milk they are so thin, and Ferdinand the [carabao] Bull is looking pale and wane. He will go to the butcher in a few days" (October 18, 1942, 141). The animals had simply been hungry; the sheep were "starving to death, having eaten all the hedges, flowers within reach," and the rabbits died of neglect and hunger. The chickens perished because of both starvation and disease (141).

The camp garden as of November apparently was producing some vegetables, including the familiar onions, lima beans, and cowpeas; it also provided native vegetables such as camotes and cincomas. The garden provided only a limited amount of vegetables per person, however, especially for 146 internees; the result seems to have been an improvement more in taste and texture, rather than in amount (Vaughan, November 16, 1942, 158–159). The meals improved only marginally, owing to the small amounts involved, despite slaughtered stock, onions, cincomas, and high hopes.

Regular meals on the Line at Bacolod, then, continued to be somewhat thin. Breakfast consisted of one cup of weak coffee (beans roasted over an open fire in camp) and a "big spoon" of rice, as well as "a bit" of coconut honey (made from camp coconut squeezings cooked down with a little sugar). Lunch varied, but the main dish, not surprisingly, was "always rice," although there was a second helping for those who wanted it (two "big spoons" perhaps?) and possibly fresh garden produce. Tea time also featured rice, but it was served with vegetables and sometimes spinach juice (Vaughan, 125–126).

The emphasis on fresh fruits or vegetables was an innovation since September. After the kitchen reorganization, the Bacolod Line tried to feature (as the trained dietitian, the new head of the kitchen, recommended) more native foods, fruits, and vegetables and not so many of the camp's purchased canned goods. To do so would provide more vitamins and save the "emergency" canned food supplies for any future hard times. Increasingly, the kitchen filled out meals with such native foods as *tintola* (fish head soup) and *patola* (a stringy, okra-like vegetable boiled in coconut milk), which internees tried to accustom themselves to eating (Vaughan, November 9, 1942, 153).

Despite these economies, however, food still had to be paid for—from whatever source. Some, including Vaughan, worried about the drain on camp finances: "Since we are civilians the Japanese have made no effort to stop food supplies from coming in as long as we ourselves have to pay for it, cash or credit (all is on credit), but we know this can't go on indefinitely" (September 17, 1942, 128).

Not only money, but soon certain stores, necessary both for consumption and for fuel, began to run out. Alcohol (even for medicinal purposes) vanished from camp, except for whatever some of the men produced secretly in a hidden still using ginger root and molasses. Not only drinkers were distressed at the lack of alcohol (except for their own crude and probably dangerous product), but so too were those cooking in the camp kitchen, because its stoves used alcohol as fuel. Vaughan explains that the camp commandant demanded that, owing to the alcohol shortage, camp food be cooked outdoors over wood fires (internees also had to purchase the wood). As Vaughan notes with disgust in her diary, the camp rice "is cooked to a smoky, sticky mess" over open flames (November 30, 1942, 162). This alcohol shortage was very odd, because both earlier and later Vaughan saw Japanese trucks pass the camp with huge drums "filled with alcohol from nearby sugar central's alcohol distilleries" (September 21, 1942, 130).

Later, on Negros Island, even salt became a "rare" commodity. Vaughan tells of a notice on the camp bulletin board put up by the authorities that announced, "no more extra table salt can be allowed . . . and we live in sight of the sea! But we have no coconuts (such a useful fruit in cooking) and there is a large grove just outside the fence which separates the camp and the free (?) world outside" (December 5, 1942, 166). Along with the alcohol and salt, Vaughan once again saw the Japanese shipping out supplies, in this case tons of sugar, though the internees were "almost out" in a camp that was literally between two sugar mills. It was not that stores of sugar or salt or alcohol didn't exist but rather that the Japanese authorities refused to give any to the internees; instead, the stocks of salt, sugar, and alcohol were sent on to the home islands or to the Imperial troops (Vaughan, 165).

In spite of these depredations Bacolod camp did its best to observe holidays, though even festive meals reflected a growing imbalance in the diet. During holidays the camp brought out the best food it had — often supplies that the camp had saved. Even so, the picture was still somewhat grim, as Vaughan's description of Thanksgiving Day 1942 inadvertently shows, although she seems delighted with the meal that smuggled wine, ingenuity, limited stores, and available vegetables produced:

> Dinner consisted of native port, native sweet potatoes (camotes), a vegetable goulash, and squash pie without crust. The "special" was an awesome "turkey" lying

in state on a table in the center of dining room. A large pumpkin-type squash, shaped surprisingly like the torso of a fowl, had legs of long bananas fastened on with copper wire, which also formed the feet sticking high in the air. The turkey's wings were long curved slices of camote, the neck was the stem of the pumpkin painted darker than the rest of the body. The handsome fowl lay on its back on a large platter of red rice which looked, at first glance, like dressing. (November 26, 1942, 160)

For dessert, Vaughan talks about the chocolate coconut candy "the women of the camp" made over "an open fire for several successive afternoons." Fighting flames, coughing, and fanning away smoke for several days, they made over a thousand pieces of fudge so that all 146 people could take "several pieces" each back to the room (160).

For Christmas, Vaughan mentions that the camp was the beneficiary of two live sheep, paid for and brought to camp by Mr. and Mrs. Simke, a German-Jewish couple who were friends of Vaughan. The sheep, notes Vaughan, were "the first gift of food to the camp since we came in"; everything else sent in for the camp (and for Christmas dinner) had to be purchased. The Simkes also provided Vaughan and her two children with a special food package containing such wonders as a can of Carnation milk, a small can of pineapple butter, three eggs, six bananas, lollipops for Beth and Clay, and also a valuable bar of "Lifebuoy soap" and several meters of cotton cloth (December 12, 1942, 166).

Back in Santo Tomás, while food remained a vital concern, medical facilities had slowly improved—and none too soon, according to some internees. Late August 1942 saw the establishment of a "new" hospital across the street from Santo Tomás in the Santa Catalina Convent. Having housed a former girls' school, the convent now provided space for between 175 and 200 patients—almost twice the capacity of the hospital on the college grounds (Davis, 30). This new hospital presented the Japanese with a unique problem: How did they prevent a literal parade of sick Allied internees from creeping across the street under the all-too-compassionate eyes of the Filipino populace? The solution involved lining the entire passage from the campus to the convent with a high board fence (Davis, 30; Hartendorp, I, 247). However restricted the passage to health was, the camp rejoiced at having more space. According to Lucas, by the end of 1942, "nearly everyone in camp was suffering from some form of vitamin or mineral deficiency" and beds were at a premium (Lucas, 61).

As I've indicated before, no real medical facilities graced Bacolod camp. One room in the manual arts building served as a place to put the sick—one in which sheer space and general freedom from noise was the sole benefit of this bleak refuge. There was no medicine, nothing for fevers, not even bed-pans or hot water bottles. Sick internees had to bring their own bedding, cots, medicine (if they had any), water, and food, and they had to nurse their own sick if they were not too sick themselves (and often, even if they were).

It is not so surprising, in light of primitive medical and public health standards in the camp at large, when Vaughan reports that her barefoot two-year-old, Clay, stepped on a nail on the way to the showers. A terrified Vaughan, discovering that the camp lacked anti-tetanus serum, was frantic to do *something* to try to help. While waiting for the Japanese-appointed Dr. Jara to arrive (Dr. Smith isn't mentioned again), Vaughan held a screaming Clay down as one of the camp nuns "squirted iodine with an eyedropper into [the] hole in Clay's foot and forc[ed] iodine through to the bottom opening" (August 9, 1942, 116). Fortunately for Clay Vaughan, Dr. Jara, after ransacking the town, obtained serum from a private stock and gave Clay a 1,500-unit injection immediately. This was not, however, done out of the goodness of anyone's heart or because of the provisions of the Geneva Convention: It cost Vaughan $25, because she had to buy the entire 5,000-unit vial. It was $25 she had to borrow. She tried later to sell the remaining serum (minus Clay's second injection) back to the camp hospital, but the authorities were "not interested," despite the prevalence of rusty nails, tin can lids, and animal droppings littering the camp.

Even with the serum, medical care was so poor that Clay almost died from a reaction to the shot, even though the doctor insisted he had only some sort of infection. Clay's fever shot up over 102° F, he developed a stiff neck, and hives swelled his face so badly his eyes were nearly closed. After fruitless medical treatment with hot compresses and icthyol ointment, only a timely adrenaline shot at the town hospital stopped the dangerous swelling and helped clear up some of the other symptoms of serum reaction (Vaughan, August 12, August 20; 116–118).

Occasionally, odd sorts of medical supplies would suddenly materialize in camp. Vaughan notes in an October 27 entry that Dr. Jara arrived in camp one day with a 25-gallon drum of cod liver oil (from what source, no one knew). The camp, whether it wanted it or not, was charged $180. Jara informed the assembled (and surprised) internees that "The oil will be doled out in small quantities for emergencies only" (146). No one seemed clear what those might be, especially given the heat and nearly constant sunlight (and the obvious presence of at least Vitamin D) in the area.

By the beginning of April 1943, medical problems had become increasingly obvious, and nutrition had gradually worsened. Despite different geographic locations and individual differences among commandants at the different camps, no internee escaped nutritional problems and the increasing severity of the Japanese as the tide began to turn militarily. Though manifestations of both malnutrition and punishment may have differed somewhat in the particulars between camps, the general pall cast by both was inescapable. It would only get darker as 1943 moved into 1944 and finally 1945.

6

Hunger Time

April 1943–February 1945

The next eighteen months in camp saw several important benchmarks in terms of health and food. The Davao camp closed, and its internees moved to Santo Tomás, then to the newly established Los Baños camp; a typhoon hit in November 1943; and the first (and only) U.S. Red Cross food packages were distributed. The next year, 1944, as mentioned earlier, saw the end of outside food supplies (the package lines, the vendors); additionally, by December, the Baguio internees found themselves shipped out of their camp and into Bilibid Prison in Manila. During this last year a small but growing death rate hit both Santo Tomás and Los Baños as starvation rations increasingly became the rule and health, the exception. The rescue of internees in both camps and in Bilibid Prison during February 1945 came not a moment too soon, for those internees were reduced to eating foliage.

Back in the latter half of 1943, however, no one expected the situation ever to become so severe. Certainly, camp life still continued much the same in May and June, though prices for produce and camp supplies in Santo Tomás and Baguio were climbing and the food on the Line was decreasing slowly in amount and nutritive value. Sometimes a view from outside the camps, or by those just entering, can provide an interesting perspective. Doris Rubens, a former journalist and English teacher, and her novelist husband entered Santo Tomás in late April 1943, after being captured in the mountains of northern Luzon where they had been hiding since the outbreak of the war. Accustomed in the last months to living almost entirely on wild fruit and the occasional haunch of game delivered by sympathetic mountain natives, the Rubenses' reaction to camp amenities and food is particularly vivid, especially if the latter had been supplemented. To the Rubenses, after approximately one and a half years spent in leaky bamboo and sawali-sided huts, Santo Tomás appeared to be the land of plenty and comfort. After a hot shower, some clean used clothes, and shoes, the Rubenses sat down to a meal provided out of private (not camp) funds by their friends, the Jenkses. Mrs. Jenks treated the couple to breakfast in the internee "restaurant," where, for ₱ 1.40, they were served hot cakes and syrup, scrambled eggs, and fresh coffee and cigarettes (Rubens, 208–209). Such things were possible for those with money in 1943 before the Package Line closed and vendors and restaurants were outlawed.

The regular chow line meal, to which the Rubenses soon became accustomed, provided corn mush for breakfast and rice and mung beans for dinner, with an occasional banana for dessert (Rubens, 209). The couple soon began using the chow line and buying extra food whenever possible (once they were able to float loans with other internees).

The Rubenses were not only given a solid breakfast their first day in Santo Tomás, but they were treated medically as well—this time by the camp clinic. Once again, Doris Rubens's account gives us a midwar look into standard camp medical practices at this largest internment camp. The day the Rubenses arrived, they were treated almost immediately for festering cuts and tropical ulcers, as well as given standard shots for cholera, typhoid, and dysentery. They were also, embarrassingly, de-wormed (Rubens, 221).

According to the 1956 HEW Report, almost every one of the prisoners had intestinal parasites of one kind or another from late 1942 until release. Constant deworming seems to have gone on whenever possible in Santo Tomás and also in Los Baños, because even purgatives, while effective in ridding the body of worms, could not prevent reinfection. Regarding both *ascaris* and another, less frequent, worm, *strongyloides*, Blacklock and Southwell, two wartime experts on nematodes, explain that while "boiling water renders [them] innocuous" and prevents parasites, "it is not only by drinking water that the risk is run." In water the parasite larvae can directly penetrate the skin; they suggest, therefore, that both bath and domestic wash water be boiled as well for safety's sake — a precaution the internees did not seem to know about or practice (229–230). Obviously, at every stage, from eating raw talnium greens and private garden produce, to using untreated and second- or third-hand wash water (a practice Carlson describes earlier in Cebu), to walking barefoot, internees continued to become repeatedly reinfected. Concern over parasites was shared by those in all of the camps; Elizabeth Vaughan, for example, tried to make her children wear *bakas* (wooden platform sandals) to keep their feet off the ground. Even so, given the dangers the toddlers ran from falling with the shoes, Vaughan eventually decided to risk parasites rather than see, for example, Clay or Beth stumbling on their *bakas* and cracking their skulls open after falling off the unrailed concrete barracks steps at Baco-lod (Vaughan, September 1942, 129). Bacolod apparently did not have any deworming medicine, only the limited usefulness of boiling water for preven-tion. Even this primitive prophylaxis proved difficult in both Baguio camps (Hay/Holmes). In mountainous Baguio, boiling water was quite a chore. In fact, as Halsema points out, hot water was such a rare and jealously guarded indulgence that one of the few times he actually had hot water was a special indication of the camp's care and concern for him after he'd been tortured by the *kempei tai* — one of the few circumstances that seemed to demand this treatment (Halsema ltr, April 21, 1997).

Health and food both became an even larger issue in Santo Tomás when Japanese orders sent some of the camp's internees to Los Baños, a new camp. As we have seen in the previous chapter, the perils of this new camp were many. Los Baños was fortunate that the Japanese ordered a former Santo Tomás doctor, the peripatetic Dr. Leach, to accompany the first 800 men and the 12 volunteer navy nurses to the camp. With the help of the nurses, Leach fashioned the best hospital he could out of the facilities that existed, despite a lack of potable water and the risk of malaria (Hartendorp, I, 527–528; Davis, 30).

Davao camp, prior to its closure, presents an interesting contrasting case in terms of medical supplies and treatment. Though there was a Mission Hospi-tal close to the camp with missionary doctors, the Japanese often refused the internees medical treatment or visits from the Mission doctors. With food sup-plies getting thinner and internee medical supplies almost gone, these refusals had serious consequences, somewhat echoing the problems at Bacolod. Frank

Cary, for example, discusses the stubborn and painful tropical ulcer he had contracted. Starting from an insect bite or an open cut, Cary explains, "the original cut gradually spreads its area, goes deep and then sideways. Some of them get as large as a baseball in diameter" (April 8, 1943, 25). In a later letter he describes the crude medicine he had available to him to deal with this disabling problem — a problem that in some POW camps, incidentally, could lead to eventual amputation of limbs as the ulcer ate its way down, then into, the bone. For Cary, his only defense was to treat the ulcer with what boric acid crystals were on hand — a treatment that "burned" for "several hours" afterward (April 20, 1943, 27). Though this treatment seems to have helped somewhat, Cary later explains that even though the ulcer apparently healed over for a time, it later broke open repeatedly. It was not until 1944, in Santo Tomás, that Cary was able to clear it up for good using sulphathiazole, which came in with the Christmas 1943 Red Cross shipment (April 8, 1944, 54).

Food and medicine were needed in all camps but especially in newly organized Los Baños. The Santo Tomás internees, however, managed to raise more outside money to send to all the camps partly from the American Red Cross Relief funds sent through an account in Tokyo and from the Bessmer private fund. Los Baños camp, for example, received over ₱ 20,000; Baguio camp, ₱ 22,700; and even Davao on Mindanao got ₱ 20,800 over the next six months (Hartendorp, II, 18–19). There is no mention, however, of any money for the Bacolod camp, probably because by March 1943 the Japanese started breaking up the camp and sending boatloads of internees over to Luzon and, ultimately, to Santo Tomás (Bryant, 140–141). Santo Tomás's share of the money — ₱ 50,000 — went, by Executive Committee vote, to buy even more food and medical supplies, as well as clothing for those in camp without such things, including Doris Rubens and her husband (Vaughan, June 7, 1943, 229).

Internee health was suddenly and violently threatened — and then almost miraculously spared — because of a typhoon and flood on Luzon (November 13–19, 1943). Santo Tomás was hard hit, though Los Baños came in for part of the storm too. Heavy winds and pouring rain began at 11:30 A.M., November 13, 1943, and it rained steadily for the next five days. The wind snapped trees, collapsed many private shanties in camp, and decimated private garden crops. Internees counting on extra food from their gardens were devastated: "Papaya and banana plants that the internees had cultivated with such loving and expectant care were flattened by the wind," and the dispensary, the outpatient clinic, and the doctors' offices were flooded with water a foot deep inside. Other buildings suffered water damage throughout (Lucas, 118–119). Notices, hastily nailed up in the rain, called for everyone to boil water or drink only safely collected rainwater because the Manila filtration plant was down and the sewer lines backing up. Worse yet, by the third day of the storm, gas pressure fell, and this resulted not only in a loss of refrigeration (and, therefore, in food spoilage) but also in ruined vital vaccines and serums in refrigeration as well (Hartendorp, II, 28–29).

Santo Tomás internees found themselves wading, sometimes waist deep, to vital parts of the camp. Toilets with first no, and then low, water pressure had to be primed with buckets of floodwater, and in some buildings, such as the annex where plumbing was overwhelmed and washed out, the women and children had to resort to chamber pots. These were emptied every day by stoic men sloshing through the flooded areas carrying large collection barrels (Magnuson, 61).

Luckily, although the floodwaters did rise to within an inch of the floor of the food bodega, food stores escaped soaking, though the baggage and clothing bodega was completely swamped by the rising waters (Hartendorp, II, 28–29).

The last three days (November 17, 18, and 19) the floodwater receded, and by the twentieth, the Santo Tomás campus was reasonably clear of water. In all, the storm had produced broken shanties, ruined gardens, layers of mud, waterlogged baggage, and a total of twenty-seven inches of rain. Notes Hartendorp solemnly, "No serious illness developed as a result of the experience, though there were some colds contracted. No doubt the recent inoculations against cholera, dysentery and typhoid averted more serious consequences" (II, 30).

Apparently, the damage to both Los Baños and Baguio was insubstantial. Crouter, for example, makes no mention whatsoever in her diary of any weather problems from November 13 to 19 (Crouter, 236–238), though Hamilton mentions winds and heavy rain (71). Halsema agrees with Crouter, claiming that Camp Holmes was not affected at all by the storm, which was much more south and generally inland (ltr, May 21, 1997). Nor is there any report from Bacolod, because most of the camp (including Bryant and Vaughan) had already transferred to Santo Tomás before the storm hit.

In an interesting side note, Vaughan tells of the storm as it hit Manila proper. Outside Santo Tomás, in Remedios Hospital because of illness, Vaughan saw the town's devastation firsthand: "Torr.r tial rains fell for three days and nights until water in the streets rose to waist level and hastily constructed bamboo rafts (bamboo poles tied together with strips of rattan) replaced motor . . . traffic" (Vaughan, November 14, 1943, 245).

Her two small children, staying with a friendly Swiss couple, also watched the storm goggle-eyed. Here Vaughan inadvertently suggests a strange perspective — in this case, how children growing up inside an internment camp saw Japanese abilities and power. On a visit to Vaughan in the hospital, her three-year-old daughter Beth turned to her little brother and announced (as she looked out the window onto the flooded streets), "Look at what the Japanese have done, put all this water here!" (November 14, 1943, 247). To small children shushed, watched, lectured, and warned about the guards, the Japanese undoubtedly seemed capable of imposing *any* hardship on their prisoners, even a typhoon.

A few weeks after the storm, all the internment camps finally received the long-awaited U.S. Red Cross parcels. The *Teia Maru* had brought the parcels on its return trip, and they were distributed to three camps: Los Baños, Santo Tomás, and Baguio (internees from Davao and Cebu having already been or in the process of being moved to one of the previous three larger camps). According to figures that Carroll Grinnell supplied to Hartendorp, Baguio received 520 food parcels and Los Baños 1,020. Santo Tomás, with the largest population, obviously received the greatest number of kits—over 5,000 (Hartendorp, II, 53). Briefly, everyone not only had enough to eat but also had such luxuries as butter, chocolate and meat paste. Here indeed were vital supplements and a means to stay healthy when the chow line was only able to provide two slim "meals" a day to adults—meals of squash, moldy rice, and greens; even bananas had disappeared in Santo Tomás's Line (Lucas, 106). The bonanza had arrived earlier on trucks at Santo Tomás on November 30, 1943, but was not distributed immediately because the Japanese insisted on inspecting the parcels. Grimly, the Executive Committee members watched as, "By order of the Japanese officers, internees ripped off the straps [binding four kit lots together] with screwdrivers or whatever was handy. The Japanese tore open the parcels with knives and chisels and dumped out the kits. Then they opened these in the same way. They began by thrusting the chisels into cans of meat and salmon" (Hartendorp, II, 49–50). Luckily, only two lots of four were actually searched and ruined this way at Santo Tomás, though on Christmas Day at Baguio camp (Hamilton, 69) Japanese *kempei tai* ripped open several packages searching for inflammatory cigarette package wrappers stamped with "I Shall Return." The Baguio commandant Tomibe, however, as mentioned earlier, prevented both the final confiscation of loose cigarettes (he had them returned) and the destruction of entire kits, making sure the correct number of whole parcels evaded guards, police, and looters to reach Baguio camp safely (Tomibe, 42).

Grace Nash in Santo Tomás perhaps describes most movingly a typical family reaction to the arrival of the parcels—one kit of forty-eight pounds each, for every person, including children and babies (Nixon, 55). For the Nash family this meant five packages in all. These were not only treasures but lifelines:

Ralph carefully lifted out one section of the first kit. Fingers were all thumbs in the excitement and we wanted to shout to the rooftops when we beheld the delicacies inside: one pound of powdered Klim milk, a package of processed cheese, vitamin-ized chocolate, canned meat, packets of bouillon, prunes, tiny Vitamin-C pills so needed to offset the all-starch camp food! It was simply unbelievable! This wonder-ful food! We cried with joy and gratitude. (Nash, 137–138)

It is important at this stage to understand what the kits actually contained and the actual amounts, because it was the presence of this food supplement that helped most internees survive the year and two months until rescue. Each individual food parcel contained the following:

14 cans of preserved butter spread (oleomargarine, Vitamin A); 8 cans of corned beef; 6 cans of corned pork loaf; 4 cans of Spam; 4 cans of chopped ham-and-eggs; 4 cans of pate; 1 can of "party loaf"; 1 can "Prem" pork; 4 cans of salmon; 16 small envelopes (vegetable) bouillon powder; 4 cans of powdered milk; 4 packages of processed cheese; 4 packages of dried prunes; 4 cans of jam; 8 cans of soluble cof-fee [instant]; 8 cakes of chocolate; 4 packages cube sugar; and 24 Vitamin C tab-lets. (Hartendorp, II, 51)

Apparently, some kits were designed especially for invalids and so differed slightly in content, emphasizing different and richer foods (Hamilton, 70).

The extra vitamins, fats, minerals, and calories served, with extensive indi-vidual private rationing, to add to daily requirements for the next year, and, as we see in many accounts, they also provided special-occasion meals as well. Hamilton mentions several special birthday meals of hot cakes and syrup, as do Magnuson and Nash. Others tell of tiny family celebrations with meals cooked privately over native charcoal burners or of birthday food on the chow lines brightened by extra meat paste in their portion of stew or a teaspoon of precious jam on a portion of dinner rice. In Baguio, midnight "suppers" and even "picnics" were sometimes celebrated with long-rationed Red Cross par-cel food, as Halsema's 1944 diary attests.

Food, however, was not the only thing the Red Cross shipped to the camps, as medical supplies were also sent. Desperately needed drugs, bandages, medicine, and cases of surgical instruments made their way to Los Baños and Baguio, as well as to Santo Tomás. Additionally, supplies contained enough vitamins for a year for every internee, essential drugs (such as sulphathiazole) to treat tropical diseases and ulcers, surgical equipment, and even blood plasma, in addition to body and laundry soap, toothbrushes, and other per-sonal hygiene supplies (Hartendorp, II, 53; Nixon, 56). These, along with the extra food, helped lower what would have been a much larger death rate in the camps than actually occurred by the end of the war. One can only wonder what the morbidity and mortality rates would have been had *all* of the

American Red Cross parcels sent to the camps actually been delivered instead of the single distribution in December 1943, which was the only U.S. Red Cross food and medicine shipment both internees and POWs ever received in the Philippines (Waterford, 48; Rubens, 223).

The number "missing" despite recorded shipment is illuminating, even astounding. According to a report issued by the *Comité International de la Croix Rouge*, American and other foreign national Red Cross parcels and crates were being shipped out approximately every two months in 1942: 6,993 crates in July on the *Asama Maru*; 48,818 crates on the *Tatsatu Maru* in September; and 47,210 crates in October on the *Kamakura Maru*. By October 1943, 140,000 individual *parcels* were shipped on the *Teia Maru* (part of which arrived for the camps). A portion of these shipments may indeed have appeared in December 1942 in Santo Tomás as the Canadian and South African Red Cross parcel distribution. Both these and the other later shipments, such as those containing 80,000 multivitamins, which were shipped *weekly* in 1944 (Waterford, 43) were intended exclusively for POW and civilian internees in the Pacific (*Comité International*, vol. 1, 477, in Waterford, 49, n21), of which the largest number were in the Philippines. No shipments were seen after Christmas 1943.

Why then did the internees in the Philippines (and the POWs) generally receive only one parcel in all the years of confinement? There are several interlocking answers to that—and a fair proportion of blame falls on both the Japanese and the American governments. As Corbett explains in his discussion of the repatriation issue, the Japanese government agreed to allow the U.S. government to send relief supplies of food and medicine to the prisoners *only if* those supplies (and even mail) went on an exchange ship. In essence, if the repatriation and exchange process broke down, then vital supplies would not be sent (Corbett, 92–93).

Throughout the war, the repatriation effort suffered from some fairly bizarre problems—sometimes at the hands of the American FBI and the Southwestern Pacific Area (SWPA) commander, General Douglas MacArthur. As the shipment of vital supplies was tied to personnel exchanges, when the head of the FBI, J. Edgar Hoover, unilaterally violated a previous agreement with the Japanese made by the State Department and Special Division (in this case, performing body searches on Japanese repatriates), the Japanese, in a rage, not only held up the second repatriation but threatened to cancel it altogether (Corbett, 70). This exchange was the one carrying the 1943 American Red Cross parcels that the prisoners needed so desperately. Even though the Special Division's angelic second-in-command, James Keeley Jr., managed to smooth ruffled feathers and patch up an agreement so that the second repatriation could proceed, Hoover continued to cause trouble.

According to Corbett, the proposed third repatriation and exchange of 1944 died not so much thanks to J. Edgar Hoover as to General Douglas MacArthur, who refused to allow a combined number of 331 Japanese pearl divers and ship pilots held in Australia to be put on the exchange list: "MacArthur consistently advised against their [the pearl divers'] repatriation on the grounds that they possessed vital military information on the territorial waters of Australia" (99–100). Unfortunately, MacArthur's official view of the espionage risk posed by the pearl divers—with their supposed knowledge of the Australian coast—convinced the Australian government to deny their release, even though by this time the coastline was secure, thanks to American and Australian efforts earlier. MacArthur once more had shown his importance and power to those, including President Roosevelt and General George Marshall, who he felt were not supportive enough of his efforts and genius.

The result of this muscle flexing on MacArthur's part was the loss of the third exchange, even though the general was fully aware that the exchange ships were the only means of sending food and medicine to the prisoners. In 1944, the year of the worst starvation and disease in all the camps, this was a death sentence for many internees and especially POWs—most of the latter MacArthur's own former troops from Bataan and Corregidor. At the same time, MacArthur also managed unknowingly to ruin a British exchange as well (Corbett, 100–102).

What supplies did get to Manila didn't always reach the prisoners. Where did these vital supplies go? One answer may lie in what appears to have been a fairly regular Japanese practice—to confiscate the parcels and either divert them to the Imperial Army or store them in warehouses for possible sale at a later time back to the internees. As Hartendorp notes (and the Tokyo War Crimes Trials transcripts confirm), such practices occurred regularly. In 1942, for example, the Japanese kept Red Cross medical crates of sulfaguanadine, blood plasma, bandages, tape, and gauze, among others, in warehouses in Manila and then *sold* them back to the very internees for whom they were intended initially throughout 1942 and part of 1943 (Hartendorp, I, 331). Why did the Japanese do this? In the Tokyo Trials, during questioning of Suzuki of the Prisoner Information Bureau, Prosecutor Mornane investigated this question:

Q: With regard to Red Cross goods, did you authorize your staff to take Red Cross goods supplied for the use of prisoners of war?
A: Yes. (IMTFE, Reel 21, 27,224)

The defense, on a redirect by Counsel Freeman, seemed to attempt to rehabilitate the client by having him elucidate further (obviously expecting some sort of rationale to be given. It wasn't).

Q: Mr. Suzuki, why did you authorize your staff to take away Red Cross supplies?
A: That was lack of wisdom and virtue on my part. (Reel 21, 27,225)

Christmas festivities in 1943, made possible by those Red Cross parcels that did arrive, were somewhat elaborate, as the extra food infused additional energy and spirit in the internees. Carol singing, Christmas dinners, productions of the *Messiah* (complete with 100 voices and Lactogen can floodlights and borrowed evening gowns for the women performers in Santo Tomás [Nixon, 57]), and many other activities were put on in all the camps. Despite the deaths (three or four a week in Santo Tomás [Lucas, 100]) of those who had waited too long for the parcels of food and medicine to arrive, the internees did their best to try to celebrate the season, even though many were depressed to find themselves in internment for another Christmas. A somewhat grim little couplet expressing this sentiment soon made the rounds of Santo Tomás camp: "We were wrong before / But we'll be out by '44" (Magnuson, 62).

The year 1944 brought further disappointments rather than rescue, however. Food and health soon began to deteriorate with increasing rapidity. This was, of course, when the so-called "soldier's ration" was *officially* and openly applied to the internees. As we have seen earlier, the Japanese never truly provided this ration, though they kept repeating this claim during both the Manila and Tokyo Trials.

The Japanese gave several reasons for the insufficiency of the supposed soldier's ration, especially in the Manila area—beyond an obvious lack of desire to feed an enemy. Rice supplies in the Philippines, always in need of outside supplementation even before the war (they claimed), were low because of heavy U.S. Naval submarine activity. Enemy blockades prevented rice imported from Indo-China from reaching the Philippines. Secondly, according to the Japanese, they had little transportation to get the food to the camps, and what trucks or rail cars they possessed had to bring supplies from outlying provinces not only to internees and POWs, but to Imperial Army soldiers as well (IMTFE, Ishikawa testimony, Reel 21, 27,631–27,632).

Each of these rationales is simultaneously true and false by turn. Certainly, transportation was limited—though not unknown, especially for those with rank. The question of prewar rice production in the Philippines has already been partially addressed in the previous chapter but perhaps bears repeating here. Despite claims that "The Philippine Islands, though originally an agricultural country" had been importing rice from Siam and French Indo-China "even in ordinary times" (IMTFE, Muto testimony, Reel 25, 33,144), Wickizer and Bennett, and especially Horner, disagree. As Horner points out, citing figures in the *Orient Yearbook, 1942* published in Tokyo: "the import of rice . . . was relatively unimportant in the immediate pre-war years. For instance, in 1935, net rice imports totaled less than 5,000 metric tons while national production exceeded 2,000,000 metric tons. . . . [Before the war] the Philippines was virtually self-supporting in foodstuffs" (*Orient Yearbook*, 1942, 1029; qtd in Horner, 88). This is a fact with which Wickizer and Bennett's figures seem to agree (63ff). Though the Philippines, as of November 1941, had to import *some* rice, it was due probably to the 1938 and 1941 weather disasters (both flooding and drought) rather than to an endemic production problem (Danquah, 62–63).

In any event, Danquah points out that even weather disasters "cannot wholly explain the food shortages in this predominately agricultural country" (63) and goes on to cite, among other things, warfare, Japanese rice-buying practices in the Philippines, the amount of food shipped from the Philippines to the Japanese home islands, guerrilla activity in the provinces, the use of intraisland shipping and ship-building for military, rather than cargo, use, and the regular Japanese troop habit of confiscating food. As far back as December 1941, the invasion and fighting coincided with harvest time for rice and corn in the Philippines. Japanese military landings in Pangasinan and Pampanga and sorties through Tarlac and Cavite over land were, unfortunately, also invasions through major rice-producing regions. Because of the fighting, 30 percent of the rice crop and 20 percent of the corn crop that year were lost (64).

The Japanese accommodated for this scarcity by falling into a pattern that they would follow throughout the rest of the war in the Philippines: Troops "requisitioned" local harvests, as well as stray animals. They also slaughtered indispensable plow animals (such as carabao and cattle) to "fill in" for shortages of meat when meat shipments were delayed (Danquah, 64).

Japanese authorities also bought up all the rice they could find using an Imperial Army procurement agency in Manila, the *Beiko Kuba*, which regularly outbid local buyers, thereby stripping the area of grain and often other foods. What was left to the Philippine residents, under the Japanese-imposed Laurel government, was then rationed through *Bibasang Bayan* (BIBA), a procurement and distribution agency which supposedly preserved food stores for Filipinos. Historian William Pomeroy claims that BIBA "was the instrumentality for taking the staple food from the mouths of the people and channeling it to the Japanese" (123). Historical arguments aside, the lion's share of the rice went repeatedly to the Japanese and not to legal Philippine markets, given the terrible shortages evident in Manila, a metropolis that Lucas says by April 1944 resembled a "ghost city" with pinched-faced children and adults peering through the window (131). In regard to this misery, explains Lucas, the Japanese food administrator told the *Tribune* cryptically that "Filipinos should learn to suffer as suffering is a precious investment" (115).

Because rice production in Japan itself was weak (six months into the war, six major Japanese cities were rationing rice), the government decided to produce food in the conquered regions—both for home use and to feed occupation and invasion troops. The emphasis, on one hand, of trying to force Filipino farmers to conform to Japanese planting methods (including adding cotton as a crop, which took up rice-growing space), the constant Japanese confiscation of what *was* grown, and the continuing large-scale theft of private food and animals soon produced a near-famine in the urban areas of all the major islands, but especially around Manila on Luzon. These actions (and Japanese rice hoarding) soon caused a steady migration of people from Manila to outlying areas. Despite Japanese propaganda to the contrary, "food abounded in the rural areas, but [was] virtually inaccessible to urban markets due to Japanese army requisitions" (Danquah, 65–67). In the mountain provinces on Luzon from 1943 to 1944, for example, dried water buffalo meat, dried fruit, wild pig or fresh deer, fresh eggs, and often chickens could be had cheaply. Eggs ran about 1¢ each and a large chicken, 15¢ (Danquah, 72).

The problem, besides Japanese confiscation (and probably because of it), was that constant guerrilla action in the outer provinces often prevented rice crops from making it to the urban areas; this, in turn, made the Japanese army even more savage in its policies and in its "requisitions." Confirmation of this comes from an interesting source: the guerrillas themselves. A famous American female guerrilla leader on Luzon, Yay Panlilio, describes the situation and the insurgents' feelings:

> Guerrillas and civilians alike clawed for food. . . . He got the grain of rice who reached it first, and over and over again, the Japs reached it first! Jap patrols guarded the reapers in the paddies, not from "misguided elements" but from the very hands reaping their own self-planted seedlings. . . . Jap ship after ship *left* Manila heavy-laden, low in the water and sluggish. [italics mine] (Panlilio, 214)

As we saw from Vaughan's entries, among others, the Japanese regularly bled the islands of food and supplies to supply Japan.

Because of this situation and the manner in which the Japanese stripped the Philippines of its own products to benefit Japan, the "Harvest Struggle" began. Anti-Japanese guerrillas ordered head men in villages to secure all harvestable rice crops either by threshing and hiding them from the Japanese or by setting the crop on fire if there was no time to get it harvested and hidden. The "directors" of the struggle were also responsible for ordering Japanese threshing machines to be burned or otherwise disabled and for forbidding food to be sold even to Filipinos from urban areas if only to ensure enough food for local villagers. In addition, guerrillas plastered every available surface in rural areas with slogans such as "No Rice for the Enemy" and "Keep the Food of the People" (Danquah, 74–75).

To see that "scarcity" was a term on Luzon applying primarily to the law-abiding, or the Manilaños, one has only to read spy Claire Phillips's account of Manila during the war. She discusses the large storehouses of rice in the city ready to be shipped to Japan and the flourishing black market trade run by Japanese officers. Phillips, posing as a black marketeer, made a deal with a Japanese naval officer in charge of one of the warehouses. He sold her, directly from the warehouse, a substantial number of sacks of rice for P 100 a sack. Her men came secretly to the back of the warehouse, loaded the sacks on a truck and took them away. Later, without Japanese knowledge, Phillips smuggled the sacks and purloined medicine back into POW and internee camps, especially Cabanatuan (Keith, 115–118). According to Phillips, even in Manila in 1944 there was rice to be had—for the right price and by greasing the right palms (130–131). By late 1944, however, even the black market tightened, as supplies from conquered Japanese territories, even from the major rice producer in the Pacific, Vietnam, failed to arrive in transit to Japan. There were, according to Danquah, just too few transport ships to carry the grain— a condition only *in part* due to American submarine depredations. As Danquah points out, the Japanese Empire lacked adequate tonnage even at the beginning of the war. The Japanese had deliberately limited their production of cargo ships before the war to make more military ones (78). With the Japanese tripling the occupation forces in the Philippines in 1944 (from 64,000 to approximately 192,000) and their lack of transport, obviously rice was at a premium (65; 75). The black market was only available to those with money and only then for a limited number of goods. Those without money starved outside the camps, as those in the camps were to do also by late 1944.

During this same year, the "soldier's ration" began to shrink ominously. The Japanese military, instead of continuing the previous monetary per diem, now switched to a ration "in kind" to substitute for the per diem. This ration started not at the promised 1,750 calories (the soldier's official ration), but at 1,600 per person (half for children). By September 1, this dipped to 1,350 calories a day; by October, it was down to 1,100 (Butler, 642).

It is interesting to understand the exact nature of the so-called "soldier's ration" and to explore why this ration proved insufficient, even for nonfighting civilians, the elderly, and babies. The Japanese Imperial Army drew up a set number of grams of rice, fish, vegetables, oil, and salt to constitute the soldier's per diem ration. This ration, according to the Hague Agreement and parts of the 1929 Geneva Convention, was supposed to apply to both civilian internees and POWs. Unfortunately, the actual ration the internees received did not remain constant and diminished quickly. In the first place, the 250–300 grams of rice (an official two-day ration) was given in *unhusked* rice (Evans, 463); according to experts, at least for rice grown in a monsoon country such as the Philippines, husks make up 25 percent of the total weight of the rice — 25 percent, that is, which cannot be eaten (Wickizer and Bennett, 102). By this reckoning, already the official 150 grams per day actually means 102.5 grams of edible rice. This, however, was probably not exact either, because the kind of rice the Japanese gave the internees, in addition to being unhusked, was "paddy or rough rice" and usually contained bits of stalk, rat droppings, and possibly dirt and pebbles (Wickizer and Bennett, 63) — hence the need for the internees to "pick" and "clean" the rice as a work assignment. Obviously, debris not only might have added weight, but also might have decreased the sheer amount of usable rice.

Even these official camp figures were probably optimistic. They did not, for example, account for the deliberate and continuous short-weighting of rice sacks that went on (as indicated in the Manning report from Los Baños, in which a 5 percent short-weight on the sacks was consistent [Hartendorp, II, 443, n1]). Obviously, no one was truly getting 100–150 grams of rice a day either; indeed, the Japanese included the *accompanying* vegetables the ration promised (actually camote tops, talnium greens, and occasional mung beans) in the "extra rations" category (above the "normal" ration) in September 1944 — and their weight was deducted from the original allowance in Santo Tomás. The promised fish materialized, if at all, as fish heads and eyes, though occasionally a handful of tiny fish went into soup for several thousand diners. No internee mentions getting a ration of oil, and indeed salt was frequently held back as a punishment.

Those with an eye to the future started making provisions for even harder times to come. One of these, Mrs. Jessie Bell Hanson in Santo Tomás, told Frederic Stevens she made preserves from rationed remnants of the Red Cross parcels, as well as from local stores she had earlier bought from "outside." With these, she concocted "bomber bread," a kind of emergency hardtack that wouldn't spoil, made of salt and rice flour, soda, shortening, and vinegar. When baked, after being cut out with a discarded corned beef can top, this produced small, hard, square loaves that were easily stored (Stevens, qtd in Waterford, 74).

"Bomber lotion" was perhaps another way of preparing for even harder times. This was illegal alcohol made out of fermented raisins and orange and pineapple pieces in a secret camp still. It was, says Lucas, "specially designed to soothe the nerves in times of crisis" (107), and it certainly preserved the raw ingredients in a resourceful and compact manner.

The internees dealt with the food crisis starting that August with their usual grim aplomb. Eva Nixon points out that, although the increasingly inadequate rations led to arguments, friction, and ill-feeling even in family groups and among friends, internees managed to avoid civil wars through a strict application of democratic rules:

> When everyone was hungry, equal division became all important. In the days when there was enough rice, my friends and I who ate together would get three rations of rice in the same container. We then helped ourselves family style to as much as we wanted and gave the rest away or saved it for the next meal. But when the ration was slashed, there would always be only a spoonful of rice or gravy left in the can. "You take it, you need it more than I do. . . ." "No, I think you should have it because you have to work on night duty." So the one who finally did take it felt like a glutton as the others sat watching in agony. We solved the problem by beginning each meal with carefully measured equal division. (65)

Camp practices in terms of food and sanitation also reflected the tightening of rations in Santo Tomás. Camp rules would soon forbid any can owner to lick out his or her private can (filled on the communal chow line) after eating—not because of a fear of germs so much as because of the waste of possible food: "The cans had to be rinsed out and the rinsings put back into the soup or mush for the next meal." Not even stray crumbs could be wasted. Burned rice at the bottom of the huge camp cooking cauldrons, once thrown away as inedible, later was given on a first come, first serve basis to those waiting in line for the scrapings. Eventually, the burned rice was kept and ground up to be put back in the soup (Nixon, 65).

Baguio (Holmes) camp also saw the doubtful nature of any "in kind" measure of official rations. A February 1, 1944, entry from James Halsema's diary explains:

> The food problem now rests more or less on the shoulders of the Jap Army quartermaster and we're still worried, more or less. First consignment of chow, including a case of Japanese tea, sugar, local Price in wooden buckets, fish, a small pig, about 30 sacks of Saigon rice, pickled radishes, cabbage brought in today. . . . Food bids fair to be a foul problem. Meat and fish are short-weight. J QM [quartermaster] would not allow them to be weighed before our truck brought them from Hoover rice bodega. (1944 diary)

Los Baños was faring as poorly or even more so than Santo Tomás and Baguio at this time. By July the internees had used up most of the Red Cross kits, and families faced the beginning of real deprivation. Even this would, perhaps, be merely a prelude to something worse in the future — or so internee actions indicated. They rationed whatever meager supplemental food they had left. No longer optimistic, they planned on yet another Christmas in camp. The little jingle from a year before now turned bitter: "Out in '45 / If we're still alive" (Magnuson).

Margaret Sams, after transfer to Los Baños with her son, David, her new baby Gerry Ann, and her future husband Jerry Sams, contemplated the dwindling supplies not with panic but with a kind of grim determination:

> We decided we'd pool our Red Cross kits and use one can a day to supplement the rice and soup that we were given on the Line. We thought the cans might last the duration, but before many weeks passed it could easily be seen that they would be a thing of the dim, dark past long before we were liberated. We decided to save a can of salmon for Thanksgiving, and a can of Spam for Christmas. We set aside a can of Gerry Ann's precious powdered milk to cover all eventualities. (214)

Rations in all the camps continued to fall shorter and shorter, or to arrive sour, spoiled, or inedible. Rations of fish did come to Baguio camp, for example, but they were usually dumped in a filthy pile on the supply-shed floor, half spoiled. Their unsavory condition could be directly traced to the use of dynamite to catch them (Halsema, 1944 diary, February 15).

The internees continued to try to make the best of an increasingly severe situation by substitutions. Mary Ogle mentions a number of these — and they provide an unexpected index to the internees' determination. The native root vegetable *gabi* (earlier grown by Ethel Chapman), for example, was "not bad" if seasoned with onions, cut up, and fried as hash browns or put in chunks in mock potato salad. *Chayote* (a gourd earlier brought to the Philippines from Guatemala), when used as a filler for stews was palatable and even better if baked and served with tomato sauce. Sweet potato leaves could be eaten as salad greens, and cassava root, after being sliced thin, sun-dried, and ground into powder, made decent flour. The latter thickened sauces beautifully, though after the food cooled the thickening tended to deteriorate. Green papayas, ground up, substituted for applesauce, and mashed bananas, whipped hard, could be used in place of increasingly scarce eggs in baking, or served as the main dysentery diet (Ogle, 211–212). Coconuts, while they lasted, served as the all-purpose food item and camp "cow." The coconut liquid from the center was saved "for fermentation to use in our baking to provide the element for soda to work on" (213). Shredded coconut meat, covered with water and steeped, then squeezed out, provided "milk" for morning cereal; it could also be browned over low heat and made into a sweet to eat. Coconut "milk" let stand overnight would provide a thick cream-like substance that rose to the top and could be made into "butter" (213–214). There was even a form of bread on which to put this coconut butter, because the "chief scientist finally succeeded in developing yeast and the bakers began to bake." All families, incidentally, were allowed a start of yeast for personal baking, if they chose (215).

Mary Ogle's recipe for "corn bread" made near the end of 1944 in Baguio provides a sense of both the wit and the shortages in camp:

> Take one cup of soft rice left over from breakfast, one cup of corn-meal mush, one cup of water and three tablespoons of vinegar made from soured coconut water, one cup of corn meal and one cup of rice flour or cassava flour, one teaspoon of salt and one teaspoon of soda. Dump it into a greased iron skillet, slap on the lid, and stick it under a firebox of hot coals under the large caldrons in which food for five hundred is cooked. If it doesn't burn up, it will come out wet and soggy on top and is guaranteed to give indigestion to the strongest man. (217)

Soon, for the hungry internees, dangerous foraging while on outside work parties for the camp or forbidden secret arrangements with the less ferocious camp guards became worth the risk. Jerry Sams, at Los Baños, did both, managing to trade with a guard for duck eggs and fresh milk for the baby. He also gathered fresh ginger and tiny native tomatoes in his jacket while out chopping wood. He was lucky. The right guard was on the gate and let him through without close scrutiny of his clothing (Sams, 215). Later, people would be shot for foraging, even though Los Baños was located in the middle of an experimental agricultural station with acres of bananas and coconuts. As Sams explains, "I thought then, and still am inclined to think, that the Japanese have a perverted sense of humor. They could as easily have let us collect coconuts, or bananas, or cassavas, or any of the other fruits that were there for the taking. But no, we could have [only] wood with which we could cook our miserable handful of rice, if we weren't too tired to walk after the wood, that is" (213–214).

By July, Santo Tomás was also experiencing indifference to internee hunger, as an indignant nurse, Tressa Cates, describes in a diary entry:

> One of the cruelest things the Japanese did to a group of desperately hungry people was to refuse to accept the carts of food that were sent to our camp by Manila organizations. Day after day, fruit, vegetables, and eggs were sent in pushcarts, which were left standing outside the gates, while representatives of charitable organizations pleaded with the Japs to permit them to give us the food. But our benevolent jailers told them that we had sufficient food, and we sadly watched them wheeling away the carts. For this cruelty and falsehood, we hated them. Our hate intensified when we saw the listless children and the old men and women in advanced stages of beriberi and other deficiency diseases. (Cates, July 13, 1944, 209)

Butler agrees, pointing out in his article that, after July 1944, "the food at the camps became extremely inadequate; weight loss, weakness, edema, paresthesia and beriberi were experienced by most adults," as was a significant and accelerating weight loss (640).

Thus began the last seven months of increasingly acute deprivation. Internees such as Magnuson, who had earlier turned up their noses at weevils and cockroaches in their lugao, now ate them down hungrily as possible protein sources. Plants of all kinds—sometimes poisonous and deadly—began appearing in private dinners; pigweed, hibiscus flowers, climbing wandering jew, and lily bulbs (the last nearly fatal) gradually, then progressively, supplemented internee portions (Nash, 161; Cates, November 20, 230–231; Carlson, 133).

New camp rules at Santo Tomás also illustrated the depth of the hunger and the edge of desperation that had crept in. Near the end of 1944, "the camp made a rule against picking weeds for *personal* use. One millionaire, in fact, received a fifteen day [internee] jail sentence . . . by the Committee on Order because he picked some pig weed for his own private use" (Nixon, 65) (italics mine). Internees whose job it was to peel the camp vegetables and who had, in the past, gotten to take home any peelings or seeds, were forbidden to do so anymore. According to those checking the tables, the peelings were becoming dramatically thicker. The usual "mad scramble" for garbage under the kitchen tables was also forbidden, and a ration system for refuse was instituted after a woman "accidentally" cut another woman across the hand with a knife when the victim struggled with her under the table over a choice piece of garbage. Finally, even rationing garbage and peelings had to stop: "The vegetables were not peeled. They were washed, cut up, and put in the soup or gravy, peelings and all, to make enough to serve the camp" (Nixon, 66). "Garbage" ceased to exist.

Repeatedly, Japanese officials cut the camp rations as their military losses increased and MacArthur's expected return drew nearer. Nurse Tressa Cates's account reveals the internee hunger in its inexorable march forward. On September 15, 1944, Cates writes that the Santo Tomás commandant cut the camp ration, and the following entry describes the effect: it was "a bitter blow. Our people were desperately hungry. They looked like scarecrows with their scrawny bodies, listless manner, and with that anxious mask that we all wore those days" (September 16, 217). An October 13 entry speaks against the increasingly severe diet in camp and the internee protests—both verbal and written—which the camp commandant repeatedly brushed aside with the same maddening answer: "The Commandant repeatedly reminded our leaders that we were on the same rations as the Japanese soldiers" (221). The drumbeat of hunger continued with both a November 15 and November 20 rice cut. Cates's diary on November 29 notes, "Six of our neighbors . . . became violently ill today from eating lily bulbs" (232).

Baguio (Holmes) camp, too, felt the pinch. An October 1, 1944, entry in Halsema's diary mentions that there were a "surprising number of normal men" (that is, not obviously sick) who now weighed possibly twenty or thirty pounds less than they did at the beginning of internment. A later entry (October 4) notes that the Executive Committee finally voted to distribute emergency food reserves.

An anecdote about Los Baños camp in December 1944 offers yet more evidence of the skimpiness of rations—as well as many internees' ability to make light of their hunger. According to Jane Wills, once she arrived in Los Baños, she ran into one of the men she had known earlier at Davao. Merle invited her to join his bridge group, which played every week. The stakes alone tell the story: "We'd play all afternoon with the stakes of maybe an egg or a banana. I never knew where the treats were coming from, but I didn't ask questions. Merle and I frequently won the set. Merle was always a gentleman and gave me the prize to take back to my family" (23).

These last seven months in the Los Baños camp saw the actual face of sadism appear as second-in-command Lt. Sadaaki Konishi, a supply officer, arrived from Santo Tomás. His obvious and often-expressed hatred of Caucasians soon put a shiver of despair down the spines of the prisoners. Grace Nash, just transferred with her family from Santo Tomás, had no doubts of Konishi's intentions and of what would be the nature of life under him: "Lt. Konishi arrived to instruct us in the inferiority and degradation of the white race and the superiority of the Imperial Japanese as exemplified by General Homma . . . he [Konishi] was the ban[e] of our existence in Los Baños camp. Our rations were cut severely; petty persecution, continuous orders and change of orders began. And there would be more, and more, and more" (152).

Konishi's deliberate cruelty became evident almost as soon as he arrived in camp. In mid-fall 1944, Konishi told Bennett and a group of other starving internees they had permission to carry away as many hundred-pound sacks of rice from the Japanese storage shed in camp as they could and put them in the camp kitchen. After watching the emaciated and weakened prisoners struggle gamely for an hour to carry out as much rice as possible, Konishi waited until they were finished and then informed the panting men he had changed his mind *and ordered them to carry all the sacks back into the shed* (Arthur, 109; Terry, 71). They did not receive even one ounce of rice for this exercise, except what stray grains the children could sweep up from the ground after the move.

Nor was Konishi satisfied to turn the screw using only simple cuts in calories or false promises. He also confiscated produce from the Los Baños internee private gardens and, as an added insult, declared that all such produce was now to be regarded as part of the official ration per person—no longer as a private source of supplementation. Next Konishi cut the salt ration and watched as, soon afterward, internees writhed with salt-deprivation cramps in the hot sun. His explanation was that the salt was needed in Japan for "munitions." Eventually, he did restore the salt ration—but only because its lack incapacitated too many internees and prevented them from working (Arthur, 109; Lucas, 167). He next threatened the camp children by cutting their rations in half and eliminating eggs. This especially affected those under age five, who had, despite camp restrictions and by tremendous camp sacrifice, been given an egg a day. Adult rations in Los Baños were also cut repeatedly, and soon even obviously plentiful bananas, camotes, and beans were rarely seen.

Konishi's cruelty needs to be mentioned here if only to refute the notion that his part in the seeming policy to starve internees was due merely to circumstances, rather than to his own desires. According to Anthony Arthur's research, Konishi had a truckload of fruit dumped unceremoniously on the asphalt just inside the camp. The supply officer told the internees they could return at 4:00 P.M. and eat as much of the fruit as they wanted. For four hours the fruit sat piled on the blacktop in 110° heat; when the internees returned at 4:00, "the fruit had already rotted into a fly-blown, putrid pile of garbage" far beyond scavenging (109). (Internee Carol Terry remembers the incident but recalls that the pile was made up of fresh greens, instead of fruit [71].)

No one seemed to know why Konishi did these things, though everyone in camp suspected it had to do with his racism—after all, he called himself "the strongest white race hater in the army" (Nash, interview). As Dower points out, it was not impossible for a Japanese soldier to be a racist. After all, "The problem of racism is often approached as if it were a one-way street named white supremacism. . . . The many attitudes that come together to comprise racial consciousness, however . . . are hardly a monopoly of white people" (179). Still, racism may not have been the complete answer. Others believed Konishi's cruelty was due to mental deterioration brought on, possibly, by either alcohol or syphilis (Nash, interview). For whatever reason, a variety of internees recall Konishi telling them that before *he* was through with them, they would "eat dirt and grass." (In other internee versions, it is "rocks and dirt" or "sticks and dirt.") Nor were the internees the only ones who tried to avoid his ire; Lucas remembers that "even Masaki, one of the friendly guards admitted . . . that he was worried about the camp. In his opinion, the Commandant was a coward and Konichi [*sic*], a crazy drunkard" (Lucas, 182).

Other guards, including Ito, a Japanese Christian whom Carol Terry mentions, also feared their commander. When possible, Ito would allow bits of food in from the outside but only small amounts and always while looking nervously over his shoulder (72).

Other guards also showed that racism was not always a trait of Japanese soldiers. The Carlsons' three-year-old, Larry, was a favorite with many of the Los Baños camp guards. Even in the later, food-starved months of 1944, they frequently furnished him with tidbits of food, on one occasion giving him "a coconut so large he couldn't carry it home." Carlson explains that Larry kicked it all the way back to their barracks, though besieged by other internees who jokingly called him the "littlest collaborator" and pretended they were going to take his coconut. Larry, however, was adamant, explaining that "I can't give this to you. I'm going to take it to my Daddy" (134).

Other times, Imogene Carlson had to try to limit not only the guards' generosity to Larry but even, once or twice, that of several internees as well. Even during these terrible times, as he toddled around the camp, the guards (and an occasional internee) would give him "a bite of this, a spoonful of that, a sip of cocoa or lime juice everywhere he went." This soon produced stomachaches and vomiting, which wasted all the nutrients Larry had managed to acquire in this fashion — and from family meals earlier. Despite the camp hunger, then, Imogene pinned a note on the back of Larry's sunsuit reading: "Please do not feed me anything!" (133).

Being the parents of a popular child had its advantages. Carlson adds that another guard, "one of Larry's admirers," brought a small bag of desperately needed salt to the Carlson family and gave it to them, in honor of their son (137). Another soldier, also fond of Larry, visited the little boy and saw how meager were the portions to be split among the four Carlsons. "The soldier, shaking his head sadly, said, 'Very little, very little.' He looked sad and sympathetic with our poor rations and left right away. The next morning, he came in again with his chow bucket filled with rice cooked with tiny fish and gave it to Ray" (138). Given this sort of behavior by some of the guards, obviously, Konishi was distinctive for his sadism rather than common in his excessive xenophobia and racism.

What Konishi's antics show (besides his cruelty) is another dark fact: Even late in 1944 food was available. The Japanese authorities, for whatever reason, simply refused to give it to the prisoners. Fruit, greens, vegetables — none of these came into the Philippines by ship. Like the Red Cross parcels stuffed away in Japanese warehouses, this was food easily available and not subject to the supposed depredations of the U.S. Naval blockade. A deliberate policy to starve the internees seems to have existed, since not only a lunatic like

Konishi cut rations, but so too did those apparently sane officers in Santo Tomás and even, finally, in Baguio (Holmes).

Tragically, Konishi's mad threats seemed to come true by late October and early November in Los Baños camp. By then, the internees were trying to exist on about 900 calories per day (unsupplemented). Many began regularly picking through the Japanese guards' garbage for scraps, fishing out and boiling stripped carabao bones and gagging down bits of rotten vegetable (Arthur, 97). No plant or even invertebrate was safe. In addition to the earlier mentioned pigweed or lily bulbs, the hungry internees now stewed morning glory seeds and tomato leaves, fried banana skins, and slugs. Snails, earthworms, cornsilk, grass, and even a cactus plant got consumed in the desperate rush for supplemental calories. Rubens, now in Los Baños, explained that she and her husband had to quit eating their cactus plant, despite its "fresh apple-like flavor," because it "lacerated" her husband's stomach lining (226).

There was a rumor that stray dogs and cats were filling out the meager official ration (Lucas, 171; Arthur, 97). Arthur's famous anecdote about the demise of the Currans' pet dog at the hands of Dr. Nance, who wanted a nutritious stew for the children and the sick, is supported to a degree by other sources. Doris Rubens confirms that the dog was killed. She was one of the camp judges brought into the case, but the details of the dispute are hard to confirm (Rubens, 225–227; Arthur, 116–118). In any event, dogs, the court ruled, were not "private property" in a concentration camp (Rubens, 225). Certainly, anything from the animal kingdom that moved was eaten—along with anything vaguely edible that didn't.

Carol Terry describes the daily foraging activities she and her husband both watched and participated in at camp. She talks of collecting invertebrates and plants and explains:

> We gathered weeds and ate them. Someone put up a sign, "Keep off the grass. We eat it." We all ate garbage. When the Japanese let us have a banana, we ate it skin and all. We gathered slugs and ate them, but the cooking of slugs is a bit of a trial. They would keep crawling out of the frying pan and had to be continually pushed back until life was cooked out. There were a few dogs and cats in camp, and gradually they began to disappear as hungry Americans ate them. (67)

She adds sardonically, "Incidentally, cat is much more tasty than dog!"

Imogene Carlson apparently lacked Carol Terry's iron constitution—or perhaps her culinary skill. She discusses the problems in preparing nontraditional foods such as grass, explaining that when grass is cooked "it just turn[s] stiff and hard like straw" and becomes impossible to eat. Carlson adds that she herself couldn't eat slugs, though Ray ate them twice "and finally turned vegetarian again" (133). For some, apparently, there were limits to what one would eat even when starving.

Nor were things much better at Santo Tomás and Baguio camps. The Santo Tomás dietitian, Elvessa Stewart, reported that desperate foraging occurred in the large camp, and, even without Konishi, rations continued to be cut. Internees, according to the dietitian, soon "picked lawns and shrubs clean to eke out starvation rations" ("Manila Infamies," 52). The cuts at Santo Tomás also eliminated any special or extra food for children older than two years.

Even more of a general threat to life was the sad fact that whatever food the Executive Committee had squirreled away for emergency rations was soon confiscated by the captors. According to Hartendorp, the Imperial Army confiscated over *sixteen tons* of food from Santo Tomás, Los Baños, and Baguio (Holmes) camps between February and November 1944 (II, 440, n6; 442, n6). In all the camps, internees began to barter with the guards for a sack of mung beans or a kilo of extra rice or two bananas in exchange for wedding rings, engagement diamonds, Elgin watches (the guards refused inferior brands), and especially Parker pens (Rubens, 226; Nash, 175). The food the internees received after trading with the guards was often from food the latter had stolen from the bodegas in camp (Nash, 175). By the end of 1944, according to Cates in Santo Tomás, "Many of us believed that the Japanese planned to kill us by slow starvation" (December 20, 235). Frank Cary, too, despite his initial sympathy with his captors, agreed (ltr of January 21, 1945, 107).

Grim figures bear out at least the fact, if not the Japanese command's intention, of prisoner starvation. December 1944 saw Santo Tomás's internees existing on between 800 and 1,000 calories per day, while those in Los Baños lived on just below 1,000, and Baguio internees struggled on 900 a day (Butler, Table One, 640; Pearson, Table V, 1,000). Internees dreamed about food and sometimes woke themselves up snapping their teeth in hurried dream eating (Hartendorp, II, 436). Some, including missionary Judy Hyland in Baguio camp, were distressed to discover that their spirituality, as well as their stomachs, suffered under the sledgehammer blows of privation and hunger:

> To my dismay, I found the less I had the more grabby and thing-centered I became. Lack of material goods did not make me more spiritual. When one is hungry, it is not easy to concentrate on spiritual matters. The craving for food interfered with prayer life. How many times at night I would begin to pray—only to waken in the morning realizing that my mind had drifted off into a fantasy of bacon and eggs and pancakes. (Hyland, 76–77)

Health problems increased almost exponentially as malnutrition grew. By December 1944, 75–90 percent of the adults in Santo Tomás had edema (in camp called "wet beriberi," and a sign of hypoproteinosis), while Los Baños dealt with not only edema but additional cases of beriberi, pernicious anemia, scurvy, and dysentery (HEW, 35; Arthur, 107). Epidemics of measles, whooping cough, and influenza also swept through both Santo Tomás and Los Baños camps. By the beginning of 1945, edema was nearly universal in all camps. Described in an earlier entry, nurse Tressa Cates of Santo Tomás describes how this combination of lack of protein and low Vitamin B produced grotesque features: "By now, we all knew the symptoms. Each day, we examined our faces, hands, and legs for the telltale signs. Most of us had some symptoms, but what we feared most were the edematous legs that resembled useless and dead stumps of wood. Worse still were the distorted and large faces that resembled grinning Halloween pumpkins" (August 2, 1944, 212–213). This "famine edema" as it grew in the camps was a sign of critical malnutrition and caused more and more deaths. Malnutrition touched everywhere and everyone—even physicians. Bryant remembers a Santo Tomás doctor, Dr. Taylor, a formerly pudgy fellow of large appetite who left for Los Baños in April 1944. He later died of starvation, less than ten months before liberation of the camp in late February 1945 (173).

Camp Holmes internees in Baguio soon fared even worse than those in the other two camps. In the gray dawn, several days after Christmas, 1944, the prisoners found themselves bouncing out of camp in three groups of trucks that took them to Old Bilibid Prison in Manila. After a long, rough, and jostling two-day trip down partially destroyed roads, they finally passed through a series of three locked gates and arrived in front of a two-story building with iron gratings over the empty windows next to the compound of an emaciated and diseased group of American POWs, a sick remnant of survivors from Bataan and Corregidor. The internees were then assigned to cell blocks on their own side of the compound. Hyland tells about their introduction to life in the decaying prison: "We stumbled off the truck. Herb Loddigs fell in a heap and was carried off to the hospital cell blocks, unconscious. We had hardly any heart to try to make a place for ourselves on the dirty cement floor. There was no soap, so we had to try to clean out our spaces as well as we could with cold water" (96).

Food, if anything, was even scarcer at Bilibid than it was in any of the camps. From a ration of 900 calories a day at Baguio, the unfortunate residents of the prison now fell to only 700 calories a day—a ration completely lacking in vitamins A, B Complex, or C (Butler, Table One, 640). Medical facilities on the internee side were also unworthy of the name. Though the internees set up a "hospital" to be ready to deliver at least two expected babies, the hospital consisted of a "cold room, a tea strainer for an ether mask, a desk drawer for a crib . . . [the hospital] was in a cell on one side of the main building. This whole structure had been the hospital at Bilibid before the prison was condemned [by American authorities before the war]" (Shaplen, 68).

Jim Halsema's 1945 unpublished "Bilibid Diary" shows both of these aspects. The January 1, 1945, entry describes life in Bilibid:

> My moral[e] was low on the morning of my 26th birthday. For three days I've been lying on dirty sheets, myself only partly washed, bitten by ants, cooties, mosquitoes and an occasional scurrying bedbug. . . . The hospital, equipped and organized in Baguio for all medical work, is reduced [here] to beds, pills, and the few workers who carry on. Its esprit de corps is gone. The doctors are still fussing over their own family affairs. Most internees are tired, buggy and bitten. From my bed I see a high stone wall, above which is the roof of the [current] Bilibid hospital with a large Red Cross.

Halsema goes on to describe the diet of internees until rescue. Camp food consisted of cracked corn or rice twice a day along with "sometimes wormy and rotten camotes, soybean residue, camote tops" (January 23). Halsema also notes continuing trouble with "big green flies" and mosquitoes hovering over the open sewer ditch latrines in camp. Internees attempted to keep old mosquito netting over the latrines to prevent later food contamination, but it seemed to be too little too late, as dysentery swept the prison on both sides of the compound (January 27; January 23).

Santo Tomás inmates, without the grimness of prison walls and on a slightly larger number of calories per day (800, compared to Bilibid's 700), still twisted under increasing hunger. Cates's entry of January 26, 1945, is indicative of the state of food and mind in Santo Tomás shortly before rescue: "Hunger had become a living thing, like cancer. It ate into our bodies and minds. We thought of nothing else but food and hate" (242).

Again, as Hartendorp and others point out, this kind of hunger was completely unnecessary. According to Hartendorp, the following food supplies were *on hand* in Japanese bodegas in Santo Tomás camp on January 25, 1945, a day earlier than Cates's entry: 1,200 kilos of corn; 9,700 kilos of rice, and 3,400 kilos of soybeans. At a hypothetical consumption rate of 800 kilos per day, the supply would have been sufficient for the whole camp for at least thirty-one days (Hartendorp, II, 506), which would have lasted well past the actual rescue dates, even the late one at Los Baños.

On January 29–30 the Japanese, however, trucked away six loads of food supplies from Santo Tomás, releasing only 100 kilos of rice to the internees, along with some corn and soy refuse, mixed with 110 kilos of soybeans and 100 kilos of green papayas—thin supplies to feed over 5,000 internees. This resulted in a watery corn-soybean-papaya "stew" and an additional small spoonful of greens for supper that night. The next day, the Japanese had 4,000 kilos of the remaining rice from the bodega resacked into smaller bags; of this, they trucked away 3,200 more kilos of rice and sent it to the Japanese army. They substituted soybean refuse for the rice and sent this to the internees (Hartendorp, II, 511–513).

Without even the energy to scavenge by late January 1945, children in Santo Tomás and Los Baños camps showed the mental as well as physical effects of hunger. They sat and talked obsessively about future meals. Notes Cates, "The tremendously active kids that used to tear around the campus like savages were now little old men and women. Hollow-eyed, skinny, and listless, they sat around and talked about food."

Nash also discusses this change in Los Baños and the change in the children "too weak to romp or run" who leaned against the camp sawali fence and talked of nothing else by the hour but "the food they would eat when liberated. There was no conversation about movies, comics, or toys; just food" (181). In her own family, the only bedtime stories her children wanted the exhausted Nash to tell them at the end of the day were stories of the imaginary meals (in painful detail) that they all would eat after they were free (182). One sight in camp seemed to confirm the desperation Nash describes of those days: Imogene Carlson points out that her two children, Robin and Larry, "no longer played soldier. Now their game was funeral—funeral, imitating what their childish eyes saw everyday" (139).

As the deaths in various camps increased, so, too, did the Japanese administrative nervousness over the causes listed on internee death certificates. With American bombs exploding in the distance, visible squadrons of American war planes constantly flying over the camps, and news of American forces already on Luzon, undoubtedly the fear of future criminal charges had something to do with repeated orders the Japanese gave internee doctors to eliminate the official diagnosis of "starvation" from the hospital files.

The Japanese were well aware of the advancing and victorious American forces approaching the prison and civilian internee camps. This may even have been a contributing factor leading to the "Camp Freedom" period in January 1945 at Los Baños camp. At 3:30 A.M., January 7, internees awoke to hear the retreating sound of car and truck engines. After arising, a few adventurous souls found the camp deserted of officers and guards. Straining their eyes in the dark of early morning, they could just make out the last trucks pulling away from the main gates. Internees, still half asleep, poured out of the nipathatched barracks into the central compound as others yelled the news: "The Japs are pulling out of camp! They've turned it over, lock, stock, and barrel to our committee" (Ale, qtd in Nash, 192). They then renamed Los Baños "Camp Freedom" in honor of the occasion.

Grace Nash describes the camp chaos following the discovery of freedom:

> People were going crazy with the news. As we pushed aside the curtain over our entrance, we heard the last of the Japs driving their trucks out through the front gate. . . . Our friends and barracks inmates were rushing pell-mell through the *sawali* fence just across the road, into the Japanese barracks. Children and adults alike were milling and yelling into their quarters to loot—each one trying to get ahead of the other!
>
> Soon they streamed back, loaded with furniture, army boots, souvenirs, small sacks of rice or sugar—anything and everything. (192–193)

Though Grace and Ralph were disgusted by the looting and refused to let their boys participate, they and their friends celebrated freedom by breaking out almost the last of their hoarded food. Grace, Ralph, and friends were soon drinking real coffee with sugar, as they laughed and joked—the first real coffee (and probably true laughter) they had experienced in quite some time. A joyous camp committee issued double portions of mush for breakfast and reintroduced a noon meal of rice. Soon, Filipino traders returned to the camp to sell or trade with the internees in exchange for molasses, fruit, rice, and even carabao. The fact that the Filipino suppliers in the area had food to sell suggests that the Japanese claims of lack of food in the area were false, as Lucas points out (176).

The chow line meals in the camp improved steadily—so much so that almost all internees became ill from overeating, as their shrunken stomachs swelled with unaccustomed sufficiency. With rare foresight, however, the Internee Committee gave each person an extra five kilos of raw rice from the Japanese stores to keep for "emergency rations"—something that the Nashes did, but others did not (Lucas, 176; Nash, 193–194). For the next six days, using both its own emergency camp rations and supplies from the Japanese storage bodega, the camp ate well, and deaths by starvation briefly ceased.

On January 13, only a week later, however, internees were again shaken out of their sleep around midnight. This time the surprise was depressing and frightening: The Japanese were returning. Nash once again describes the scene: "Soon we heard their boots stomping up the road outside, a string of abusive profanity heralding their arrival. Our hearts sank in despair and fear. We got up quickly and hid our reserve ration of rice" (196).

The Japanese reoccupation of the camp had some severe repercussions. As Nash and Lucas both speculate, and Jim Halsema concurs, the Japanese were humiliated by their retreat, rebuffed by the superiors to whom they were supposed to report, and then forced to return. Additionally, when they returned, they found their quarters looted, illegal radios blaring, and the food bodega nearly cleaned out. Stern retribution was demanded. All looted goods had to be returned immediately (on pain of search, seizure, and death). The camp rice ration was cut, this time literally to a handful a day (Lucas, 176–177; Nash, 197). Fortunately, the secret emergency rations given at the beginning of the "Camp Freedom" period were still in many people's possession, hidden behind a wall or under a floorboard—available to supplement what was obviously an official starvation ration. In addition, the rice the Japanese now issued was the notorious unhusked *palay* rice. Internees had to roll each husk previously dried in the sun between boards repeatedly to get the grains loose. It was an expensive caloric effort for malnourished people to make for a very minimal nutritional return (Evans, 463).

Santo Tomás and Bilibid did not have even this illusion of freedom nor any sudden abundance of food (however short-lived); whether this was worse or better for the internees is hard to judge. The cruelty of the return and the reduced rations were harsher than daily life at Santo Tomás, though life there was also lethal by February 1945. Cates's diary entries describe the desolation and hunger gripping the camp. The Japanese butchered a carabao "while hundreds of starved people stood in a circle watching, hoping, and praying that they would receive a handout." After the carabao's carcass was taken away to feed the guards, the internees were allowed the "leavings": "Men, women, and children rushed to the spot and, like voracious dogs, they clawed around the blood, entrails, dust and grit, searching for tail, ears, hooves, or anything that resembled food" (Cates, February 1, 1945, 244). As Nixon points out, "Mothers soon disposed of the hide [which they were allowed to salvage] by deftly cutting it up and making food for their families." Other, more desperate souls who perhaps did not manage to get any hide took to cooking rats (66).

Two days later, Santo Tomás was liberated, and food began to flow into the camp, first from K-rations from individual soldiers and then from army supply kitchens. The soldiers gave the prisoners chocolate bars and other rich rations, despite medical warnings to the contrary. The young soldiers couldn't help themselves when they saw the condition of the Santo Tomás internees: "Their bodies were . . . wasted by hunger. The youths were pale and gangling and the old people were feeble and sick with diseases of malnutrition" ("Santo Tomás Is Delivered," 28). Their generosity cost some internees their lives. Just as in the case of Los Baños, the first food the prisoners received was often too rich and in some cases caused severe illness and even death. Quickly, the army learned to feed the liberated internees gruel, then mush, then more substantial fare.

In the dark confines of Bilibid Prison, the former Baguio internees sat waiting for release, existing on whatever food they had rationed. James Halsema describes their condition five days before liberation by American troops:

And here we sit, nearly 500 of us, hungry for decent food, for news of the world and our families, for comfort, for variety, entertainment, for freedom. Our every hope is pinned on the prompt arrival of our army—yet 3 weeks after the initial Luzon landing we know nothing of its progress. We live in a world of corn meal mush, mysterious explosions, boredom, partial exhaustion. Almost everyone has had or is having a debilitating bout of mild fever, sometimes accompanied by bone aches and nausea, which is called dengue for want of a better diagnosis. Sanitary conditions are very poor, health undermined by general malnutrition. ("Bilibid Diary," January 30, 1945)

Down to only 700 calories a day, sick internees forced themselves to eat camote greens or mush if they could, while those comparatively well found themselves stretched to the breaking point by having to husk their own rice.

Bilibid Prison was finally liberated on February 4, after the Japanese guards, in a move initially reminiscent of the Los Baños false dawn, silently left the camp after posting a notice that the prisoners inside were free (Halsema, February 4, 1945).

Los Baños camp, though it usually had more food than Bilibid, suddenly had less; its rations were cut even further—to none! Starving, they waited, and on February 23, a U.S. Army tactical group, along with a number of different guerrilla groups, liberated the camp in a dramatic end-run around Japanese troops in the field, taking the internees out on amphibious vehicles. Some internees at Los Baños were so sick, malnourished, and weak when relief arrived that the soldiers literally had to carry them to the vehicle and load them aboard. Hunger had left an indelible mark psychically on many, however, even during rescue. Ralph Nash, despite the pleas of his wife to get aboard the amphibious tank, continued, with the former barracks on fire overhead, to load a suitcase and to retrieve whatever personal food rations were still in their quarters. He made it out, barely, before the ceiling collapsed in flames. No matter what, he intended, it seemed, to make sure that his family wasn't going to starve (Nash, interview).

Others also could not seem to square hunger and rescue. Nash describes the chaos as internees hurried (or were carried) to waiting army vehicles to be spirited to safety; time was essential. However, "The sight of fellow prisoners plodding down that road toward the tanks ahead is one I shall never be able to erase from my memory. . . . Some had nothing in their hands but a tin of corned beef, ripped open, and they were stuffing the precious morsels into their mouths. Others were scooping out handfuls of cooked rice, eating it as they walked. It was hideous, and pathetic" (219).

Ultimately, liberation came just in time. By rescue, the average weight loss among internees was 52.9 pounds (or 32.5 percent of average body weight) — 20 pounds of it in the last four months. It is important to note that a 40 percent loss of original body weight usually results in death (HEW, 30; 34–35). Fortunately, the average weight going into internment had been slightly heavy, or the statistics of starvation would have been more severe. Pictures after liberation show the noticeable weight loss, especially the pipe-stem arms and legs of the men who gave up their food for women, children, and the sick. The next thinnest in the photographs are the women, who, in turn, often gave up their food for the children (ages two to twelve), who appear almost normal. Despite being only slightly underweight, they were noticeably short for their age group—a possible result of the calcium shortages (Butler, 647). The babies under two years seemed the least affected of all. Butler notes only a few cases of growth retardation; of the eight he discusses, only two were underweight at birth to four weeks, and only half were lacking an inch or two of normal length (Butler, 647). Again, the camp policy (in all three camps) of giving the children and infants under certain ages eggs and milk while supplies lasted was probably responsible for the relatively normal health of the very young.

Finally, though internees were not tortured or murdered outright, there can be little doubt that, at least at the level of the camp commandants and above, starvation was a situation *allowed to exist consciously*, even if not secretly ordered. This much is obvious from both the HEW reports and postwar doctors' examinations, as well as from internee diaries and retrospectives. On an individual basis, some guards showed great kindness to certain internees by secretly giving them extra food. One guard at Los Baños, for example, enjoyed Nash's violin playing so greatly that he privately requested pieces and repaid her with life-giving mung beans and eggs (Nash, 180–181). Another guard, this time at Bilibid Prison, helped Fern Miles by privately easing up to her when she was by herself and dumping a helmet full of Japanese rations in front of her saying, "You hungry. You eat" (Miles, 160). Generally, however, the Japanese were either indifferent or (more rarely) they were like Konishi or Abiko. Certainly, whatever extra food made its way into camp (whether on an individual basis or on occasions of charity to the whole camp) produced only a temporary blip upward in a larger, general downward pattern of calories and health. Only the timely arrival of American troops ultimately saved many prisoners' lives.

7 A Roof over Their Heads
Shelter in Civilian Internment Camps

If food and related health problems would prove to be the overreaching concern of the internees — and the aspects of camp life they usually remembered most vividly — still the nature of their housing and the work they did to fill their hours and keep up their domiciles occupied many paragraphs in both private diaries and later retrospectives. After all, the square footage of private space is so important to the quality of life in an internment or prison camp that there are specific requirements about it in the Geneva Convention (IMTFE, Reel 21, 27,124). The physical nature of housing, after all, affects personal privacy, marital relations, family life, and community relations; housing limitations by necessity also require utopian social policies and demand that the community's needs come before the individual's. Personal space soon becomes a thing of the past, and the snores, coughs, wheezes, and effluvia of a room crowded with fifteen to fifty people reoccur as a normal aggravation every night. Even (as was the case in Santo Tomás and eventually Baguio) with infants and small children housed with their mothers separately in another building, crying babies and screaming toddlers invade even the sanctity of the next building's peace. Noise is endemic in a camp, just as are lines, crowding, and personality conflicts.

The internee problem of overcrowding and lack of privacy becomes clearer when we consider the actual physical spaces involved, both public and private, in the different camps. Citing a specific population count for each camp is difficult, because it varied over time. An overall approximation, however, where it is illustrative of conditions, seems warranted. According to Waterford, there were 7,800 civilian internees in the Philippines. This number was made up of 4,200 men, 2,300 women, and 1,300 children, of whom the vast majority (6,000) were American. The next largest proportion were British or from the Commonwealth (1,500), and the rest were Dutch, Polish, Italian, Free French, Norwegian, and even Egyptian, among others (Waterford, 261; Pearson, 990). The majority of these either started, or ended up, in Santo Tomás Internment Camp in Manila.

Though Santo Tomás Internment Camp was the largest of the camps at between forty-three and sixty acres (depending on whether one counted the Fathers' spaces), as well as having six principal buildings to use for housing, it also had the largest number of internees (over 7,000 at one point) and the worst crowding. For those unable to live other than in the university's classrooms or gymnasium (and later, the annex, dormitory, and education buildings), it also presented the greatest problems for privacy. Indeed, as internees from outlying camps, such as Bacolod, Cebu, and Davao, found themselves transferred into the more centrally located Santo Tomás, the crowding became so alarming that, by May 1943, the Los Baños camp opened to help relieve the congestion. It is important in any description of space and housing to note the date; housing was at a premium, and dormitory rooms, classrooms, and the main gym exploded with the extra population right before the transfers to Los Baños (May–October 1943) or during the last six months of internment (September 1944–February 1945) when the Japanese finally interned those missionaries who had signed the cooperation pledge earlier in 1942. In the early months at Santo Tomás, however, when the population was between 3,000 and 4,000, people weren't sleeping in the halls or stacked shoulder to shoulder, although the camp was still crowded.

As predicted back in mid-1941 by the American Coordinating Committee,

Santo Tomás University with its campus grounds and buildings proved to be the best physical space for a decent internment camp. Its four-story concrete main building, the education building, the gymnasium, and the wooden annex housed the first 3,050 internees in early 1942, with the main building and its classrooms housing the largest number (1,500 initially). It is important to recall that each of these classrooms housed anywhere from 30 to 50 people, and the average floor space per person varied from 22 to 16 square feet (Hartendorp, I, 11).

Vaughan, transferring from Bacolod in April 1943, describes what might be called the "mature" camp — after the initial days of war but before the swelling population of the last six months. The main building housed most of the female internees, as well as the internee administration offices and some classroom space (ground floor); the second and third floors provided the majority of the classroom spaces for quarters, and the mezzanine floor held the camp library and the sewing area (with machines). The gymnasium housed the men; the balcony seats were torn out and extra cots for the men were put in their place, while every inch of the basketball floor held cots swathed in mosquito netting. The education building with its three stories had previously been a women's dormitory but now also housed male internees. A one-story cafeteria became the Japanese commandant's office (complete with a "Do Not Enter" sign over the door), and the annex in the rear of the main building was set aside for infants, children, and mothers, with a children's dining room, children's hospital, and a clinic. There was also a "well equipped" playground between the annex and the dormitory. The dormitory was a small building that housed older children and their mothers; once children reached twelve years of age they had to switch to the main building (Vaughan, April 19, 1943, 204). Two internees' accounts of their accommodations — one in the main building classrooms and the other in the annex — accurately portray the conditions under which most internees lived.

Frieda Magnuson, and her two-year-old daughter Susan, lived in Room 72 of the annex. In August of 1942, their classroom of approximately 20 by 22 feet housed eight women and twelve children. Even with only twenty bodies (rather than the thirty or forty that would come later), things were crowded: "Slabs had been constructed for our single mattresses with storage space underneath and mosquito nets overhead. We each had 36" of aisle space and heaven help anyone who infringed on the next person's space" (Magnuson, 53). To understand the quality of life in this limited space, we need to see the room in context, to remember the children quarreling, as well as the stumbling mothers, half awake, trying to arouse toddlers in the middle of the night to put them on the potty seat, and, of course, babies crying.

Alice Bryant transferred from Bacolod in mid-1943, eventually living in two different rooms. The first of these was a large room with approximately fifty women in it on the first floor of the main building. The only free bed was in the center of the room. Bryant remarks somewhat ominously that she "felt thoroughly unprotected" in the center bed. Possibly because of that — and also because a Bacolod friend's room had free space — Bryant transferred to a front-facing room on the second floor of the main building, right behind the flag-pole. Somewhere along the way she had gotten "custody" of a cot-sized wooden bed (with no springs), which she dragged into the room; luckily, the space assigned to Bryant was just long enough for the cot and 40 inches wide. She goes on to describe life in such a room: "The few inches of space not required by the bed, added to my neighbor's, Mrs. Forest's, few inches, formed a narrow aisle where we could dress and bump into each other. Fortunately she was a superior woman, and our collisions were only physical" (164).

As Hartendorp explains grimly, "Additional space in the rooms was not obtainable either by purchase or favor"; internee officials, despite some compatriots' suspicions, "were not a whit better off than anybody else" (I, 43). Here, too, understanding the ambiance of even this restricted space requires a more complete picture, especially about the nature of the night. Under curfew, internees could not roam after 10 P.M. and so were forced to be inadvertent and surly auditors of whatever went on. One internee remembers,

> Molly's bumping was indeed the major issue of the summer of '42 for Room Five, taking precedence over the battles of the Coral Sea and Midway Island. Molly accused Gill of kicking her twice in the night but, as Isla and May had proved, it was quite impossible to kick through two nets. "Someone else must have shaken you to try and stop you snoring," Isla told Molly. Molly's incredible grunts and snorts kept everyone awake. (Lucas, 42)

Alice Bryant speaks for many when she describes her distress over the lack of privacy she suffered in internment which was brought on by overcrowding and the "sub-steerage way of living" all experienced involuntarily in Santo Tomás:

> Hard as the hunger was to endure, for me the complete lack of privacy, of a moment's solitude was equally hard. . . . Oh for an opportunity to get away from them [roommates] and from everyone else! However, the only alternative to sitting in the room on my hard wooden bed was to go into the noisy corridor, which was worse. I bathed in public, jostling and being jostled in the crowded bathroom. Month after month I milled about in a mob. (168–169)

Nor was Bryant alone in such an assessment. Lucas even claimed that, due to heat, tension, lack of privacy, and overcrowding, from January to September

1943 the hospital was "crowded out with mental cases" (82). Though this perhaps overstates the case, a great number of internees from all camps recorded their obsession with space and their fury at the lack of personal privacy. Washing, sleeping, talking, sewing, cooking, reading, writing: None of these activities seemed to be done anywhere but in a crowd.

To maintain minimal civilization, camps such as Santo Tomás, as had other classic collectives and utopias in history and literature, decried individual taste and freedom of movement and instead instituted a jungle of rules. As Eva Nixon explains, there was "a rule for everything: when to talk, when to be silent, where to throw garbage, how to stand in line, how to walk down the hall, when to take a siesta" (27).

Breaking these rules infuriated others and threatened the camp's tenuous harmony. In such close quarters, even small violations of the rules loomed monstrous. As Dr. John F. Russell explains in an article dealing with the psychological effects of captivity, "The mundane becomes important" (252). Nixon, for example, once approached the laundry troughs with her wash only to discover that someone trying to get through the breakfast dishes more quickly by avoiding the mealtime wash line had used the facilities set up for laundry instead. A stern sign, all capitals, hung over one of the spigots: "NO WASHING DISHES HERE! THIS MEANS YOU!" (27).

Internees came to depend on rules to maintain whatever private spaces they could find. Regulations became barbed wire that fenced off one's own "property" — either physical or psychological.

Bryant, as did so many others around her, had to struggle to create personal space and a sense of privacy through stern imaginary boundaries and sheer determination. A friend lent Bryant a card table and two straight chairs. With these, a ragged tablecloth, and a flower, Bryant created a parlor for herself and the "Gov'nor" by placing the table and chairs next to a window in a downstairs corridor. She explains, "This, and the few feet of space it occupied in the crowded corridor, were our nearest approach to home" (165). Here she and the Gov'nor and sometimes friends worked sorting and making up bunches of the surplus greens from the Gov'nor's garden to give to friends in need. Here, too, Bryant and her husband ate their meals, rather than in the "crowded, noisy, and smelly" dining hall (165–166). Despite grumbling, other internees respected the Bryants' "squatters' right" to the space by the window in the corridor. Possession of space in the camp was not nine-tenths of the law, but all of it.

These squatters' rights also applied to personal resting places on the lawn or steps (for those without stools or camp chairs) and even to outdoor cooking spaces for those who wished to cook additional food (or their camp rations) on their own for themselves and their families (Hartendorp, I, 43). Bryant, for example, "inherited" Mrs. Miller's cooking space when the latter went to the hospital. Even with a reserved cooking place, however, all was not smooth sailing. A cook also needed fuel of some kind — something very hard to find by early 1944. Most fences and some trees had already disappeared, so great was the need. Bryant was blessed, however; others, poor creatures, did not have the Guv'nor for a husband. As Bryant explains, she was able to "fan up a fire made from trash the Gov'nor found while rummaging through dumps of refuse in search of compost." Soon "wonderful" meals appeared — for example, one made from a third of a can of corned beef (from the Red Cross parcels), spiced with withered cloves of garlic and fried in slightly rancid margarine (175). With a bit of sour rice cooked several days before, and a "considerable quantity of green stuff" from their garden, Bryant was able to invite a neighbor, Mr. Easthagen, to come to dinner at the "private" table in the corridor.

As Lucas and Bryant both pointed out, however, publicly cooking one's food could imply hoarded stocks of food and it seemed wrong to prepare their food in front of those whose stocks had already run out. Indeed, even a bit of bone obtained by stealth from the Japanese officers' mess lost much of its appeal because of fear of camp censure and misjudgment: "We were afraid that those who saw it — we had to eat in public — would think we had stolen it from the *camp* kitchen, to which the enemy did sometimes donate bones" (Bryant, 177, italics mine).

Lucas describes a typical morning scene in Santo Tomás, as various private cooking fires, dotted around the patios and grounds, smoldered away: "Cooking in the open was hell. The whole camp seemed to be an inferno of smoke and the ragged, emaciated internees . . . looked like the tortured devils of some medieval paintings as they crouched painfully over their little charcoal stoves desperately fanning the fading flame, their eyes sore and streaming from the grimy clouds" (129).

Despite the continuing struggle with wet wood, eye-streaming smoke, and makeshift meals, the illusion of a personal or family life represented by having a "home-cooked" breakfast or dinner together, rather than being lined up and served institutional food in a mess hall, was vital for many emotionally and spiritually.

Such a desire for personal and familial space — free at least in theory from eavesdropping, prying eyes, and general crowding — probably explains the phenomenon of the "shanties" in Santo Tomás, which started to appear as early as the second month in camp, possibly even in January (Hartendorp, I, 49). According to Whitesides, the shanties originally started as an entrepreneurial project on the part of several ex-contractors in camp. Enterprising builders, using old furniture thrown out and discarded lumber, as well as bamboo, built crude nipa-thatched shelters initially on the patio and then on other bits of discarded or unused ground. Here families could sit and eat or talk together, though the shanties initially could only be occupied during daytime. As Nash explains, this provided "some semblance of family life" and "to get away from the crowded rooms for part of a day was gratifying" (77).

The concept soon caught on, and prices for shanties rose as the huts became more sophisticated and lumber, palm thatching, rattan, and fresh bamboo could be purchased and delivered to the camp. The first shanties cost internees ₱ 50; by 1943, they were up to ₱ 350 (Vaughan, April 19, 1943, 205).

What did the internees get for their money, besides a gathering place with a sliver of privacy? After all, the shanties, according to Japanese order, had to be open on three sides so the guards could see in and theoretically prevent unwanted pregnancies from occurring. (Despite the rule, five surprise bundles of joy arrived anyway.)

The basic shanty doesn't perhaps sound very attractive, but to the men and women who were cramped and jammed into classrooms with fifty others, the shanty was the epitome of freedom. About 20 square feet of space, with a wooden floor and nipa sides, as well as an overhanging sloping roof also thatched with nipa, the shelter contained very little. The well-equipped shanty had, probably, a native charcoal stove the size of a medium clay flower pot made out of terra cotta or clay, along with a supply of kindling or charcoal. Here family members cooked meals as if on a modern hibachi. Many shanties also contained at least three clean five-gallon gasoline cans — one to serve as a baking oven for rice or little cakes and the other two for carrying dishwater and laundry water back to the shanty where such things could be done in private. Other necessary amenities included a rough table, individual place settings (tin plates and cups, knives, spoons, and forks), personal folding stools, chairs or small benches, and a cupboard nailed to the wall (Whitesides, 18).

The indefatigable and endlessly talented Ray Carlson, fresh from Cebu, initially purchased a space outside to accommodate a family dining table with a canopy made of bamboo poles and nipa shingles. This he gradually redesigned until he had transformed the dining area into a true shanty, which was almost immediately flattened by the November 1943 typhoon. Ray was not discouraged but as usual saw this adversity as an opportunity to improve on the past, and, while doing so, he startled his wife once again with his seemingly endless abilities and competence: "He extended the posts a littler farther . . . so our finished shanty was quite a bit bigger than our former one. Ray did all the work himself. I hadn't realized before that he knew so much about carpentry. When I asked him, he said, 'Oh, I had a little manual training in Junior Hi and a year of it in High School too'" (Carlson, 118).

In many ways, these shanties had the make-it-yourself pretend charm of a suburban tree house or a child's clubhouse—a place fixed up with odds and ends that children truly believe they could live in if only their parents would let them. Unfortunately, they themselves were now adults, and these "clubhouses" had become coveted. They were regarded as mansions in Santo Tomás; to those still living in crowded rooms, the inhabitants became a "shanty aristocracy."

At first, the internees and their families were not allowed to stay in the shanties at night until overcrowding in 1944 made it a necessity. In the meanwhile, the shanties became pawns in the camp. As punishment, the Japanese banned families from the shanties during most of the day; then they banned everyone from using the shanties; finally, they raised the ban. Eventually, 576 families moved into the shanties to live and sleep during 1944 and into early 1945 (Magnuson, 63; Lucas, 39–40).

"Several different villages" of shanties—Glamorville, Froggy Bottom, Jerktown and Upper Jerktown, Shantytown, Jungletown—ultimately sprouted and surrounded the main buildings. These Topsy-like (referring to a slave girl in *Uncle Tom's Cabin*) shanty towns, in turn, each elected its own mayor to represent the town with the Executive Committee. Finally, a planning, registration, and licensing subcommittee came into existence to control the future size and location of shanty developments (Whitesides, 43; 17–19; Lucas, 39–40; *Internews*, 1, November 1942).

Regarding this description of Santo Tomás's space and housing, it is again necessary to provide a certain context. Santo Tomás appeared wonderful to those being transferred in from the rough and ready accommodations and primitive housing of some of the internment camps on the other islands, especially from Cebu and Bacolod. Bryant and Vaughan, both inmates of Bacolod camp, remember their first view of Santo Tomás in mid-1943:

> Fed as we were on optimistic rumors rather than news, we had no idea that this enclosure would represent our world for two whole years. . . . Those who greeted us looked comparatively well-fed, well-dressed, and carefree. Indeed the whole place seemed to us like a big picnic. . . . At night music was broadcast in the plaza before the Main Building, and people sat in folding chairs to enjoy the evening coolness, or strolled back and forth. It reminded one of a European spa. There were classes and lectures for adults as well as for young people. (Bryant, 147)

Vaughan also mentions the private shanties, the well-trimmed hedges, the spacious lawns, the baseball diamond, and the soccer field. Vaughan, however, notices the drawn looks on the faces and recognizes that this was not a spa

(April 19, 1943, 202). Vaughan's perception was prophetically accurate as 1943 closed and tighter discipline made itself felt early in 1944.

Bryant's glee a year earlier over her transfer to Santo Tomás (even under stricter discipline) is understandable, given the space and accommodations of her last place of internment: the primitive Bacolod camp. On the Negros Occidental side of the island, Bacolod was essentially a block of classrooms and a few out-buildings on eight acres of land, surrounded by barbed wire (Waterford, 260). There was a single nineteen-room classroom unit, holding eventually all the internees (approximately ten per room), a separate home economics laboratory, a separate manual training shop, and a storage shed. The Japanese soldiers were quartered in the former school principal's house, directly across from the main school building. Two of the front classrooms were also set aside for the quarters of the Japanese commandant (Vaughan, "Community," 24–25; 35–36).

Initially the internees had three classrooms assigned to them. Vaughan and her children, Clay and Beth, were sent to the "children's room" along with three-month-old Douglas White and his amah, and Mrs. Oss and Thora Ann. They joined others who, like Bryant, had come in from Negros Oriental earlier and established themselves in the room. Vaughan describes the rooms as "filthy, cockroaches on [the] floor, heavy cobwebs on the wall" (June 7, 1942, 96). Privacy was at a premium, and the small space for each family group of mothers and children in the room presented hard choices and required strict disciplining of the children which was often heartrending in its painful yet absolute necessity.

Lack of privacy can lead to a debilitating envy when the woman in the next bed or her children have more necessities, and even luxuries, than others in the crowded room. Vaughan's September 17, 1942, entry gives a pitiful example of the nature of "home" under such conditions and the way in which internees, even children, had to adjust to space limitations:

> Beth and Clay have at last learned that only one corner of our small room is our "home," as they call it, and that to get from our "house" to the door of the verandah they must pass the "houses" of three other families—though no line and no division for privacy mark the boundaries of each "house." Always open to view, the toys of children in two of these families whose "homes" are in the same room with us are not to be touched. (126–127)

While Vaughan made her children "understand" the rules of private property and privacy, she could not stop them from looking and longing, especially when another child roughly Beth's age, Thora Ann Oss, sat her pretty dolls, tea set, and blocks on the table between the beds and then refused to offer them to Beth for play. Vaughan agonizes over the obvious injustice, and her inability, as a parent, to explain to her children that they also once had nice things; the toys the children saw

> kept Beth and Clay in such an unhappy state of mind because they could not touch them. It required many spankings to teach them. How Beth has looked long-ingly at Thora Ann's doll carriage, but she has not been offered the "push" of it once these three months she has eyed it daily. And how she has softly cried, asking me if she might not sit in Thora Ann's child's rocking chair when Thora Ann is not using it—and how I have had to deny her and try to explain at the same time that her own little rocking chair and other furniture do not exist any more as they were lost (along with toys) in the Central fire. (127)

Crowding soon took a toll, even in simple daily routines, irrespective of envy. Vaughan's July 20, 1942, entry discusses the fact that

> everyone here [is] trying to tell others what to do, and especially what *not* to do. Everyone [is] spying on everyone else, especially kitchen workers to see if food is taken from kitchen, trying to see what is in packages delivered from outside by families and relatives, and the unending gossip about people who do not wash floor-mop clean after using, who "flit" [spray insects] through mosquito net in face of nearby bed occupant, who get extra service from kitchen, who take up too much room on clothes line, etc. (109)

Bryant too suffers from crowding and yearns for privacy, although, in her case, it is her muse, not a child, who suffers. Intimate expression of private feelings comes slowly if less poetic souls look over the writer's shoulder or make suggestions; mourns Bryant, "I should have liked to resume my attempts at verse-writing but I led too much the life of a goldfish. It was hard enough to live in a room with so many miscellaneous women without increasing my difficulties by openly and deliberately putting myself into the category of the freaks who write verses" (127).

If private quarters in Bacolod were depressing, general accommodations were no more uplifting. The rest of the camp provided nothing more than "a few chairs, an old stove, water faucets which did not run, and a toilet which did not flush" (June 7, 1942, 96). A dilapidated manual training building served as dining room and kitchen. The camp commandant—a civilian who spoke English—was even worse than the accommodations: "He was an igno-rant, dirty, dwarfish little man who, before the war, had been employed as carpenter by a sugar central (or mill) in the province" (Bryant, 126; 129). His former job, perhaps naturally, gave him a certain edginess, even nastiness, with internees who had been part of the former society of his employers. Not one aspect of camp life appeared even a bit auspicious.

Unlike those in Baguio or even Santo Tomás, authorities of Bacolod camp obviously were deadly serious from the very beginning about the internees staying inside the camp confines. The wire fence (originally to keep in early Japanese internees), in addition to being barbed, was also electrified, and there were machine gun emplacements at the corners of the camp, fortified and disguised by grass and sandbags. They were also manned by "truckloads" of soldiers, according to Vaughan, equipped with hand grenades and "small bombs" (Vaughan, September 21, 1942, 130; October 22, 1942, 145).

Those same soldiers apparently took up peeping at internee women as a regular recreation. Once again limited space and inappropriate housing denied the internees even normal privacy, as did lax control of the guards. Explains Waterford (and Vaughan confirms this charge),

> Throughout the administration of one Japanese commandant, the guards were out of control; complaints about them from the internees were futile. Guards amused themselves by sitting in their second-story windows across the road from the camp with field glasses focused on the internees' bedrooms. . . . The guards also peeked into toilets, showers, and bedroom windows as they walked about the grounds and entered living quarters unannounced. (Waterford, 63)

Vaughan matter-of-factly explains that the women in her room soon learned to struggle into some basic garments by their beds and then "we [could] only duck low beneath [the] window sill" waiting for the guard to pass by. After he passed, Vaughan and the others would then gingerly stand up and finish dressing. Despite these precautions, she notes that the next morning, after crouching on the floor beneath sill level to pull her dress over her head, she emerged just in time to see the guard leaning in the window, staring. Unlike some fortunate internees in Santo Tomás, Bacolod had nothing even resembling private shanties. Internees simply had to dress stoically and hope they timed it right. As she commented in a grand understatement, "This kind of thing is annoying" (July 6, 1942, 106).

Cebu and Davao camps offered many of the same problems, though imprisonment in temporary camps earlier made the official camp appear to be almost comfortable. On Cebu, for example, the first confinement the civilian internees suffered in 1942 was in a provincial jail. The sixty-two Americans and British internees were assigned to "a number of one-storied cell-blocks, surrounded by a 14 foot concrete wall, enclosing a small yard. The people slept bed to bed about 30 to a room, the women and children apart from the men" (Hartendorp, I, 316).

The cell blocks featured wooden slat beds set on short wooden legs. These butted head to head with little or no space in between. Women and children slept in one cell block, the men in another, and in both it was "fiendishly hot" (Hartendorp, I, 316; Carlson, 76).

Eventually moved to the junior college campus of the University of the

Philippines, the internees found themselves housed in classrooms, though in Cebu they were not nearly so crowded as those in Santo Tomás. As in so many other camps, water was initially limited because of either Japanese bombing or later American sabotage of the waterworks on the island. Communal closeness came with the conditions. Things as simple as doing the laundry, bathing, washing hair, and even flushing the toilet demanded that internees share. As Imogene Carlson explains, "We washed our clothes out-of-doors in buckets or cans, using any container we could find. When we finished our clothes, we passed the soapy water on to others who were still washing. The last of that water was saved to flush the non-functioning inside toilets, which were used at night only. The rinse water was passed from person to person, too. What was left was used for baths" (86).

Davao camp on the island of Mindanao was a fairly large camp — at approximately 280 men, women, and children, larger than Bacolod camp (148 internees), though not nearly so well documented in internee diaries or memoirs. One of the few internees from Davao to keep a contemporaneous letter-journal collection, Frank Cary, pointed out that, similar to those on Cebu, Davao internees were moved a number of times before settling in a real camp. First captured and moved into the "Foreigner's Club" (and restricted to the library) on December 23, 1941, the Allied internees lived an "extremely cramped life." This library room, though screened, was without rugs on the floor and had only four long wicker lounge chairs to use as beds. Most slept on the floor until they were moved, on January 3, 1942, to a private residence. Cary says nothing particularly about this new residence camp, except that it was "just opposite a brothel!" (5) and seemed to be in a line of cabarets. (Jane Wills identifies this place as the former "Happy Life Blues" dance hall [19].) Whatever its nom de guerre, the camp itself was filthy and had to be cleaned up; internees had to dig toilets and also prepare a place for cooking.

This location was also rich with vermin of one sort or another, not just with the usual bedbugs or beetles inside but with rats and snakes in the open around the building; explains Jane Wills, "There was a black cobra in the area, and I just hated to walk outside. I wouldn't go anywhere in the dark for fear I'd stumble across it" (19).

Ultimately, the internees were moved again to yet another place, because, according to Cary, the Japanese officers wanted the previous private residence to live in themselves. The internees were taken back to a school compound in town (Hartendorp, I, 260; Cary, 6).

People seemed to be everywhere. Eventually, Davao camp became so crowded that the Japanese, as they had in Santo Tomás, allowed shanties to be built. For internees with a personal sleeping space of 3 by 8 feet on the hall floor, shanties were an extremely attractive alternative (Wills, 19). Davao internees constructed their shanties with many of the same materials as those used in Santo Tomás, including bamboo, reeds, palm fronds, sawali sides, and congon grass thatch. At Davao, however, the huts were more sophisticated, partly because, unlike the shanties in the larger camp, these could be closed on all sides by immovable walls. Both Jane Wills and Frank Cary speak warmly of these cherished private spaces. Wills explains, "In spite of bugs, it was just heaven here after the bedlam of being in the 'fish bowl' of this concentration camp with absolutely no privacy" (20). Cary goes further and describes the building of his piece of heaven in an April 8, 1943, letter; in it we see more leniency in Davao than at Santo Tomás in obtaining materials:

> By building on stilts we had a living room (really a porch) 6 feet above the ground and a bedroom 2 feet higher. For materials we were permitted to go to the hills and fell trees for the main posts. Lack of nails made us pin it with pegs. For flooring we were lucky enough to get boards for the bedrooms, but split off the armored bark of palma brava for the porch. . . . For tying we used rattan strips. Crytzer [another internee and former Luzon Stevedore Manager for Davao] is clever at using the inadequate tools with which we must work, and has made us some bamboo settees. (24)

Back on the island of Luzon, the internees at Camp John Hay, then at Camp Holmes near Baguio, lived under circumstances similar to those at Cebu but not as privately as in Davao camp, and in markedly better conditions than at Bacolod. Both Camps Hay and Holmes were well above the malarial zone and in the mountains previously used by government officials as a summer retreat; moreover, thanks to internee guards that paced the grounds at night and strong central Japanese control, Japanese guards never offered the kind of indignity offered to female internees at Bacolod.

The first camp, John Hay, however, initially was hardly inspiring. It housed the 500 men, women, and children who were captured around the town of Baguio and from northern Luzon in a partially burned and demolished Philippine Scouts single-story barracks, originally built in 1906 to house Igorot soldiers (Halsema ltr, May 21, 1997). The Japanese authorities housed men and women in segregated quarters in both John Hay and Holmes for most of the war, and cohabitation was forbidden, even (especially?) between married couples. All children under ten lived with their mothers in the women's barracks, but all *boys* over ten lived with their fathers in the men's barracks. As Bloom points out, both Japanese soldiers and internees assumed that the mothers were responsible for all child care of those below ten and of all girls (Bloom, "Death," 78).

The rooms at John Hay were bare and rude. Crouter describes them in an entry entitled "Notes jotted in late January, 1942": "There are bare rafters, shelves around the windows, nails for hanging clothes, and lines down the middle for laundry drying. We all sleep on mattresses on the floor, surrounded by bags. We have pillows and blankets, but not sheets" (17).

Each person had approximately 33 inches of bed space (Bloom, "Death," 78) for himself or herself and all possessions. As Natalie Crouter mourns in a February 19, 1942, entry, "What a *small* life it is, so bounded and detailed by checking and numbering. The floor space is being measured now to see how much each occupies. My back aches every night now. Being in the middle, it is hard to turn over, with three of us sleeping on a three-quarter mattress" (21–22).

In an April 1 entry, Crouter goes on to describe the ambiance in the barracks at night: "Mosquito nets look so queer at night. Some are square, some oblong, some peaked, some round, others just little face veils. In the dusk it looks like a cobweb city of fantastic shapes" (34).

After great effort, the internees finally adjusted to the limited space and poor quarters assigned to them at Camp John Hay. In three months internees "hadn't moved an inch" in or out of their designated personal space, and Natalie Crouter points out that "each one hangs on to his allotted spot like grim death" (March 28, 1942, 33). In mid-April, however, this delicate balance shattered as the internees found themselves trucked to another camp near Baguio, this time eight kilometers away. This was Camp Holmes (Hartendorp, I, 168–169).

The camp facilities, formerly those of the Philippine Constabulary, consisted of living quarters for at least 800 people and featured three main barracks, two of them double-stories, along with a small officers' quarters. The single-story barracks ("Green Barracks") became the one that housed women and children, while one two-story barracks held men and the other, the kitchen and dining area on the ground floor. (The upper floor housed more men.) Eventually, the Constabulary Officers' Quarters were transformed into the "Baby House" for infants (Halsema ltr, May 21, 1997). Rather than mattresses on the floor, Camp Holmes featured double-decker bunk beds fitted into the available space. Even though conditions were crowded, Crouter described the barracks as "light, airy, built on the tropic style with sliding shell-paned windows, [and] much pleasanter" (April 21, 1942, 42). The camp also eventually sported a clinic and camp hospital compound, supply sheds, and bodegas, as well as the dining room area, which featured tables and chairs rather than merely benches (Bloom, "Death," 78).

Holmes had several advantages. In addition to buildings in better physical shape, customs and space restrictions were an improvement. Families occasionally got to gather to eat together in the dining hall or to enjoy a snack, thereby reasserting their status as a family. In addition, for a while the commandant gave permission (as Tomibe did frequently, for example) for mixed groups of internees to go on picnics in the hills surrounding the camp. Husbands and wives could sit together and children could talk to both parents, especially those kept from them by gender segregation in the barracks.

Eventually, by early 1944, families were beginning to "burrow dugouts beneath the barracks" to have a place in which to live together. Faced with such a situation, the Japanese authorities relented and unilaterally announced that co-habitation was acceptable, despite some internee advocates of segregation who "raised alarmed cries about the imminence of a population explosion" and its effect on the food supply. Under the new rules, protests not withstanding, specified barracks went co-educational (Bloom, "Popular," 802–803).

Holmes could also claim another big advantage over most other camps. Unlike the crowded conditions at Camp John Hay, Cebu, Davao, Bacolod, or even Santo Tomás, Holmes at least offered an inexpensive escape in the form of a scenic vista, as well as a modicum of privacy in the hills. Even without the money to purchase the materials for a shanty, an internee or a family could still attain solitude. This was important because, as Crouter explained, "People's traits are emphasized a thousand times where there is no privacy, no possibility of concealment under social graces" (April 18, 1942, 38). It was a terrible blow in mid-1944 after the escape when the hills were declared off-limits and the camp eventually fenced with barbed wire.

On December 26, 1944, the Baguio internees' situation deteriorated sharply when the Japanese Imperial Army units claimed the strategic advantage and the (now improved) housing of Camp Holmes. Once again, internees were told to take their belongings and leave, this time to be sent to infamous Old Bilibid Prison in Manila—most recently the last stop for POWs. Judy Hyland previously mentioned the lurching, several-day truck ride down from the mountains; dawn saw the internees enter Bilibid Prison, there to waste away until the war ended or rescue came, along with the POW survivors of the Bataan and Corregidor campaigns in the hospital cell blocks across the wall in the next compound (Hyland, 96).

Many of the internees were stunned by what they saw. As Mary Ogle describes it, when the trucks pulled up in front of the prison, "We had heard we might be going to a hospital and so had had visions of a fairly well-equipped building. What a surprise! There was no one there to meet us. The place was dark except for one dim bulb that burned in the front hallway. We were shown a stack of mattresses and told what wing of the building we were to occupy, and that was all there was to it" (283).

Illness soon spread in the crumbling cement cells. With only cold water with which to wash themselves or their surroundings, the personal spaces were soon rife with insect life because disinfectant spray was completely absent. Despite this, families continued to be able to live together even in a prison setting. Families, for example, were put in rooms on the lower floor of the main building, and single girls on the upper floor. Single men lived in a separate "flimsy" building with 4-inch boards, 2 inches apart for walls (Ogle, 287; 289). According to Ogle, "Each family just marked off the space they needed, hung up a few sheets, and set up housekeeping on bunks" (287). War correspondent Robert Shaplen gives a sense of the actual space involved. Using the Smeddle family quarters (housing Mr. and Mrs. Smeddle and twenty-year-old daughter, Betty), which was around 7 by 14 feet, as an example, he explains, "Nearly everyone had a cot and a mattress, ample clothing hung on hooks, and trunks and suitcases had been set up as furniture. All in all, the Baguio internees appeared to have fared very well, far better, as I learned afterward, than the civilian internees in Santo Tomás" (68).

Shaplen's report is overly favorable; he points to the obvious advantages of the family spaces in Bilibid, but he does not mention food and medicine, which, as we have already seen, were in very short supply. Space is indeed one way to measure advantage; however, sustenance is a more direct and immediate criterion.

Certainly, Los Baños camp, located forty-five miles from Manila in southern Luzon on twenty-five acres of the former University of the Philippines agricultural college campus, would have appeared to be paradise to the Santo Tomás and perhaps even the now-incarcerated Baguio (Holmes, now Bilibid) internees (Hartendorp, I, 528; Waterford, 259). Los Baños, however, had its own set of problems, one of which involved the degree of overcrowding in camp—and by whom.

Until mid-1944, space in Los Baños, at least after the efforts of the first group of 800 internees, was adequate—though barely so—for the 1,500 or 1,600 internees eventually sent there. Los Baños featured a variety of dormitory barracks, including a barracks set aside for a kitchen, as well as eight small bungalows, a two-story YMCA building, and a gymnasium, and a twenty-bed hospital. There seemed to be room in the camp for all the 1,600 internees sent there (though they were somewhat cramped). The barracks, for example, had floors made of split bamboo, sides of matting, and a roof of palm branches. Each barracks held ninety-six people; there were sixteen cubicles measuring 20 by 12 feet in each barracks, and each cubicle held six people (Terry, 59; Hartendorp, I, 528). Jane Wills, eventually sent to Los Baños from Davao, gives a somewhat less favorable picture of the living quarters, describing the barracks as "big long shed-like building[s], divided down the middle with divisions like horse stalls on each side" (22). The bungalows were used by families, as were some barracks.

The July addition of 520 missionaries (among these some twenty mostly elderly and ailing Catholic priests and nuns, as well as Protestant missionaries from Baguio) needless to say did not please the internees already in residence. The bulk of these new arrivals were originally from Manila or Santo Tomás as well as some nineteen others from the Cagayan Valley. The missionaries were not welcome (Hartendorp, II, 282–283). By the summer of 1944, food was scarce, buildings were crowded, and many believed that the missionaries had been collaborators who signed the infamous "cooperation" agreement with the Japanese. Grace Nash, for example, held the agreement against the newcomers and in her own words and heart "just disconnected them from American nationality," even suggesting that it would make sense if they lost their citizenship (Nash interview; Arthur, 71). She was not alone in her feelings.

The infamous "pledge," after all, included some rather startling provisions. The first condition the Protestant missionaries had to sign stated that they would "gladly cooperate with the Japanese army as it proclaims the military administration in the Philippines." (The Catholic hierarchy made a private agreement with the Japanese.) The third provision demanded that signatories laud the idea and spread the word that "the great ideal of the Greater East Asian Co-Prosperity sphere is on the road to its realization." They were also to state their belief "that the very fulfillment of that great *ideal is to attain world peace*" (Nixon, 33–34, italics mine). This and other like provisions were signed by almost all the Protestant missionaries except for those who volunteered to stay in Santo Tomás during the first release in January 1942 (Nixon, 30).

Missionary Carol Terry understood the other internees' enmity but pointed out that the missionaries were threatened if they did not sign; indeed, according to Nixon, four missionaries (of which she was one) refused to sign the pledge. In a series of meetings with the Japanese covering almost a full week, gradually signatures accrued as threats and relentless demands continued. Even those who absolutely refused to sign the document did not escape later censure. In the end it made no difference; the Japanese published a list of all those who signed — including the names of the four who actually had not done so (Nixon, 34).

The fact that four missionaries refused to sign and that there were other missionaries, such as Harry Fonger and all those at the Baguio camps, who volunteered to stay in internment camps from the beginning seems to cast doubt on the seriousness of the death threat. Untortured and still alive, Fonger was sent to camp, not to an early grave. Partly because of the general animosity of the other internees or perhaps (as some claim) because they were forced to do so, the missionaries lived together. In the last four months they also tended to eat their private rations in a group in their own section behind a sawali fence in the upper part of the camp; this section was soon dubbed "The Holy City," while the rest of the camp was sardonically referred as "Hell's Half Acre" (Lucas, 157).

The "misshies" (as some of the more disgruntled internees referred to them) were a problem not only because of their numbers but because of their attitudes as well. Those who disliked them did so not merely because the missionaries had strong religious beliefs; so too did their co-religionists, the Catholic sisters. The nuns in Los Baños, some of whom internee women had known during the internees' stay at Assumption Convent in Manila (Alice Hill, interview), were reasonably well liked. Internees noted their volunteer nursing in the hospital, their hard work, and their generosity with whatever food or clothing they had. Such generosity did not prove to be true as often of the missionaries, who, according to several internees, not only didn't help others but hoarded food and refused to share what they had. Jane Wills talks not only of hoarded food but of the use of extortion as well. According to her, "There were a lot of missionary families in camp, and one family had a grinder. They'd let people use the grinder for a portion of their rice" (26). Near the end of internment, when most supplies had to be treated before being eaten (unhulled rice, whole dry corn, and so forth), to demand payment of what may very well have been a family's lifeline — rice — put that missionary family beyond the pale with the other nonmissionary internees, who saw this as religious hypocrisy.

Again, unlike the missionaries, the Catholic sisters performed well publicly among the other Los Baños internees. According to Isla Corfield, the nuns who arrived "quickly cleaned up their barracks" and set "their few possessions neatly in order" when they got to camp. In contrast, the Protestant missionaries arrived in confusion and stayed that way for some time, sitting among their possessions and consoling themselves with their Bibles, while testifying loudly that "God will help!" (Lucas, 158).

Waiting for God or MacArthur's forces to save them would take at least two more months. For Margaret Sams waiting in a Los Baños dormitory, for Vaughan and her children in the annex, or for the Carlsons in their shanty in STIC, as well as for Jim Halsema and Mary Ogle managing to survive in crumbling Old Bilibid Prison compound, the next months would be a test of nerve and strength unlike any the internees had faced before.

8

Idle Hands Are the Devil's Playground
Work in the Camps

Under the best of circumstances, being crowded in with others and lacking basic privacy cause friction, even without disliking fellow internees personally. The fact that the missionaries were people many of the other internees would have avoided, as the missionaries would have ignored them had they not been in a camp with them, made the friction even worse. Signs of distress began to appear at Los Baños. Explains Carol Terry, "Nerves are tested to the breaking point. The way another ties his shoes or combs his hair may get on one's nerves until he has to get away from the barracks and walks up and down the camp roads until nerves are quieted" (57).

The fluctuating camp population—at one point 2,146 internees in Los

Baños, 3,785 in Santo Tomás, and 468 in Baguio/Bilibid (Hartendorp, II, 466), demanded a variety of work be done both to make the overcrowding bearable and to maintain reasonable public health standards. Work functioned, then, not only as a necessary means to a healthful end but also as a way on a regular basis throughout the war for internees to pass the time productively and to keep from driving each other crazy in close quarters.

According to internee Alice Bryant, all "able-bodied internees who were not superannuated" were supposed to work (151). Both the kinds of shelter and the work connected with each camp varied among the camps, as did food supplies, administrative rules, and health. "Able-bodied" also meant different degrees of "ableness" in different camps, as illness and malnutrition increasingly decreased the ranks of those able to pick up a bucket, gather firewood, or sweep out quarters with a twig broom.

To understand the nature of the work with which the internees filled their time (or which they did to maintain the camp), "work" needs to be defined in terms of both the public good and self-maintenance. Understanding this thoroughly reveals not only the pressure, grievances, and attitudes of internees but also their unremitting labor and basic courage in insisting on a bearable existence, if only through their own unrelenting efforts. As Jim Halsema notes, these efforts were "a common characteristic of American-run camps" because of "the determination of their inhabitants to improve their environments, not to accept them as found" (Halsema ltr, May 21, 1997). Examining work in a variety of camps (Hay/Holmes, Bilibid, Bacolod, Cebu, Davao, Los Baños, and Santo Tomás) helps illuminate the daily tasks they performed (some more physically demanding than others, in more primitive camps).

Normally, life itself wasn't threatened by the work the internees did as it was in the case of the POWs, who were forced, despite international law, to build airstrips, roads, and railroads for the Japanese military. Normally, public works for the internees were only in support of camp requirements or personal sanitation; internees were rarely used for military slave labor, though there appears to have been an exception made in Davao Internment Camp on Mindanao. There internees were forced to load rock and sand into trucks, repair bridges, and load supplies (sacks of rice) for the military on a ship as well as other unspecified but "illegal" duties (Cary, April 14, 1942, 5; IMTFE, Reel 10, 12,800; Wills, 17).

Forced internee labor also happened in Santo Tomás, though, unlike that in Davao, it didn't directly aid the military and supposedly was legal because it "improved" internee safety. Acting Commandant Onozaki ordered internees to dig post holes, string wire, and construct a barbed wire fence around the wall and near the gym, as well as to replace the sawali on the fence around the seminary grounds. Despite protests by the Executive Committee and Grinnell himself, in addition to strident citations of the Geneva Convention, internees started the fence — under protest. The Internee Committee, facing threats of punishment both to themselves and to any able-bodied men who refused to work on the fence, agreed to the work but picked men for the job rather than forcing them (as the Japanese initially wanted) to volunteer. Through this, they actively participated in keeping themselves prisoners as they strung barbed wire intended to mark the perimeter of their prison. To be forced to "volunteer" to string the wire, which both symbolically and literally kept the internees inside the camp, was an insult to them (Hartendorp, II, 291).

The more common pattern in the internment camps was for jobs to be listed by internees and assigned to other internees for the benefit of the internee community at large — this was true throughout the war. As we have seen, in the first six months of internment (and to a significant degree thereafter), the Japanese camp authorities (both civilian and military) made no particular effort to supply food, adequate shelter, or basic standards of sanitation. These the internees grimly but doggedly provided for themselves as they could. Public works, then, became a necessary part of every adult internee's day, if only to keep the threat of exposure, starvation, and pestilence at bay. In Santo Tomás, for example, the Executive Committee soon formed sixteen operating committees, of which one was the "Work Assignment Committee," which posted camp jobs needing workers and then tried to match an internee's wishes and skills with a suitable job. Jobs included, among other duties, picking up, hauling, and burying garbage, weeding the communal vegetable gardens, cleaning drains and gutters and emptying chamber pots from the rooms into the toilets, serving as a porter to carry packages, planting shrubs, trimming grass, censoring mail, carrying away stones, shooting rats, killing bedbugs with disinfectant, serving food, cooking, washing dishes, mending clothing, teaching both children and adults, digging drainage ditches, nursing at the camp hospital or serving as an aide, repairing books in the library or fixing machinery, building new facilities, plumbing, wiring, working in the Executive Committee office as stenographers, typists, interpreters, or secretaries, or preparing vegetables, cleaning rice of stones and weevils, and assisting newcomers. Each of these jobs fell under its own department, such as camp sanitation or food service. Other jobs of a professional nature, including professional entertainment and newspaper publication, as well as medicine, dentistry, and religion, were also deservedly listed as camp jobs (Stevens, 24). As internee Karen Lewis remembers, "Everyone had a camp duty according to their talent or desire, in addition to KP and bathroom monitor" (81). She also points out that every child "over the age of twelve had regular bathroom monitor duty" (80). As

Whitesides explains, "This daily work could in effect be considered a form of tax paid to the internee government" (16).

Of all of the jobs, those related to public health loomed the largest in daily life. At the beginning of internment, for example, Santo Tomás boasted "wholly inadequate toilet, bathing and laundering, as well as cooking and dishwashing facilities" (Hartendorp, I, 26–27). Margaret Sams remembered that initially there were only five toilets in the main building for over 500 women and children (Sams, 61)

Undaunted, the internees quickly set up a Sanitation and Health Committee led by R. E. Cecil, a former employee of West Coast Life Insurance Company. He and the other committee members feared an epidemic among the crowded (at that time approximately 3,000) inmates if nothing was done about sewage. With a volunteer workforce of over 600 men, Cecil's committee (of which a number were former engineers, carpenters, and plumbers) built and then installed additional flush toilets, fifty additional shower baths (as supplies became available), and long washing troughs with multiple faucets for washing clothes or personal dishes. The new showers could not relieve the crowding completely, as women still had to shower with others throughout the war; notes Sams, "Later, much later, I was [finally] able to share a shower with ten or fifteen women without cringing, while dozens of other women waited their turn and other dozens marched in and out of the bathroom" (61).

In addition to these measures, Cecil's committee constructed additional pit privies (until more plumbing supplies came into camp), connected camp sewer drains into the city's system, eventually got gas piped to the kitchens, and increased Santo Tomás's water pressure by getting permission for and then constructing new inlets into the Metropolitan Manila Water District mains. The committee also had a regular detail that picked up garbage and buried it in trenches dug in the rear of the grounds, where it served as fertilizer for future garden space, though as the internees are quick to point out in their memoirs, garbage disposal was not a problem after mid-1943 — the starving internees left none. In the first year of the war, however, Santo Tomás disposed of a ton and a half of garbage a day (collected three times a day) — garbage that had to be buried initially, because the Japanese refused to allow garbage carts (with possibly hidden passengers) to travel in and out of the camp (Magnuson, 53; Hartendorp, I, 26–27).

Even garbage duty lent itself ultimately to internee humor. A former Manila banker, now on the garbage crew, with a nod to Shakespeare's *Romeo and Juliet*, labeled the two wheelbarrows used for the chore "Rose" and "By Any Other Name" (Nixon, 23–24).

Public health consisted of more than mere garbage dumps or extra plumbing, important as these were. Under Cecil's leadership, there was a camp-wide campaign to eliminate mosquitoes, rats, and flies, as well as snakes. His crews cleared hectares of brush, weeds, and sinks to trap cobras and rats; they also filled in pits, holes, and open drains to eliminate breeding grounds for mosquitoes; and they had fly traps installed by every garbage can and toilet in camp. Bedbugs were ruthlessly hunted down and scalded with boiling water or sprayed with a camp-concocted insecticide. Alice Bryant, in one of her first jobs in Santo Tomás after transfer from Bacolod camp, "earned my daily beans by fighting bed bugs." She was not completely convinced that these efforts were effective, as she explained: "My work was to fill up and give out spray guns filled with a fluid made up in camp out of whatever material was available. Although I poured gallons of it into the guns, I had no faith in it; for a while it was used for killing bedbugs, it would not do so unless there was enough to drown them" (151).

Nor were members of the sanitation squads the only predators of the bedbugs. Room residents were also enlisted in the bedbug eradication campaign. The February 24, 1942, *Internews* (camp newsletter-paper) announced the commencement of the war with the slogan, "kill 'em or scratch yourself." The Sanitation Committee set it up as a contest, explained eradication procedures, and served as judges to announce winners—those room residents with the "highest individual batting average against bedbugs." The committee told the internees to use exposure to sunlight, boiling water, and camp disinfectant or chorine wash on the mattress seams and bed frames, as well as on the room corners and floors (1, col. 2). Winners were rewarded often with some kind of candy or baked good.

The bedbug eradication project was unending. They—and other noisome insects—were everywhere. Martin Meadows remembers as an early teenager the unforeseen consequences of mosquito nets in the rooms, at least in terms of the universal war against bedbugs: "The nets were attached to strings that spanned the rooms, and these strings gave the ubiquitous bedbugs an additional means of travel from bed to bed." He goes on to mention one of the men who bunked next to him, "a bearded hygiene-challenged ex-seaman . . . whose belongings were literally covered with bedbugs—sheets, pillow, towel, mosquito nets (the corners of which were packed with the critters)" (ltr, July 27, 1998).

Meadows does point out, however, that the mosquito nets also repelled some pests beyond mere mosquitoes. Possibly because the room had once been a science lecture theater and had ranges of wooden steps, it was infested with cockroaches as large as three inches or greater: "These used to fly around the room at night slamming into the nets" (ltr, July 27, 1998).

Other internees remember Santo Tomás especially because of the bedbug campaigns. Says Doris Rubens, "I also think of bedbugs—flagellated by the ever-vigilant Sanitation Committee, we were always either looking for or killing bedbugs" (222). Rubens's comment suggests that, despite massive efforts, the Sanitation Committee never truly eradicated bedbugs. The problem remained an itch needing to be scratched, so to speak, for the rest of internment.

Contests as a means to attain public health goals soon became endemic in Santo Tomás camp. A camp-wide antifly initiative enlisted not only adults but also children; those with the most dead flies (these to be brought to the committee headquarters to be counted *individually*) won prizes weekly.

The *Internews* announced the chartering of a "Junior Swat-the-Fly Club" under the direction of Carl Gabriels, head of the Insect and Rodent Control Department of the Sanitation Committee. Each week "leading fly annihilators" received prizes of candy also (March 17, 1942, 1, col. 3). The *Campus Health Bulletin* (no. 3) on March 20 announced that the first winner of the junior contest, Stan Thompson, killed 5,370 flies, while ten other children (eight boys and two girls) qualified for the "1st Class Swatters" title by killing over 1,000 flies each (1, cols. 2–3). As Lewis, then age nine, remembers, "Children were set upon the flies, armed with glass jars, waxed paper and rubber bands. I remember the prizes were awarded to the winning fly catchers, but not being one, I don't know what they were" (80).

Another favorite weekly contest, the "Cleanest Room Contest," played to communal pride on the part of room residents and applied social pressure on those who ordinarily weren't very clean. The Sanitation and Health Committee made weekly inspections of all rooms in all the buildings and determined the cleanest single room and the most sanitary suite of rooms. As a February 21, 1942, *Internews* explained, points were awarded for the cleanliness of the floors, ceilings, and sills, dust-free furniture, closed garbage cans, and neat personal effects storage, in addition to clean mosquito netting and the presence of a prepared weekly sanitation report (1, col. 1). Some internees, especially men with strong arms and backs such as Frank Cary, were enlisted initially to sweep the fifteen-foot ceilings for spiders and cobwebs in the men's quarter—a tiring and, by 1944, exhausting and nearly impossible job, given the rations (Cary, 51).

Back in 1942, however, internees still had strength and a desire for prizes. The prize for the cleanest room was a large cake that went to the room inmates. In the first contest, two women's rooms tied for the prize—Room 18 in the main building (American women) and Annex Room 66 (British women and children). In this case, the kitchen staff whipped up two cakes for the co-winners (*Internews*, March 3, 1942, 1, cols. 1–2). Men occasionally won the "cleanest room" award, as did Room 41, main building (American men), on March 10 of that year (*Internews*, 1, cols. 2–3), and as Room 43, Martin Meadows's room, did on July 3, 1943; as he suggests, this must have been after the unhygienic seaman left the room! Imogene Carlson and her two boys were in one of the annex rooms that once received the "Camp High" award for being the cleanest room in camp. She admits that "competition was keen" and that the room's residents felt "quite honored" (109).

By March 13, 1942, the Sanitation Committee had added other requirements for those hoping to win the title — again, it seems, intended to plug an unforeseen public health hole: the communal areas in the building not under any group's purview. The rooms inspected for the contest now would be judged "entirely on sanitation." The twist was that "each room bordering on the same corridor [would] receive the same number of points allotted to that particular section"; therefore, room inmates in the contest were now responsible for the condition of "corridors, toilets, stairways and fire buckets" used communally and would gain or lose points accordingly.

This new wrinkle in the rules introduced a necessary but unpleasant kind of work into the life of internees: toilet cleaning. On a rotating basis (assigned by the room monitors usually) room inmates cleaned and disinfected toilets by hand on each floor of the buildings (and also public ones) until their rescue in February 1945. Memories of those internees so assigned remain vivid, even after half a century:

> "Toilet duty" was nauseous, but necessary. We had a bucket of disinfectant and a cloth, and after each visitor we wiped the porcelain object with the cloth which had been dipped in the bucket of disinfectant. We used the bare commode, without benefit of seat or lid. I never felt that it was beneath my dignity to clean up after people . . . but I did despise putting my hand in that awful old bucket of smelly, oily-looking disinfectant. (Sams, 62)

Toilet duty could also mean being the "paper lady" at the door. Given the difficulty in camp of obtaining fresh supplies, the camp rationed toilet paper; those going to the bathroom had to indicate whether they needed "one sheet or two" depending on the nature of the visit. Handing out toilet paper squares itself became a camp job for both sexes. Toilet paper, initially rationed at five sheets per person, dropped to three sheets, then to two, and eventually to one — soon to be replaced by squares cut out of the inner cardboard of toilet paper rolls (Lucas, 101). Children over age twelve participated (as room residents) in such duties. June (Darras) Alden, for example, at thirteen years old was assigned to hand out toilet paper and to "squeegee the shower floor" in the bathroom (Questionnaire, 1991, 2).

By late 1943, sometimes job, location, and attire clashed, given the existing supplies of available used clothes and shoes (the handing out of which was yet another duty). One of internee Alice Hill's jobs at Santo Tomás was to distribute clothing to those internees who had just arrived or who needed clothes to replace the near-rags they were wearing. Supplies of clothing came from a number of sources: some from recent Red Cross shipments but many from *local* Red Cross boxes packed just before the war by somewhat affluent Americans to help "the poor." Hill remembers a friend of hers coming into the supply shed and telling Alice that she (the friend) *absolutely needed* shoes — that she couldn't stand the wooden clogs, that her feet were narrow, and that getting anything to stay on them was a problem. Alice Hill remembers her friend was "pleased as punch" when Hill found her the only pair of shoes that fit — a pair of white, high-heeled "party shoes." They made a ludicrous combination with the remnant of a tea dress she was wearing and the Chinese "coolie" hat on her head to keep off the rain. On her way to perform her camp job for the day, her friend teetered back into the common area of the compound, bringing an odd touch of high society to whatever duty she had been assigned. Whether her duty was handing out toilet paper, washing dishes, or eradicating bedbugs, Hill doesn't specify (Hill, personal communication).

Women weren't the only ones to bring a demented touch of raffish charm and class into camp life and labor. In a May 1, 1943, entry, Vaughan describes the scene at the dining hall one morning: "In the breakfast chow line this morning behind two patriarchal looking internees stood a man in black evening trousers, the shiny silk braid on the dusty trouser legs slightly out of place at this hour of the morning. Above the black trousers he wore a faded and patched blue denim shirt" (214).

Another camp job, certainly with its own touch of peculiarity, bears mentioning here as well — at least in any sort of modern Western society since 1910. With an obvious shortage of sanitary napkins, during their menstrual cycles female internees had to use rag squares sewn together. These (with names and room numbers embroidered on them) were turned in to the laundry after use where a number of volunteers washed them out, dried them, and then put them in the clean laundry to be returned to the proper person and room. Magnuson remembers clearly and even gratefully: "When Kotex ran out, a former society butterfly (I wish I could remember her name as she was one of the heroines) volunteered to wash the pieces of flanne[l] we were issued on which we embroidered our names. She got a hand-crank washing machine from outside and did this unpleasant job throughout internment. Her job was made easier the last year when 80%, including me, of women stopped menstruating [due to malnutrition]" (54). Lucas notes that the nature of conspicuous consumption among the "wealthy" changed; by 1943 women brandished their prosperity at the less fortunate by carrying sanitary napkins to the bathroom, taken from an ostentatiously displayed box in their quarters (102).

Another public health requirement for the contests mentioned earlier involved fire prevention. Each room kept a filled fire bucket of water by the door and had an appointed fire squad; room occupants also voted when or if to forbid smoking in the rooms during the day, during the night, or at any time. Smoking in bed was always forbidden. The worry was that fire would break out in the overcrowded sleeping areas where mosquito nets and cots almost touched. This was especially true of the men's gymnasium, which had huge festoons of mosquito netting over the entire space. The fear was that a mere spark or a carelessly put-out cigarette would catch fire to the netting or the frame and everything would go up in flames in a second. Notes Hartendorp, "No doubt because of these precautions, there was never a serious fire" (I, 28), though there was a constant seesaw dispute between fire squad members and mothers who insisted on bathing small children in the fire buckets.

Other public health communal jobs involved washing dishes and cleaning pots and pans in the kitchen. Sascha Jensen's father, for example, was head of kitchen sanitation (Jensen, 40), and Alice Bryant, relieved from bedbug duty, soon took up dish washing in the dining hall as her camp duty. Here she washed the communal dishes, occasionally helped people wash their personal dishes, and rinsed, dried, and handed dishes back. Eventually, the Sanitation Committee ruled the entire dish washing operation "unsanitary" because the water was not hot enough to kill bacteria (Bryant, 154).

Camp jobs were not always connected to public health concerns, however. Camp routines and personal lodging maintenance also required able bodies. A variety of jobs existed, as indicated earlier. Many women, such as Sascha Jensen's mother, worked on the "vegetable detail," which involved cutting the spoiled parts off vegetables. Another job most female internees performed at least once in camp was rice cleaning. Supplies of rice, especially in 1944 after the Japanese procured them, had to be picked over before they could be cooked; this was somewhat boring, but not backbreaking work, as Bryant notes (having moved from dish washing to rice picking); she speaks of rice picking specifically for the diet kitchen: "The work my companions and I did was easy and sociable. We sat around the table gossiping, and each of us rolled rice around in a plate or tray and took out stones, worms, rodent excreta and other foreign objects" (155).

Doris Rubens remembers the more general rice cleaning and picking for the camp, rather than the diet kitchen, very well: "To this day, when I think of Santo Tomás I think of worms — worms wriggling through the mush and rice" (222).

Still other jobs involved the camp garden: watering, weeding, planting, or picking hungry insects off the plants by hand. Bryant's husband, "the Guv'nor," was especially good at gardening, not only helping produce a large crop of greens for the central kitchen, but finding and using compost from under old trash piles.

Many other tasks involved usual "domestic" duties now done on a large scale. A number of women, for example, sewed and mended for the camp, which proved invaluable as camp life progressed and manufactured or new materials grew scarce. Starting with three sewing machines given the camp by the Red Cross and placed in the corner of the main building to the left of the staircase, Mrs. R. E. Baskerville and Mrs. W. C. Parker were the first to sew for the camp. More women joined, and soon, from six in the morning until four in the afternoon, the group turned out mosquito netting, mended clothing, sewed on lost buttons, altered old ROTC pants so they could be worn in camp, and cut out and made aprons for the kitchen, as well as sheets and pillowcases for the hospital. They did not, however, do sewing for women initially, but either for the camp itself or for men who, supposedly, couldn't sew for themselves. When the sewing department added six more sewing machines, one was later set aside for use by the internee women (Hartendorp, I, 32–33).

Another former domestic duty, cooking and serving, also became a camp job, the former particularly popular as food became more and more scarce after 1943. For most of the war a dietitian was in charge of the kitchen and ordered the meals, came up with the mass recipes, and chose the cooking staff. Those women chosen, in addition to men, now cooked not for a family of four, seven, or ten, but for a group of over 3,000. Other women had the camp job of ladling out the food on the serving line; still others washed dishes and cleaned the area.

Specialists, such as doctors, nurses, and dentists, as well as engineers, plumbers, chemists, entertainers, newspaper editors, teachers, and ministers worked in their specialties for the camp. Chemists, for example, managed to produce soap, disinfectant, and hydrochloric acid, as well as Epsom salts recovered from refining salt. T. A. DeVore, formerly a chemist with the Philippine Smelting Company, headed the lab and "factory" (the latter set up on the roof of the main building using a variety of cobbled-together materials). Due to this sort of expertise, in addition to antiseptics and disinfectants, the lab produced calcium hypochlorite to purify the drinking water (Hartendorp, II, 481).

Obviously, those with a thorough knowledge of Japanese also found their skills called on professionally. Several men spoke the language well. Frank Cary, for example, a missionary who had spent most of his life as a boy and later as a clergyman in Japan, served at both Davao Internment Camp and then at Santo Tomás as an interpreter—a job that was more labor intensive than it might initially seem. Explains Cary in a May 27, 1944, entry,

> Roll call completed I report myself at the [Executive] Committee office, receive any order and then take my station on a bench where I can be quickly available to anyone needing my services. Some days I am busy all day, other days only for a few moments.
>
> The jobs may run from getting cooking permits for folks with sick children who want to cook in their shanties. . . . I may be taking directions for the building of a fence, or even by supervising the work if it is outside the lines and a soldier guard be necessary. By supervising I mean being ready to interpret whatever comes up from either side, rather than overseeing the job. (65)

Interpreters were not the only internees serving in an official capacity whose consciences and even lives would be affected by Japanese methods. The Executive Committee members (both appointed and later elected) had an often-thankless task—trying to soften yet carry out the increasingly hostile and vindictive orders emerging from the commandant's office in terms the internees would accept. Sometimes they were accused of treasonous complicity; in other cases, ineffectual efforts. Alice Bryant mused about the nature of the Executive Committee jobs, noting, "It constantly, with great danger to its members, had to battle Japanese on our behalf in an effort to get sufficient food, decent living conditions, and liberty and our own organization within the camp" (201). The actual nature of that great danger manifested itself, as mentioned earlier, with the execution of four Executive Committee members just before rescue.

Fortunately, most of the jobs in camp—professional and otherwise—were not life-threatening or complicitous, though perhaps volunteer teachers such as Bryant grew to think they might be the former. Because parents wanted their children to maintain and then exceed their former grade levels, teachers provided their expertise. Other adult internees agreed, seeing this as an excellent way to keep the children from running through the camp and getting in everyone's hair.

Santo Tomás boasted an educational system of K–12, as well as college, adult, and business education classes. Thanks to the broad collection of Americans and British citizens at the beginning of internment, Santo Tomás was blessed with professional educators at every level. The head of the camp's education department, Don W. Holter, was the ex-president of Union Theological Seminary; other members of the department who planned curricula included Luther Bewley, the former education adviser to President Quezon;

Lois F. Craft, the former principal of the American School; Ralph L. Lautzen, the former principal of Bordner School; and Helen J. Blue from the Philippine Normal School. According to Gleeck, 90 percent of the primary school teachers, 94 percent of the intermediate teachers, and 70 percent of the high school teachers "had professional teaching experience before internment." Other well-educated internees, including Bryant, though not professional teachers, filled in the gaps (262).

All children and teens of school age were required to attend a half day every day except on Sunday. Alice Bryant, who taught in the Santo Tomás school "district" after having finished her stint as dishwasher, taught seventh- and eighth-grade classes. Accommodations for learning were not optimum: Teachers held classes initially outdoors, using chairs and desks moved out of the classrooms to make room for the new internee beds; later, the classes were held in one of the old labs, a long narrow room on the fourth floor of the main building (Lewis, 84). Vaughan explains in an April 26, 1943, entry that "Classes were opened [after internment started] with unmatched and insufficient textbooks, almost no chalk for blackboard work, and stubs for pencils" (210).

Despite limited supplies, the classes had some useful tools. There were often enough textbooks to share (generally one for every four students); if there were too few copies of a text the books were put on reserve. The camp library also included, in its "reference section," four sets of encyclopedias and four dictionaries (Gleeck, 262; Lewis, 84).

Thanks to the practice of sharing books, the fact that classrooms were divided indoors only by blackboards, and the "enormous" size of the classes, teaching was a trying business. With facilities not even as good as those found in a nineteenth-century one-room schoolhouse, teachers were challenged professionally. For the few nonprofessional teachers, including Alice Bryant, teaching was often an exercise in insanity: "On one side of my section was a class so unruly that it had six history teachers in the course of the year, only one of whom was able to keep it reasonably quiet — and he taught it only two weeks! I had to talk at the top of my voice to enable my pupils to hear; and when they recited I had to repeat what they said, if the class was to get any benefit from the recitation" (153).

Middle school classes were somewhat less rowdy than high school classes but also less attentive. Bryant reports on one student who noted despondently that some students wrote, some talked, and some played cards during class: "The teacher was teaching, but not one person appeared to be paying any attention to her" (153–154). Teaching was such a nightmare to Bryant that, after only one year, she voluntarily went back to the camp work assignment desk and returned to a job in the kitchen. Despite Bryant's qualms, however,

examinations were given regularly, and on Monday, April 26, 1943, Santo Tomás held its first "Class Day" exercises. Twenty-one high school seniors
"graduated" from "Santo Tomás Internment Camp High School." (Teachers
and administrators carefully recorded test scores, lesson plans, and grades to
allow students to be given credit after the war [Vaughan, 210]). A student from
that internment school system, Karen Lewis, provides the eulogy for such an
unusual experience: "I look back with awe and respect for those amazing
teachers, so challenged, so inspired, and so brilliant, who, with so little, taught
us so much" (84).

Adults also made use of available educational expertise, taking informal lessons from knowledgeable or professional instructors in camp in foreign languages (Spanish was popular, as was Japanese), history (but not modern history or political science — both forbidden by the Japanese authorities),
theology, physics, geology, cosmology, astronomy, mathematics, and literature.
A "substantial portion" of the Santo Tomás adults participated. As Gleeck
comments, "The community had been uninterested in adult education during normal times, but in internment, both technical and non-technical lectures could be sure of an appreciative audience" (264).

Learning turned out to be a major means by which to avoid boredom and
ignore the indignity of both internment and crowding. Lessons for both adults
and children, however, tapered off as food grew scarcer and concentration by
even the most diligent became physically less and less possible.

Until July 1, 1944, Santo Tomás could boast professional entertainment as
well. Master of ceremonies and professional comedian Dave Harvey (actually
Dave Harvey McTurk), a Shanghai entertainer who had arrived in the Philippines in 1939, soon established a "Theater under the Stars," a series of regular popular entertainments for the camp inmates (Gleeck, 231). Harvey, a
veteran nightclub manager and radio personality, regularly concocted an
amusing pastiche of acts and entertainment on the wooden stage the internees
erected at one end of the plaza (Gleeck, 231; Bryant, 159). There were quiz
contests, occasionally an old American feature movie (sometimes a Japanese
feature movie), a Mickey Mouse cartoon, and Japanese propaganda films and
travelogues. There was also singing, dancing, instrumental concerts, speeches,
declamations, and Harvey's comedy routines often involving (in dialect) his
persona of Charlie McGillicuddy — an immigrant in an Americanization class.
Charlie even "ran" for a position on the Executive Council — the election
results of which were "followed" on stage and announced as McGillicuddy
won (Bryant, 160). As Hartendorp points out, the self-mocking songs sung in
the shows, making jokes about bedbugs, meals, rumors, crowding, and release,
especially infuriated the Japanese, who could not understand how or why pris-

oners would laugh at conditions of their imprisonment (II, 297). What the Japanese did not understand was that such satiric squibs kept spirits up. As Gleeck explains, the Harvey shows made "a major contribution toward building and maintaining camp morale" (264).

In addition, internee choral groups also performed on stage in the "Theater under the Stars" for the rest of the camp. Bryant joined the women's chorus to help sing Handel's *Messiah* on Christmas Day 1943, as did Ray Carlson in the men's, though Bryant claimed she "was no great addition to it, for the war literally and progressively took my breath away" (159). Ray Carlson, in addition to being an expert at inventing things, doing double shifts in the garden, and taking care of his family, was also "in all the other Christmas programs," and he also sang in a mixed quartet (Carlson, 115).

Almost a year and a half earlier, on May 16, 1942, an internee male chorus of forty men, directed by Karl Kreutz, had performed a deeply meaningful program, ending with "Gounod's 'By Babylon's Wave' after Psalm cxxxvi." When Kreutz introduced the selection, he explained to the internee audience (and their Japanese guards and staff) that "the words referred to the Babylonian captivity of the Jewish people and added that they might be taken 'as applying to some other situations'" (Hartendorp, I, 115). Several of the verses were poignantly applicable:

> Here by Babylon's wave
> Though heathen hands have bound us,
> Though, a-far from our land,
> The pains of death surround us;
> Zion! Thy mem'ry still
> In our heart we are keeping
> And still we turn to thee
> Our eyes all sad with weeping. . . .
>
> O Lord, tho' the victor command
> Our captivity sad and lowly,
> How shall we raise thy song so holy
> That we sung in our fatherland. . . .
>
> Woe unto thee! Babylon, mighty city,
> For the day of thy fall is nigh! (Hartendorp, I, 115, quoting Gounod)

Always somewhat nervous about the shows, the Japanese authorities stopped the entertainments in 1944 after one show in which Harvey told the internees in a thinly disguised vaudeville routine that there was "going to be a hot time in the old town tonight" and indicated he meant Paris—this, after having learned from a secret radio message that the D-Day invasion had occurred (Bryant, 161).

In addition to performing camp duties internees needed to maintain themselves and their own quarters, not only for public health reasons but for personal dignity as well. Bryant describes the typical daily maintenance routine among the 800 women on the second floor of the main building: "Upon arising one took soap, towel, washrag, paper (if any), toothbrush, dentifrice (if any), drinking can, boiled or chlorinated water, and juggling all this paraphernalia, walked to the bathroom. Here one stood in lines, and shared a shower with two or three others. Everyone wore *bakya* or wooden clogs, to avoid infection with athlete's foot" (165).

Initially voluntary, maintaining the condition of one's things and keeping them neat, at least in Santo Tomás, soon became compulsory because of the elected position of room monitor. In the mothers' and children's annex, there were no elections, but each mother took a regular monthly turn being a room monitor. In all cases, twice a week beds had to be moved out and cleaned underneath, with personal belongings tidied up and temporarily stowed on top of the beds and any mosquito nets tied up; floors had to be mopped and disinfected, with sills, ceilings, and furniture dusted daily. Each internee (including the monitor) was responsible for her own personal space and belongings, though all rotated communal jobs inside the rooms such as mopping and dusting, as well as (for those in rooms facing the front) cleaning pigeon droppings off the balconies (Bryant, 164).

Early in 1944, the women in Alice Bryant's room in the main building elected her room monitor. In addition to maintaining cleanliness, the room monitors' other duties eventually assumed vital importance as the war ground on and food and energy became increasingly limited. Bryant, for example, had to collect bread pieces and small eggs at the main dining hall and hand these supplies out to the room inmates, who were increasingly too weak to stand in the long food lines. The room monitor had to divide food as equitably as possible and make sure that all room dwellers got a fair share and in reasonable condition. Bread had to be broken (literally) into equal pieces with the same amount of crust if possible and the room monitor had to collect payment for any available "extras," such as eggs, sold in the room, make change, or decide to accept IOUs.

Room monitors also had to fill out forms each time a room inmate moved in or out, as vacancies occurred or people temporarily went to the hospital. Overcrowding developed as internees from smaller camps (in addition to Bacolod, Cebu, and Davao), such as Iloilo and Tacloban on other islands, swelled the ranks of the main camp at Santo Tomás. The increase in population taxed the judgment, patience, and fairness of every room monitor, as limited spaces had to accommodate an ever larger number of people. This overcrowding often led to complaints about snoring, space, and slights. Room monitors were expected to adjudicate these issues.

People in positions such as Bryant's also had the unenviable task of assigning public cleaning duties, including the various bathroom jobs, to residents of the room. Wise room monitors did their best to rotate the worst duties and to compensate for those too sick to work at the hardest jobs with useful but less strenuous work (Magnuson, 53).

Roll call (often more than one a day) was another onerous duty for the room monitor; there had to be an exact count (and the reason for any absence recorded on the log) of every room inmate legally registered in the room. The room monitors made reports to the floor monitor, who then made them to the inspecting Japanese officers. Originally, this was done in a rather cursory fashion at 9:00 A.M. each morning; during the first months of 1944, however, there were at least two roll calls a day, one in the morning and one in the evening. Sometimes there was an additional one and this time instead of just the room monitors standing at attention outside the room all of the residents had to line up stiffly in the building corridors. Miscounting had serious consequences. If the count the room monitor gave did not match the registered number in the room (assuming explained absences), then the entire floor would begin the count again. As people grew weaker and sicker from both dysentery and malnutrition, as well as cursed with edema-swollen feet, standing at attention for hours was often unbearable. On occasion, the Japanese officer misunderstood the count given or misread the logs for the rooms; despite this, the count would be repeated until it came out "right." A good room monitor had to be able to think quickly enough to avoid recounts (193–194).

Bryant describes the procedure in detail as it occurred in early 1944 in Santo Tomás:

> Each time I had to fill out a form which I held in my hand as, wearing an armband, I stood at the head of my double line. Sometimes the roll call, which usually took about twenty minutes, would last two or three hours, and no one would get anything done. A few times we had special roll calls, once at two o'clock in the morning. If a Japanese passed I would say, "Ready, bow!" and theoretically the room bowed as if in one piece. An instant later I would say, "As you were," and it assumed an upright position. (193)

Not all work, however, was communal or for private maintenance or camp routine. Some of the more enterprising devoted time left over from camp jobs to entrepreneurship or personal needs. Until early 1944, Santo Tomás eerily resembled a small town, complete with its own rudimentary economy and marketplace. Whitesides comments, "By the time one year had elapsed most of the basic economic and financial elements of a flourishing American economy were being applied under a free enterprise system, in a prison where the jailers did absolutely nothing to provide for their prisoners" (19).

He goes on to explain that self-help and internee initiative were responsible and, in doing so, defines what he means by "flourishing": "By the end of April 1943 we had become a flourishing but overcrowded community of nearly 6000 people. Flourishing we were compared to the standards of living that we would have endured without the economic and financial wizardry we conjured up with our own devices" (20).

Both Celia Lucas and Whitesides list a number of clever internee enterprises that made their mark on the camp economy during the first fifteen to eighteen months. Barber shops appeared, for example, and ex-employees of Pan-American Airways "developed a process for pasteurizing coconut milk" and set up a dairy, called the Coconut Cow, which sold "Milk from Contented Coconuts" at 15 cents a pint both to individuals and to the central kitchen (Whitesides, 18; Lucas, 46). Other internees repaired shoes and made bakyas, while still others skillfully beat out cups, water carriers, and plates from old tin cans. Those who could crochet advertised "brassieres to fit" or knit shirts (using split string as the thread). Some women whittled knitting needles out of bamboo. Others created shorts for sale or made stuffed animals from their own old clothes, summer dresses, and trousers. As Lewis remarks, "There most certainly was some sort of barter or payment for these skills" (81–82).

Restaurants also flourished, selling various hard-to-come-by foods. "Lefties," for example, served coffee and hotcakes made from corn mush, as well as hot meals at one peso per dish. Doris Rubens and her husband were treated to just such a meal (at Lefties, apparently, based on their description) when they were brought into Santo Tomás in April 1943 after being captured in the hills of central Luzon. Friends provided the meal, which included not only hotcakes but cigarettes and eggs as well (Rubens, 208).

Candy makers and bakers also sprung up, selling cakes made with duck eggs and rice flour, and coconut or molasses candy, the latter especially popular with "the large number of business executives who had been deprived of their customarily large daily consumption of alcohol." Cornbread, muffins, cookies, brownies, and popcorn soon followed (Whitesides, 18; Nixon, 36–37).

Eva Nixon credits a friend of hers, Art Whitman, with "spark[ing] the spirit of business" in camp. Immediately following the fall of Singapore (in February 1942), he told Nixon he believed that they would be imprisoned for a "number of years"; facing this, and knowing how necessary both absorbing activity and money for extras would become, he started a business making candy — initially, only fudge. As Nixon explains, however, his fudge was excellent, so he branched out, concocting cream-filled chocolates so good that people started buying boxes of his specialty chocolates for spouses or girlfriends or just for themselves (36).

Private "shop" owners also set themselves up, if only in a small way. A lamp store sold floating-wick lamps made out of carved coconut shells powered by coconut oil; a beauty shop of sorts made its presence known, as did a stationer and a fortune- teller.

Businesses were so numerous and camp space so limited that soon the Executive Committee had to make a rule that "each vendor had to secure a license to operate a business." To secure such a license, a vendor had to pass a health inspection and pay a fee to the Internee Relief and Welfare Committee (Nixon, 37).

On January 6, 1943, Kuroda gave permission for a camp canteen "to be operated as a community enterprise under the direction of the Executive Committee" (Hartendorp, I, 339). Camp internees provided capital to start the canteen, to buy the building materials and initial stock, and to pay for utilities. The store originally intended to sell such merchandise as toilet articles, clothing and sundries, and later, "home-made" sundries such as jelly, peanut butter, and "grapenuts" made from toasted coconut. The canteen did a brisk business selling at cost with only a "a nominal surcharge." Nonsalaried internees worked behind the counter, and by order of the Executive Committee, once again, "all profits accruing [were to] be donated to a relief and welfare fund for the benefit of indigent internees" (339).

Even a somewhat elaborate camp magazine/newspaper evolved. The *Internitis*, a newspaper taking the place of the earlier, short-lived *Internews*, had cartoons, competitions, a gossip column, jokes, cooking hints and substitution recipes, short stories, crossword puzzles, and horoscopes. Dave Harvey also published a humorous camp magazine called the *STIC Gazette*; the two together provided all the above plus the sports scores of the internee British vs. American league baseball and soccer games, as well as chess, dart, and bridge tournaments. Card games, according to Gleeck, were the principal quiet recreation in Santo Tomás; there were at least fifteen to twenty poker games every evening and over forty bridge foursomes (Gleeck, 264).Other entertainment included music — either the evening's recorded musical programs or live performances on stage, with performers like violinist Grace Nash. For these, as well as for dances and parties, the two publications listed times and places (Lucas, 46–47).

Obviously, as conditions worsened by mid-1943, the number of baseball games and parties, as well as humorous reports about those activities, began to shrink. Vaughan, for example, notes in an entry dated April 19, 1943, that despite the flowering trees, the spacious lawns, the baseball league, and the four-hole golf course, "There is tragedy in every group, a tightness about the mouth of a seemingly carefree ball player, furrowed brows, quick and cautious whispers after a furtive look around to see that no one is in earshot" (202). The growing lack of food and the tightening of Japanese regulations soon made games (as well as the energy or optimism to play them) fading events of the past.

Even if they did not make items to sell, the internees improved personal conditions through work on private projects. Labor was expended making clothing, utensils, tools, and necessities for private life and survival.

The summer of 1943 through May 1944 saw clothing becoming more and more threadbare and embarrassing. Finally, the commandant gave each internee eighty "clothing points" or coupons for the period ending in May. One yard of cotton print, 36 inches wide, cost ten points; men's denim (enough for a pair of shorts) ran twenty-five points. Many internees decided to pool their coupons, so the clothing department could buy wholesale and get the most cloth for the least money (Lucas, 102–103).

Women now sewed for themselves, their husbands, and their children to fill out their meager wardrobes. Even though Red Cross relief supplies (in the famous Christmas of 1943) had included enough playsuits to go around (one each), the children's clothing and other garments still required either making, altering, or mending (Cary, May 27, 1944, 64). Because of the tight cloth rationing, however, women in camp soon achieved a tiny measure of freedom: Women's shorts, originally outlawed because of Japanese ideas of female modesty, later were allowed (because they took less cloth to make). The only requirement was that the shorts be *no more than four inches* above the knee, this having been established, apparently, as the absolute line of visible virtue (Lucas, 103).

Margaret Sams was also a seamstress when conditions made it necessary. She was not, unfortunately, a tinker. Luckily, a friend was capable of improvising in that department. Margaret rhapsodizes over the inventive abilities of Jerry Sams (her future husband), who managed to make life easier for both Margaret and her son through his ingenuity and hard work. One of the things Margaret wanted most was a washboard; without one it was almost impossible to get clothes truly clean. Jerry brought Margaret one—seemingly materialized out of nowhere. She goes on to describe it: "And what a washboard! He made it from pieces of iron, a board, and a large tin cracker can. Where he got the board or the iron strips or the can or the tools with which to make it I didn't ask him, but he bent the tin can over the iron strips which he had secured to the board in the conventional washboard pattern, and I loved it" (107).

Nor did Jerry stop with the washboard. He soon solved a daily problem: carrying food back from the food line. Sams found she could not carry both her portion and David's back from the line to a place to eat alone; David, a small boy, had to carry his own. Inevitably, it slopped or spilled out. Jerry made David a little pail to carry his food in. This, too, was constructed out of an old cracker tin (Jerry seems to have made the best of refuse piles and old dumping grounds). Jerry took the tin, cut it off at the right height, then folded the sharp edges over and made them smooth. He soldered a partition on the inside of the pail so that the mush would not run into the greens and then soldered a handle on the pail itself. This marvel he then painted, adding David's name on it later. For some, love comes with roses and candy; for Margaret Sams, it came with washboards, extra food, and a little boy's pail. Long-stemmed roses and Whitman samplers were from another life.

Private gardens were another, perhaps more vital, regular means of improving the present life of oneself and loved ones. Allowed small plots of land in waste areas, internees raised not flowers but as many vegetables as possible to supplement the diet of their families. Though the Japanese allowed only one hour a day (7–8 A.M.) for private garden work, internees still managed to raise enough produce to supplement their increasingly thin diet — at least until 1944, when Japanese authorities confiscated much of the private produce and made it part of the official camp ration and demanded more area be cleared and tilled.

Bryant's ever-resourceful husband, the "Gov'nor," made a flourishing garden on a cast-off space between the gymnasium wall and the barbed wire perimeter fence. Sorting through old piles of camp refuse, Mr. Bryant eventually took away wheelbarrow loads of compost he found. After ditching and draining the somewhat swampy land and mixing in the compost, the Gov'nor planted his first crop using seed he brought with him from Negros and some he received from private individuals and the camp garden. During the dry season, he personally watered his plants by hand with a watering can; in the wet months, he kept ditches open to drain off excess water. He weeded, loosened, and aerated the soil daily.

When his first crop of lima beans and salad greens such as pechay and talnium matured, he plowed it back into the ground; the second crop, including lettuce, talnium, onions, radishes, and, occasionally, cucumbers and tomatoes, helped make the difference between life and death for himself and Bryant in the last months of internment (157–158). Indeed, during that time, his garden even helped others; explains his wife, "During the worst time in

Santo Tomás, from twenty-five to twenty-seven persons were getting something out of his garden every day. Some observant people suggested that, if he had been in charge of the camp garden, there would have been enough greenery for everyone." Despite their generosity, the Bryants still had enough left over to trade with others for a bit of rice or cornmeal mush.

Bryant was particularly impatient with and disapproving of those who sat on the sidelines idly, envying her produce; her attitude echoes that of the Little Red Hen: "Sometimes when people saw me bringing in a big tray of garden produce they would exclaim, 'You are lucky to have a garden!' I was fortunate to have a husband who possessed a great deal of energy and initiative. If I had admired him before the war for being a dirt farmer, my admiration now increased when I saw other men with hungry families sitting around reading novels" (158).

She notes somewhat scornfully that others could certainly have done the same as her husband, and points out that, in addition to the Gov'nor's hard work, his foresight was also exemplary. Before he plowed under the first crop, Mr. Bryant saved seeds and put them in a tin box to keep them safe from insects, as well as giving seedlings to others. To Bryant, hunger was a problem at least partly due to laziness and lack of imagination; she and the Gov'nor survived until rescue due in no small part to Mr. Bryant's garden.

Baguio camp (at this point, Camp Holmes) had a smaller administrative organization than that of the largest camp. The internee "General Committee" (initially appointed and then later elected) simply divided the necessary camp work and put it loosely into "departments." According to internee Jim Halsema, assignments then followed an elaborate "Master Sheet," drawn up by internee Gus Skerl, that "would have done credit to the operational studies of a major corporation." Skerl's list attempted (as usual) to match talents and occupational preferences with necessary labor (Halsema ltr, May 21, 1997). Once again, although five hours a day of work were required of each male internee and three hours a day for women, internees generally were allowed to choose the detail on which they would work (Ogle, 191–192).

With no package line similar to Santo Tomás's, in Baguio jobs such as porter, checker, or storehouse clerk didn't exist; other jobs, unknown in Santo Tomás, did exist, such as goat and pig herder — the latter usually done by teenage or middle school internee boys (Hartendorp, I, 169; Bloom, "Death," 78). The different departments included the kitchen department, the hospital, the department for camp sanitation, the garbage department, the "mechanical" department (which fashioned pots and water cauldrons, did mechanical repairs, and even produced aluminum false teeth [Ogle, 199]), the internee guard department (similar to Santo Tomás's camp police), and the room cleaning department. Unlike the larger camp, Baguio had no room or floor monitors. In most cases the camp duties were done by male internees, because women had their own General Committee that assigned them to look after the children and to wash and mend their own and their families' clothes, though they also worked in the kitchens, helped in the hospital, and occasionally cleaned up garbage inside the camp. Male internees, for example, were the only ones allowed outside the camp to gather supplies from town, dispose of garbage, herd and tend animals such as pigs, goats, chickens, and eventually cattle, or allowed to cut firewood (Halsema, 1944 Diary, Feb. 7; Ogle, 198–199). Women (except for nurses) stayed in the restricted world of the camp, away from dangerous unofficial activities such as smuggling food or radio parts back into camp (Bloom, "Death," 78).

Other more strenuous duties included daily gutter cleaning details (referring to the ground gutters between the walk and the approach to each building, which tended to fill with dirt and debris), and after the few cattle arrived, "slaughtering details" (Ogle, 199).

One of the more popular details needs explanation. Garbage detail, which required men to load garbage cans daily into a four-wheeled cart that they themselves had to pull, provided access to the outside world, as mentioned earlier. The garbage dump was a mile outside camp down the road. This meant, among other things, that the garbage crew had access to, and could buy, extra food such as eggs and mangos at a small store on the way back to camp. Jim Halsema, a member of the crew, also ran a single-sheet, typed a "daily newspaper" (using the news drawn from a secret radio in the camp hospital), thereby diverting suspicion from the camp and suggesting implicitly that he got his news outside the camp on his garbage trips. This sheet was posted in camp and enjoyed by everyone (Ogle, 196; Halsema, "Oral," 9). A copy of it is now on display in the new National POW Museum in Andersonville, Georgia.

Internees who were in the professions tended to work in their specialties—especially in health care and laboratory work, though engineers took their place, for example, on the "fuel" committee. Halsema enumerates the following different professionals in camp as of January 1945 (numbers are approximate): 4 engineers, 1 geologist, 1 chemist, 13 teachers, 1 dentist, 43 miners, 1 pharmacist, 6 mechanics, 8 doctors, 10 nurses, 1 journalist, 4 lumbermen, 17 assorted "businessmen," over 120 missionaries and family members, and one interpreter ("Oral," n1, Appendix D).[1] The bilingual, bicultural daughter of an American Episcopal bishop serving in Japan, Nellie McKim, served not only as the camp interpreter but, according to Bloom, as "a valuable liaison with the Japanese commandants and guards" as well ("Death," 78). Unlike

Frank Cary in Davao and then at Santo Tomás, she seems to have had no difficulty in drawing an emotional or ethical line between her sympathies and her countrymen. She clearly aligned herself with her countrymen.

Another professional activity was teaching. Like Santo Tomás, Baguio camp intended to push the camp children beyond their previous grade level. Though there was no school for the first four months at Camp John Hay, after the move to Camp Holmes, there were regular classes for both elementary and high school pupils. Unlike the students in Santo Tomás, Baguio's students had enough textbooks — those brought in from Brent School — though they were severely censored by the Japanese. All discussion of "dangerous ideas" (which were unspecified), and of forbidden subjects such as geography and history were the Japanese censors' particular targets. If the objectionable portions of the text were too long to be blacked out, the Japanese simply tore out the pages until the text was once again "safe." (Jim Halsema mentions that he secretly taught just those two forbidden subjects using information he collected from town on the garbage detail or from the secret radio smuggled into camp in a box of medical supplies by Dr. Dana Nance ["Oral," 9].)

Because there was no place to hold class except underfoot in the dining area, school, which started on May 27 of the first year, was initially held outdoors under the trees or in some other reasonably quiet spot. Later, during the rainy season, the internees petitioned the Japanese to provide a building. The Japanese then brought into camp a shack from outside to serve as an elementary school building and offered a small cottage by the guard house for the high school (the latter moved repeatedly over the next year). Neither was particularly spacious nor well equipped. Both consisted of only one room with no desks or seats but just "a miscellaneous assortment" of rough tables and crude benches. Paper, of course, was at a premium, as were pencils, tablets, and chalk. There were a few blackboards and rough wrapping paper or the backs of wallpaper samples to serve for paper (Ogle, 231–233).

The teachers made up for the lack of materials or space. As at Santo Tomás, Baguio's teachers were professionals — mostly from Brent School, though some from other places as well. These — and several professors — made up the K–12 and adult education divisions. There were even graduations from high school after every semester, complete with diplomas fashioned by the camp carpenter shop to resemble "small wooden balls and chains." Betty Smeddle was one of several students who completed high school in Camp Holmes (Shaplen, 69).

Similar to those at Santo Tomás, the internees at Baguio were great readers. The Japanese allowed them to take the library of the John Hay Officer's Club with them to Camp Holmes, and this was supplemented eventually by all the books from the Brent School library and part of the library of a local Anglican bishop. To keep track of the books, the camp chose an official librarian and also a bookbinder to keep the books repaired. But Ogle notes, "The number of really good books . . . was limited, and they were the ones in constant demand, and there was always a long waiting list for them" (236–237).

Other camp entertainment, though not professionally performed or organized like Dave Harvey's in Santo Tomás, did provide programs of one kind or another to supplement the inevitable bridge playing. Almost everyone came to the dining room to listen to musical programs, oral readings, lectures, quiz games, and especially camp-written and -produced plays. According to Ogle, Mrs. Lucy Vincent was the usual author and director of these thespian affairs and favored satiric and comic plays about camp life such as her highly popular adaptation, "Camp Hamlet" (237–239). Camp Holmes also mounted a well-received version of Thornton Wilder's *Our Town* (Halsema ltr, May 21, 1997).

One last perennial entertainment involved sports. As at Santo Tomás, Baguio had two standing baseball teams, in this case the Miners and the Missionaries. These teams, until debility from hunger and disease became too common, played on the parade grounds before enthusiastic crowds of partisan internees. There is no mention of soccer or any other game (Ogle, 239).

Crouter, Halsema, and others also mention in passing in their journals the more ordinary camp jobs. Halsema, for example, mentions shoe repair (and amateur cobblers) (1944 Diary, January 24); others discuss the camp "playsuits" made from material courtesy of the Red Cross, and still others speak of egg gathering, feeding the stock, handing out rationed toilet paper, and cleaning up litter. Halsema adds floor mopping and fly swatting (though not as a contest) and cutting and hauling firewood to the list of duties ("E. J.," 300).

Not everyone saw work as noble under all circumstances. In a June 23, 1942, entry Natalie Crouter writes, "I'm tired of garbage and washing out three cans every morning. Tomorrow I will see the dignity of labor again but today it's off!" (66). Other internees complain of fixing toilets, cutting up vegetables, or cleaning the mess made by other people's children in the crowded barracks. Generally speaking, however, most internees, no matter how much they disliked the camp work, saw it as a necessary evil—and even the price one paid for a communitarian existence.

For most camp members, the inevitable camp job involved rice picking, called by Crouter "a common communal activity for everyone," though it had started out (and stayed) primarily a female activity. Everyone was supposed to pick over and clean at least one plate of rice a day. The so-called "Rice Detail" met at one side of the vegetable room, where on a long table internees picked rocks, insects, and detritus out of the rice spread before them. As at Santo Tomás, the chore was boring but not terribly laborious, though it was very hard on the eyes; just as in the larger camp, people gossiped while doing it or sang (Crouter, May 7, 1942, 45; Ogle, 196).

Women in particular were expected to help with preparing the raw materials for meals by doing such humdrum chores as washing and cutting up vegetables for the camp kitchen. This was the vegetable detail and involved around forty women regularly. Assembling in the vegetable room on the ground floor of the men's barracks, the women would cut up, clean, and slice out mold or rotten spots on the various produce brought in, at least early on, in crates, bags, and bundles by the camp buyers from Baguio market. The female internees had the vegetable detail highly organized. Everyone went to work at 7:00 or 7:30 A.M., stopped briefly for breakfast at 8:00 A.M., then went back at 9:00 A.M. and worked until 10:30 or 11:00 A.M.. Sitting on benches, they peeled camotes, chopped cabbage at the table, snapped green beans, cleaned green onions, and hunted out slugs in the pechay (Ogle, 192–194).

Once in a while, some female internees, to the disgust of others, would refuse to do this (or any other) work. Explains Crouter,

> [She] says she has two children to look after. She is too good to do hard work. . . . Like many others they [this woman and her daughter] wash too often and as many clothes as they would have washed at home. It can't be done here with so many shortages — soap, water, pails. There are about forty mothers who do no communal work, simply look after their children. If many more of our workers leave camp, these others will have to help cut vegetables or they won't get any. (April 15, 1942, 38)

Baguio mothers were expected (and socially pressured) to do communal work; their initial assumption that they didn't have to do so makes this camp very different from Santo Tomás. There, from the very beginning, women with small children — Frieda Magnuson, Margaret Sams, Elizabeth Vaughan — all had specific jobs to do.

Even in Baguio, however, women were expected (whether mothers or not) to keep their "private" spaces clean by mopping and dusting, and their personal goods (netting, bedrolls, boxes, clothes) on a shelf or in a box. Cleanliness and neatness were demanded by the majority of room residents; given the limited living space, babies frequently had their diapers changed on the floor (Crouter, March 6, 1942, 27), and women had to sleep shoulder to shoulder.

Sewing for oneself and one's family, repairing broken necessities (sandal straps, eyeglasses, watches), and scraping together food sources were a large part of everyday life for the women. They did the family's laundry, too, using fire pails for washtubs. It was, says Ogle, "a bit of an ordeal," especially during the rainy season when lines for wet clothes had to be stretched out during the day in the barracks (202–204). Women also sewed clothing for their children out of discarded garments, perhaps the same ones these very women — or others of their class and position — had put in Red Cross boxes just before the war. Here, as in Santo Tomás, a certain surreal quality intrudes. Crouter, in a June 30, 1942, entry, explains that the clothing Nakamura gave them to replace their own was not only inappropriate but also a mocking reminder of their prewar lives:

> The gowns are a strange collection for us to carry in. . . . They are not practical for camp wear, even for dressing gowns or housecoats, for the material is too elegant to be worn before the eyes of soldier guards who are curious. . . . Their appearance [the gowns'] aroused mixed sensations. . . . There before us in smooth, shining black satin, diamond shoulder straps, silver lamé, suave cut, shape and design . . . we had not seen such beauty of line for six months and it mixed oddly with the barracks mops in kerosene tins, garbage tins, and waitresses. (64–65)

Unlike the evening gowns and diamond shoulder straps, the mops and kerosene tins were the truth of daily life now. Internees wrung what they needed out of what was available. June Crouter even took a Red Cross triangle bandage and made a daring sun top for herself. Several older ladies collected scraps of used material and made quilts ("concentration camp gray," one resident noted). Jerry Crouter fixed his daughter June's broken glasses frames one day and dug through garbage for a bone with marrow for Natalie on another.

With a population of only 148 people at its largest (Waterford, 260), Bacolod camp on Negros Island demanded even more primitive work of its internees than did Baguio. Bacolod had almost no facilities (especially for health) and, as has been mentioned, what run-down buildings of the former elementary school existed had to be cleaned, repaired, and modified by the first group of internees. They even had to build a wood stove on which to cook (Vaughan, June 7, 1942, 96–97).

Fortunately, to deal with such circumstances, Bacolod could claim a well-trained and diverse population. According to Vaughan, Bacolod internees were comprised of twenty-one Sugar Central executives, seven other employees of the Central, five lumber mill executives and eleven lumber mill employees, one doctor, one lawyer, three teachers, nine Protestant missionaries, nine collective Catholic nuns and priests, eleven "other" employed, and forty-two "unemployed or non," of which housewives undoubtedly made up a large proportion ("Community," 30).

Unlike the Santo Tomás or Holmes camps, in Bacolod whole buildings or floors weren't set aside and sexually segregated, but instead, different school rooms housed each sex. Work was also assigned by sex. Men herded and tended camp animals (a carabao, chickens, rabbits, and pigs) and cut wood, as well as tending the camp garden and boiling the rice and drinking water. When necessary the men also pitched in with both carpentry and plumbing jobs; Vaughan, for example, mentions a series of privies the men built.

The women's jobs tended to follow an enlarged domestic arrangement in Bacolod as well as in Baguio, though women here (lacking an interned male chef) did most of the cooking and served food, took turns preparing vegetables, and cared for the sick (Bryant, 126). Despite lack of experience or even interest, any woman could be assigned to cook, though the camp did have a dietitian who organized the menus. Disinterested or inexperienced cooks, however, often made nearly inedible food, including the "extra" food given to those men doing heavy manual work. As Bryant reports: "There were sitao beans, black beans, and mung beans, the last so old that many were flinty and inedible. They were cooked without any meat or grease, and often peppered and salted until they were most unpalatable" (147).

Everyone capable of working was expected to do so and in fact was assigned some task. Camp work itself took about two hours a day for each internee — in addition to personal housekeeping and room upkeep. The personal chores involved taking turns sweeping out the rooms daily and scrubbing and washing the walls and floors of the rooms once a week. With only a tiny bit of disinfectant and limited soap, the cleaning was more a matter of intention than of results (Bryant, 126).

Alice Bryant complains about the materials she had to work with, pointing out that the "broom" was simply "a little bundle of twigs that had no handle" (127). Bryant and her roommates bent over the short brooms for ten or more minutes at a time — and even then they could not sweep up dust and debris very well because of the crude broom straws made of twigs.

Women also were responsible for washing their own and their families' clothes. Approximately every two or three days, often between 9 and 11 A.M., women carried their meager garments to the long wash trough the men had built earlier and "rubbed away in cold water." Alas for Bacolod residents — unlike Margaret Sams, no one was blessed with a washboard (Bryant, 127; Vaughan, June 7, 1942, 97). The results, at least according to Vaughan, were not inspiring; colors ran, garments got stained by native water, and the constant hand scrubbing soon wore holes in the clothing. Vaughan's towels were "now a pinkish yellow from stains, poor soap, mineral water, and just poor washing on [my] part" (October 18, 1942, 140).

Women internees also spent their time sewing and mending their children's clothes. In an entry dated January 1943, Vaughan talks about taking an old maternity smock she had among her possessions (she wore it carrying Clay) and making a "new dress" out of it; she also talks about children's skirts and sun suits made from old tablecloths. Similar to the heroine in *Gone with the Wind*, she and the other women turned home furnishings into clothing: "Scarlett O'Hara was not the only war-harassed self-stylist who saw wearing possibilities in window draperies. Bedroom marquisette [sheer mesh fabric for mosquito nets] has gone into ladies' air-conditioned undies in camp, and heavier curtains and odd pieces of draperies have appeared as original concentration camp dresses" (185). Such inventive alterations were particularly necessary for Vaughan. Clothing she had worn while hiding up in the hills during the months before capture constituted her entire wardrobe; these were worn almost through (November 20, 1942, 160).

Work and camp duties (both public and private) soon fell into a hard but regular routine in Bacolod. Elizabeth Vaughan's June 7, 1942, entry gives a typical "order of the day" schedule for the camp in the summer of 1942. Despite the fact that there were no room monitors or bureaucratic machinery, the numbers of internees still had to be carefully noted. In the case of Bacolod, this was done not only through the roll calls (two per day) but also by a series of bed checks at night. Vaughan shows the early morning hours of June 7 interrupted at least four times (midnight, 2:00, 3:00, and 4:00 A.M.) by bed checks in which Japanese guards marched into the various rooms and shined flashlights suddenly in the eyes of those trying to sleep to ascertain if anyone had escaped. This series of interruptions was not unusual (97). With this in mind, we look now at Vaughan's schedule to get a sense of the work and activity (on limited sleep) at Bacolod camp:

> A.M.
> 7:00 Breakfast
> 8:00 Roll call on front steps
> 9:00–11:00 Housekeeping (scrub floors, do laundry)
> 11:30 Lunch
> P.M.
> Noon–2:30 Siesta (quiet)
> 3:00–5:00 Sewing, cleaning, laundry, bath
> 5:00 Tea
> 6:00 Roll call on the front steps
> 9:00 Lights out. (97)

It is interesting to compare this well-documented camp on Negros with several less-documented camps on other islands—specifically on Cebu and on Mindanao—in terms of work conditions.

Cebu internees, for example, had no jobs for an "Executive" or even a "Central" committee similar to those in Baguio or Bacolod. The Cebu internees chose two representatives to speak for them to the Japanese commander, but the results were frustratingly negligible. Nothing was done. Protests also failed to stop either the overcrowding or the two roll calls per day (8 A.M., 6 P.M.). Protests also didn't prevent the guards from passing through the cells every two hours supposedly to detect escape (Hartendorp, I, 317). "Work" as such was minimal in the provincial jail, though there was more to do in the next locations when the 23 British internees moved to Lahug Primary School and the 100 or so Americans, along with a few stray Norwegians and Dutch, moved to the junior college campus.

Jobs at the internment camp at the junior college branch on Cebu reflected the destruction that had happened earlier. Because water, electric, and gas supplies were unavailable, camp work at the new location would include not only chopping firewood or making charcoal for fires but also drawing and carrying water from wells and carving, then filling, coconut shell lamps for light. Hartendorp notes that, despite the much roomier conditions at the junior college branch, it was also exceptionally filthy and dirty, having been previously occupied by the invading army, many of whom had never seen a Western bathroom before (I, 317). Cleanup took quite some time, especially given the lack of power and water.

The nature of camp life and the various jobs in Davao internment camp seem closer to those at Santo Tomás than one might expect. Davao, too, had an Executive Committee (Cary explained that even though he had important language skills, he couldn't be on it, because his interpreting work would complicate his job). The camp also held formal religious services. Cary, a missionary apparently affiliated with the Congregational church, performed religious duties, including holding formal church services, every week. He rotated these duties with other clerical internees, among whom were several Catholic priests, an Episcopalian reverend, a Baptist minister, and a Society of Friends (Quaker) missionary. (He was also on an entertainment committee, though what it did other than sing at Christmas is not clear.)

Because the camp had a garden, obviously watering, weeding, thinning, and keeping the plants pest-free were camp jobs to be done communally. Cooking and food preparation were also done communally, as was public area cleaning. In another entry, Cary indicates that wood also had to be gathered and cut for both cooking and hot water. In this same passage, he points out that laundry had to be done by hand as well (ltr, January 28, 1944, 50). There was also a clinic that had to be ready for inspection.

Additionally, rooms had to be cleaned, mopped, and dusted in time for Saturday morning inspection by the Japanese, although Cary makes no mention of roll call. Cary also discusses having to wash the floor of his dwelling and tightening the slats on the palma brava over the porch, although his main job was still serving, he says, as on-call translator (ltr, May 15, 1943, 34).

The Davao Internment Camp does not seem nearly so primitive as either Cebu or Bacolod. Cary's daily schedule for April 14, 1942, is interesting to compare with that of Vaughan's at Bacolod:

> 5:00 A.M. Go down to grate and press out "cocoa-nut milk" for gang's breakfast
> 6:30 Help clean floors
> 7:00 Breakfast
> 7:30 Cleaning continues
> 8:00 To garden to work
> 11:30 Bath
> Noon Lunch/Reading
> 3:00 P.M. Coffee/reading
> 4:00 To garden to water
> 5:15 Bath
> 5:30 Supper
> 6:00 Bridge or reading
> 9:00 To bed (9)

One wonders what Elizabeth Vaughan, the "Guv'nor," and Alice Bryant would have given to have two baths a day, no roll call, and at least six hours for reading.

Even so, Frank Cary found Santo Tomás, at least initially, a camp with many more creature comforts than Davao. He noted in January 1944 (just after his transfer from Davao) that in Santo Tomás there was running water in the showers *at all hours* and that cooking was all done by gas, not wood—which eliminated jobs such as chopping, carrying, and stacking. He also mentions in his January 8, 1944, letter that the Santo Tomás floors were cement and "insect-proof" (which would come as news to the bedbug brigade) and that the weather was comfortably cool (Cary, 48). Santo Tomás, he explains, had eliminated a number of more primitive jobs and "civilization has been at work." In mid-1943, "Laundry can be sent out for starching" by those with money, instead of being hand laundered (50), he notes approvingly.

Undoubtedly, this relative "civilization" was one of the biggest reasons that internees in Santo Tomás were reluctant to transfer to the new Los Baños camp 68 kilometers south of Manila. As Hartendorp explains, "it was not that Santo Tomás was an ideal place to spend one's life in, month after month, season after season; but much had been done to make living conditions at least tolerable" (vol. I, 523).

Thanks to early Red Cross funds, personal money, and loans, Santo Tomás sported many camp improvements, including hospital facilities, "dorms," full sanitary facilities, and a well-equipped kitchen. A significant proportion of internees also had personal shanties they had built at some expense. Work for the camp and for self-maintenance followed a regular, predictable, and even tolerable schedule. No one had to lug water, cook food for the entire camp on smoky wood fires, or concoct primitive sanitary facilities. For a variety of sound reasons, it was definitely a case of better the devil they knew than the one they didn't.

And there were some very disturbing rumors about the devil they didn't know. As has been noted earlier, despite the glowing reports about Los Baños in the Japanese-controlled *Tribune*, internees were suspicious of the elaborate paeans to scenery, tranquil surroundings, and fresh air—all, incidentally, equally true of a cemetery. The camp would require, even by Japanese accounts, a great deal of additional work to make it fully habitable.

After the first 800 relatively strong and healthy internees arrived in mid-1943, they were immediately sent to finish the barracks complexes, as well as upgrade the toilet and shower situation previously mentioned. They also were forced, as were internees in Santo Tomás later, to string a six-strand barbed-wire perimeter fence around the camp—all of which involved heavy work, such as digging innumerable post holes and then gingerly stretching the wire. With only wood stoves in the kitchen, there was also a wood chopping detail, along with the initial preparation of a camp garden by cutting grass, digging, and turning soil, as well as the initial weeding and planting. By the time later truckloads of internees (married couples, children, and seniors) arrived, the camp was a bit less primitive and more similar to what the internees had left. Here, too, every internee who was able-bodied had to work two hours at heavy work (usually males) or three hours at lighter work (women and seniors, usually). There was an executive committee and a series of subcommittees: kitchen, sanitation, health, welfare, administration, education, and food distribution (Hartendorp, II, 446, n1). Briefly classes, both high school level and adult in a variety of subjects—from foreign languages (especially Japanese and Spanish) to science and literature—were a part of the camp during the summer of 1943 and partly into 1944 (Arthur, 80). After this point, the internees' scramble for food and survival once again made any effort not connected with finding or consuming food and carrying out the most basic camp duties unlikely because of the listlessness and weakness caused by growing malnutrition.

Before extreme ration shortages became the norm, however, a variety of camp jobs were connected with the subcommittees. In Los Baños married couples were allowed to live together in the newly built "married barracks." Room maintenance then became the duty of a family or a couple, rather than thirty others. In some ways it was bliss to have the privacy and extra space; in others it was more difficult, because there were fewer hands to do necessary work. Even in the barracks for singles, room sharing was more regularly among four to six rather than thirty to fifty.

Although there were no room or floor monitors, Los Baños had barracks monitors (such as Jane Wills's father) elected by each housing unit every six months who were responsible for the "discipline, sanitation, health, welfare, and feeding" of each barracks (Hartendorp, II, 446; Wills, 22–23). As in other camps, a roll call was required, and barracks monitors were responsible for the numbers under their charge. According to Calhoun and Fonger, both former chairmen of the Executive Committee, Major Tanaka, the first commandant of the camp, was a decent individual and refused to require any extra or middle-of-the-night roll calls, unlike the continuing practice at Santo Tomás (Arthur, 55).

Internees at Los Baños in late 1943 and early 1944 could expect to work as cooks, servers, produce buyers for the camp kitchen at the "shed," bathroom cleaners, nurses, doctors, aides, members of the camp administration, teachers, plumbers, engineers, office workers, and gardeners, as well as wood foragers and choppers (Hartendorp II, 445). Once again, health professionals continued to work in their specialty. U.S. Naval Lieutenant Commander Laura Cobb, for example, the head of the navy nurses, then supervisor of all U.S. Navy, British, and two Filipino civilian nurses, worked, along with doctors, aides, and volunteers (both men and women), in the makeshift Los Baños Hospital (Evans, 462; Davis, 30). Dr. Dana Nance, previously in Baguio, was transferred to Los Baños, where he served as head of the hospital.

To serve in the hospital required not only professional skill but often ingenious tinkering. Despite the fact that, due to aid money in May, August, and October 1943, Los Baños was able to purchase some basic supplies (Hartendorp, II, 18–19), others materialized seemingly out of cleverness and thin air: "Yankee ingenuity constantly outdid itself in converting the seemingly impossible into the utilitarian" (Evans, 463). Old Japanese beer bottles from the dump, for example, had their necks cut off and the cut polished smooth to become hospital glassware; internees soon fashioned the discarded bottle necks into patient "call bells," by hanging a bit of steel inside the neck on a piece of vine (Evans, 463). Odd pieces of metal, wire, and wood found themselves transformed into bedpans, signs, instrument holders, and other paraphernalia. Ultimately, however, doctors had to treat internees—and even operate—with few or no supplies or even medicines in some cases. For example, in November of 1944 Dr. Nance had to perform an appendectomy without anesthetic on an internee—who actually lived. Tending those in need of care also became a camp job for willing volunteers.

Unlike others in the camp, many of the missionaries did not choose to deal with any of the sick not already in the hospital — they even refused to perform any home nursing duties for one of their own in the camp. Carol Terry's terrible bout with impetigo revealed a particularly nasty side of her co-religionists. Terry believed that she had acquired the infection from the Japanese trucks that had transported her to Los Baños, and she waited for the disease to clear up as it did with others. With Terry, however, it did not. Infected, itching, and ill, she could not seem to get aid from the other missionaries: "Other people began getting better, but I continued to get worse. It was thought I was reinfecting myself from my sheets, but no one cared to wash them for me or to loan me theirs, for fear of getting the disease. My clothes were covered with purple medicine [probably Gentian Violet] and pus and needed changing, but no one wanted to wash them, and I was supposed to keep my hands out of water" (53). In addition to other miseries, Terry soon developed impetigo sores around her eyes, which prevented even the escape of reading. Another missionary did grudgingly read aloud to her, but she insisted on sitting far away and reading only one particular book of the Bible — the book of Job. Said a disillusioned Terry, "Job's troubles on top of all my own were too much" (53).

Eventually, a former housemate and missionary friend of hers, Mrs. Paget, along with her husband, found out what was happening and risked infection by having Terry to dinner and washing her bedding. Terry explains that the Pagets "realized the difficulties of my situation" and discusses how they "hauled water and washed every soiled thing I had." They also applied fresh hot compresses and kept both her and her laundry clean so that, eventually, the impetigo cleared up (53–55). Comments Terry ruefully, "As a leper apart, I learned what it meant to have practical help as well as prayer. I determined . . . works would have a much larger part in my . . . life" (55).

Some found nursing of any kind, professional or communal, too distressing. A variety of jobs that didn't involve the sick existed, luckily. Internee gardens also provided work. Internees had to lug water for the plants, weed, loosen the soil, and remove insects from the vegetables. Some female internees, rather than working in the garden or as volunteers or aides in the camp hospital, performed office work for the Executive Committee. Carol Terry remembers that after being cured of her initial bout of impetigo she became camp secretary. At that time she could type six to eight hours a day at the camp office (Terry, 69). Other internees remember constructing camp benches and picnic tables for central camp dining, digging latrines, tending camp animals (pigs and chickens purchased with relief funds earlier), cutting grass, and cooking and serving food.

It is extremely important when discussing camp work to understand some basic distinctions, because they influenced the nature of the jobs. Los Baños camp was different from other camps because it began much later in the war after Japanese fortunes began to turn sour. Food (and Japanese patience) was shorter at Los Baños for a longer period of time than even at Santo Tomás, not only because it started that way but because the camp was relieved later. This meant that food shortages affected the workforce sooner and longer. For these reasons, work at the camp soon followed a different pattern. For example, by November of 1944 (about six months after its establishment), Los Baños found itself with 113 new cases of avitaminosis and 162 new cases of asthenia (debility or weakness), all of which were due to malnutrition. At least half the camp "ha[d] clinical signs of starvation" (Butler et al., 643). In December of 1944, only the most basic jobs could be done. The Manning Report of December 5, 1944, explains the situation: "Due to restrictions on diet, all non-essential camp activities have been abandoned and heavy work on essential details has been overstaffed to relieve the burden . . . universal conscription [of] every male in the camp between the ages of 18 and 40, rotat[ed] throughout barracks in lots of 50 per day or more if required" (qtd in Hartendorp, II, 445, n1). Essential camp work ultimately meant those jobs involving food or health. Given the growing level of infirmity, barracks monitors had the additional duty of delivering food lots to the barracks and distributing them to individual rooms rather than having the internees go to a dining hall (Hartendorp, II, n1).

Such weakness told. As Carol Terry explains, working or even searching individually for food was counterproductive by that December: "It was a losing fight. We used up more calories gathering weeds than we gained by eating them. If we worked in our gardens for an hour, we became dizzy, things swam before our eyes, and black spots dotted our vision. . . . Signs of starvation became evident in everyone. We became weaker and weaker; people began to faint" (69).

Jobs were modified more and more as hunger grew. Even office work couldn't be done full-time. Terry now typed not six or eight hours a day but only one, and that exhausted her strength. Other work details changed as well. Instead of building or repairing picnic tables, for example, internees were tearing them apart. Picnic tables provided firewood and, given the growing starvation, another necessity — coffins. One of Los Baños's new duties now demanded that a group of men be detailed "to do nothing but dig graves and build coffins every day" (Terry, 63; 75). This job evolved as both food and materials increasingly came into short supply, as Evans explains: "At first, the men planed and finished coffins for the dead. Later on, they could only fashion them out of rough-hewn bamboo poles. Finally, the dead had to be buried in such strips of sheets as were left" (463).

Ultimately the only "private" entrepreneurship left in camp was profiteering. Earlier, a cockney internee in Los Baños named Sniffen whose origins "were obscure" made deals with many of the older men when they arrived in camp, trading them cigarettes for the cans of Klim processed milk these men still had from their Christmas 1943 Red Cross kits. As the hunger grew into 1944, Sniffen sold his store of Klim to desperate parents who needed it for their children. Sniffen and the Japanese guards worked in tandem, Sniffen collecting jewelry, pins, watches, or whatever internees had on hand, and the guards selling them in town and splitting the profits. Sniffen also loaned invasion "Mickey Mouse" money and took IOUs in exchange; the latter were to be paid back at 6 percent interest *in U.S. currency after the war*—obviously worth a great deal more than the inflated pesos he traded. Currency trading and extortionate pricing were jobs he could manage, despite cuts in even his rations. Camp rumors credited him with over $10,000 in IOUs gathered at Los Baños. He lived on, and apparently managed to collect, most of these debts of honor after the war (Arthur, 72–74).

The promised rescue finally came, indiscriminately saving the lives of both the worthy and the unworthy, the Sniffens and the Nashes, the Sneeds and the missionaries. Baguio, Bilibid Prison, Santo Tomás, Bacolod, Cebu, Davao, and Los Baños finally were emptied of their involuntary former inhabitants. They would spend the next half century and more pondering the meaning of it all.

9 *Angels and Tanks*
Rescue Comes

The cavalry arrived in February. From the out-of-the-jaws-of-death raid on Los Baños camp to the simple retreat of the guards at Old Bilibid Prison, no rescue duplicated another, and, predictably, internee reactions varied widely as well. The threat to internee lives also seemed to shift, from the rumor of a Japanese "kill order" to an innocuous evaporation of guards. Santo Tomás internees (and, incidentally, those in Old Bilibid Prison as well) sat on the north edge of the Battle for Manila only one kilometer from the front lines at the Pasig River. Snipers, falling shrapnel, and misplaced artillery shells were a common danger, while later at STIC, over 240 internees ended up as hostages in order to secure safe passage to their own lines for the remaining Japanese in camp. Despite these differences, American-led forces liberated all three camps with very few Allied or guerrilla deaths and over 5,000 internees rescued, although the local Filipinos near the camps did not fare so well, especially at Los Baños.

To realize the full significance of these numbers, it is important to understand in general what was going on militarily at the time. Considered within this context, the rescues seem even more astounding in both their planning and their execution.

June 1944 witnessed the approach of American troops to the Philippines. That month's Battle of the Philippine Sea, called by a former Japanese naval officer "a devastating defeat," was the prelude to the actual invasion of the islands, and it cost the Japanese heavily in terms of trained personnel, especially valuable air crews (Koyanagi, 357). October 1944 brought the U.S. landing at Leyte and later that month the Battle for Leyte Gulf, the "largest naval battle in history," and, according to Ogawa, the worst military disaster in the history of Japan, resulting in the crucial loss of most of the Japanese fleet, including two of the world's largest warships (33). By mid-December 1944, U.S. Armed Forces had landed on Mindoro, just south of Luzon, putting the United States in position for the early January 1945 landing at Lingayen Gulf. The Battle for Manila followed, with U.S. troops fighting in the surrounding areas, as well as on the outskirts of the city, from street to street and, finally, from house to house. The battle began in early February and didn't end until early March with the first clearing of Manila Bay (Owens, xi–xii). The other islands with substantial Japanese forces fell one after the other: Palawan (February 28, 1945); Panay (March 18); Cebu (March 26); Negros (March 29); Bohol (April 4); and Mindanao (April 12) (Pomeroy, 134).

It was during this military chaos and the Battle for Manila that the rescues took place. Combat veterans (such as the Eleventh Airborne Division) from New Guinea and points south of the Philippines, as well as those from other units, were pulled out of the fighting for Manila and sent to rescue the internees (Flanagan, "Jove," 43–44).

In light of the apparent strategic importance of Manila and the rest of Luzon to the strategy of MacArthur's Pacific War effort, it seems strange that MacArthur would deploy fully seasoned combat troops for rescue rather than for the continued reconquest of Luzon. Los Baños, for example, had little strategic importance; taking the camp would achieve nothing militarily (Bailey, 54). To deliver Santo Tomás, Bilibid Prison, and Malacañan Palace, a "flying column" of 700 men (an element of the Eighth Regiment, First Brigade, of the First Cavalry Division, motorized), of which 200 would go to Santo Tomás, would have to strike out ahead of the main body and risk being isolated and possibly surrounded by the Japanese (Bailey, 54; Williams, 207; Hartendorp, II, 531). Why did rescue operations have a higher priority than military needs?

The answer lies inside one of the more opaque questions of the Luzon campaign: whether the threat of future Japanese massacres of internees and POWs was imminent. MacArthur himself seems to suggest the probability as he explains in his *Reminiscences:*

> I was deeply concerned about the thousands of prisoners who had been interned at the various camps on Luzon since the early days of the war. Shortly after the Japanese had taken over the islands, they had gathered Americans, British and other Allied Nationals, including women and children, in concentration centers without regard to whether they were actual combatants or simply civilians. I had been receiving reports from my various underground sources long before the actual landing on Luzon, but the latest information was most alarming. With every step that our soldiers took toward Santo Tomás University, Bilibid, Cabanatuan, and Los Baños, where these prisoners were held, the Japanese soldiers guarding them had become more and more sadistic. I knew that many of those half-starved and ill-treated people would die unless we rescued them promptly. (246)

Maxwell Bailey also considers this concern legitimate, explaining that guerrilla forces had told MacArthur "grisly details" of a December 1944 brutal POW massacre on Palawan (Bailey, 54), as well as other atrocities on Luzon, especially as the Battle for Manila progressed. MacArthur feared that a pattern might be emerging: As U.S. forces advanced, prisoners in the immediate area would be killed.

Nor was local guerrilla information all that caused MacArthur to fear for the lives of both military and civilian prisoners. Common knowledge from China to Java suggested it. As one Japanese social critic and historian, Saburo Ienaga, states, the Imperial Japanese forces were known throughout the war for their brutality to civilians in occupied countries, to POWs, and even to their own forces: "World War II brought atrocities on an unprecedented scale, and they were an infamous hallmark of the Japanese military . . . the Greater East Asian war which has been glorified [in Japan] as a moral cause, was a dirty war of sadistic cruelty" (Ienaga, 181).

Lord Russell of Liverpool, author of two comprehensive studies dealing with atrocities during World War II, concurs with Ienaga. He points out that "no less than fourteen" different POW massacres occurred between April 1942 and August 1945 in the Far East and the Southwestern Pacific (Russell, 110).

Ienaga goes on to point out the ruthless treatment the Imperial Army meted out to its own troops—supposedly a form of triage in the name of survival, victory, and efficiency. Those Japanese soldiers too badly injured to continue on the campaign without burdening others, "were forced to kill themselves or be shot" (182). In fact, any soldier taken prisoner was expected not only to commit suicide—blowing himself up was a popular option—but to take as many of the enemy with him as he could (184)—an attempt, incidentally, that internees at Santo Tomás would see firsthand. The Japanese parents of a son killed in battle were forbidden by the government to mourn because it was considered treasonable. In one typical case, the dead soldier's father and mother had to hide their sorrow by going far into the mountains to weep (Ienaga, 291, n55). Given these cultural and political dictates and assumptions on the part of the Imperial Army, how much consideration could POWs or civilians expect from the conqueror?

All too frequently the answer was "none." The catalogue of atrocities was infamous and helps to suggest the basis for MacArthur's fear about the mass execution of prisoners. The Philippines had already witnessed the Bataan Death March and heard rumors (soon to be confirmed in late February) of the three year torture and finally murder of suspected Allied sympathizers and spies in Fort Santiago. In February 1945 (the month of the internee rescues), during the Battle for Manila, drunken mobs of Japanese soldiers and sailors directly under the command auspices of Admiral Sanji Iwabuchi shot, burned alive, bayoneted, blew up, and machine-gunned 60,000 Filipinos, among them babies, young girls, children, elderly, and patients in hospitals (Linderman, 176). Dubbed the "Rape of Manila," the destruction of people and property by the Japanese from February 17 to March 3, followed at the end by Allied bombing, was so immense that only the desolation of Warsaw rivaled it.

Former white colonists and members of the Commonwealth also were included in massacres, both in Manila and on other islands. One particularly infamous one involved eleven Baptist missionary-teachers formerly on the faculty of the Central Philippine College, as well as six other Americans, on Panay in December 1943 ("Hills of Panay," 90; IMTFE, IPS Exhibits, #1393, Roll 42). Among these, in addition to seven women, was a nine-year-old boy; all were "probably beheaded" because they were suspected of being guerrilla sympathizers ("Hills of Panay," 90). Another instance, the massacre of ninety-seven civilian workers earlier on Wake Island on October 7, 1943, probably was not yet widely known, though it would come out during the Tokyo Trials. The reason given for the massacre seems to support Allied contentions. According to a Japanese witness, Katsumi, the prisoners were executed because the Japanese feared the Americans were going to land on Wake Island (Reel 11, 14,931).

News of the infamous December 1944 massacre of POWs at Puerto Prin-cesa camp on Palawan was one of the most horrendous reports to reach Mac-Arthur's headquarters; it was particularly memorable because of its recent and singular brutality. A survivor, Gunnery Sgt. Douglas Bogue, describes the scene after the Japanese guards sloshed gasoline on the POWs and then, inside the air raid shelter (into which they had been ordered), set them on fire: "As the men were forced to come out on fire, they were bayoneted or shot or clubbed or stabbed. I saw several of these men tumbling about, still on fire, and falling from being shot" (IMTFE, Reel 12, 15,234–15,235). Most of the forty other POWs who escaped the fire and tried to run were hunted down and shot on the beach or in the surf of Puerto Princesa Bay (IMTFE). Over 140 POWs died. Only five POWs survived, of which Bogue was one. A day later, true to Japanese fears, U.S. forces landed across the Sulu Sea on Min-doro, where they established an air base (Owens, xi).

Some internees, too, had heard terrible rumors and frankly feared for their lives before, during, and especially after the invasion of Luzon itself. Lucas, for example, notes the following frightened entry in Corfield's diary from February 3, 1945, when she believed that she heard tanks approaching: "The rumble persisted, grew louder, filled the air with a clanking rattling rolling grinding roar as it advanced inexorably toward us. Relentless doom for the enemy? Or annihilation for us? Would the Japs dare? Of course they would. Hadn't they already stopped our food entirely?" (201).

There is some historical disagreement about whether or not an actual Japa-nese order existed to either massacre the camp inhabitants or to treat them benevolently in the case of Japan's defeat. The arguments for either side are complex, though ultimately the evidence doesn't support a civilian internee death order in the Philippines. The varying versions, however, remain intrigu-ing. A Japanese staff officer in the Philippines Fourteenth Army Group, Shu-jiro Kobayashi, for example, explained that he had been privy to particular written orders regarding prisoners. Kobayashi claimed that in mid-December 1944 (the same month as the Puerto Princesa massacre), "The divisions con-cerned were instructed to deliver war prisoners and internees peacefully to the U.S. Army when they arrived there [for example, Americans on Luzon], to have them carry provision for one month at least with them, and to escort them against bandits" (IMTFE, Reel 21, 27,734).

Another Japanese soldier, Ishikawa, testifying in the earlier Yamashita trial in Manila, seems to concur with Koybayshi's testimony. According to him, there was indeed an order for the release of POWs and civilians that "came from Tokyo, from the Army Commander through Yamashita and it was issued to the various internment camps" (IMTFE, Reel 21, 27,633). The substance of the order of December 1944, he said, was "to treat prisoners in a friendly manner and in case the Americans should approach, to leave as much food and medicine as possible for the internees and prisoners. The third item was not to treat the prisoners or internees in any atrocious manner whatsoever before retreating" (IMTFE, Reel 21, 27,634). Ishikawa goes on to state that the order was written, not oral. When asked where this order was, Ishikawa explained that he had been forced to burn all the papers in his possession at Cabanatuan camp before the rescue. There was, therefore, no copy to show the Tribunal (27,634).

Halsema offers significant support for the possibility of a benevolent order when he points out that "Bilibid was the only civilian/military POW camp whose Japanese commander had *the opportunity* to obey the order for a peaceful hand-over" (italics mine). Halsema notes that rescue at both Santo Tomás and, ultimately, at Los Baños, as well as at Cabanatuan, featured surprise attacks in which "American rescuers stormed the gates" (personal communication, April 10, 1996)

While Ishikawa's version of the order did not acknowledge Japanese violations of such a benevolent order, especially at Puerto Princesa POW camp and on Panay, it seems obvious that the voluntary release of the internees from Old Bilibid Prison by their captors represents some version, however imperfect, of what the Japanese claimed to be doing everywhere.

An anecdote further supports the probability of such a benevolent order. Halsema relates a conversation he had after the war with Shimichi Ohdaira, the former quartermaster of Los Baños Internment Camp. Ohdaira explains the peculiar disappearance from camp by Japanese troops the week of January 6–13, 1945, the so-called "Camp Freedom" period. He claims that the commandant actually did follow the guidelines of the order. Believing (due to a strategic feint) that the American forces were about to land on Luzon, Major Iwanaka pulled all his troops out and left the internees in charge of the camp, warning them to stay inside the camp for their own safety. The contingent then went to Manila to join other forces. Their return a week later was due to the discovery that the Americans had landed not on Luzon but at Leyte Gulf. According to Ohdaira, the commandant was "admonished" at Japanese Headquarters in Manila and "sent back in disgrace to take revenge on the internees" (Halsema, personal communication, April 20, 1996).

Ultimately, despite this suggestion of revenge (which of course could easily have meant starving rather than shooting them), Halsema does not believe that any order existed to massacre the internees, even in the special case of Los Baños camp. He explains, "Contrary to the widespread rumor still believed by many ex-POWs and internees that the Japanese intended to massacre their prisoners when the Americans arrived, the order had been given to release them in any event" (Halsema, "Biblio," 89).

It is important, however, to consider possible evidence to the contrary, despite the fact that the preponderance of information supports the existence of a benevolent, rather than an execution, order. A review of other Japanese testimony might cause a researcher to be wary. Shujiro Kobayashi, for example, continues to claim in his testimony that such benevolent procedures were actually practiced, not at Bilibid, but at Santo Tomás Internment Camp. He explains, "After negotiations were repeated and as the representatives of the internees gave U.S. Army an advice [*sic*], saying 'These Japanese looked after us very well,' the U.S. Army replied that they would comply with the Japanese proposal and they would immediately lead the way to a safety zone" (IMTFE, Reel 21, 27,740–27,741).

Even if this represents a garbled version of the safe conduct eventually given some of the remaining Japanese in camp, it overlooks (even denies) the fact that the safe conduct only arose because of a hostage situation. To be fair, perhaps this situation occurred because, as Halsema suggested, this was the result of a surprise attack that allowed the Japanese no time to do otherwise. Perhaps, too, as Lord Russell and Van Waterford both suggest, the local commandants in both Santo Tomás and Los Baños might have decided not to obey the order and then killed all the prisoners (Russell, 65; Waterford, 182).

Kobayashi, however, goes on to insist that the Imperial Army ordered nothing of the sort: "The Shimbu Group, in accordance with the . . . instructions, delivered some 4,000 in Manila and Saint Thomas [Santo Tomás?], and 3,000 in Losbagnios [Los Baños?] to the U.S. Army peacefully" (IMTFE, Reel 21, 27,734). Kobayashi adds that the Shimbu Group did all this in both camps without "resorting to any fighting and through peaceful negotiations" (IMTFE, Reel 21, 27, 740–27,741). Internee hostages held in Santo Tomás's education building and those internees later clambering aboard amphibious vehicles at Los Baños camp would find such a description odd.

Whether either order—benevolent or deadly—ever existed is not important in the end, because it may have lacked any effect on the local camp decision. The difference between the Japanese lack of action at Bilibid Prison and the ferocity at Santo Tomás, for example, continues to suggest that the nature of any action or conduct in the camps was still within the province of—and at the personal whim of—the camp commandant. Higher Japanese authority had made only sketchy checks over the years to ensure compliance with official camp orders (Russell, 65) and had seemingly allowed commanders maximum autonomy of action, so there was little reason for commanders to obey official orders. MacArthur undoubtedly ordered his men to rescue both the

POWs and internees because insubordination of the commanders and subsequent massacre of the internees was a strong possibility. Halsema himself points out that, although there was probably no kill order, "They [the internees] were so far behind the American lines that anything could happen. The American Army did not know what the Japanese intended to do with the internees ("Oral," 26).

Certainly, the fact that in that same February the Japanese massacred a number of civilian prisoners (Americans among them) by burning them in their cells in Fort Santiago rather than freeing them suggests that such atrocities continued throughout the war (IMTFE, IPS Exhibits, #1431, Doc. #2817, Reel 42, 3).

The Santo Tomás Rescue

The largest rescue of internees was from Santo Tomás Internment Camp (STIC) in Manila. To internees who perhaps didn't realize the difficulties involved in rescuing prisoners from a camp in the middle of the city where a battle for possession was ongoing, the rescue must have seemed slow in coming. This was especially true after repeatedly seeing U.S. planes flying over the camp and hearing distant guns since September. The unhappy practice of rumors and speculations about liberation raised spirits briefly, but cast those believing them into a deep depression when the rumors turned out to be false. Denny Williams describes the emotional seesaw on which many internees found themselves: "As I fought off lassitude and tried to get through my work, I kept hearing talk of how close and how soon. Nobody had anything else on his mind, only Liberation and the food, food, food that would surely arrive with the troops" (199–200). She remembers forcing herself to stop picking a day when she believed the troops would arrive to free them. She had been wrong earlier too many times, and each time it resulted in a terrible letdown.

Still, even for the wary inmates of STIC, there were some encouraging signs. Vaughan, for example, talks about the first real bombing of Manila by the Americans and the internee reaction to it in a September 21, 1944, entry: "It has happened! Manila has been bombed! A week ago today we underwent two fruitless air raids. So far bombs were falling within hearing distance, but today the real thing happened. At 9:30 A.M. the sky suddenly blackened with planes as they swooped down from high clouds into the misty morning air below. Immediately heavy anti-aircraft batteries went into action" (295). She also points out the paradoxical danger hovering over (or falling on) the internees due to Japanese defense efforts against American planes:

When we realized it was the real thing—something for which we had waited for almost three years—with great joy we hastily gathered children together and got under our beds none too soon. A heavy iron cap off an anti-aircraft shell hit the tin roof of the annex with a terrific thud and rolled noisily down the sloping tin to hit the ground below. . . . A cr-a-a-ash and the sound of glass splintering on concrete came from the road directly across a narrow, uncovered corridor from mine. A six-inch iron splinter had pierced the window pane, scattering glass over the room and corridor. (295–296)

Vaughan, as did other internees, felt less and less joyous as the weeks and months dragged on and nobody came—except Japanese supply trucks building a quartermaster headquarters inside the camp. The Internee Executive Committee protested hotly that the internees should not be used as human shields to protect food and ammunition. The Japanese loftily replied, "It is an insult to the Imperial Japanese Army to say that we might use the internees as a shield" (Vaughan, October 15, 16, 18, 20, 1944, 298–299). After all, the commandant pointed out coolly, the Santo Tomás grounds were not known as protected territory; therefore, the Imperial Army could not possibly be using them as a shield to protect itself. Vaughan and others greeted this piece of chop-logic with scorn, explaining that all their mail had been addressed to Santo Tomás Internment Camp and the Red Cross had sent packages with that address as well (298–299).

Despite the earlier definite signs that the Allies were on the way to rescue them, time slowed to a crawl for the internees after December 23, 1944, when they began eating only a 200-gram rice ration per day. As Vaughan notes grimly in her January 30, 1945, entry, "On this day eight deaths" (Vaughan, 300).

Santo Tomás internee Robert Y. Robb seems to agree, and emphasizes even more strongly the unspoken fear among thoughtful prisoners that the rescue was also a race—with starvation. Based on the secret diary he kept during the entire internment, he is able to recall his emotions some weeks before rescue, especially when another internee told him that "it'll probably be four weeks" before liberation. According to Robb,

> That's a nice conservative estimate, four weeks. "Out in ten days!" they used to say, the confident ones, back in February, 1942. But here we are caged on the second floor of the Education Building, and starving, and it's February, 1945, and I won't be around a month from now. Not me, with my weight down to less than a hundred pounds and my energy gone. I got a date for St. Valentine's Day, me and my fluttery heart. Me and a lot of fellows aren't going to be around. (64)

Indeed, Hartendorp flatly states, "In Santo Tomás a deliberate policy was being carried out, a man-weakening and man-killing program, when there was food in the camp bodegas which might at any time have relieved the situation" (II, 510). By this time food (due either to retaliation or whim) was so meager that death was imminent for the internees.

Exhausted and depressed, the internees held on, given hope by the planes flying over, some waggling their wings. Finally, a personal message came from one of the planes. It swooped low over the camp and dropped something. Wrapped around a pair of pilot's flying goggles was a message: "Roll out the barrel. Santa Claus is coming Sunday or Monday" (Williams, 199–200). It didn't take that long. Rescue came at 9 P.M. that same night.

The actual rescue was peppered with unexpected events beyond anyone's ability to plan or foresee. Santo Tomás was the first of the three camps to be relieved — on February 3, 1945 — and MacArthur's flying column came none too soon.

As Cates pointed out, the death rate was accelerating week by week. From January 1, 1945, to February 3, the average internee (denied supplementation from outside vendors or packages sent in by friends) was receiving between 700 and 800 calories a day, of which less than twenty grams were protein (Butler et al., Table One, 640). Camp deaths and the listlessness brought on by malnutrition and illness characterized many in the camp even on the day of rescue itself. Robert Robb described the scene in his room, 216, in the education building at the end of the day on February 3: "The nervous ones talked excitedly about the American planes that had strafed Jap troops in Manila during the day. The sober ones, the sick and disheartened who had had their fill of rumors of imminent liberation, were lying on their cots in their rooms. Their mosquito nets were in place, and perhaps they could sleep a while before hunger pangs tormented them into waking with a start. It was bedtime, almost nine o'clock" (34).

Most of the internees in Robb's room, as well as those in many other rooms, had reached the point of merely trying to stay alive on the limited calories. Exhausted with hypoproteinosis and cursed by swollen feet and ankles, they did not witness the first moments of rescue, even though the sounds of mechanized vehicles approaching were evident (Robb, 34). Denny Williams, however, remembers those first moments vividly, especially what she heard immediately before the tanks entered the compound:

> The rumble stopped. Dead silence at the gates. Dead silence in the building. Full darkness now, and not a light showing this side of a glare on the horizon. Dead silence and black darkness while the whole world held its breath.
>
> "Where the hell is the front gate?"
>
> A good American male voice that made me tingle all over brought me to my

feet pounding somebody's shoulders, all of us screaming, joining our voices to others which rose all over the building.

"It's the Americans! God Bless America! The Yanks are here! Our boys have come!" (201)

Williams goes on to note that the troops sent up flares in order to see whom they would be attacking (and to avoid the internees). The flares "pitch[ed] the compound into relief with the drive, the half-opened main gate, and the guardhouses in stark outline" (201–202).

Amid a cheering pandemonium from the buildings and shouts of "There are no mines! It's okay, come on, come on!" (Lewis, 97), a tank from the First Cavalry Division ground ahead, plowing through the sawali fence hiding Santo Tomás internees from the outside world.

Various accounts mention different specifics about that moment, not surprisingly. June Darras Alden, then a teenager in camp, remembers: "The First Cavalry Division literally burst through the gates in their tanks, catching the Japanese guards by surprise. There was some resistance before the Japanese surrendered" (Questionnaire, 1990).

Tressa Cates at the time speaks of the tanks knocking down not only the sawali fence but part of the wall as well when they entered Santo Tomás (245). Williams in recollections also gives a vivid description, though perhaps it is not as accurate as Cates's contemporary diary account:

Then a metallic monster tore through the sawali fence, and a search-light on its nose swept around the Plaza. Little enemy soldiers ran shrieking and shooting before it, while two American officers on foot, guns at the ready, led the tank as it lumbered relentlessly forward to a stop facing the main building.

One of the officers looked up and said, "Hello, folks!" (Williams, 201–202)

Three more tanks quickly followed the first, and a fifth went around to the rear of the building. Infantry soon followed "mowing down the enemy or driving them ahead in flight" despite "several grenades" going off, thrown by retreating guards (Williams, 203). After the shooting stopped, the internees tumbled out of the building into the still-lit compound.

Things then turned riotous. A whirlpool of grateful faces and clutching hands surrounded each tank and man on foot as, "jabbering and weeping and touching and kissing the soldiers," the internees tried to convey their gratitude and relief (Williams, 204). The crowd grew denser as additional men and women pushed their way out of the main building.

However grateful the internees were, they were inadvertently hampering the soldiers' military efforts. Even as soldiers wiped their eyes and gave starving internees candy bars and cans of fruit from their jacket pockets, they continued shoving the grateful horde back inside the buildings, away from the spitting gunfire that still continued. Their efforts were sometimes in vain; frantic with hunger, some internees who had received candy bars, fruit, or other food plopped down right on the ground and, despite the milling crowd, "crammed their mouths full" (Williams, 204). The soldiers seemed touched and horrified at the same time; one soldier, "tears streaming down his face," turned away. "It makes me sick to watch them, they're damn near starved to death," he said (qtd in Williams, 205).

Robb, having finally made his way down from the education building to the patio, after wading through mobs of other internees on the stairs, walked painfully up to one of the soldiers and said, "Nice seeing you fellows. . . . Thought you'd never get here. You've done a grand job." The soldier seemed embarrassed, especially as he eyed Robb's pencil-thin body, his bloated belly, and his incongruously swollen legs. He told Robb that it was "nothing" and indicated that he and the others were happy to be there (67).

During the confusion, some surviving Japanese soldiers ran into the education building and hid themselves among the internees. The tanks countered by rolling up and training their 75 mm guns on each wing of the building, while the first tank parked across from the front entrance and aimed at the ground floor. Through the noise, American soldiers yelled for everyone on the patio to get inside the main building and to "vacate the shacks" (possibly referring to the shanties). Repeatedly, GIs warned the heedless and jubilant internees that there still was shooting and that they were in danger (Robb, 64–65). Slowly, the mob started to edge back toward the main building.

The internees who were in, or had returned to, the second- or third-floor rooms in the education building, unaware of the Japanese soldiers' previous escape into their building, were now more in danger than their milling friends in the compound below. They soon discovered they were not alone: "Five Jap soldiers in full field uniform blocked the doorway. Their rifles, bayonets in place, covered us. As they motioned us to keep back, a squad of Nips carried our beds, mattresses, rickety chairs and stools into the corridor" (Robb, 64).

The internees were then ordered to sit down on the floor, as the soldiers used internee bedding to cover the windows and block the north stairwell access. This procedure continued in other rooms, possibly on the third as well as the second floor. Squads of Japanese either guarded the internees in their rooms or were stationed in the corridors. As the tanks outside stopped moving and a silence fell, Robb details his sudden, frightening realization at that moment: "We were the hostages of the jittery Japs who had barricaded themselves in on the North Wing—in the internees' quarters on the second floor. Every-one in rooms 215, 216, and 217 was a hostage. Above us on the third floor, were more internees, perhaps 200 in all" (64).

A voice from the patio then cut through the silence as the officer in the central tank stood up in the open turret and yelled at the education building: "We'll give you Japs just three minutes to come out with your hands in the air! . . . If you don't come out walking, we'll blast you out" (Robb, 65). As the officer (according to a fearful Robb, "hard-faced" and "mustachioed") made this last threat, terrified internees, looking through gaps in the bedding-blocked windows, saw the gun snouts of the tanks apparently pointing directly, it seemed, at their rooms.

One internee, convinced the tanker would start firing when no Japanese ap-peared, shouted out a second-story window: "We're up here on the second and third floor. We're Americans." Another added, "The Japs got us cornered here!"

Internee fears, according to Robb, were not really allayed by the brusque acknowledgment the tank commander sent back: "Keep your nerve and you'll be all right" (65). Shortly thereafter, the tank commander prepared to shoot, despite the internees who continued wailing that there were civilians in the building. The tank commander was steely: "You internees up there on the second floor, can you hear me? You guys hit the deck, lie flat on the floor, face down, and get behind any shelter you have. Use your beds and mattresses as shields. Keep away from the balcony. Get as far back from the windows as you can. Get back in the rear corridor" (Robb, 65).

Blocked from taking the tanker's advice, because the Japanese were already in the corridors, and mattresses and bedding were already being used to shield their captors, the internees inside were understandably frantic. The possible irony of dying at the hands of their rescuers was all too obvious. The tanker, ignoring calls and cries, didn't hesitate another minute:

> Then it came. Cr-r-r-UMP! The wooden floor we hugged bounced up to smack us in our faces; it groaned and creaked. The guns outside—the 75s, the .30 and .50 caliber machine-guns—raked the first floor from right to left and back again. Tommy guns and rifles crackled. Above the almost deafening noise piped a high voice: "Mommy, are the Americans going to kill us?" (Robb, 65)

The tanks fired several more times before falling silent. Still the Japanese inside the education building failed to surrender their arms. During a long cease-fire, Robb recalls several of the internees around two o'clock in the morning deciding to try to climb down the twenty-five-foot fire escape rope that still hung undetected from the room's balcony. Three of the room's in-mates tried but fell to the concrete below, because they couldn't keep a grip on the rope. He explains that "you can't hold on to the rope, not with . . . fingers so swollen with beriberi" (67). (Robb doesn't say, however, how badly those who tried were hurt or why the Japanese didn't discover the attempted escape after hearing them fall.) The internees continued to wait, marooned by illness and hoping to avoid being blown up by their rescuers or shot by their jailers.

At some point during the lull, after the tanks ceased, Commandant Hayashi sent two lieutenants and a pair of civilian interpreters out of the education building under a white flag to negotiate safe conduct and a passage to Japanese lines for the remaining sixty-five soldiers inside (Williams, 211).[1] The American officers on hand received the group and took the officers' swords and side-arms. One of the two officers (it seemed to watchers to be the hated Lt. Abiko), as he returned his hands above his head, suddenly reached for something over his shoulder. An observant major in one of the tanks immediately shot Abiko four times. When they examined the pouch on Abiko's shoulder, they found that it contained a hand grenade; if it had gone off it would have killed everyone close by, something the major had seen happen before (Williams, 209). Once again, Ienaga's discussion of suicide and murder, rather than surrender, comes to mind.

Surprisingly, Abiko was not yet dead but lay on the ground moaning. Internees from the main building who were still outside ran over and kicked, spit on, cut, slapped, and pummeled him in a fury. Unrestrained, several women even burned him with the ends of their cigarettes. Dr. Stevenson stonily ordered everyone away from the wounded soldier. Although only recently let out of solitary confinement, Stevenson now had Abiko (still alive) taken into surgery. Internees protested angrily as they remembered the policies of deliberate starvation, the slaps and kicks administered to the elderly, the sick, and the frail for bowing incorrectly, the sadistic roll calls in the middle of the night, the "interrogation" and torture of men who had been caught trading for food with the Filipinos over the wall—all specialties of Abiko's. Williams, almost against her will, helped Stevenson move Abiko. Even as Stevenson turned him over on the table, another grenade dropped out of his coat. It was caught just before it rolled off.

Despite growing hardness of heart, Williams performed her nursing duties, helping Stevenson as he worked on the Japanese lieutenant. Together they cut away his clothes, splinted a broken arm, put salve and dressings on his burns, and stopped his bleeding, as well as dusted his wounds with sulfa and dressed them. He was then, after some internee protests, put into an infirmary bed where he died four hours later without regaining consciousness. Stevenson said sternly that war could make "animals out of any of us" and refused to let himself or Williams watch a patient—even Abiko—simply die (Williams, 209–210).

According to Nixon and Robb, the Japanese did not release the hostages in the education building until two days later (Williams thinks it was only one day). As they left, the Japanese troops removed the barriers at the top of the stairs, and Robb and the others were finally free. When the Japanese marched stiffly away, passing between restraining lines of American troops guarding them from angry Santo Tomásians, some internees cheered, while more furious voices yelled, "Kill them! Kill them!" (Williams, 208).

Following the exodus of the former captors, the tanks pulled back and began to direct their fighting to outside the camp. Internees continued to try and greet the American soldiers, even as they were urged to go back into the buildings for the sake of safety. Earlier, Carl Mydans, *Life* photographer and former Santo Tomás internee repatriated early in 1942, caused a sensation among the crowd as people recognized him (Williams, 203–204; "Santo Tomás Is Delivered," 25). He, like MacArthur, had promised as he left to return; he had. Anything was possible.

Internees continued trying to familiarize themselves with freedom, wandering here and there, absorbing what they could and asking soldiers where they were from, even as other soldiers—or possibly the ones they were addressing—traded shots with snipers outside the camp. They also tried to learn a new American vocabulary. As one internee said, "We're three years behind; we got to know what 'G.I.' means and why everybody's called 'Mac'" (qtd in Robb, 67).

During this time, Denny Williams ran into Lt. Mann Yancy among the troops, a kind of "Kissin' Kin" because Mann's sister had married Denny's brother. Delighted to see him, Williams hugged him tightly. Upset by her obvious weight loss (61 pounds), Mann filled her hands with chocolate bars and sugar from his pack until something more nutritious could be found. As Williams chewed on a piece of chocolate, Mann explained that only 200 men of the 700-man "flying column" had come to the relief of Santo Tomás; they had accomplished their mission by a surprise attack—and the fact that 100 of that relief force had split off, scaled the back wall of the camp at the southwest corner, and attacked the guards right before the tanks burst in, thereby ensuring their success (Williams, 207).

Despite this "rescue," however, the Japanese outside continued to shell the camp and surrounding areas. Snipers blasted away from the top of walls, on roofs, or high in trees near the camp. Grenades went off, and American forces thundered back with artillery and rifle fire. The internees were still not safe, though starvation had ceased to be a threat. They now ate "tons and tons of food" and were treated medically for a variety of conditions with "medicines by the barrelfull" (Robb, 67).

The army served the hungry thousands of Santo Tomás a breakfast suitably light initially (to avoid injuring starvation-shrunken stomachs) made up of tinned fruit juice, thick bowls of mush, milk, sugar, and real coffee. They also invited stunned internees to have "seconds" if they wanted! (Williams, 211–213). Despite their best efforts, the army inadvertently caused a number of internees intestinal distress because of the protein-heavy stews filled with beef or pork they later served following the earlier days' regimen of mush and soup. As Alice Bryant explains, even the careful Gov'nor (who had lost nearly 100 pounds during internment) had problems: "Until our liberation I did not realize how desperately hungry the poor Gov'nor was, as he never complained. Now, for a while, he could not seem to get enough. He was careful not to overeat, but he would take to his room everything our friends did not want, especially anything starchy, such as breakfast mush, to eat between meals. In spite of his discretion, the rich stews soon gave him indigestion, which checked his gain in weight and caused him considerable distress" (229–230).

Three days after the army entered the camp, the internees were still not free to leave. Harsh and sporadic fighting continued, wounding internees as well as soldiers. Bryant gives a taste of that time as she recalls, "A few days after our liberation I was almost killed. I had taken our tray of dishes out behind the main building to wash them after luncheon. It was late, and everyone else had finished this job. Just as I got outside, something struck near me with an immense crash. I quickly dodged under the dishwashing shed and crouched, still holding my tray. Down on the corrugated roof above me shrapnel rained thickly" (219).

Another instance illustrates not only the internees' trust in the soldiers but also their obviously automatic return to camp routines even after the army came. Bryant continues,

> I was harvesting lettuce [from the Bryants' private garden] in our usual fashion, one leaf at a time, so that the plants would keep on growing and putting on new leaves. The Gov'nor had gone away for something. Shells kept whizzing right by my ear and exploding the instant they passed it. I did not enjoy this. Indeed, it annoyed me, but there was a soldier on guard nearby, and I though[t] he would tell me to leave if it was dangerous.
>
> "Those shells aren't aimed at us," I told myself optimistically. "They sound nearer than they are."
>
> They sounded as if they passed just three inches from my ear.

Finally, I was so annoyed that I asked the soldier, "Is this a good place to be?" "Well I don't know, Lady," he answered doubtfully. He had on his helmet and was crouched in a fox-hole. No one else was in sight. (229)

Ultimately, before the army released the first group of internees on February 11, nineteen internees were killed and more than ninety seriously injured (Williams, 207). For some, the injuries and shock after rescue were almost as dangerous as camp itself. Sue Magnuson, age four, was blown out of her bed by an exploding shell and, though only scratched, was in shell-shock. Peggy (Peters) Read suffered so much from the firing and the bombardments that, after liberation, she did not speak "for quite a while" (Read, Questionnaire, 1990). Others were hit by shrapnel and bits of masonry, including Karen Magnuson, then a small child, who was hit by falling debris while recovering from polio and tuberculosis in the camp hospital (DeVoe, Questionnaire, 1990). Eva Nixon even remembers seeing a friend, Gladys Archer, literally beheaded by shrapnel (88), while Karen Lewis watched her friends, a pair of twins, felled by an explosion on the plaza (Lewis, 100). On the other hand, many others, such as Teedie Cowie Woodcock, claimed they were not touched by bullets, masonry, shrapnel, or even intestinal distress (Questionnaire, 1990). It seemed to be a frightening matter of luck.

After February 11, groups of internees strong and healthy enough to leave began to do so. Denny Williams, as one of the army nurses, was sent out in the first group after being told that President Roosevelt had awarded each of the army nurses a Bronze Star with two oak leaf clusters and a Presidential Citation for conspicuous gallantry. As Lt. Col. Forrest of the relieving troops remarked as the nurses finally left Santo Tomás after almost three years following the fall of Corregidor, "The Army Nurse Corps has outdone itself in the past three years" (Williams, 220). Williams recalls her thoughts and what she gazed on as she left Santo Tomás that day:

> Then we climbed into a big truck and drove slowly down the long drive to the gates, where the guardhouses were empty and half-collapsed now. I turned to look back at the main building where our room had been. To my left was the Fathers' Garden and the Seminary where I had gone to seek Father Ahearn . . . to my right was the "finishing school" which became Santo Catalina Hospital. . . .
> No, I felt no grief on leaving Santo Tomás. (221)

Old Bilibid Prison Rescue

Bilibid's internees were also ill and starving as they waited for a rescue that came, finally, a day after that at Santo Tomás, on February 4, 1945. In January there were three days of air raids over Manila, leading the more hopeful in the camp to expect release in thirty hours or (if not that) then in only a few more days (Halsema, "Bilibid Diary," January 8, 1945). Bilibid internees, like their fellows in Santo Tomás, were also the beneficiaries of a sudden snow of propaganda leaflets, several days after the third air raid. Jim Halsema, while glad of the evidence of the closeness of U.S. forces, did not seem particularly enamored with the nature of the pamphlets, as he shows in this January 10, 1945, entry:

> Bobby Patton found our first American propaganda: a leaflet extolling the virtues of Doug MacArthur (6 pictures showing him in various parts of the sw Pacific looking handsomely grim) plus a message asking recipients to watch for further instructions to be given by the doughty general over the radio and by leaflet. Baguio internees, still smarting over being deserted by Dugout Doug, are sore because "his leaflet shows we haven't landed yet." [Actually, the American forces had — on January 9 at Lingayen Gulf (Owens, xii).] ("Bilibid Diary")

Unlike the crashing rescue and firefight following the release of the internees at Santo Tomás, the deliverance of the Bilibid prisoners was almost comic in its lack of dramatic events. American tanks didn't release the prisoners; the Japanese did — with an official proclamation. The commandant, Major Ebiko, assembled the internees and read them an official proclamation announcing their release. The guards then simply left, telling the internees that, though they were "free," for their own safety they should stay inside the camp. According to Major Ebiko, a written version of the circumstances of their freedom and its conditions had been posted on the front gate, facing south on Azcarraga St. The liberators, by breaking through the west wall of the prison, did not see it. The notice read (in English):

> MESSAGE. Commandant Major Ebiko. 1. The J[apanese] Army is now going to release all prisoners of war and internees here on its own accord; 2. We are assigned to another duty and shall be here no more; 3. You are at liberty to act and live as free persons, but you must be aware of probable dangers if you go out; 4. We shall leave food stuffs, medicines, and other necessities of which you may avail yourselves for the time being; 5. We have arranged to put up sign-board at the front gate, bearing the following contents: "Lawfully released Prisoners of War and Internees are quartered here. Please do not molest them unless they make positive registance [*sic*]. Sensu bun." (Halsema, "Bilibid Diary," February 4, 1945)

Unfortunately, there is no indication that any "foodstuff, medicines, and other necessities" (other than what prisoners already had) were left, nor did the Japanese guards offer to move the internees safely through the fighting to the American lines, as Kobayashi stated was supposed to occur. R. Renton

Hind recorded events following the de facto release in his diary. Mary Ogle's comments, made some years later, agree with Hind's. He describes the scene: "Mounting a desk in the lobby Eschbach [internee chairman] read the message to the assembled internees immediately after the Jap guards on the roof with their bottles of gasoline had filed down the stairway and made their sullen way out of the building" (266).

Ogle further mentions that the voluntary noon departure of the Japanese — marching away "without looking to the right or left" — gave a peculiar distinction to the Bilibid [Baguio] internees: They were the only camp "officially released by the Japanese" (296–297). Hind continues his account, mentioning that, "Spontaneous shouts of joy followed the announcement, an American flag, laboriously made in Baguio by the camp's women-folk and smuggled in to Bilibid was unfurled, followed by a singing of 'God Bless America.' . . . The reprieve and pardon was, in a sense, as sudden as it was unexpected" (266). Later, an American officer from the POW side of the now-freed camp yelled that the flag should be taken down immediately, because it was being used as a target. Internees complied swiftly after an enormous explosion hit close by (Halsema, "Bilibid Diary," February 4, 1945).

For those, such as Jim Halsema, still ill with malnutrition and fever, this release could not have come soon enough. Many internees in camp had dengue fever, the usual hypoproteinosis, beriberi, and other maladies. Halsema's brother-in-law, Rupert Foley, for example, was still recovering from an emergency appendectomy performed by internee doctors in a sheet-draped makeshift operating room. That procedure, as well as other therapeutics, had required a blood transfusion from another internee (Halsema, "Bilibid Diary," January 30, 1945; February 3, 4, 1945; Halsema ltr, May 21, 1997, 11).

Both the ill and the not-so-ill, however, rejoiced at the news that the Japanese had left and that they were "free" (though not able to go into the streets, which were crisscrossed by stray bullets and fighting). Once again Hind describes what even the fact of freedom meant to men and women interned over three years and slowly starved for the previous four to six months:

> After three years, release was a matter of hours only; that release that we had hoped and prayed for so long. It meant news again, the radio, an end to beriberi and malnutrition, it meant that we would soon be going home where there would be soap, civilized clothes, the moving picture, telephone, telegraph, butter, eggs, milk, sugar, wheat flour, meat, table cloths, napkins, knives and forks (not a sole dessert spoon at the table) but more than anything it meant privacy again. . . . Think of it! — there would be bath tubs and a bath room door that could be locked. (265)

Another somewhat ironic turn occurred before the proclamation, however. Though Santo Tomás was swarming with American troops, soldiers in the street outside passed Bilibid by. According to both war correspondent Robert Shaplen and Bilibid internee Mary Ogle, military intelligence knew nothing of either the civilians or the POWs at Bilibid, though MacArthur's *Reminiscences* don't make this point clearly (Shaplen, 65; Ogle, 297; MacArthur, 246). Intelligence, for example, knew that the prison had been used earlier to confine prisoners but believed that the POWs had been transferred to another camp or maybe to the Japanese mainland; additionally, it was thought that the Baguio internees were still up north (Shaplen, 65).

Consequently, on February 3, sounds of rescue clanked and growled down the street—and then passed, after an exchange of complaints and (according to some) profanity about directions to Santo Tomás. According to Bilibid internee Fern Miles, two of the First Cavalry's tanks apparently got separated from the rest of their unit and "came down the street just outside our back wall." She continues, "One stopped and an American soldier stuck his head out and yelled, 'Hell, Harvey, we're on the wrong street!'" (161). Another missionary internee, Judy Hyland, remembers the incident but with three tanks instead of two and in less profane language: "Through a crack in the gate [one prisoner] saw the first tank stop and heard a voice call out, 'Should we go on, or should we go back the way we came?' Then he heard a voice from the third tank back reply in a beautiful Southern drawl, 'Let's go on and give 'em the works, Haa-vy!' Beautiful American voices! Those really were American tanks" (104).

Diarist Jim Halsema writes an even different version of the event: "A tinny siren down Rizal Avenue, sounds of a tank making the corner, then a burst of fire across the wall. . . . A large and several small jeeps with 37 mm cannon, and 10 wheel trucks swept down the road. Guns popped, upstairs residents scurried down. Walker and Carter, on the roof, claim that they heard a Southern drawl shout, 'Goddamit, Hahvey,' and saw FEU building riddled with fire" ("Bilibid Diary," February 3, 1945).

All three accounts can be reconciled to a degree. Certainly, tanks (and probably jeeps and trucks) passed on their rescue mission to Santo Tomás; at some point they passed Bilibid Prison, which was only three blocks from the larger camp (Shaplen, 65). It is also true that real rescue didn't come until the next day after the reading of the proclamation. All three accounts mention a Southerner and someone named Harvey at whom the Southerner was swearing; this suggests that the internees did hear one of the tank drivers as his machine stopped, then finally rumbled and bumbled its way past.

The next day, February 4, under orders to check the prison's physical condition and appropriateness as a future, if temporary, base for the returning army command, jeeps and trucks drove up to the prison. The discovery of the internees and POWs fell short of an action-adventure movie, however. There are several versions of the discovery, though their thrust is essentially the same. War correspondent Robert Shaplen, for example, reports marching along with the "rear elements" of the Second Battalion, 148th Regiment, 37th Division. With a squad of ten men, Sgt. Rayford Anderson began to circle and inspect Bilibid. Shaplen relates what a surprised Sgt. Anderson claimed he saw: "After his detail reached the prison, he made sure there were no snipers in the nearby houses and looked over the penitentiary wall. To his astonishment, he saw several hundred men, women, and children standing about in an enclosure. It was still twilight and he had no trouble attracting their attention by waving to them. They waved back" (63–64).

According to Shaplen, Anderson next discovered the POWs. Exploring further by checking inside an empty room, Anderson saw a boarded-up window and a small uncovered chink through which he peered. Spotting POWs, he rammed his rifle butt at the wood, breaking the old boards and opening a hole. He then yelled to the closest group that the "Yanks" had come. There was no response; Anderson speculated about this lack: "They wouldn't budge. I guess they thought it was some Nip gag. After a while a man edged over to me and I shoved my hand through the broken boards and shook his hand. 'I'm Sergeant Anderson,' I told him. 'I'm here with some American soldiers. We're all around you. You got nothing to worry about'" (Shaplen, 64).

Mary Ogle adds details to the scene, but she critically reverses the action and order of events. When the POWs heard what they thought were tanks on the streets outside the wall (jeeps and trucks, probably), in a frenzy they (not the relieving forces, according to Ogle) began trying to rip loose boards on a corner. A near tragedy was narrowly averted: "When the soldiers in the street saw those boards moving they thought it was Japanese on the other side getting ready to fire at them, and so they raised their guns ready to fight, but when they looked in, they saw white faces!" (Ogle, 297).

Although accounts differ, we should note that both are secondhand: Ogle was not on the POW side of the prison, and Shaplen got the story from Anderson. In terms of contemporaneous accuracy, however, Shaplen's piece is dated March 5, 1945 (approximately a month later), and Ogle's book is a reminiscence thirteen years after the fact. Although her subsequent details of conversation between the POWs and the rescuers add fillip to the account, the neat symmetry of the remarks suggests the account may be apocryphal: "'Who are you?' they [the soldiers outside] exclaimed. 'We are war prisoners,' the fellows inside replied. 'No, you are not,' came the answer. '*We are here now!*'" (297).

The last word should probably go to Jim Halsema, whose diary of events, unlike the other two accounts, is both firsthand and contemporaneous. As in all his other articles and in his book, *E. J. Halsema: Colonial Engineer* (1991), Halsema continues to show a singular accuracy about even the tiniest matters, as a quick survey of the notes in both his articles and his books attests. Further, Halsema's diary entries (complete with his own editorial corrections after the fact) in this study have consistently proved themselves to be short on fancy and long on facts. He also relates the interaction between the rescuers and the POWs, though not quite as Ogle remembers: "Prisoners heard banging at [the] wood wall plug, saw 6 strangely helmeted faces with drawn guns. 'How the hell do you get in this place?' they asked. 'How the hell do you get out—we've been trying for three years,' they [the POWs] replied" ("Bilibid Diary," February 4, 1945).

Later, troops rediscovered the civilian internees. According to Shaplen, further reconnoitering around the prison led Anderson eventually to break into one of the doorways in the West Wall, where he then saw the internees who had earlier waved at him. The first internee he talked to was Betty Smeddle, "an attractive twenty-year-old girl who was wearing a white blouse, striped red-and-white shorts, a red ribbon in her hair and powder and lipstick." He adds, "She looked healthy" (67).

Though Betty Smeddle might have looked "healthy," many others did not—especially because most of the adults had given portions of their food daily, from the beginning of internment, to children and teenagers. Certainly, the large number of internees either on bed-rest (such as it was) or in the hospital area were not in good condition. That anyone at all looked "healthy" was probably due to the fact that, at least until a month and several days before Bilibid, the Baguio camp had fewer internees (approximately 500, rather than more than 1,000), more doctors, better medicines, and, for a time, better food. Additionally, compared to the brutalized human skeletons in the POW camp next door, the internees, whose treatment was less abusive and severe, undoubtedly looked more normal. "Better," however, is a relative term. Even with the earlier camp advantages of Baguio, the later 700-calorie-a-day diet and crude medical conditions at Bilibid had reduced many to staggering wraiths of their former selves. Finally, the healthiest internees, free from fever and in the compound, were obviously the first to meet the soldiers—something Shaplen later admits (67).

Crowds of internees, as usual, sought out the small relieving force. Many wanted just to touch an American GI. Though the majority of the soldiers were needed to patrol the walls and gates, as well as keep a lookout on continuing actions outside, the internee chairman asked that at least one soldier be allowed to come to meet the internees. One did. Mary Ogle remembers that first GI vividly and, incidentally, repeats a common description of American soldiers that would be given by the internees in all camps: "My, we thought he was the biggest and huskiest looking man we had ever seen. We hadn't realized what an anemic, skinny group of people we had become until we saw this real he-man from the good old U.S.A." (298).

The luckless GI was besieged with questions: Had Italy surrendered? Had John Barrymore died? Were the Allied troops now fighting in Germany? Had Roosevelt been re-elected? Who was vice president? (Hind, 267).

The GI answered as many questions as he could, but he was stumped by the question about the vice president; after thinking hard for some moments, he offered a name, "Harry Truman." The GI didn't know what state he was from but suggested that the vice president wasn't important anyway (Ogle, 298).

As with Santo Tomás, Bilibid was not truly safe, despite the absence of Japanese troops inside the compound. The Battle for Manila raged outside, possibly even closer to Bilibid than it was to Santo Tomás. Bullets flew everywhere, and shells exploded nearby, even at one point knocking some of the masonry off the camp walls. Finally, Manila began to "burn in earnest" the night of the American troops' entrance into Bilibid; Mary Ogle describes the scene, as flames and smoke partially obscured the front of the prison: "As the sky darkened to the north, it grew brighter in the South. One after another, every hotel, every office building, restaurant, and residence in downtown Manila took fire. Over the sound of the flames we heard rifle shots and the rattle of machine guns. . . . By nine-thirty the fire was less than a hundred yards away" (70).

It was time to evacuate the internees and POWs rather than let fire do what their jailers had ultimately not done: take their lives, especially as gasoline storage tanks were nearby (Halsema, quoting Stanley Frankel, in ltr, May 21, 97). Women and children, along with those who were ill or feeble, were taken on trucks or jeeps. The able-bodied men, at least initially, started walking, carrying only essentials, leaving all other possessions behind. Eventually, trucks picked up all the walkers after half a mile and carried everyone to the safety of the countryside and an abandoned shoe factory at Ang Tibay, ten miles outside town. After the internees and POWs were settled at the shoe factory, the trucks and some troops of the Thirty-seventh Division returned to pick up as many mattresses as they could so that no one would have to sleep on concrete (Shaplen, 71; Ogle, 299–300).

The next morning, February 6, the army fed the former prisoners breakfast—a wildly extravagant meal by the old prison standards. Cereal, milk, sugar, coffee, wheat bread, bacon, and eggs graced the tables the army set up, as both internees and former POWs lined up in four long lines to eat "homeside" food (Hind, 269). Again, too, some became sick with the luxury of meat, eggs, and wheat.

The fire near Bilibid had apparently burned itself out short of the prison, so the army returned both internees (sick and well) and POWs to Bilibid temporarily until the authorities could arrange transportation to a collecting point at Santo Tomás or a hospital, and eventually home (Shaplen, 71).

The trip back to Bilibid was uneventful, but the return was upsetting for the internees. While they were gone, some army personnel unwittingly told the neighboring Filipinos that the internees would not be coming back. Not surprisingly, internee possessions vanished. All personal effects, all memorabilia, as well as suitcases, clothes lines, laundry, kitchen utensils, a microscope and other hospital equipment, a corn-grinder, underwear, socks, and books were gone. With so little of their own, the internees had now, ironically, lost everything because of their rescue. Some of the losses were poignant:

> Well, there we were, bereft of everything. For three long years men and women alike had taken pains to save a complete outfit of clothes to wear when we went ashore in the States. Regularly these clothes had been aired; when an iron was available, they had been pressed; the suit cases or bags had been sunned at intervals when Baguio's weather permitted and we had all become increasingly shabbier as the years of internment passed. However, we had one presentable outfit laid away for the trip home. Now it was gone. (Hind, 269–270)

Despite this last and unexpected blow, the morale of the camp began to rise little by little. Good food helped. The easy, low-key familiarity of the soldiers and the sound of English eased spirits too. Unlike Santo Tomás, the soldiers at Bilibid were merely on alert, not constantly fighting the Japanese. Though the internees had to settle down, minus their possessions, to the "primitive camp life" of earlier times, food had ceased to be a problem, and the children of the camp (eighty of them under age ten) ran almost wild with delight and the novelty of everything (Halsema, "Bilibid Diary," February 1, 1945). They mobbed the soldiers with a proprietary air: "They thought the soldiers and their guns and their jeeps were their personal property. As soon as a jeep drove into our yard, the children swarmed over it. They wore the soldier's helmet and even wanted to play with his gun" (Ogle, 305).

Hind also noticed the interaction and the kindness of the soldiers who played with the camp children, even though the latter "plagued them by playing with their equipment, trying on the soldiers' helmets, and generally interfering with their duties as sentries" (267). The reasons for this forbearance were soon obvious; the children, the soldiers often said, reminded them of their own at home.

A meal, with the U.S. Army now in charge, was a celebration to those who previously had felt lucky six months before to get a few tiny, dried fish heads in their lugao. Regular meals soon proved to be as mind-boggling as breakfast had been at the shoe factory earlier. An average day's menu follows:

Breakfast: Wheat cereal; stewed apples; coffee with milk and sugar
Lunch: creamed salmon; cold asparagus
Dinner: Pork with gravy; Irish potatoes; mixed vegetables; tea (Hind, 272)

In *addition* to the regular meals, Hind notes with wonder that each internee and POW received a "snack" of bread and butter, jam, cheese, tinned fruit, sugar, and milk *every day* (272).

As with the breakfast at the shoe factory, the Bilibid prisoners, although they were warned, soon had trouble with initially limiting their intake to those kinds of food not richer than mush, weak tea, or soup. Hind explains the problems sympathetically: "Not to have butter for a long, long time, and then, suddenly, to be issued nearly a pound a day by a sympathetic army meant only one thing—unless, of course, one was strong willed enough to practice moderation. Strength of will, however, is not developed on empty stomachs" (273). As he points out, the food was rich; cooks and compassionate army mess-mates secretly continued to urge the sickly, and sometimes skeletal, internees to have as much food as they wanted: "From an intake of seven or eight hundred calories a day, it jumped to three or four thousand" (Hind, 273).

The results were typical. Many in camp came down with stomach cramps, nausea, dizziness, diarrhea, and other gastrointestinal complaints. Many of, as Hind calls them, "the unwise and reckless," actually went into the hospital to recover. Others, "strange to relate," adds Hind, suffered appetite loss, and their weight continued to fall in spite of available food. Hind notes enigmatically, "There were many who were slow to recover their old-time vigor for mere food was not enough" (273). Even so, after at least two months, the last of the Bilibid internees left for transports to the United States or parts west. Others transferred, as mentioned earlier, to Santo Tomás to wait there and be entered on the centralized transportation lists (273).

The end of the beginning of freedom left some still in a state of shock. In "Bilibid Diary," Jim Halsema's entry of February 4, 1945 (the day of release), reads, "The kempei-tai can go to hell—I'm free of their attentions. Anti climax. Stunned unreality."

The Los Baños Rescue

On February 23, 1945, Los Baños, the last camp to be relieved, experienced by far the most theatrical rescue—one about which there is still controversy concerning, again, the reality of a possible execution of prisoners, this time *specifically* at Los Baños. To find a way through the arguments and counter-arguments about the threat, it is useful to consider the actual rescue element by element and in context, showing the precarious physical and mental position occupied by the internees, the information that the U.S. Army had received about them, the part played by various guerrilla groups, and, finally, the nature and date of the raid.

In the waning months of autumn of 1944, the internees at Los Baños were delighted at first to see "their" planes flying overhead. It was obviously the "beginning of the end." One internee, missionary Carol Terry, describes her memory of the same September 21, 1944, bombing run that Vaughan describes from Santo Tomás:

> In the North the sky was filled with black specks. "Look! Look! They've come! THEY'VE COME!" For five minutes I just jumped up and down yelling and pointing. The roads in camp began to fill with people. From every direction internees came running, all pointing, all yelling, all uncontrollable with joy. . . . They were flying over Manila, thirty-five miles away. We strained our eyes and gave vent to our joy until the Japanese guards sent us inside the barracks.
>
> Inside the barracks we could still hear the bombs. No one worked: no one even sat down. We laughed, we cried, we ran up and down the aisles of the barracks. Men punched one another, women hugged each other, half-crying with joy — the long-for moment had come. We were bombed at last! (60)

The Los Baños internees could make a joke out of that last statement. Unlike their compatriots in Santo Tomás, the bombs were not close enough to them to drop shrapnel and bits of exploded earth on their heads.

With expectations high that day, as Lucas reports, "Everyone delved into emergency supplies and the next morning the garbage cans were full of tins" (161). It would be five more months before rescue, however. As the internees trudged back to the barracks to get under cover, they searched the sky, looking for planes. According to Terry, "Straight over our heads they flew. We strained our eyes to read the insignia and instead of the usual fried egg, we saw the white stars and bars. People went wild; they shouted, they waved their arms. The planes dipped their wings in salute. Not even lack of food could dim the spirits of the camp that day" (62). For three weeks delight reigned every time the air raid siren howled. Acting out these feelings, however, by loudly demonstrating happiness and support became dangerous early on when the Japanese posted punishments for staring at the sky.

Another somewhat disturbing event followed in the Los Baños camp which was similar to that in Santo Tomás. During October 1944, the Japanese administration and guards moved into camp barracks, and the guard sentries moved their sentry boxes inside the camp (Lucas, 162). Though the Japanese denied it, this move was obviously intended to protect them from air strikes or bombs. American bombers flew over the camp with fighter planes dashing in and out among them, looking, to a peeping Isla, "like dolphins" (Lucas, 163). Were the Japanese right? Did the planes know that Los Baños was an internment camp? Supplies came from Santo Tomás as did packages. What were the possibilities that Los Baños camp, despite such an indirect identification, might unwittingly become a target of both the bombers and the "dolphins" because of the new arrangements? It was a fearful internee question never addressed nor answered by their captors.

Early January 1945 saw actual acknowledgment of the internees below: According to Arthur, the planes flying over the camp fired their machine guns together in what would be soon a familiar historical rhythm, "duh-duh-duh-DUH"—the first bar of Beethoven's *Fifth Symphony*. That pattern—dot-dot-dot-dash—was also the Morse code for "v"—for "Victory"—the signal both Allied civilians and military personnel flashed to each other (120).

Far from deciding to dig in and use the internee camp as protection from the all too evident American forces who were quickly retaking the island, however, the Japanese detachment at Los Baños made the unexpected move mentioned earlier. After a strafing incident involving Major Iwanaka's car and a P-38, as well as the disheartening discovery that the Americans did know where the internment camp was, the Los Baños contingent simply left. After hastily telling the head of the Executive Committee that they had left food "for two months" (but only if counted in the same starvation portions), the Japanese guards and their leaders then warned the internees to stay inside the camp. With this, they left, their trucks lurching out of the gate in a grinding, headlight-bouncing convoy. At 6 A.M. internees awoke to reveille and a miraculously empty camp. The "Camp Freedom" period had begun (Arthur, 120–125; Terry, 75).

In the continuing (even repetitious) quest to pin down the truth about a specific kill order, it is important to point out that this period of false freedom began on the same date that the Bilibid "Freedom" proclamation of February 4 is actually dated: January 6. This again supports the possibility that a benevolent order was sent to all camps.

One interesting irony appears in Imogene Carlson's account of this period. Looting of the absent Japanese officers' quarters produced a radio (in addition to Jerry Sams' illegal set) on which they could pick up KGEX in San Francisco, along with MacArthur's "Voice of Freedom" program. On the latter the internees heard that the U.S. Sixth Army had landed earlier with 68,000 men at

Lingayen Gulf, only a hundred miles northwest of Manila (Arthur, 129). The first popular American song that floated to them over the airways was, amusingly, "Don't Fence Me In" (Carlson, 143–144).

"Camp Freedom" ended as suddenly as it began. At 3:00 A.M., January 13, 1945, the Japanese returned and retook control of the camp.

Even during the Camp Freedom daydream, however, a warning note sounded under the merriment. George Gray, secretary of the Los Baños Executive Committee, treated the infected arm of one of Konishi's staff who had scraped open his arm on a thorn bush and then crept back to the camp hospital for treatment. As he explained in credible English (inadvertently confirming Ienaga's earlier report), "The Japanese ha[ve] little time for troops wounded in action" (qtd in Arthur, 131–132).

Nor was this all the soldier told Gray. Perhaps in return for the care, he told the Executive Committee secretary that the Japanese would eventually return and reoccupy the camp. Even though the soldier believed that ultimately the Allies would win, he warned Gray that "there [will] be hard fighting . . . and the internees [will] be in great danger" (qtd in Arthur, 132).

Although I earlier dismissed the possibility of a general order to massacre, the possibility of a threat to the Los Baños camp itself needs to be analyzed. A variety of internees, at least one commentator, and one military historian seem to believe that the Japanese had particularly marked the Los Baños inmates for death. We remember Ohdaira mentioning the order to "take revenge on the Los Baños internees." States Michael Onorato, a prominent analyst and oral historian of the internment, "It seemed that the Japanese having lost Manila earlier in the month were bent on taking out their frustrations by killing the internees at Los Baños" (xii).

One argument possibly supporting this involves the camp's isolation and clear distance from the bulk of American troops at that time. Apparently away from any immediate interruption (or reprisal), and able to do with the prisoners whatever they wanted (the guards were already starving them to death), the Japanese might have carried out such an order. Unlike the more restricted conditions in a camp such as Santo Tomás, which was on the edge of the Battle for Manila and in which fighting was almost hand to hand in some areas, theoretically no American troops would be nearby to save or avenge the prisoners. Between the internees and the American forces was the Japanese army and a large lake—Laguna de Bay. Geography and the rage of the Japanese might suggest such an action.

As Halsema pointed out earlier ("Biblio," 89), many internees believed fervently that a specific order for their massacre existed—some even claim to have heard of it. The story of how the internees might have come to know about such an order varies. One internee, Dr. Jay Hill, tells of a Baptist missionary he knew in camp (he doesn't give the name) who, unknown to the Japanese, spoke and understood their language fluently. While cleaning the outer office, the missionary apparently overheard the commandant speaking on the phone and repeating an order incredulously that he appeared to have just been given by his superior. The order was to machine-gun all the internees on February 23 (Jay Hill, interview).

Another Los Baños internee, Imogene Carlson, mentions something similar. According to her,

> A few days before our release, a Japanese order for the massacre of our whole camp was discovered by an internee. He had been a missionary in Japan and spoke Nipponese very well. The Japanese had required his services as an interpreter in the commandant's office. The internee *saw* the order in a desk [drawer] which said that all the internees in Los Baños Internment Camp were to be machine-gunned at 7:00 A.M. roll call on February 23. (Carlson, 147; italics mine)

Grace Nash, on the other hand, says there was a written starvation order—one she believes she saw on its way later to the National Archives in Washington D.C., but she does not mention seeing a "kill order" specifically. (Certainly, camp rations suggested the former was true.) Nash did mention, however, that the paratroopers who rescued the internees told her and several others that intelligence information had been sent to them about the intended Los Baños massacre and that this information (and the specific date) were the reason for the raid (Nash, interview).

What emerges is a curious congruence. In two of the stories there is a Japanese-speaking missionary who works in or around the commandant's office. In Nash's anecdote, army intelligence knows about the massacre and plans the raid. The variations (verbal, written, overheard, seen, told) suggest several slightly different versions of one story. This original story resembles a rumor, because no one saw or heard the deadly information *firsthand*—a traditional aspect of folklore. Hill and Carlson got the information secondhand, and Nash seems to have gotten it "thirdhand" if possible.

Yet another snag waits in various accounts of the information and how it got to the American forces. Supposedly, the eagle-eyed (or owl-eared) missionary hurried to tell the Internee Committee chairman about the kill order. A young internee, chosen for health and stamina by the chairman, then supposedly broke out of the camp at night via the deep ravine running through, then outside, the camp. Once away, the story continues, he tried to contact either MacArthur's forces or the guerrillas to give them the information (Carlson, 147). The young internee in many accounts is Pete Miles; in some he is Ben

Edwards. In another version the guerrilla historian Mojica claims that the three men were Pete Miles, "George Zervoulakos," and someone named Robert Schaeffer (588). No other accounts mention Schaeffer, though scholar Sondra Chapman quotes the *New York Times* article of March 1, 1945, in which a supposed fourth member is not Schaeffer but someone called Jack Connors ("Sondra Chapman," 94). In all the other accounts it is also Freddy, not George, Zerveloukas (not Zervoulakos).

To shed some light on this, we need only consult Ben Edwards's account of the raid and its planning published in the April–June 1985 issue of *Bulletin of the American Historical Collection*. According to Edwards, there were *three* young internees who escaped to try and contact the American or guerrilla forces: Freddy Zerveloukas, Pete Miles, and himself. Flanagan and Bailey both accept Zerveloukas, Miles, and Edwards, although there may be some circular citation here, because Flanagan lists Bailey as a source and Bailey lists Flanagan's earlier work, *The Angels* (1948).

The second discrepancy arises over the simple issue of who told whom about the massacre. Why did the young man (or three men) risk being shot to slip out of camp to find the guerrillas or American forces, if not for the overwhelming necessity of preventing their own (and the rest of the internees') death?

According to Ben Edwards, on February 12, well before any such massacre, internee Freddy Zerveloukas returned from an illegal foraging trip (one of many) to a nearby Filipino village. In the village he found fresh American cigarettes and other things that could only exist if the villagers had been in recent contact with American forces (60). In addition to the cigarettes and newly minted Philippine coins, one guerrilla also showed Zerveloukas a written message from Major Vanderpool of guerrilla headquarters for central Luzon. The message instructed a local guerrilla unit to "take steps" to liberate the Los Baños Internment Camp (qtd in Edwards, 60). No reason was given. *Terry's Hunters* author Proculo L. Mojica, however, offers an explanation. After the rescues at Santo Tomás and Bilibid, as well as the earlier January 30 rescue of the POWs at Cabanatuan, these successes provided "inspiration to liberate the Los Baños internees" (573–574). It then makes sense when Edwards denies that he and the other two internees sent a message to the guerrillas or told them about any massacre threat. The army (and the guerrillas) told *them* and then only that the camp was going to be liberated. Indeed, Mojica denies that the escaped internees ever mentioned such an imminent massacre. The intended rescue was supposedly planned originally for February 19, not February 23 (Mojica, 574–576), but that did not prove practical in terms of either logistics or organization.

The variation in accounts becomes more pronounced when Edwards explains what came next. The following morning after Freddy's contact with the guerrillas, he showed the note to both Pete Miles and Ben; the three friends then took the message to the Camp Committee secretary, George Gray. After Gray had shown others on the committee, Edwards explains that "it was decided" (he doesn't say by whom) for all three men to try to contact both the guerrillas and the American forces to "relay up-to-date information, on the condition of the internees and other pertinent information about the camp" (Edwards, 60). Edwards mentions nothing about a kill order or a specific date or time.

Actually, the three intended initially to see what the first friendly guerrilla or U.S. Army group they reached proposed to do for them—perhaps to supply them with arms or ammunition for a fight within the camp (Mojica, 576– 577). The three also planned to provide information about the nature, size, and routines of the camp, as well as the position of sentries, pillboxes, guard barracks, and the commandant's office, to help with any raid. They also included a schedule for roll call, noting that the sentries would have their guns stacked while they were doing morning calisthenics (Edwards, 60–61).

The three did escape from Los Baños camp at nine o'clock at night on February 18 (one day before the earlier proposed rescue), sneaking out of the hospital building after helping a "sick" Pete Miles to the building. They slipped under the two barbed wire fences and then into the deep ravine running through, then outside, camp—one naturally well camouflaged by foliage. Already in the ravine hidden from view was an armed guerrilla whom Freddy had contacted earlier. He took them to meet his commanding officer at Barrio Tranca, President Quezon's Own Guerrillas (PQOG) Colonel Espino, whose nom de guerre was "Colonel Price." Here they also met Sgt. John Fulton of the 511th Signal Company, who said he would accompany them to the camp of Col. Gustavo Ingles of the Hunters ROTC Guerrillas.

The three internees then split up so that there would be a better chance for at least one of them to contact the Eleventh Airborne south of Manila. Freddy and Ben had orders to go to the guerrilla stronghold on the east side of Laguna de Bay (Barrio Nanhaya); Pete Miles was sent to the Eleventh Airborne. If he didn't send back a message confirming he'd made it, Ben would then attempt to contact the Eleventh (Edwards, 61).

Pete did reach the Eleventh Airborne, and Freddy and Ben arrived on February 19 at Barrio Nanhaya, where they were taken to guerrilla leader Col. Abinago Ortiz. Here they met two men from the Eleventh Airborne who brought orders for both Freddy and Ben to accompany them to the internment camp area and explain the terrain and buildings surrounding the camp. At that time they were also to identify a possible drop zone for paratroops and the best road into the camp (Edwards, 62–63).

Once again, military necessity and strategy seemed to suggest the 7:00 A.M. attack, not knowledge of a particular date and time for a prisoner massacre. At that time the guards would be unarmed, changing shifts, and slower to react. The date apparently resulted naturally from the requirements of intelligence gathering, planning, and acquisition of troops. Guerrillas needed to be contacted and collected, and necessary American forces would need to be pulled out of the fight for Manila and surrounding areas.

A few last words from U.S. Army sources and military historians seem to settle the issue. Certainly, Douglas MacArthur, never one to hide his light under a bushel basket, does not mention a specific emergency requiring a daredevil, carefully timed, strategic raid to save over 2,000 internees' lives. It is hard to imagine that he would not have dwelled lovingly for many pages on such a highly romantic and dashing action had it been in response to imminent civilian slaughter; his *Reminiscences*, however, makes no mention of anything along those lines. Even granting him incomplete recall at age eighty-four (when he published his *Reminiscences*), his own preface tells the reader that he is "not relying strictly" on memories but basing his account on "recollections of events, refreshed [with] a reference to my own memoranda and a free use of staff studies and historical records made under [my] direction and supervision" (MacArthur, v). Surely, the Los Baños raid and its reasons would have been prominently mentioned in both studies and records.

Additionally, although he discusses the mechanics, planning, and execution of the raid (using "After Action" reports and "Combat Notes" as well as a February 1945 "Summary of Operations") in his analytical article, "Raid on Los Baños" in *Military Review,* military historian Major Maxwell Bailey never mentions a kill order as the reason for the rescue (51–66).

Indeed, the careful planning for the raid, as much as anything else, suggests that this complex, coordinated action was hardly a spur-of-the-moment rescue effort in response to a sudden emergency. The inability of army forces, apparently, to support a relief effort earlier due to lack of specific forces illustrates this. In fact, by February 10, one of the most important units in the raid, the Eleventh Airborne, had already been assigned to join XIV Corps in its attack on Manila (Flanagan, "Jove," 9). Continues Flanagan, concerning the period of February 10–February 30, 1945: "Most of the time the Eleventh staff fought the big battle against the defenses of Manila, but part of the time, albeit a small part, the staff considered, planned for, and sought intelligence about a place it barely knew existed: Los Baños" (10).

Planners for the actual rescue at Los Baños recognized early the unique nature of the operation: The camp was accessible by land, water, or air—a situation that could provide a unique opportunity (as well as obvious problems in coordination) for a multi-unit attack.

Unlike the rescues at Bilibid and Santo Tomás, this one required a highly complicated, highly organized, and highly coordinated network of small unit raids well behind enemy lines. Flanagan sums up the nature of the raid and its dangers well; it involved:

> well-trained, disciplined, battle-tested troops; extraordinary heroism by brave, young internees; heroics by fractious guerrilla bands; and appropriate and reasoned decision-making by tactically sound commanders on the ground. It [was] an operation performed under the stress of battle, with commanders wary of the fact that any moment their small units might suddenly be engulfed by a much larger enemy force. . . . [It showed] commanders working under extreme pressure of time and distance with an unruly mob of excited, hilarious civilians, suddenly free and unaware of the dangers that persisted even though the big, suntanned, exuberant Americans had arrived. ("Jove," 10)

The Los Baños raid, in terms of tactics and strategy, is a classic. This work, however, deals only with those aspects that most directly apply to the internees; anyone interested primarily in the flawless execution of this multi-unit raid should review detailed military studies of it. Further reading in works by both E. M. Flanagan Jr. and Maxwell Bailey as well as consultation with their bibliographies would add additional sources and illuminate questions of a professional nature. Anthony Arthur's more general narrative work about the raid is also superb. For this study's purposes, however, only those aspects that made the raid difficult for the rescuers—aspects that affected the rescue of the internees—need review.

Beyond even the unique problems of combined, multiple forces, the Los Baños raid faced several problems within the command structure itself. The military principle of strategic simplicity obviously couldn't apply—and this was to affect how soon the raid could be made and how long the internees would have to wait. As Bailey points out, even without any changes in orders or commands, airborne operations were generally complicated by their very nature. In this case the Ringler paratroopers of B Company, 1st Battalion, 511 Parachute Infantry Regiment faced over three command changes in a short period of time. Bailey explains, "On the ground at Nichols Field [Ringler] was responsible to Soule, the Los Baños force commander. In the air, Anderson, the 65th Troop Squadron commander, was in charge. On the drop zone and through the attack, Ringler himself was the senior officer on the scene. However, upon arrival of the first amtrac, command reverted to Major Henry Burgess, the 1st Battalion commander" (65).

Even if possible command conflicts were solved, to draw up viable plans staff officers required detailed intelligence about the area, the camp routines, the number of Japanese forces, and which guerrilla units were willing to aid in the attack. Essentially, the Eleventh Airborne planning staff got its information from three sources. The first of these consisted of their own intelligence officers who had "infiltrated into the guerrilla units operating in the area" (Bailey, 55); among the latter were Terry's Hunters (the Hunters ROTC Guerrillas), the Hukbalahap, the Fil-Americans, Marking's Guerrillas, the Chinese 48th Squadron, and the PQOG (Mojica, 589–590). The three escaped Los Baños internees were the second source of information, especially Pete Miles, who worked directly with division G2 officers. Miles was an engineer and could help intelligence assess possible launch and jump sites. The third source of information came from Army Air Force reconnaissance photographs. As Bailey explains, the use of all these sources allowed "the Eleventh Airborne's intelligence section . . . to piece together an extremely detailed sketch of the camp, including sentry locations and guards' quarters. Additionally, the guerrillas and Miles reported that the camp guards nearly always began their day with an 0700 exercise period" (57).

Other intelligence assignments involved checking roads and bridges to determine whether they could stand up to traffic; deciding on launch and amphibious landing sites around Los Baños; and, finally, assessing enemy strength. This assessment extended beyond enemy forces in and around the camp to those nearby in places such as the gravel quarry, Mayondon Point, the San Juan River, and especially the Alaminos-San Pablo area, which contained a large number of Japanese troops — approximately 6,000 of which were strongly concentrated in the southern hills (Bailey, 57).

Ultimately, both intelligence and the aim of the mission determined the number and kind of forces to be included. Major General Joseph Swing, the planner and genius of the Eleventh Airborne Division (the so-called "Angels" Division), selected three forces, which he put under the mission command of Colonel Robert "Shorty" Soule. The first force consisted of army "Pathfinders" (those who would infiltrate the area along with guerrilla units) — in this case, the Eleventh Airborne Reconnaissance Platoon (under Lt. George E. Skau). This group would slip into the area prior to the attack, kill the camp sentries, and mark the drop and launch zones immediately before the parachute assault on the camp. The second team consisted of the Airborne Assault unit (the paratroops) under Lt. John Ringler. Their mission was to kill remaining Japanese sentries and guards and then collect the internees for transport, while securing the camp area. The third force consisted of the combined Amphibious Assault units under Major Henry Burgess, an Amphibious Tractor Battalion under Colonel Joseph Gibbs, and a Parachute Field Artillery Battalion, an Airborne Engineering Battalion, and also two companies of the 511th Parachute Infantry Regiment—all, including the Amphibious Tractors, under the coordinated control of Major Burgess (Bailey, 59; Flanagan, "Angels," 96–97). At the same time the paratroops were dropping, the Burgess Amphibious Attack force was to land at Mayondon Point and proceed across the lake to the camp to pick up and transport internees back across Laguna de Bay to American-held territory.

This combined force was hardly large enough or well equipped enough to fight off large numbers of Japanese troops by itself; therefore, Swing planned a diversion—a ground attack well away from Los Baños camp at the same time as the raid, by a group under Lt. Col. Ernest LaFlame (Bailey, 59; Flanagan, "Angels," 96–97).

Given in what physical condition General Swing expected to find the internees, he also insisted on the establishment of a "secure area for quartering and hospitalization of the freed prisoners" inside American-held territory (Bailey, 57). The Army XIV Corps would find the facilities and provide supplies (60).

The timetable the army drew up was also complicated, requiring pinpoint coordinated accuracy in timing the attack. For example, the Division Reconnaissance Platoon was expected to infiltrate the area surrounding the camp with the help of guerrillas. These combined forces would make their way in by water and be in place by "D-Day Minus 2" (February 21, 1945). By this time, the reconnaissance patrol would have prepared the means to mark the parachute drop zone as well as the amphibious vehicle landing area. They would also have coordinated local guerrilla units (approximately 300 men) and set each group a military object to meet in the first five minutes.

The guerrilla units presented a series of potential problems. The various groups were rivals territorially and ideologically in Rizal and in some of the other southern provinces (Mojica, 277–310). Normally, in a state of war with each other, trading shots, kidnapping members of each other's gangs, stealing weapons, and declaring contradictory control over immediate territory, the various guerrilla groups for this raid had to forge a fragile alliance. The U.S. Army would have to try to keep the peace and coordinate the various unit attacks—something the leaders of these units might resent. Despite their history of feuding, the units put aside their deep differences and accomplished their assigned unit objectives.

There were different objectives. The army command assigned the PQOG guerrilla group to guide the Recon Platoon to the area and help them meet up with Terry's Hunters. Terry's Hunters (along with the Recon Platoon) were then to eliminate the perimeter sentries and most of the camp guards before the latter could reach their weapons (Mojica, 581–582; Bailey, 64). Swing assigned the Huks to mark the jump site with smoke and secure the area, protecting the paratroopers as they came down and got out of their parachutes. The Chinese 48th Squadron guerrillas were expected to guard the junction, along with the two companies of the 511 Parachute Infantry, and prevent Japanese reinforcements from aiding the camp personnel under attack. Finally, the command chose Marking and the Fil-American Guerrillas to identify and secure the amphibious landing site after the Engineers swept for mines (Bailey, 63–64). The amphibious vehicles would arrive here and then leave the area (Mojica, 589–590). These were the preparations that needed to be accomplished immediately before the actual beginning of the raid.

The Parachute Infantry (the 155 paratroopers) planned to be over the drop zone at exactly "D-Day, H-Hour" (7:00 A.M., February 23, 1945). Once on the ground they were to follow in the earlier footsteps of the combined guerrilla and Recon Platoon forces moving into the camp. There, with the help of Terry's Hunters, they were to get the prisoners quieted and organized into groups for a speedy withdrawal from the camp; they were also to make arrangements to transport internee baggage (Bailey, 54–57).

The Amphibious Assault forces were to leave two hours earlier than the paratroopers. Transported by the 672nd Amphibious Tractor Battalion, they planned to enter the water at Mamatid on D-Day, H-Hour minus 2 (0500 23 FEB 1945) to reach the far side of Laguna de Bay by 0700. Once there, the force would travel to Los Baños (guided by Marking and the Fil-American Guerrillas) at the same time that the paratroopers were jumping, intending to rendezvous with them in the camp itself. Together they would load prisoners on the fifty-four amphibious tractors (amtracs), shuttling them first to the beach and then back across Laguna de Bay to American-held territory at Mamatid beach (Bailey, 57–60), in two waves, coming and going, if necessary.

Meanwhile, also at D-Day, H-Hour, the Diversionary Attack Force was supposed to attack Japanese forces far from Los Baños at the same time as both the parachute jump and the amtrac landing. Once over the San Juan River near Calamba, after taking the Lercheria Hills, they were to "seize and hold the bridgehead and [eventually] move overland to contact the forces at the internment camp" (Bailey, 59; 64). In case the amphibious vehicles had a problem withdrawing with the internees because of hostile fire, the Diversionary Attack Force, upon arrival, would engage the enemy and retake the camp if necessary, "in strength." Finally, the attack force would pick up any of the paratroopers still in the camp after the fighting, using the last amtracs (Bailey,

59–60). xiv Corps, finally, planned to set up quarters, hospital facilities, registration, and mess facilities for the rescued internees once they landed after their escape across Laguna de Bay (Bailey, 60).

All in all, the sheer variety of troops and avenues of attack, the combination of scouts, regular army infantry units, amphibious vehicles, guerrillas, and paratroopers, stuns the imagination. If ever a raid should have failed, it was this one, if only on the basis of difficulty of coordination and degree of complexity. Instead, it succeeded brilliantly, freeing over 2,132 internees (see Bailey, 66, n36) and losing only two American troops from the Diversionary Attack Force and four or five guerrillas (Mojica, 599–600). (Guerrilla and army accounts differ on the number of irregular troops lost.)

The Amphibious Assault Force commander, Major Henry Burgess, the man who was supposed to evacuate all the internees and any wounded or tarrying paratroopers or recon men, had two very large worries. The first of these was how he was going to organize a group of hysterical civilians, including non-ambulatory cases (the number of which he had been told might be as high as 600), and get them loaded onto available vehicles in time to escape any Japanese forces in the area. His second difficulty was contingent on the first: if the internees could not be loaded quickly enough, how was he going to defend them and the camp, given its unprotected location, with the limited number of Diversionary Attack Force personnel at his disposal, even supposing they arrived in time to help? (Flanagan, "Jove," 165; Bailey, 65). Despite these concerns over the raid, the plan proceeded.

The guerrilla history of Terry's Hunters contradicts official army reports about what happened first. According to Mojica, during the time *before* 0700 that the guerrillas were expected, along with the Recon Platoon, to have infiltrated into the parachute and amphibious landing zones, the guerrillas engaged in a brief firefight on Faculty Hill just outside the camp. Mojica claims that Japanese sentries at two western guard towers spotted Captain Tan of the Hunters and his group and opened fire on them at 06:25, thirty-five minutes before the "surprise" landing and attack. This firefight consisted, says Mojica, of "pandemonium," which "broke loose" between Tan's group and the sentries, involving at least three minutes of fighting with the men in the watchtower and eliminating three machine gun nests as well (597). The guerrilla history describes the hand-to-hand combat that followed the first shot and that saw "the use of bayonets, trench knives, boloes, and pistols" (597).

This combat broke off abruptly as Terry's Hunters left for their rendezvous at the parachute drop zone, apparently after winning. Mojica comments that the Hunters were in place on time: "At 7:00 o'clock sharp just over the cornfield east of camp where two billowing white smokes [*sic*] reached up into the sky, the first of the paratroopers' parachutes blossomed beautifully under the morning sun. Momentarily, Japs and guerrillas were distracted from their deadly business of killing each other" (599).

Although neither Bailey nor Flanagan describes any 6:25 A.M. firefight just before the drop, that does not mean that there was none, though the possibility of such an extensive engagement seems somewhat remote. Guerrilla efforts in this and other raids have often been either overlooked or underreported in some army publications; however, given the fact that Faculty Hill (the scene of the firefight) was relatively close to Los Baños and, from the description, that the watchtowers seemed near or in camp, "the element of surprise" would almost certainly have been lost. Perhaps this fight took place farther away or a day earlier, and accounts have inadvertently been combined. Mojica, by his own account, bases his history not on "the greater portion of Hunter records," which were lost through fire and enemy depredations (iii), but principally on interviews with participants, on oral unit histories, and on unpublished Philippine manuscripts by guerrilla lieutenants Guerrero, Ingles, and Adevoso (iii; 635).

At Los Baños camp, the morning of February 23 dawned gloomily as internees slowly made their way to the 7:00 A.M. roll call. Many of the Japanese guards, already stripped down to loincloths, were preparing to start yet another daily round of calisthenics. At that same moment, planes droned near the camp and the first parachutes opened in the sky. Aiming at a drop zone of no more than 3,200 by 1,500 feet, "with trees on three sides, a railroad track on the other side and a powerline across the northern end" (Bailey, 61), the paratroopers jumped at an altitude of only 500 feet. Ringler chose this short jump to limit the length of time his parachute troops would be in the air and exposed as hanging targets to any Japanese riflemen.

The nine C-47s delivered their jumpers safely to the zone previously marked by phosphorus grenades. Bailey notes that while the combat report he used claimed that "all landed in a tight pattern with no injuries," in fact, eight of the jumpers landed outside the drop zone, with two landing in the trees and one on a power line. Authorities still reckoned the jump as a success, however, because all of the paratroopers survived without injury—even the man on the power line (Bailey, 66, n30).

As the first chute opened (their signal), the Reconnaissance Platoon and the guerrillas went into action and surrounded the internment camp, opening fire. Bailey describes the action next: "The first shot was a bazooka round fired by the platoon leader that destroyed the pillbox at the main entrance to the camp. The rest of the men bayoneted, shot, or grenaded the remaining sentries and most of the camp personnel who were exercising as predicted" (62–63).

As the first chute opened, the Japanese in camp saw the paratroopers beginning to float down. They quit their exercises, and the relief guards ran for their weapons. The drop and the subsequent attack were so unexpected that "the loincloth clad guards . . . milled about for a time" before running back to the barracks for clothes and guns (Flanagan, "Jove," 154).

If the Japanese were surprised, so too were the internees. Some didn't even recognize initially that the longed-for rescue was under way. Father George Williams, S.J., who had just finished celebrating early mass that morning, was late, on his way to roll call, when the paratroopers jumped. He saw "some planes" coming across the lake but paid little attention, because "planes had been a common sight in recent days." In fact, when Father Williams saw "little objects" being dropped from the plane, he initially thought that they were encouraging propaganda leaflets from the U.S. Army command (Flanagan, "Jove," 158).

Other internees were less blasé, recognizing immediately what they were seeing. Carol Terry, for example, recalls, "Suddenly I heard people outside the barracks gasp. I rushed outside. The sky was full of parachutes. Bullets began to whistle around our heads" (79). To Grace Nash and others, the paratroopers looked like something unearthly — angels, perhaps, or in Grace's case, "Greek gods coming from the heavens!" (215).

For other internees, the sight of the word "RESCUE" painted in "large yellow letters" on a low-flying plane made the event real (Lucas, 195; Flanagan, "Jove," 155).

Margaret Sams also remembers the soldiers "gracefully floating down out of a blue-blue sky." Jerry Sams, still not quite aware, snarled at a friend outside the barracks who yelled at him to "come here!" that he couldn't "come here" because "I haven't got my pants on yet." To this the friend replied heatedly, "To hell with your pants, come here!" (Sams, 278).

Almost simultaneously with the sight of parachutes, the internees heard the crack and crump of rifles and grenades, as guerrillas and members of the Recon Platoon eliminated camp sentries and perimeter guards. The attack by combined forces was swift and sure; as Bailey points out, everything proceeded so smoothly that there was little left for the incoming paratroops to do except "search out and kill the few surviving guards who had fled to the prisoners' barracks" (Bailey, 63). The internees themselves ran for cover, either in the barracks or outside; Flanagan mentions one group of nuns hiding under their barracks' beds, busily repeating the rosary, while another nun continued calmly to cook the morning (and the only) meal of the day from under another bed (Flanagan, "Jove," 153–154).

Terry's Hunters provides a vivid description of the rescue after the second group of guerrillas ran ahead of the paratroopers toward the camp: "[They moved] over already cut barbed wire fences and across a field strewn here and there with dead Japs. At first they [guerrillas] advanced cautiously but when they saw what was going on, they broke into smiles and put down their guards" (Mojica, 599). By the time the airborne units arrived, the internment camp was essentially secure, with most of the guards either dead or in hiding.

All the work was not done, however, by members of the guerrilla units or the Reconnaissance Platoon. An occasional internee helped out. Ben Edwards came in with one of the guerrilla units, as did Pete Miles. Edwards explains, "There was considerable fighting for a few minutes and I vividly remember thinking that the tracer ammunition that someone was firing looked like tennis balls floating through the air" (66).

Pete Miles also fought his way in (although he was wounded); he claimed that part of the gunplay and fatalities he saw among the guerrillas came from two undercover groups firing at each other, "each thinking the other was Japanese" (qtd in Edwards, 66–67). Mojica does not corroborate this. He states that several of Terry's guerrillas died fighting "enemy fanatics" dug in under a building (600), and that a hidden Japanese guard killed one other guerrilla, Sergeant Atanacio "Tana" Castillo, a fervent patriot who received his death wound charging the Japanese and spraying them with bullets (Mojica, 589).

Unlike Ben Edwards and Pete Miles, one internee volunteered her help from inside the camp. Margaret Whitaker's middle-aged mother, "not willing to sit around doing nothing while waiting to be rescued, spotted some recon men and guerrillas trying to break through the barbed wire. Mrs. Whitaker found a wire clipper somewhere and helped them cut through the fence" (Flanagan, "Jove," 154).

This peculiar moment is partially supported. One GI, Corporal Jason Smith, said he and two guerrillas had a shoot-out with several guards hiding in the brush. Smith claims to have seen, under weapons' fire, "a person [probably Mrs. Whitaker, says Flanagan] hand a tool that looked like a cutter" to another soldier (Flanagan, "Jove," 155).

Meanwhile, the internees hugged the floor of the barracks or hid under the beds unless, like Imogene Carlson, one had a husband with foresight, like Ray. Earlier in the month, Ray had thoughtfully dug a tiny air raid shelter "under one of the cubicles" of the barracks. This just fit the Carlson family, who sat safe from enemy fire and watched what they could of the battle (Carlson, 147).

Carol Terry, not so fortunate, clutched the barracks floor and hid behind a frail barricade of suitcases. She peeked out the window from time to time; a glance showed her the moment of rescue had come: "An American shouted at us 'Be ready to leave in five minutes. Take only what you can carry. Get into the tanks.' We had no time to pack; we just fled" (80).

Imogene Carlson heard something similar, as another American soldier, above them in the barracks hall, yelled: "You are free, liberated! Pack up and be ready to leave in five minutes. Take only what you can carry!" (147). Ultimately, Carlson was able only to pack "a broken-down overnight bag" with nothing more than "a change of ragged clothing" for each family member, Bibles and hymnbooks, baby cups, and their remaining spoons. Ray, always ahead of the game, also insisted they each carry a blanket and mosquito net with them (149).

Grace Nash also had a thoughtful husband. Earlier, Ralph Nash and a friend had dug a shelter for the family—not as elaborate as the Carlsons', to be sure, but a family foxhole. As the fighting started, Ralph had Grace and the boys get into the foxhole and then forced his way slowly into the barracks to grab the boys' bed frames. These he struggled with and dragged out, somehow succeeding in hoisting them over the top of the hole. For added protection, despite the fighting going on, he went back and retrieved a mattress, which he added to the bed frames. Grace was frantic during these adjustments:

> "Get in, Ralph, hurry, quick!" I said. He pushed the mattress in place and climbed inside—none too soon, for bullets began spitting and hissing all around us.
> Stan and Gale, still in their pajamas, were squatting down in the mud and gazing out through the opening of our shelter to view the planes that were flying back and forth over the camp. They shouted their reports every second. . . . Suddenly Gale turned around and, looking so serious, said, "Mommie, do you suppose we could open that can of meat today? The Americans are here!" (Nash, 216)

The Samses did not have an air raid shelter under the barracks or a family foxhole with a barricade cover. At the sounds of shots, they jumped into, and hid in, a drainage ditch just past the barracks. They watched for a short time the battle they "had been longing to see for three years." Another figure suddenly appeared above them in the barracks, just visible to them:

> Suddenly the shooting became less intense and we looked up in time to see what looked like a pair of dirty pants sneaking down the hall. We felt sure it was a guard trying to make his escape, but just as Jerry reached the hall he gave us a big wink and we looked again and recognized, through the dirt and filth and grime of battle, a Filipino. Not only was he on our side, he was generous. He gave Jerry an egg that had come through the thick of things—unbroken. One lone egg, but such a lovely sight. (Sams, 279)

Soon after this, Sams saw "the most wonderful-looking American boys I have ever seen" marching toward the barracks yelling to get ready to move out in five minutes (280). She took a bundle of clothing and retrieved photographs from the picture albums. With this bundle, the Samses made their way to the center of the camp.

The camp was in an uproar, even as the amtracs, after coming several miles from the beach (Flanagan, "Angels," 96) groaned and roared into the area. Explains Carlson, "Some of the internees in their joy at being liberated took a long time saying their 'thank-yous' to the men" (150). Others became caught up in giving thanks to a higher power; one internee, Sister Mary Kroeger, a Maryknoll nun, said she saw a priest halting midway to the amtracs to kneel down and give thanks. She continues, "An American soldier, realizing that any delay could mean the death of us, went over to the priest and said, 'Come on, Father; let's get the hell out of here'" (qtd in Flanagan, "Jove," 168).

Still others (according to Ben Edwards, mostly a group of older men) "refused to leave without their trunks, boxes and belongings." Edwards reasoned that the older men's belongings were "probably just junk," but the men thought they were "treasure[s]" because they were all they had. He explains further, "Some did have canned goods they refused to leave, and others were just so confused they didn't know what to do" (Edwards, 67).

Faced with orders to move the internees quickly to the rescue vehicles, but with the older men still flatly refusing to leave, Edwards was driven to desperate measures: He set fire to a far corner of their barracks. He adds, in something of an understatement, "They moved out without further ado!" (67). Soon the flames had leaped to other barracks. Carol Terry remembers fleeing too as her own "paper-thin barracks were afire" and their walls became sheets of flame (Terry, 80).

Despite the confusion caused by internees trying to shake hands with, or kiss, the relieving forces and people refusing to leave without their "stuff," the soldiers themselves were models of patience and kindliness, according to most accounts. Says Carol Terry, "Our soldier boys were wonderful. They were kind and thoughtful, perfect gentlemen, and as brave as ever a soldier was made. They made me proud to be an American" (81). Carlson remembers the careful handling especially: "We were not rushed or hurried, but the soldiers efficiently got people walking in the right direction" (150).

The soldiers continued to be gentlemen even when faced with what must have seemed to them dim questions from internees. One female internee, for example, as she was being led toward the amtracs, repeatedly asked the soldier with her if he were a Marine. He replied that he wasn't; she then expressed bitter disappointment, explaining that she had been having dreams of rescue — and rescue was always at the hands of the Marines! The soldier, somewhat nonplused, continued, however, to guide her to the waiting vehicle (Flanagan, "Jove," 170).

Grace Nash's account of another such off-key exchange is particularly poignant, even if amusing. She had finally slipped from the foxhole up to the barracks hall when she met a perspiring soldier. She poured him a glass of water from her jug and queried him:

> "Are you going to take us out of here in a few weeks," I asked, breathless with excitement.
> "No," he answered, looking at me strangely.
> "In a few days?" I asked.
> "No, in a few minutes!" he replied.
> "In a few minutes," I repeated dazed and unable to comprehend.
> "You bet," he said, striding on through the barracks. (Nash, 218)

For all the internees, the next minutes would be remembered only as a blur of activity and confusion. "Five Minutes" echoed repeatedly throughout the camp, as internees struggled to grab precious personal possessions, clothes, and even food. Trying to decide what to take as the seconds ticked away caused frenzied activity for some and terrified paralysis for others, especially if they were not yet in line for the amtracs. Nash recalls grabbing her own as well as Stan's violin, a handful of clothes, music, and toys. She then told her sons to gather their clothes and take whatever they could carry. The sense of speed infected even the children. Nash's son Gale started crying as the family packed, "Mommie, Daddy, hurry! Come or we won't be saved! The people are all going!" (Nash, 218). Ralph continued systematically loading a suitcase; unlike the older men earlier, Ralph was oblivious to the flames spreading between the barracks. Nash frantically called for him to come with them. Ralph ignored their appeals, even though Grace could feel "the heat of the flames from the Japanese barracks, soaring and crackling a few yards away" (Nash, 219). Finally, in desperation Nash, Gale, Stan, and the baby started out. (Eventually, Ralph was just able to make it to the amtracs in time, giving Nash a terrible scare.)

The camp was now in what might be called "organized chaos." Internees with armfuls of belongings stumbled toward the waiting amtracs, while some, such as the Nash family, got separated and searched frantically near the amtracs for lost family members. A number of internees tried to go back to the burning barracks to rescue more belongings, but determined soldiers pulled them back (Sams, 261). Margaret Sams, however, was amazingly calm. After rolling up bundles of clothes and obtaining selected pictures, she, Jerry, David, and baby Gerry Ann trudged toward the vehicles: "Very shortly then, we were lined up in the road waiting for our turn to climb up into a tank [amtrac]. I felt most inadequate when I had to have help getting up into it. The barracks were beginning to burn as we went down the road" (280).

Despite the desperate hurry and fear of the Japanese returning, Ray Carlson was still capable of real wit. The Carlsons were the first internees to reach the amtracs. As they approached, Ray raised an interrogatory finger and jauntily called to the driver, "Taxi?" (150).

Soldiers everywhere continued to shepherd the sick, those on stretchers, nuns, missionaries, the elderly, women, children, and male internees toward the vehicles. Again, Flanagan stresses the carefully casual manner assumed by the GIs as they tried to hurry the internees along but not frighten them more than they already were. The soldiers continued, according to one internee, "helping people along, calling good-natured replies to witticism, but wasting no time for all their easy good nature" (qtd in Flanagan, "Jove," 169–170).

Struggling along carrying Roy, and trying to pick up two pieces of luggage, Grace Nash remembers with deep gratitude the aid she received: "A voice said, 'Here, let me help you.' I looked up, way up, to see a giant paratrooper swing my luggage up effortlessly. I held Roy and tried to keep pace" (Nash, 219).

Along the way, giddy with rescue, the internees found many things hilarious. One of the amtracs, for example, had mostly nuns aboard. Only after they got under way again, did anybody remember the name painted on the side: "The Impatient Virgin." The amtrac trundled down to the beach trailing somewhat hysterical laughter.

Inside the amtrac was a different world. Nash describes her first impression of the rescue vehicle: "At last our turn came. The strange, huge tank let down its rear gates and we climbed inside, twenty or more people, several priests and ourselves. As I sank down on a piece of luggage, I offered a 'Thank God' for this miracle! It was the most beautiful limousine I shall ever see, I thought. The rear end closed now and we were deep inside, in the bottom of this giant vehicle" (220).

Not all internees could fit onto the limited number of amtracs, however. Burgess and his troops tried to take women, children, and the ill first, but many women and children refused to leave family groups. Finally, the vehicles took on all the internees they could without further discrimination and, with the rest of the internees following behind, left for the crossing at Laguna de Bay. As part of the command arrangements, guerrillas (because they lacked full field packs) took charge of any heavy baggage that wouldn't fit on the amtracs; these arrangements were no surprise. General Swing much earlier had explained that civilians, unlike POWs, always had too much baggage. As the internees on foot trailed after the amtracs, companies "A" and "C" from the Amphibious Assault Force left their original blocking points on the road and formed, along with the previously assigned guerrillas, a moving defensive perimeter around the last of the internees and, ultimately, one around the launching area on the beach (Bailey, 64).

One of the drivers of an amtrac, Arthur J. Coleman, remembers his first impression of the internees and the way they ate whatever they were given — or sometimes simply took what they wanted: "The internees looked very thin and were dressed in worn and tattered clothing. They were very hungry and ate our rations without asking for them. We had boxes of 10-in-one rations partially emptied of the better items, with crackers and less desirable items remaining. They ate everything but the boxes" (qtd in Flanagan, 162).

Nor were the amtrac drivers the only ones to remark on the internees' terrible physical condition and clothing. Earlier, as forces began securing the camp after the sentries had been killed, even the guerrillas, hunted, ragged, and poorly fed themselves, felt pity, though for some imagined, as well as true, deprivations: "They were in a pitiable state of health. Their clothes, which were never changed nor replaced in three years of imprisonment, hang loosely about them. Even their bottom wear, were more rags than pants. . . . The Hunters were all pity for them for they offered a sight that was quite different from their former prewar images" (Mojica, 600).

Surrounded by a mob of internees, Burgess himself coordinated the evacuation, which, according to Flanagan, was "a military commander's nightmare." The internees were hardly soldiers, and their slowness in responding to commands was both frustrating and frightening as the time slipped past. Flanagan describes the scene: "The ragtag, chattering, stumbling mob of men, women and children walking along the road amid the rumbling, dust-raising amtracs that were loaded to the 'gunnels' with cheering, scrawny people and piles of boxes and suitcases made Burgess wonder if he could control this rabble long enough and move them fast enough to evacuate all of them to safety" (Flanagan, 177).

At the beach the first amtracs slowly slid into the water. Splashing in next, columns of three followed, and all began the two-hour trip across Laguna de Bay to the safe haven of the Mamatid landing. As the vehicles churned their way across the lake, Japanese soldiers in the hills fired both rifles and bazookas at the amtracs. The remaining internees on the beach, guarded by soldiers and guerrillas, ate and waited, confident the amtracs would return to take them away too. The amtracs, despite being shelled and fired on (some shells coming close enough to splash internees inside), moved "casually as if they were doing it on stage." Looking back, internees could see two waves of amtracs along the lake, moving dauntlessly (if slowly) and zigzagging, their U.S. flags streaming in the breeze (Flanagan, "Jove," 178).

Imogene Carlson remembered how the soldiers dealt with the enemy firing as the internees did what they were told and squatted down on the floor of the amtrac: "Our rescuers ground out machine-gun bullets as casually as if they were shooting movies instead of enemies, cracking jokes as they worked. I don't know if that nonchalance was their natural way of working or if it was elaborately done in order not to frighten us civilians. It seemed very spontaneous to me" (151). Seeing the soldiers firing at their former captors, the internees offered extravagant images of their saviors, naming them "angels," "heroes," or as Sams called them, "young gods from another planet" (281) as they swung their guns here and there, shooting. Both Sams and Nash comment on the "ping" of empty machine gun shell casings as they fell into the bottom of the amtracs; both women mentioned also that some of the casings burned theirs and their family's arms, hands, and legs on occasion (Sams, 282; Nash, 221). Despite this, the voyage to freedom went very well. Eating C-rations, crackers, and candy, the internees eventually were "riding as smoothly as if we were on a paved road in a high-powered motor car" (Sams, 282).

After disgorging their first load of passengers and their bits and pieces of baggage, every amtrac in succession turned around and headed back to the 500 or so people still waiting on the beach across the bay. According to former navy nurse Dorothy Danner, one of the last to be picked up, the remaining internees waited on the beach safely for over two hours. Near the end of the time, internees could hear sporadic gunfire, and some shells splashed into Laguna de Bay, closer than before. The amtracs arrived just in time. Danner recalls: "Soldiers anxiously herded internees into the amtracs as each one came ashore, the artillery shells getting closer all the time. The last amtrac was hardly a safe distance away when Japanese soldiers swarmed onto the narrow beach, but, miracle of miracles, not a single soldier or civilian was left behind" (201).

At least two photographers earlier had covered the amtrac rescue as it proceeded down the road from Los Baños and out the gate to the beach. Another, more familiar, photographer waited for the internees on the other side at Mamatid. According to Dr. Jay Hill, a former Santo Tomás internee, Carl Mydans of *Time-Life* met them on the beach and took their pictures just as he had taken those of their friends earlier at STIC (Hill, "2-23-45," 23).

At Mamatid, the amtracs finally deposited their last passengers. The army was ready for them with water, blankets, food, and further transportation. Earlier, a tent had been set up to give the internees something to eat before their longer journey to Muntinlupa. The internees passed like locusts through the supplies. Ray Carlson, early on, hearing there was food in the tent, struggled his way in to get what he could. Almost everything except coffee was gone when he reached the tables, but he did get his empty helmet filled with some "grainy substance" and sugar. The Carlsons ate happily; explains Imogene, "We were enjoying our food but were curious as to what we were eating. Imagine our surprise when we learned it was uncooked, dehydrated potatoes!" (152).

The army then transported the first wave of the Los Baños internees to cleaner, more spacious (if not more prepossessing) quarters — the recently emptied New Bilibid Prison at Muntinlupa, whose larger quarters, bunkbeds, running water, toilets, showers, and other facilities would be up to their needs and numbers. As the trucks carrying them ground along to the new quarters, Filipinos on the road waved and cheered as the vehicles passed under bamboo festive arches papered with now-useless Japanese invasion (or "Mickey Mouse") money. A sign on one arch read "Welcome Victorious Americans and Guerrillas" (Flanagan, "Jove," 188).

The two waves of trucks carrying internees arrived at 11:15 A.M. and 4:00 P.M. at New Bilibid. Though initially the accommodations undoubtedly looked grim, after the internees spotted friendly faces, the medical staff, and housing and mess facilities waiting to welcome them, a holiday spirit took over. Internees, as they climbed down from the trucks, were wide-eyed at the "new" armaments in camp — jeeps, machine guns, tanks, and strange-looking helmets and rifles. These, along with the enormous number of supplies — large drums of gasoline, huge loads of food (loaves of bread especially visible), medical supplies in evidence — reintroduced the stunned internees to a modern America, victorious and overflowing with supplies (Flanagan, "Jove," 186–187).

Bilibid, earlier a prison for political prisoners of the Japanese, now became a healing sanctuary for former American internees. Here they were fed and settled in cleaned and thoroughly scoured former cells featuring double-decker bunks, clean sheets, blankets, mosquito nets, and reasonable personal space. The camp also had reception, registration, surplus clothing, and medical screenings for those entering. It also boasted a mess, which was, of course, the central attraction for people who had been barely surviving for some months on 800 calories a day. Housed in the Catholic prison chapel, the mess could seat 750 people at a time. After registering, the internees were allowed to go to the mess hall. Flanagan notes, "They needed no pushing, organizing or second calls. The evening meal the first day lasted from 1600 until after midnight. Many internees were not above going through the line at least four times. And no one cared" (Flanagan, 189).

Earlier, their arms laden with Red Cross chocolate bars, mail, and cigarettes, the internees were stunned briefly on their way to eat. Their move into a familiar long line for food helped revive a sense of normalcy. The army, having learned its lesson, fed internees lightly that first night. As Grace Nash recalls:

It was seven o'clock when we reached the food buckets. Stan and Gale had fallen down on the grass, but when food appeared they got up and stared at the army plate and cup containing two tablespoons of thick corned beef and vegetable stew and a third of a cup of tomato juice. The first taste, and their eyes gleamed — yet they held the food in their mouths, unwilling to swallow it. It was too good, they said. We were forty-five minutes eating that first meal.

Openly, I cried. Around us, all were weeping, some holding each taste in their mouths lest they lose the beautiful sensation. Others gulped their food down in three swallows, then screamed for more! Stan and Gale were over six and seven years old now, but they weighed less than they had at three and four when we were first interned. (222)

The medical teams had tended to the sick earlier. Surprisingly, only 107 internees out of some 2,132 needed hospitalization. It is a comment on the tireless past efforts of the internee medical staff, with only limited supplies or equipment, that this was so. One tiny baby, born only three days before the rescue, was even in reasonably good health when she arrived, though doctors immediately put the baby on richer formula.

Despite rescue and medical treatment and safety, the internees could not shake off earlier fears quickly. Lucas reports that, for the first week at New Bilibid, when the army delivered allotments of food by parachute to the camp, some of the internees would turn into a mob. If one of the parcels burst open, crowds of internees, still plagued with fears of starvation, would fight with each other to scoop anything they found off the ground, even though the authorities served large regular meals in camp every day with no limit on repeated trips through the line. Lucas also notes that it took "at least a week" for malnourished internees to stop "grubbing round the garbage cans" (Lucas, 205).

Historical accuracy calls for one final note. Despite the enormous success of these rescues *from the American point of view*, and the eventual freeing of the Philippines from the cruel grip of the "Asian Co-Prosperity Sphere," some Filipinos were quick to point out a distressing truth: The Philippines — and especially Manila itself — was almost completely destroyed, thanks to both American liberation efforts and Japanese resistance. Ironically, the "Rape of Manila" was taking place at the same time that the internees in Manila were being rescued by American troops. In an article written for the *Sunday Times Magazine* in 1967, author (and war observer) Carmen Guerrero writes about those months and their aftermath: "So this was Liberation. I was no longer sure what was worse, the inhumanity of the Japanese or the helpfulness of the Americans. . . . [The Pasig] river which bisected Manila was to decide who was to live or die, for the Americans had decided to risk the whole city for the sake of a few American lives in Sto. Thomas, and had executed a sortie into the internment camp while the Japanese went on a rampage in the south" ("Consensus of One," qtd in Gleeck, 273).

Historian William Pomeroy supports Guerrero's view and explains that the *reconquista* of the Philippines caused enormous physical damage: "For the country as a whole, the reinvasion was catastrophic: it was left in a state of utter devastation. The destruction was caused overwhelmingly by the U.S. bombing and shelling. Innumerable cities, towns and villages were reduced to ruins" (135).

Pomeroy cites the case of Manila in which the bombing and subsequent firefight between forces destroyed the entire business district, 70 percent of all public utilities, 75 percent of Manilian factories and stores, and almost 80 percent of the better residential districts (135), though this obviously was hardly the work of the Americans alone, especially given the bombing of Manila at the beginning of the war.

Pomeroy and others point out what happened to other cities in the island group during MacArthur's advance. Cebu City, for example, was completely destroyed (Pomeroy, 135). James Halsema's parents, released from the Holmes camp due to age and illness and placed in hospital restriction in their hometown of Baguio, were themselves victims of U.S. bombing as American planes worked to destroy Yamashita's command center based there. (The Baguio internees had been moved to Manila earlier to make room for Yamashita's troops and staff.) Halsema's hospitalized father died in a March 15, 1945, American air raid. Halsema's mother survived only because she was in a different part of the hospital. When Halsema was able, after his release from Bilibid, to make his way up north to see his mother and his hometown, he found it in ruins: "The place was absolutely devastated. There were sections of it, of course, that had not been bombed but the center of Baguio had been leveled. The American Army had to use bulldozers to fill in the craters in the street so they could move along. It was about as flattened as anyplace I've seen. Even Manila wasn't devastated to that extent" (Halsema, "Oral," 14). Halsema adds somberly that, "Of the Americans who were in Baguio at that time, more than half died during the battle for the town."

Ultimately, the price paid for the release of the Los Baños internees would be the most costly of all in human terms. In retaliation for the successful rescue of the prisoners, Japanese troops under Lt. Konishi gathered together all the people of the Los Baños village; quoting Burgess, Flanagan explains, the Japanese "tied families beneath their homes [most of which were built on stilts with the floors about 6 feet about ground] with their arms behind their backs around the stilts, or posts, supporting the house. . . . Men, women, and children were all tied, block after block, then the area was set afire" ("Jove," 196).

Burgess said that when his men eventually stumbled into the village, they were overcome by the "stench of the dead bodies, which were so decomposed that their identification was impossible." Estimates are that the Japanese burned over 1,500 Filipinos to death in retaliation for the internees' escape (qtd in Flanagan, "Jove," 196). Neither the U.S. Army nor apparently the guerrillas were there to stop it. Historians hotly debate the reason for this dereliction even today (see Flanagan, "Jove," 202–204). Although the raid was a "success" for the Americans, it was a catastrophe for the Filipino civilians.

Gathering the Survivors of Internment

Little by little, internees and their children became less frantic for food and less grim. Here in New Bilibid, as in Santo Tomás and Old Bilibid Prison (in Manila), the children from Los Baños seemed to be able to relax first. Nash remembers, for example, how, unlike the last days in camp when she found herself acceding to their wishes for "food" bedtime stories, Stan and Gale "managed better" and played "happily." They no longer planned, as they had before, long, elaborate imaginary meals. Instead, they got used to "spending their days with GIs riding on their shoulders or in Army jeeps, their pockets bulging with chewing gum and chocolate bars. Roy, too, climbed into the front seat pretending to drive, then shrieked with delight when the Captain took him for a ride" (Nash, 224).

For internees in all three camps now, rescue had finally come. Safe, guarded by their own soldiers, fed, and clothed, they would have to try to pick up the pieces of their lives again, either in the Philippines or, for most, back in the United States. The adjustment, no matter how long desired and dreamed about, was going to be hard. For many, the Philippines had been their home; because of the war they were stripped of their businesses, houses, and possessions and in effect exiled back to the United States. They would return as paupers.

Also, as some explained later, leaving fellow internees proved much harder than anyone had originally thought it would be. Who else could empathize with their experience or turn an understanding eye on peculiar, camp-related behaviors: children, for example, unconsciously sneaking food away from a meal and secreting it in a room or finishing dinner by licking the plates—a "habit that was hard to break," according to former internee Susan Magnuson DeVoe (Questionnaire, 1990).

Under MacArthur's orders, "unless there was a very good reason," all American internees were to be sent back to the United States as soon as possible to regain their health (Ogle, 307). By mid-April, most internees had left (Flanagan, "Jove," 189; Ogle, 308–309). Friends said goodbye and cried. However safe they were, to the internees the future now looked somehow daunting.

Dressed for the trip to cooler climes in heavy Red Cross-donated coats, dresses, suits, skirts, and pants that hung hugely on their malnourished frames, the internees finally left Santo Tomás and New Bilibid. Like the clothes, freedom too still sat largely upon them. The internees would ultimately have to grow back into both.

Epilogue

Freedom for some remained a difficult fit. As one psychiatric study about POWs suggests, some internees found that the reality of life outside the barbed wire did not live up to their expectations (Russell, 253). The 1956 HEW Report suggested that such studies could also be used broadly to describe civilian internee problems (96). Disillusionment came quickly for many. After the battle for Manila, the streets and boulevards the internees had cherished in memory had vanished, leaving nothing in their place but rubble and pockmarked walls. Old Manila—and Old Baguio and Cebu City, it seems—had been obliterated, along with their ways of life, leaving behind only moonscapes, with few landmarks, houses, or clubs left to convince former internee residents that they were "back."

Those who had lost businesses and homes in the Philippines during the war and had their former savings accounts depleted, confiscated, or made worthless by inflation found themselves penniless and struggling to find a way to rebuild. For many, such as the Nashes and the Magnusons, this meant going to the United States, even though this had not been "home" for many years. After dreaming of privacy, in reality it also meant having to live with relatives, cramped once again for space and desperate about the financial future. Nor was the United States what they expected. It was experiencing a variety of shortages during mid-1945. Housing was especially difficult; even if returning internees had money, there was frequently no house to buy or apartment to rent. In Los Angeles and San Francisco, even travelers had difficulty finding a place to sleep. Hotels limited occupation by the same person to three nights only (Magnuson, 79).

Though not stripped of money thanks to Jerry's three-year back pay and overtime from the Navy, Margaret Sams and her husband found themselves facing the same housing problem. After years in camp, they hungered for privacy and, eventually, managed to purchase a small house, beginning a pattern they would follow for the rest of their lives: with each move they would buy the largest and best house they could find. After retirement, at one point they ended up with a 10,000 square foot house with ten bedrooms, five baths, and a 40 by 25 foot living room (Bloom, "Afterword," 309–310).

For others, including Ralph and Grace Nash, money was harder to come by, and the economic future was bleak. Only four companies in the Philippines had refused to pay their interned employees' back wages; Ralph's company was one of them. Without a business, a home, a job, or good health, the Nashes lived with her sister's family for two months, during which time Ralph sought a job (Nash, interview II).

Other shortages appeared in the world they had believed had no shortages of anything. Gasoline, rubber, tires, and food were rationed (though to the formerly starving internees the amount of available food did not suggest true rationing). Even with a kitchen, a small apartment, and sufficient ration stamps, cooking a meal was a matter of luck. It was difficult to obtain basic pots and pans or anything made out of metal, because metal had been collected for the war effort. In addition to lacking cookware, Frieda Magnuson, for example, couldn't find an iron anywhere. After several years of striving to dress decently in scraps and to launder patched dresses repeatedly, her family's clothes were now clean. It upset her that they remained wrinkled. The laundries in town were not taking new customers and even had waiting lists, so the problem persisted until a friend found an early model of an electric iron in her attic and loaned it to Frieda (Magnuson, 84).

Beyond the material shortages and problems with housing, many of the internees had difficulty living with a new America they had never known. They had difficulty as well with the necessity for making personal decisions — something they found distressing. Once again, Frieda Magnuson speaks for many: "The moment we had dreamed of had come true, and suddenly we were afraid. Making our own decisions seemed more than we could handle, and we felt closer to the soldiers and internees with whom we had shared the war than to those at home who we felt really couldn't understand" (83).

Adjustment continued to be a struggle during the first six months (or longer, in some cases), because the former internees either had lost touch with the American home environment or had not known it for years. Male internees also found themselves in competition for jobs with healthy people who had never been interned.

And most internees who returned were not healthy and they continued to suffer the physical effects of captivity far after the social ones. Problems with teeth were so widespread that the former teenage internee who later became a dentist, Dr. Jay Hill, wrote of the problems to persuade the U.S. Congress to grant further aid to internees for medical problems deriving from camp life. Because of inadequate amounts of calcium, Vitamin c and b complex, periodontal disease, gingivitis, abscessed teeth, weak enamel, and poor tooth formation proved to be common failings. Grace Nash pointed out, for example, that her family's dental bills were higher than their grocery bills for over five years (interview, June 15, 1990). Another internee from STIC, Martin Meadows, has had continuing gum disease (ltr, June 30, 1998), and David Sams lost all his permanent teeth by the time he was twenty-five — something Hill had predicted (Hill, ltr to McClellan Jr; Sams, 309).

Other continuing physical problems emerged from camp life as well. Poor eyesight, due to the lack of vitamin b complex, was a lifelong affliction for many of the former internees. Martin Meadows believes his 10/400 myopia came from internment (ltr, June 30, 1998). Others picked up stubborn cases of parasites such as roundworms, malaria, and some hookworm.

Some, including three-year-old Karen Magnuson, had to be hospitalized immediately after liberation with a life-threatening case of amoebic dysentery (Magnuson, Questionnaire). June (Darras) Alden's father, Edmond, had to leave ahead of his family on a hospital/transport ship. His bleeding ulcers had become so severe that he was forced to have most of his stomach removed in camp prior to leaving. Both his wife and June were also ill with intestinal problems and dengue fever, and June had yellow jaundice as well (Alden, Questionnaire; Halsema, "Bilibid Diary"). Chet Magnuson was also hospitalized with hepatitis.

Dental problems and jaundice were not the only lingering reminders of the days in the internment camps. Psychological problems, along with difficulties in social adjustment, soon expressed themselves after release. Teenager Peggy (Peters) Read, who lived through the bombardment in and around Santo Tomás, suffered shell shock and didn't speak for "quite awhile" after liberation. Several internees, among them Chet Magnuson, fell into deep depressions after release, some ending in actual breakdowns. Others, while their mental states were not so dramatic, showed definite signs of what John Russell called "long term psychological effects which captivity induces" (250). One of these effects was their returning to earlier camp routines when suddenly startled. Magnuson's daughter Karen and a friend from camp, on hearing the daily noon siren in Los Altos, would become terrified and "could not understand that it was not an air raid siren" and that they didn't have to get down and cover their heads (Magnuson, 86).

Sometimes new experiences or unfamiliar gifts reminded the internees of their former camp life. Imogene Carlson's little boys, Robin and Larry, were given gum by a soldier as they left camp; neither knew what to do with it but with a sense of survival born from previous hunger bolted it down. Imogene explained: "'Don't eat it. Just chew it.' Robin and Larry looked perplexed and said, 'What's it for?'" Food was too serious a matter for jokes—and chewing without eating was unthinkable (Carlson, 149). Sue Magnuson, when first presented in California with room service, complete with silver flatware, was so overcome with the splendor that she reached for an unfamiliar silver fork and soothed herself by combing her hair with it (83); Grace Nash's three children continued for several months after the war to hide food away in little bits in their rooms (interview, 1990).

Carol Terry also points to the telling imprint of internment even after rescue, illustrating how the sudden transformation of valuable camp possessions to piles of refuse did not yet reach into the psyches of the former prisoners:

In internment camp one's wealth was measured by the number of empty tin cans one owned. We ate out of cans, washed out of them, carried water in them and cooked in them. They were among our priceless possessions. When we fled in the tanks [from Los Baños], we were not able to take our precious cans with us. Soon after our arrival at the Evacuation Hospital, the internees spotted a lovely garbage pit filled with beautiful empty tin cans. We stampeded for the cans. The soldiers argued in vain. They could not convince internees that one could live without tin cans! Finally the Army had to give in to us. They brought out box after box of clean, empty tin cans and gave them to the internees. How rich we felt with our shiny new tin cans! (82)

Habits of prison became hard to shake. Even Frieda Magnuson found herself retreating, like Alice Bryant earlier in the garden, into old routines. Wanting to start a fire in order to cook their rice, Magnuson gingerly asked an American soldier standing close by (who had helped relieve Santo Tomás that day) if she had his permission. "Sure," he said, "Y'Awl are FREE!" (71). This, she said, hadn't occurred to her.

Despite their status as civilian internees, Ralph Nash and several others seemed to display symptoms of a condition Dr. John Russell suggested was true of former POWs: Post-Traumatic Stress Disorder (PTSD). Russell suggests that PTSD causes memory lapses, a decreased ability to concentrate, interrupted sleep cycles, and problems with employment (Russell, 250–251). Ralph Nash, a Phi Beta Kappa engineer, seems to have experienced most of these, as well as having trouble finding a job he could "stay with" after the war. According to Grace, he "job hopped" frequently. Eventually, their financial life settled down when he was hired as an engineer by Alice Chalmers Machines (Nash interview, June 15, 1998).

Other social adjustments were also noticeably hard in some cases. Grace Nash's son Stan experienced his own form of PTSD when he entered high school a number of years after the war. Grace explains that Stan "was already an old man." He found the jokes, concerns, and chatter of his schoolmates to be "inane" and told his mother he simply couldn't laugh with his peers. Internment had taken away any sense of silliness. One internee from Santo Tomás refused to let others know that she had been in camp but dealt with the depression and the bad memories by forcibly forgetting: "I have come to the conclusion that I just can't bring back the memories. This is a period in my life that is best laid to rest" (Anonymous, Questionnaire). Others, when going through the hard process of dredging up the past in order to write an account, have written while weeping or had terrible depressions during the process as it all rushed back. It was a powerful experience that continues to affect many of those who lived through it.

All of the internees, however, did not emerge quite so scarred and even the handful I have cited rose above their debilities to secure a better future. Grace and Ralph Nash settled down eventually in Arizona, with Grace still teaching violin, making occasional appearances, and writing manuals of violin instruction. Eventually, her boys, Gale and even Stan, both went to college. Stan got an M.A. in linguistics and eventually taught at the University of Minnesota and then in Oslo, Norway, for fourteen years. Gale got a Ph.D. and became the head of the math department at Western Colorado University. The baby, Roy, grew up and eventually became an occupational therapist; he took Nash,

at age 80, to receive her Distinguished Achievement Award in music education in Tallahassee in November 1989. Ralph and Grace eventually retired in
Arizona.

Not long after they returned to the United States, Chet and Frieda Magnuson and their children were sent to Lima, Peru, by Chet's company, where
they lived for five years. Eventually, after having two more children, the Magnusons returned to settle down in San Francisco for the next two decades.
Magnuson's account of internment, *Out in '45, If We're Still Alive*, was published in 1984, the same year as Grace Nash's *That We Might Live*—both of
them superb sources about the years in camp.

Elizabeth Vaughan returned with Beth and Clay to her family in Georgia,
and after several months reentered the Ph.D. program in sociology at the University of North Carolina. She soon transformed the entire frightening experience into a clinical subject for her dissertation, a sociological study of internment. It was published in 1949 by Princeton University Press as *Community
under Stress* and remains a standard reference work in the field. She later became head of the Department of Sociology and Economics at Meredith College for Women in Raleigh, North Carolina, until she had to retire for medical
reasons in 1957 (Petillo, "Introduction," xviii). Her children went on to
school, and she saw Beth graduate from college and her son in his last year of
prep school before she died of breast cancer in 1957. The young colonial
mother who had fussed about the buttons on the maid's uniform bruising the
children had become, through the crucible of internment, a stalwart independent woman of sense and intelligence.

Margaret and Jerry Sams continued on, with Jerry conquering new mechanical and technical worlds, making good his promise from STIC as a mechanical marvel and genius at concocting necessary products. He worked at
a number of different companies, including Lockheed's Missile and Space
Division, as well as the Stanford Research Institute. He eventually retired in
1974 as the head of his own high tech company, Data Optics, which he
founded in 1969. The two ultimately retired to a comparatively modest 2,800
square foot house on 153 acres in California (Bloom, "Afterword," 310). Sams
herself published a personal account of the internment, *Forbidden Family*, in
1989.

James Halsema from Baguio returned to the journalism profession. He even
covered the Yamashita trial in Manila. He was also able, as it happened, to
speak on Rokuro Tomibe's behalf to Philippine War Crimes investigators and
repay the kindness the former Baguio commandant had shown his charges.
Halsema continues in excellent health and has become a historian of the internment, as well as the central authority on all such questions, and works

regularly as a reviewer for the Cellar Bookstore and contributor to the *Bulletin of the American Collection.*

Martin Meadows went on to become a philosophy professor at the American University in Washington D.C., from which he has just retired. He explained that one result of internment was to change his personal philosophy, as he now takes life less seriously and more optimistically, knowing from experience that things could *always* be worse. His children can attest, he says, to another continuing internment effect: He constantly nagged his children about wasting food!

The missionaries, it seems, had less professional disorientation than other internees in returning to the world, due perhaps to a more close-knit and financially sound network. Hettie and Charles Glunz from Negros returned to California on the *Admiral Eberle,* a troop ship that docked in San Pedro, where they were met by family members who then took them to the Elks Club in Los Angeles for "elaborate preparations," which had been made by "government agencies, clubs, societies, railroads etc. (also our Board of Foreign Missions representatives)." These groups advanced the Glunzes funds, set up accommodations for them, and provided a car. They remained in missionary work. Another missionary, Judy Hyland from Baguio, went on to spend thirty years in Tokyo with her husband, both as Lutheran missionaries. She explains, "Japan has been a home to us and our four daughters, and today the Japanese are among our dearest friends" (Hyland, 9).

Still other internees have had reunions at various times and with various groups. The Baguio internees met and talked with critic Lynn Bloom during one such reunion; Denny Williams attended a fortieth anniversary of the liberation of the "Angels of Bataan and Corregidor from Internment." Grace Nash's reunion group in Las Vegas was gracious enough to provide names so that I could interview some of them for this book. Various organizations have sprung up as well: CFIR (Center for Internees' Rights), Inc., is a civilian internee rights group that filed a suit against the Japanese government in 1995 to receive both reparations and an apology for mistreatment during internment. The military nurses, both army and navy, including Denny Williams, have a new national organization, WIMSA (Women in Military Service to America), which recently built a monument in the nation's capital.

In conclusion, it seems that despite some lingering physical effects and early psychological adjustment problems, most internees eventually blended back into American society. Lynn Bloom, who has attended reunions, edited two memoirs of internment (Crouter's and Sams's), and knows more about the experience than any other nonparticipant, says about the internment: "Overall, the attitude of the internees, men and women . . . as expressed in diaries, memoirs, and interviews . . . is a nearly unanimous one of positive reflection, reconciliation, [and] reconstruction" ("Death," 82).

In the end, many internees believed that the experience led them to personal maturation and understanding. It also provided them, as Martin Meadows shows, with a handy yardstick to measure what truly matters in life, as well as the sure and certain knowledge that people can do what they have to do, no matter how severe the circumstances.

Appendix

Enumeration of Portions, Food Classes, and Calories Given Japanese and
Japanese-American Internees in American Internment Camps during Different Years

I. (March 19, 1942)

A. A listing of *individual, daily* portions for those internees held
in temporary custody by the Department of Justice:

Food or Beverage	Pounds per Day
Meats and fish	0.75
Lard and cooking oils	0.15
Flour, starches, and cereals	0.80
Dairy products	1.00
Eggs	0.03
Sugar and syrup	0.25
Beverages (coffee or tea)	0.10
Potatoes and root vegetables and nuts	0.10
Fresh fruits and berries	0.15
Dried fruits	0.08
Miscellaneous food adjuncts	0.015
Spices, relishes, and sauces	0.10
Japanese food	0.06032

B. A listing of the *individual, daily* portions for internees
under the custody of the War Department:

Food or Beverage	Ounces per Individual
Meat	18.0
Fresh eggs	one each
Dry vegetables and cereals	2.6
Fresh vegetables	21.002
Fruit	4.7
Beverages	
coffee	2.0
cocoa	0.30
tea	0.05
Lard and cooking fats	1.28
Butter	2.0
Milk, evaporated	1.0
Macaroni	0.25
Cheese	0.25
Spices, relishes, and sauces	0.984

(An addendum to the record notes the "Allowance is made in the
preparation of food for Japanese nationals and racial preferences.")

Source: IMTFE, *IPS*, Doc. 10-G, 1–2, Exhibit 1472, RG 331, Roll 42.

Appendix table *continued*

II. *(July 4, 1945)*

A. Rations received *individually and daily,* adding up to a total of
4.831 pounds of food representing 4,100 calories:

Foods Given	Weight in Pounds	Calorie Count
Meat and fish	0.442	442
Eggs	0.10725	64
Milk and cheese	0.56744	302
Margarine	0.036	121
Fats, other	0.05625	230
Sugars	0.2255	351
Cereals	1.234	1888
Legumes	0.044	73
Vegetables	0.548	55
Tomatoes	0.05104	5
Citrus fruits	0.18	36
Potatoes	0.70	350
Vegetables, other	0.33526	67
Fruits, other	0.147	44
Fruits, dried	0.045	72
Beverages	0.069	—
Miscellaneous	0.04317	—

Source: IMTFE, *IPS,* Doc. 10-X, Exhibit 1486, RG 331, Reel 42.

A Note on Sources

The validity of any history depends ultimately on the accuracy of its sources. Suspect sources produce suspect history. Although many of the sources I use are standard works in the field, some of them either are the subjects of controversy or present unique historiographic problems. I intend to discuss my use of problematic sources, such as the Tokyo War Crimes Trial transcripts and the International Prosecution Section (IPS) Exhibits from the International Military Tribunal for the Far East (IMTFE) and first-person narratives (diaries, retrospectives, memoirs, group biographies, interviews, and oral histories). However valuable a trove of historical detail, these require careful, knowledgeable, and sometimes circumscribed use to provide sound information.

Questions about Using the IMTFE Transcripts and IPS Exhibits

There are fierce arguments among both jurists and Far East historians about the fairness of using the Tokyo Trial transcripts in any fashion. Critics argue over the Tokyo Trials' legitimacy, for example, in regard to the debate about command responsibility (along with making field commanders responsible for actions taken by their subordinates). They also deplore the lack of Fifth Amendment protection for the accused — specifically, the right of the defendant, among other things, to face his accusers, particularly with the use of affidavits. This is perhaps the most troubling criticism in terms of this particular study because it addresses directly the questions about the admissibility of certain kinds of evidence. The defense section repeatedly charged that "the admission [into] evidence of depositions, statements (some unsigned), documents and hearsay (occasionally three times removed) violated the due process clause of the Fifth Amendment and divested the trial of any semblance of fairness" (Piccigallo, 57). Indeed, in the earlier Manila Trials, Piccigallo notes that some correspondents in the courtroom were "shocked" by the "loose interpretation of the evidence" (57), especially in the case of third-hand depositions. The lack of a witness physically present to cross-examine, according to the defense, made any rebuttal impossible. Attacking specific allegations was equally unworkable because, with no direct response, the witness's nervousness, shifting eyes, or squirming body language was not available to cast doubt on his accuracy.

My purpose in using the trial transcripts differs in some important ways from the overall purpose of the Tokyo Trials themselves. I do not intend to establish State responsibility for prisoner treatment in the internment camps so much as to investigate the nature of command structure in the Imperial Army and how it functioned (or did not do so). I also intend to determine what the "official" record says (flawed or otherwise) so that I can, in turn, measure that source's answers against those of other interested parties concerning primarily civilian internee (but also on occasion POW) conditions. Finally, I want to use the transcripts to discuss a number of Imperial bureaus (for example, the Prisoners-of-War Information Bureau) set up to deal explicitly with prisoners, both military and civilian; to record any inspections of the camps by the Japanese, the International Red Cross, or foreign neutrals; and finally, to allow the Japanese themselves to present their own arguments concerning the state of health and the lack of food in the internment camps.

To avoid the more obvious pitfalls inherent in the deposition process, for example, I have done the following: restricted myself as much as possible to actual testimony, not depositions; used only firsthand, not hearsay, information; and made sure I used both defense and prosecution testimony. If I could not satisfy any one of these, I made sure that I used more than just the transcripts as a source. When I used testimony from another trial (in one case, for example, I used indirect testimony from Yamashita's Manila trial), I also restricted myself to that information *as it was read verbatim* from the original transcript. Finally, given the controversial nature of the Tokyo Trials themselves, I have resisted using any testimony from the trials as the *sole* basis for information. I have tried repeatedly to find corroboration from other sources as well.

However, even if I were to use only Japanese testimony, and only eye-witness evidence presented in person, there is a question about the accuracy of official translations.

Reassurance on this point seems to lie in the structure of the International Prosecution Section itself. Out of five divisions in the section, two (the Document Division and the Language Division) dealt directly with evidence needing translation either into English or into Japanese. No document—for either the prosecution or the defense—could be introduced into evidence unless the translation had followed the strict procedures and standards set by the Language Division and its translation board. The latter consisted of three independent translators—one Japanese, one American, and one neutral who was intimately familiar with both languages; all had to agree unanimously that the translation was accurate before the document could be admitted into evidence. If the board disagreed, the document was returned for retranslation and correction (Tutorow, 14). As for the defendants following the trial proceedings and being able to understand all the charges and testimony both for and against them, the court (as in Nuremberg) provided simultaneous translation through earphones during the entire trial (Brackman, 18).

All the same problems concern the use, however occasional, of International Prosecution Section (IPS) documents or exhibits. In the case of the latter, however, I have tried to use for illustrative purposes only those documents that have overwhelming support from other sources—such as the murder of the Baptist missionaries on Panay or the Puerto Princesa massacre on Palawan—or sworn statements typical of a large number of other reports, rather than unique or eccentric ones. In this latter case, I would include exhibits concerning the habit (as indicated by captured Japanese records) of herding civilians (primarily Filipino but also American on occasion) into public buildings, especially churches, and then setting fire to the building, shooting those who tried to escape. Affidavits and sworn testimony affirm that the Japanese practiced this particular procedure on a number of the Philippine Islands (especially Luzon, Cebu, Mindanao, and Leyte) and throughout the war, using not only the *kempei tai* as executioners but also Imperial Army and Navy units as well as the Imperial Marines (IPS Doc. #6918, "Opening Statement" by Associate Prosecutor Pedro Lopez, Reel 42, 5).

Problems of Historical Fact in First-Person Narratives: Diaries, Retrospectives, and Memoirs

Although it seems innocent, another controversial source can be the first-person narrative. As literary critics have noted, no piece of writing is "strictly" history; that is, every history book, every historical source (even oral history), and every document has a writer (or voice), and that writer operates behind a persona, however thin or unobtrusive. The writer selects, interprets, and presents what evidence, details, or facts he or she deems important or necessary; the personality who makes those choices and the obvious subjective values inherent in the choices flesh out and constitute the "persona" or the author the writer wishes the reader to believe is writing the work—the "Implied Author." This is particularly knotty when the history is in the form of a recorded oral interview and two personae are involved—the interviewed and the interviewer. These and the persona of written memoirs may initially seem arcane, even trivial matters to consider, until one examines the first-person narratives of, for example, Douglas MacArthur, a guerrilla leader, or a missionary. Each of these has an obvious ideological ax to grind and strives to present himself or herself in a favorable ideological or personal light. As Lynn Bloom notes, the prime audience is often one's peers who have shared the experience and only secondarily the larger court of history and reputation. Bloom explains, "These autobiographers want others who have shared their experience to see it their way, and to be aware of their peculiar role in it. In the process of vindicating themselves, these autobiographers endeavor to correct or supplement others' accounts—inevitably partial, often self-serving, sometimes erroneous, in many cases fighting fire with fire" (Bloom, "Single," 39).

A missionary writer, for example, might have been one of the internees who lived "outside" camp for most of the war—a benefit that arose when many missionaries signed an agreement with the Japanese not to undermine, contradict, or disparage Japanese conduct or control of the islands. The conquerors interned cooperative missionaries only for a short period near the end of the war. Such a writer might feel the need to defend "collaborating" with the Japanese (a designation many internees gave those missionaries who cooperated and were not interned earlier). This defense could take the form of declaring that life outside the camp was equally or even *more* grueling than life in camp; it might take the form of explaining that, although the diarist signed the cooperation document, he or she was *forced* to do so by threats and that the signature was coerced. Finally, the diarist could cast the entire narrative into a model of religious pietism that rejects misery, helplessness, or suffering. Here the author may deny her own suffering *or even that of others* in an attempt to seem "strong in faith" and truly "Christian."

One chilling example of this occurs in missionary Carol Terry's contemporary account, *Kept*, written just after release. In an otherwise factual and vivid account, Terry's interpretation of the life and death of another internee, Reverend Mr. Blair, illustrates clearly how persona can shade and shape the facts.

Initially, Terry is horrified by the fact that Mr. Blair, a builder of the "world-renowned Korean Presbyterian church" and a church leader for forty-one years, was reduced to eating slugs in January 1945: "He had been eating quantities of slugs in a valiant effort to keep alive, but after a whole lifetime of giving all that he had to the Lord, he had starved to death. Where was God? Where were God's promises?" (77).

This obvious dissonance between reality and church doctrine threw Terry, an intelligent woman, into a whirlwind of doubt and lost faith. After all, she pointed out, the Bible claimed, in Philippians 4:19, that "God shall supply all your need—according to his riches in glory by Christ Jesus" (qtd in Terry, 78). But He hadn't done so. At this point Terry is left rudderless in a sea of skepticism; after all, "If God could not supply Mr. Blair's need, no longer could I trust the promises in the Bible" (78). She also says despairingly, "If the Bible were not true, if God were not the God I had been worshipping, there was nothing left in life for me" (77). This seems to be a logical, if despairing, conclusion, based on realities around her.

This tone shifts abruptly after she reads more scriptural passages as she sits in the church moments later. Her response offers readers a chance to see authorial persona at work:

> The puzzle began to fit together [while reading the Book of Revelations] and the picture slowly became visible—a picture of a lifetime of faithful service given the highest reward possible, a martyr's crown. It was for the sake of spreading the gospel that Mr. Blair had starved to death. God's highest honor had been bestowed upon one who was worthy. He had earned his "well done" and had been promoted to greater work. (Terry, 78)

Through a terrible alchemy of Bible verses and a personal desire to find a suitable reason for such a dreadful death, Terry manages to turn the degradation and tragic spectacle of starvation into a positive, even enviable, event. To Terry, apparently, starvation leads to—or is equal to—salvation. She obviously wishes her readers to understand it in that fashion as well. How might this affect historical accuracy? If she were to be asked later by a women's group to speak about the nature of camp life, what might she offer as testimony? That things (illness, starvation, and cruelty) "weren't so bad"? The writer's personal attitude, as well as neglected facts, can distort a picture of events. Others who have experienced the same events might remember them quite differently.

These differences in memory or perception appear boldly if a researcher asks a selected audience of other internees to read a specific account and rate its accuracy, based on *their* memories. Lynn Bloom did so with Natalie Crouter's *Forbidden Diary*. Twenty-four former Baguio (Hay/Holmes) internees rated the book on a five point scale; though seven reported that they found Crouter's book "Highly Accurate," seventeen others found it inaccurate to one degree or another. One internee even refuted Crouter's account point by point, despite the fact that both accounts agreed on "verifiable facts of the three year period" (Bloom, "Single," 39).

Obviously, even if an outside critic can verify facts in a first-person account, the persona still shapes his or her interpretation. Such narratives are literary booby-traps unless the historian using them remains aware constantly that the author very well may have an agenda and that even "facts" can be skewed or contradicted. To avoid this sort of distortion, an author should try to assemble as many different sources as possible to bring to bear on the so-called "facts."

That is not to say that first-person narratives should be avoided by the prudent. Diaries, for example, are vibrantly alive, immediate, and detailed, more so than later "reminiscence" writing. Their virtue is spontaneity without the haze of memory's occasional opaqueness or intervening drapes of propriety. To this extent, they are more likely to be reliable about names, dates, details, amounts, descriptions, and events. Another positive consideration is that the diary, unlike classic and more formally mediated autobiography, provides a chronological form that mimics life. This temporal immediacy allows involvement on the part of the reader (Lensink, 43). For the purposes of social history, such a source allows the reader, to a limited but definite degree, to experience camp life personally. For the purposes of creating compelling social history, this is an axis of significance that can rarely be duplicated by secondary commentary.

Diaries, despite their gifts of color and texture, intrinsically have other limitations beyond those of personae, and these may outweigh their advantages unless diaries are supplemented by other, less immediate sources. They can, for example, seriously lack perspective about the wider world outside camp and how it affects life in camp. Vision is narrower and restricted to what the diarist can see or hear. Internees, for example, can only write about their own situation, not those of friends in other camps or on other islands, or even (usually) about the progress of the war itself.

To avoid this limitation and to give a broad picture of the internment experience in general, I have used diaries and accounts from a variety of camps: Bacolod, Santo Tomás, Baguio, Los Baños, and, to an extent, Cebu, Masbate, and Davao as well (the latter written as a series of unpublished letters to family). Using this variety prevents a tendency to generalize one particular camp's nature as indicative of all of the other camps. Baguio, for example, tended to be much more humane and healthy than Bacolod; generalizations from one experience to another can be highly inaccurate. A multiplicity of details from different camps and islands corrects this and also provides a wider perspective in terms of geography and information.

There are, however, some exceptions to this rule. Though lack of perspective and accurate information proved to be true generally speaking, it is wrong to think that individuals or camps lacked *any* outside information. Many internment camps had some sources, however clandestine and incomplete. Access to information other than propaganda was naturally limited; some "facts" were actually rumors that turned out to be unsubstantiated later; other information, sent by Filipino resistance people, trickled into camp scribbled on tiny scraps of paper; even more information came from dangerous hidden radios (if the camp had any). Possession of the radios, while evident in every camp but Bacolod, was not a fact widely known to the general population. Because the penalty for being found with a radio was death, information from such sources came to the ears of most of the camp through word of mouth — a transmission that often garbled the information. What information (or more commonly, misinformation) resulted then got recorded in diaries. Incidentally, those with direct access to the radio news were not always thrilled with it: Margaret Sams might have been "in" on the news, but she was also nervous. The secret radio was hidden under a false bottom in her sewing box.

Paradoxically, other sources of information and perspective on the wider world were available — often consisting of Japanese-controlled Manila newspapers in English (such as the infamous *Tribune*) or Japanese "official" news over the guard's radio (the Japanese-controlled Manila stations also in English). Internees in Santo Tomás camp, for example, soon learned to read between the lines of the Japanese-controlled newspapers and to patch together a picture by inference.

James Halsema is a particularly vivid exception to the generalization that diarists lack a sense of the larger picture. He is unusual in that he regularly heard secret news broadcasts, as well as those booming out of the guards' barracks at Baguio. With these bits and pieces he soon fashioned his own one-page "newspaper" that he posted — "The Camp Holmes Daily News." In his article describing the liberation of Bilibid Prison, correspondent Robert Shaplen states that Halsema understood enough of what was going on in the outside world to post what turned out to be extremely accurate "news" (Shaplen, 70). Halsema admits that he was "one of the few who had knowledge of and occasional access to a radio that was hidden in the camp" ("Halsema," 9). This and the Japanese papers were the primary basis for his famous one-page camp newsletter.

Halsema's bits of information and radio bulletins could be verified to an extent by another odd source: the packing material in the one and only Red Cross parcel that all internees and POWs received in December 1943. Bits of newspaper were recovered in many camps, though Baguio camp was particularly blessed both in the amount of news and the skill of the interpreter-reporter. As Halsema explains in a January 3, 1944, entry, "J[apanese guards]'s confiscated all newspapers they found in the Red Cross boxes but some bits were wrapped around nails and I found 4 pages from the N.Y. Times of July 19, 1943 buried amidst empty mashed cartons and torn wrapping paper piled in a corner of the bodega. Inside domestic news it's true but precious messengers from a friendly, confident American world."

News stories, pictures, and advertisements gave a vivid indication of the tenor of life in the United States. Paper scraps, among other things, demonstrated an optimistic culture now tossing around ideas for "post war make-work" — projects such as cleaning up river basins polluted by war industries or trying to establish air control procedures around major cities (Halsema, "1944 Diary," January 3) to take up the employment slack after war work ceased. This obviously refuted overblown Japanese claims of a coming Allied defeat and despair on the American home front.

Halsema's case, however, is atypical of the sources of internee news in most camps, if only because it proved ultimately to be extremely accurate. The information he collected from scraps of newspaper and overheard broadcasts (Japanese or otherwise) became famous throughout the Holmes (Baguio) camp. His skills were so great that, when Bilibid Prison was freed, Robert Shaplen commented on Halsema's collection:

Jimmie Halsema, who had been a reporter before the war on the Manila *Bulletin* . . . showed me what looked like a fairy-story book, called "James Neook of Enables." On the blank pages under its cover he had kept a precise chronology of events elsewhere in the world during internment. The book was filled with figures and maps. Halsema's information was sufficiently up-to-date to include news of the liberation of Leyte, the progress of American troops on Luzon, and recent Allied successes in Europe. Halsema had also written a weekly news sheet for the camp . . . he told me that he got some of his best scoops by eavesdropping on a radio which the Jap guards in the room next to his kept going day and night. (70)

Halsema's perspective on the world outside camp and the larger issues was not evident in most of the diaries I used. Lacking Halsema's time and news training, others endured on rumors and half-understood gossip or brooded on their personal situations.

The retrospective account — one that, for purposes of clarity, I am defining as reminiscences written after the events, but within twenty years of them — can overcome the problem in perspective. Some reminiscences are less subject to errors in detail or accuracy than others, though accuracy is obviously a problem when a writer relies solely on memory and the retrospective is considerably after the fact.

Often, this is not the case if the retrospective is a *re-written* diary. In this study this includes Cates's *Drainpipe Diary*, Sams's *Forbidden Family*, Hind's *Spirits Unbroken*, Eva Nixon's *Delayed, Manila*, and Miles's *Captive Community*. These have all been edited for grammar, accuracy, and style. Retrospective, rewritten diaries seem to have the original diaries' lively accuracy but benefit from the time to compose and polish the work.

One cannot depend on completely contemporaneous accuracy, however, even with a rewritten diary. While rewriting, the author may not only alter the grammar but some of the substance as well. As Lensink points out, there are a number of considerations that may urge an author to alter a diary, including "a nervous relative," the author's "second thoughts," or worry that other participants who experienced the same events might be offended (47). William Zinsser adds that such an unseen audience often "half-paralyze[s] authors" as, weary with care, they write with their parents, their spouses, their siblings, their friends "perched" and "looking" over their shoulders, reading the author's version of events. Zinsser wonders now, as he reads reminiscences, "how many passengers were along for the ride subtly altering the past" (7).

In fact, even the original diary might not tell *everything*; uncomfortable, embarrassing, or (to the author's persona) inappropriate moments tend to be automatically edited out. After all, in the truest sense of the word, both original diaries and rewritten ones are still "author-ized" versions (Lensink, 46, 50).

Later retrospectives based only on memory are more subject to errors, because the authors write them years after the events. I have used more retrospectives than rewritten diaries, because they are more common. It is not hard to understand why this is so. The Japanese forbade internees to keep diaries; imprisonment or even death was the punishment if the guards found one. Though Halsema states that the Japanese didn't forbid diaries (ltr, May 19, 1997), there was certainly a widespread belief to that effect among both civilian internees and POWs, both in the Philippines and elsewhere.

Dr. Thomas Hayes's POW diary about the men he cared for at Bilibid Prison was a secret diary, and Agnes Keith's famous book *Three Came Home* is based partly on tiny notes she buried in tin cans at night in Borneo. She also stuffed her little boy's teddy bear with them to be able to smuggle them out of camp. Closer to home, Tressa Cates hid her diary in a convenient drainpipe in Santo Tomás, and Natalie Crouter at Baguio (Hay/Holmes) buried her notes, wrapped in oil skin and hid them under butter or nuts. Many women avoided putting themselves or their families in jeopardy and simply waited until freedom came to write about their experiences rather than go to the extreme lengths that some diarists did by concealing notes inside cans, burying them, or hiding them on their persons. Carol Terry originally started out keeping a secret diary but destroyed it after "the Japanese started pulling the fingernails off of such writers" (1). It is unclear if this actually happened, although the Japanese certainly made such threats. Depositions for the trials in both Manila and Tokyo affirm that pulling fingernails off with pliers was a common form of torture (for example, IPS, Document #6913, 8), although whether this was the fate of many diarists is unclear.

The obvious advantage of retrospectives over diaries is that both hindsight and time allow the writer to avoid repetition, trivia, mistakes, incoherence, mysteries, and narrowness. With this form, the writer can put his or her story into a larger perspective and compare it to what others' experiences were both in camps and at home. They also seem, more than do diaries, to offer the telling metaphor and the sudden illumination of understanding that so often get lost in the day-to-day dreariness and routine of diary accounts (Cannon, 299). In a strange way, this can make them more accurate in the subjective sense. As Siebenschuh points out, "Convincing factual statement[s] and interpretation[s] are made by literary, not analytical, means"; without art, the events can lose much of their meaning (26). Distinguishing fact and art, however, may ultimately prove difficult without a number of other sources.

There is one final observation to make about retrospectives. When the author writes them, he or she is drawing on common conventions of the narrative. We have already discussed one of these — the presence of a persona, something strongly evident in any first-person account. Another tendency is for the author to use, consciously or unconsciously, earlier models of narrative of which the reader might not be aware. In an effort to create an "appropriate" narrative, language, attitudes, and even interpretation of events ultimately may be pulled into a false shape (Bloom, "Single," 42). Saints' lives, conversion narratives, heroic adventures, tales of combat, pioneer stories, mysteries, Gothic tales, even romances: All can suggest a shape for events that may emphasize some details, obscure others, or change chronology and characters. When using first-person narratives as sources, then, it is wise for the social historian to keep this crochet in mind or possibly even read a few of the implied genre to get some sense, perhaps, of its distorting conventions. This is especially useful in the case of war stories or religious experiences, which blatantly tend to follow their respective conventions.

When authors write these retrospective accounts is also important. James Halsema classifies the retrospective accounts of camp life in three "waves." The first wave began "as soon as former prisoners of war and civilian internees recovered from their ill treatment at enemy hands" ("Biblio," 86). The second wave occurred in the 1960s. These two together include most of the retrospectives I use in this study.

The following authors fit into the category of first and second wave retrospectives: Donald Baker, Edna Bell, Alice Bryant, Ethel and James Chapman, Esther Hamilton, Alva Hill, Douglas MacArthur, William Moule, Tetsuro Ogawa, Sohei Ooka (whose work was ultimately turned into a prize-winning novel), Mary Ogle, Yay Panlilio, Claire Phillips, Robert Robb, Doris Rubens, Grace Savary, Bessie Sneed, and Frederic Stevens. Although I would not normally list individual authors, I want to distinguish the accuracy of such authors (in regard to details) from the historically less reliable *memoirs*—which I define as those pieces written more than twenty years after the events, most of which Halsema classifies as the "third wave" of recollections of camp life written in the 1980s ("Biblio," 86).

It is important to understand why authors bother to write memoirs over forty years after internment. Superficially, their historical value in terms of accurate details, correct sequences of events, or even years is more suspect. These narratives are the least likely to retrace incidents unerringly because they are the farthest away in time from the actual circumstances. As Lynn Bloom points out, however, memoirs are valuable to the writer even at (or because of) such a late date. Here "the aging authors seek to get their views on record while there is still time" (Bloom, "Single," 37). Former participants in horrendous events also write down their stories to serve as witnesses. Through such narratives they hope the events will never be forgotten and that they can help the cause by contributing their mite, however late. These include the memoirs of Dorothy Danner, Judy Hyland, and Denny Williams. Finally, some authors write their memoirs to explain to their children and grandchildren what happened, because often the authors' children were too young to remember clearly. This is specifically the case with Grace Nash, Frieda Magnuson, Imogene Carlson, and Martha Hill.

In the above we see one particular strength of the memoir historically above that of the retrospective. Even more than the latter, memoirs have almost a life span's worth of hindsight. These writers, Bloom explains, have the advantage of seeing not only the whole event and knowing how things turned out but the ability as well to put those events in a larger and more mature context—one that perhaps more easily acknowledges the part played by human weakness or the towering importance of small things in daily life. The memoir then emphasizes those incidents that turned out to be most important to the author's life (Bloom "Escape," 110).

Drawbacks are inherent in viewing memoirs as historical sources despite the narrative's obvious perspective and interpretative distance. One of these is, again, the insidious nature of memory itself, especially over many years. Zinsser notes that memory "can be highly unreliable"; often it embellishes events in terms of what might or should have been, and this becomes the memory of what *was*. We tend to remember our "best selves." As Bloom explains, recollection also helps to "integrate and reinterpret their memories to fill in the gaps, offer explanations, solve the mysteries, lay the ghosts. As narrators, almost all autobiographers present themselves as the central character, the heroes and heroines of their own stories, whatever their roles in the actual historical context" ("Group," 223).

This kind of addition and reinterpretation becomes even more historically suspect when reunions of participants become the catalyst for the memoirs, and this group subsequently helps shape the eventual product through a weird kind of consensus. Reunions of veterans, both military and civilian, Lynn Bloom states, "serve not only to commemorate their participation but to reinterpret its meaning" ("Group," 222).

Bloom attended the 1989 reunion of the Baguio camp internees and observed this process in action. Forty-four years after their release from Bilibid Prison, former internees got together to become reacquainted with old friends and to reminisce about internment days. As participants cross-checked (and perhaps filled in) details, events, and names, the meeting soon turned into an exercise in aiding and abetting an unofficial, unsuspected, yet growing, *group* memory. Because such groups tend to seek harmony naturally, the participants automatically moved toward a consensus regarding what happened *as well as their reactions to* those events (Bloom, "Group," 224). This process grew even more refined as the group exerted its influence by "curtailing individual tendencies to dramatize, exaggerate, and depart from the majority view" (224).

What has developed out of this is an unusual example of an "aggregate persona" — one whose overriding philosophy can influence the final shape of both recollections and their interpretation. In this case, a significant number of those at the reunion were missionaries, just as they earlier had constituted a large part of the original internees. Due to the consensus process, such an influential proportion understandably dictated the nature and *direction* of any changes in details. Individual memories now were subject to pressures "to match or fit inside the apparent consensus of the group" ("Group," 224). While, according to Bloom, "American values" remained strongly evident in this group recollection, I would suggest that yet another force dictated its ultimate shape — Christian values, especially those of forgiveness and turning the other cheek. Circumscribing national values, such as resourcefulness, humor, justice, fairness, love of education, use of the democratic processes, and personal cooperation ("Group," 229), Christian values also seem to have left their impression on the interpretation of key events. Here group remembrance practiced the ultimate "reconciliation" among the former prisoners, their memories, and their wartime captors. The intensive group desire not to "fight old battles or air old grievances," to "take the larger view" (Bloom, "Group," 227) resulted in a deliberate rejection of private recollection and unique personal feeling. Individuals inevitably found themselves subjectively nudged to erase memories of old pains, privation, hunger, illness, isolated instances of torture, and perhaps even of needless deaths, to fit their memories into the forgiving (and necessarily forgetting) group consensus of what happened and how the internees felt about it. (Bloom ruefully makes the point ["Group," 229] that this process was made easier because of the self-selection of the reunion's participants: Many of the more individualistically inclined "disaffected" did not come.) Historical interpretations from internees participating in such a reunion should be viewed with knowledge of probable distortion, given the group memory process, even though the individual internees were present at the time and place of the events they narrate.

Such wariness about the historical accuracy of any first-person narrative (oral or otherwise) seems to be in concert with narrative critic William Zinsser. He titled his collection of essays on the art of autobiography *Inventing the Truth*. It is a warning any historian should remember when attempting to use the genre.

One way to dilute possible problems is to bring to bear the evidence of a *number* of diaries, retrospectives, and memoirs on an historical question. This process demands that facts or details that do not appear in at least two of these forms not be included in any subsequent historical work. For example, in discussing the degree of starvation in several camps (an extremely controversial issue) I stated that internees, sick with hunger pangs, eventually were reduced to eating slugs and grass. I felt justified in offering such grotesque specifics because I found corroboration for them in two sources: one, a rewritten diary, and the other, a normal retrospective (the first by Cates and the second by Carlson).

In this work, I have kept in mind both the limitations and the advantages of the unique information all these sources can provide. I believe that any possible problems with credibility can be easily compensated for by methodology; the value of the information from these unusual sources is too great to exclude them. Certainly, the absence of them would make for a much less accurate work.

In all cases, with my deliberate use of multiple sources from many different perspectives (internees, Japanese historical or participatory, official [IMTFE and IPS], media, and military) to focus on events, I hope to assure a lack of bias in any *single* direction and to give a sense of balance by mentioning alternate interpretations wherever possible. The use of multiple *forms* of information is particularly important as well. As I have indicated above, form (memoir, diary, and so forth) can dictate either the direction of distortion or the distortion itself. This can be eliminated to a great degree by using multiple forms of information—in the case of this work, stern, official sources such as trial transcripts, documents, exhibits, statements, and affidavits; less formal venues such as diaries, memoirs, retrospectives, and oral histories; the hurried, often half-correct squibs of newspapers and magazines; the ponderous punctiliousness of scholarly biographies, military histories, and cultural studies (American, Japanese, and Filipino); the careful articles in academic journals and medical studies; and finally, even the breeziness and occasional dropped stitches of coherence in questionnaires and interviews. All these have helped me to create, I believe, an accurate, coherent, and empathic social history.

A Brief Note on the Filipino Spellings Used

Though I originally intended to use some sort of standardized spelling of the Filipino words in this work because of the variant versions in a number of different texts, I soon discovered this was impossible. Because of different languages used on different islands in the Philippine Archipelago (for example, Cebuano, Tagalog, Old Tagalog [Luzon], and Samar-Leyte, among others), spellings are nearly impossible to standardize. Pineda, for example, points out that out of the 19,189 entries in that dictionary, 44.10 percent come from seven different major Philippine languages, while another

4.26 percent reflect twenty-six minor languages, and another 40.60 percent, foreign languages, especially Spanish, English, and Chinese (Pineda, 701–702). Given the wide variation in spelling or even terms for the same items or verbs, looking up words becomes extremely difficult.

For example, Pineda's *Diksyunaryong* has no listing for "lugao"—a common term in a variety of internee sources. Extensive searching at last reveals another spelling, "lugaw"—listed as a Chinese loan word, along with variations such as "linugaw" and "nilugaw," also from Chinese (414). A search for "camote," a vegetable commonly eaten in camp, eventually results in finding, after some frustration, "kamote," a borrowing (somewhat mysteriously) from Mexico (297).

To make things even more difficult, Consuelo Panganiban explains in her *English-Pilipino Dictionary* that all the spelling in her work is "according to the national standard followed in schools," and when loan words appear, they are listed, as they are taught, in their *assimilated* ("Pilipino"), not original form. This often results in strange changes in internal consonant clusters or vowel substitutions affecting pairs such as "iy" and "aw" (v–vi).

To further confuse things, there is some evidence that many Filipinos on islands other than Luzon resent and reject the use of *Pilipino* as a standard language, seeing it as a move on the part of those on Luzon and Manilianos to extend the hegemony of their island culture, primarily through well-represented Tagalog-based words. The different words from different islands, then, may or may not reflect standardized *Pilipino* spelling.

Given all these difficulties, I have decided to let the orthographic chips fall where they may, using whatever spelling of the words—*baka, bayka, baika,* for example—that I find in that particular source.

Notes

Introduction

1. Scholars disagree about the number of civilians (specifically American civilians) in the internment camps. Lt. Colonel Emmet F. Pearson, who served with the army hospital at Santo Tomás (STIC) after its liberation, puts the number of internees in Santo Tomás, Los Baños, and Baguio (Bilibid) camps at 6,399 (4,763 of these American). His sources for these figures include: (1) the records made at Santo Tomás that were not lost or destroyed; (2) secret Japanese reports; (3) "well-informed individuals" in STIC and other camps, including camp doctors; and (4) two source works by Hartendorp and Stevens (Pearson, 988). Another scholar, Van Waterford, sets the number of total internees at 7,800 (6,000 of them Americans). I have chosen to use Waterford's number (unless I indicate otherwise) not only because his sources include not just army medical records, prisoner reports, and works by both Hartendorp and Stevens but a much greater variety of Japanese documents, many found since the Tokyo Trials and occupation. He has also had access to more complete records in the Philippines. His work is also comprehensive and covers all prisoners of the Japanese across the South and Central Pacific, as well as being the most recent survey (Waterford, 261).

1. Pearl of the Orient

1. According to James Halsema, at least in the case of Baguio and environs, Japanese women and children were not forced to stay in internment but allowed to return to their homes. Many did stay, however, because of their fear of Filipino retaliation ("E. J.," 361, n7).

2. First Dark Days

1. Morton explains, however, that the U.S. government didn't entirely abandon its troops in the Philippines. General George Marshall insisted on organizing small blockade runners to sail with ammunition and food from Australia. This was ineffectual, however. Most of the blockade runners sank or were captured, and the three that did make it off-loaded their supplies on Mindanao and Cebu. All these items still had to be transported through Japanese patrols to Corregidor (Morton, 160–164).

2. Actually, another internee present, James Halsema, disagrees, noting that Mukibo's English was heavily accented and "thick with consonants"; he cites the following example: "You must obey its [Imperial Army's] commands. Arr guns must be surrendered at once or you weer be kirrud" (Halsema, "E. J.," 297).

3. The bizarre nature of the claim suggests possible misunderstanding. James Halsema points out that Major Mukibo's statement that he had a Harvard education provided by a scholarship through the Presbyterian (not Methodist) church has never been

proven. As Halsema states, "Neither the undergraduate college [Harvard] nor the Divinity School alumni offices has shed any light on the validity of this claim" (Halsema ltr, May 19, 1997).

3. Meanwhile, on Several Islands Not Far Away

1. Vaughan explains that "chow" is the equivalent of $0.10 a day plus rice, fuel, laundry, soap, lights, and the right to live on the grounds (Vaughan, 12–13).

4. Inside the Gate

1. The particular awkwardness of possible legal terminology in this regard becomes evident when one studies the confused international designation (POW or civilian) for any members of the civilian Merchant Marine caught in occupied territory. As Gibson explains, under the 1907 Hague International Convention, all crew members on captured merchant ships of a belligerent were considered "POWs." However, even the Hague Convention exempted "members of the crew of an enemy merchant ship, if they happened to be citizens of a neutral state," in which case they simply became civilians of a neutral country (articles 5–7). This remained the case unless their ship was captured while "taking part in hostilities," and then they became POWs, despite their national neutrality (article 8). Gibson adds that some merchant seamen captured ashore, on leave from their ships, were not captured POWs but civilian internees. The Philippines saw members of the Merchant Marine thrown into both POW and civilian internment camps, thereby reflecting the already confused criteria for official designation (Gibson, 188). Daws points out that even civilian construction workers on Wake Island were placed in POW camps, because they, like the marines, fought the invading Japanese (27).

2. To put this in some sort of perspective, of all the British and American POWs captured by the Germans and Italians in Europe, only 4 percent died in camp, while in the Pacific Theater, 27 percent died (Russell, 57). Waterford, citing the impossibility of acquiring accurate statistics (because the Japanese frequently didn't record POW deaths), suggests a higher figure: of 193,000+ Allied POWs, 31.4 percent died. Waterford puts the civilian internee death toll (from the entire Pacific, not just the Philippines) at less than half that rate—11.2 percent (146).

8. Idle Hands Are the Devil's Playground

1. This list represents both British and American professionals in camp, but only those who went to Bilibid Prison in January. It does not include those such as E. J. and Marie Halsema, who were released to live on the outside in Baguio (the town). Additionally, the totals I list are those I personally tallied, based on Halsema's "Nationality List from the Japanese Internment Camp #3 January 1945," in Appendix D (Halsema, "Oral"). The figures, therefore, are to a degree approximations, because some profes-

sionals appear in two categories (for example, health professionals who are also missionaries). Additionally, while I also counted missionaries' wives as "missionaries," I didn't list their children in any category unless they were over age eighteen. The approximations are intended merely to give a sense of the variety of prewar occupations represented among the Baguio internees.

9. Angels and Tanks

1. Nixon says it was only sixty (86).

Bibliography

Primary Sources

Alden, June (Darras). Questionnaire, 1990.

Baker, Donald. *Life — On Rice*. New York: Carlton Press, 1963.

Bell, Edna (and H. Roy Bell). "Trails to Freedom" and "An Account of the Guerrilla Movement on Negros Island in the Philippines during World War II." Dumaguete: Silliman University Press, 1958.

Berry, William A., with James E. Alexander. *Prisoner of the Rising Sun*. Norman OK: University of Oklahoma Press, 1993.

Brines, Russell. *"Until They Eat Stones."* Philadelphia: J. B. Lippincott, 1944.

Brown, Alex A. "From the Internment Camps." *Bulletin of the American Collection* 5, no. 2 (April 1977): 72–80.

Bryant, Alice Franklin. *The Sun Was Darkened*. Boston: Chapman and Grimes, 1947.

Buss, Claude A. "Claude A. Buss in Manila, 1941–1942." Interviewed by Michael P. Onorato in *Forgotten Heroes*, ed. Michael P. Onorato. Westport CT: Meckler, 1990, 225–318.

Carlson, Imogene. *American Family Interned: Philippines, W. W. II*. Cebu City, Philippines: Cebu Christian Mission, 1979.

Cary, Frank. *Letters from Internment Camp: Davao and Manila, 1942–1945*. Ashland OR: Independent Printing Co., 1993.

Cates, Tressa R. (R.N.). *The Drainpipe Diary*. Hollywood CA: Vantage Press, 1957.

Chapman, James, and Ethel Chapman. *Escape to the Hills*. Lancaster PA: Jaques Cattell Press, 1947.

Chapman, Maurice, and Virginia Chapman. "Experiences in the Philippines." Interviewed by Michael Onorato, in *Forgotten Heroes*, ed. Michael P. Onorato. Westport CT: Meckler, 1990, 3–48 ["Chapman — MV"].

Crouter, Natalie. *Forbidden Diary: A Record of Wartime Internment, 1941–1945*, ed. with an introduction by Lynn Z. Bloom. New York: Burt Franklin and Co., 1980.

Danner, Dorothy Still (R.N.). *What a Way to Spend a War: Navy Nurse POW's in the Philippines*. Annapolis MD: Naval Institute Press, 1995.

Davis, Dorothy (R.N.). "I Nursed at Santo Tomás, Manila." *American Journal of Nursing* 44, no. 1 (January 1940): 29–30.

DeVoe, Susan (Magnuson). Questionnaire, 1990.

Edward, B. F. "Los Baños Internment Camp: Escape and Liberation." *Bulletin of the American Historical Collection* XIII, no. 2 (51) (April–June 1985): 60–68.

Evans, David C., ed. and trans. *The Japanese Navy in World War II: In the Words of Former Japanese Naval Officers*, 2nd ed. Annapolis MD: Naval Institute Press, 1986.

Fukukita, Yasunosuke. *Japan's Innate Virility: Selections from Okakura and Nitobe*. N.p.: Hokuseido Press, n.d. [text suggests late 1941].

Glunz, Charles, and Henrietta Glunz. *From Pearl Harbor to the Golden Gate*. Unpublished typescript. 35 pages [held at Bancroft Library].

Halsema, James. "Bilibid Prison, 1945." Unpublished diary.
———. "Diary 1944." Unpublished.
———. *The Internment Camp at Baguio.* Interviewed by Michael P. Onorato. Oral History Program. Fullerton CS: California State University, Fullerton, 1987.
———. "Internment Chain." Personal communication (e-mail) to author, March 1, 1997.
———. "Internment Chain of Command." Personal communication (e-mail) to author, March 1, 1997.
———. "Japanese Guard Pull-outs." Personal communication (e-mail) to author, April 20, 1996.
———. Letter to author, January 1, 1994.
———. Letter to author, April 21, 1994.
———. Letter to author, May 21, 1997.
Hamilton, Esther Yerger. *Ambassador in Bonds!* East Stroudsburg PA: Pinebrook Book Club, 1946.
Hayes, Thomas, Commander, USN, M.D. *Bilibid Diary: The Secret Notebooks of Commander Thomas Hayes, POW Manila, 1942–1945,* ed. A. B. Feuer. Hamden CT: Shoe String Press, 1987.
Hill, Alice Gallagher Morton. Telephone interview, June 16, 1990.
Hill, Alva J. *Filipinos Are Dependable Allies: After 45 Years in the Philippines an American Lawyer Tells Why He Has Faith in the New Republic.* Unpublished but bound typescript, July 1954.
Hill, Dr. Jay, D.D.S. Telephone interview, June 13, 1990.
———. Letter to John D. McClellan Jr., copy, May 7, 1990.
———. "2-23-45." Unpublished.
Hill, Martha Mills. *Linnets and Pomegranates.* Marina del Rey CA: DeVorss and Co., 1977.
Hind, R. Renton. *Spirits Unbroken.* San Francisco: John Howell, 1946.
Hyland, Judy. *In the Shadow of the Rising Sun.* Minneapolis: Augsburg Publishing House, 1984.
Jensen, Sascha Jean. "Pigtails in Prison" [autobiography and partial screenplay]. *Interrupted Lives: Four Women's Stories of Internment during World War II in the Philippines,* eds. Lily Nova and Iven Lourie. Nevada City CA: Artemis Books, 1995, 33–68.
Keith, Billy. *Days of Anguish, Days of Hope.* New York: Doubleday and Co., 1972.
Koyanagi, Tomiji. "The Battle of Leyte Gulf." *The Japanese Navy in World War II,* 2nd ed., ed. and trans. David C. Evans. Annapolis MD: Naval Institute Press, 1986, 355–384, 524.
Lewis, Karen Kerns. "Autobiography." *Interrupted Lives: Four Women's Stories of Internment during World War II in the Philippines,* eds. Lily Nova and Iven Lourie. Nevada City CA: Artemis Books, 1995, 73–108.
Long, Frances. *Half a World Away: From Boarding School to Jap Prison.* New York: Farrar and Rinehart, Inc., 1943 ["Half"].
———. "Yankee Girl": Adventures of a Young American Who Spent Five Months

in Jap Internment Camp at Manila." *Life* 13, no. 10 (September 7, 1942):
   82–91.

MacArthur, Douglas. *Reminiscences.* New York: McGraw-Hill, 1964.

McCall, James E. *Santo Tomás Internment Camp: STIC in Verse and Reverse; STIC-toons and STIC-tistics.* Lincoln NE: Woodruff Printing Co., 1945.

Magnuson, Frieda. *Out in '45, If We're Still Alive.* Sisters OR: One-Book Company, 1984.

———. Questionnaire, 1990.

Manila Sunday Tribune. "Peace, Contentment Prevail at Internment Camp." July 12, 1942, 1–3.

Meadows, Martin. Letter to author, December 6, 1997.

———. Letter to author, June 30, 1998.

———. Letter to author, July 27, 1998.

Miles, Fern Harrington. *Captive Community: Life in a Japanese Internment Camp, 1941–1945.* Jefferson City TN: Mossy Creek Press, 1987.

Moule, William. *God's Arm's around Us.* Nevada City CA: Blue Dolphin Publishing, Inc., 1960.

Nash, Grace. Telephone interview of August 8, 1989.

———. Telephone interview of May 15, 1998 ["Interview II"].

———. *That We Might Live.* Scottsdale AZ: Shano Publishers, 1984.

Nixon, Eva Anna. "*Delayed, Manila.*" Newberg OR: n.p., 1981.

Ogawa, Tetsuro. *Terraced Hell: A Japanese Memoir of Defeat and Death in Northern Luzon, Philippines.* Rutland VT: Charles Tuttle Co., 1972.

Ogle, Mary S. *Worth the Price.* Washington DC: Review and Herald Publishing Company, 1958.

Ohdaira, Shinichiro. "The Ohdaira Story: A Vignette of a Japanese in the Occupied Philippines," trans. Frank Baba, ed. James Halsema. In unpublished manuscript in the collection of James Halsema.

Ooka, Shohei. *Fire on the Plain,* trans. Ivan Morris. New York: Alfred A. Knopf, 1957 [Japan 1952].

Owens, William A. *Eye-Deep in Hell: A Memoir of the Liberation of the Philippines, 1944–1945.* Dallas: Southern Methodist University Press, 1989.

Panlilio, Yay. *The Crucible, An Autobiography by "Colonel Yay."* New York: Macmillan Co., 1950.

Phillips, Claire, and Myron B. Goldsmith. *Manila Espionage.* Portland OR: Binfords and Mort, 1947.

Read, Peggy (Peters). Questionnaire, 1990.

Redmond, Juanita. *I Served on Bataan.* New York: J. B. Lippincott, 1943.

Robb, Robert Yelton. "Nightmare in Santo Tomás." *Collier's* 123, no. 6 (February 5, 1949): 34ff.

Romulo, Carlos P., Col. *I Saw the Fall of the Philippines.* Garden City NY: Country Press, 1942 [war-time censored edition].

Rubens, Doris. *Bread and Rice.* Foreword by Carlos Romulo. New York: Thurston Macauley Associates, 1947.

Sams, Margaret. *Forbidden Family: A Wartime Memoir of the Philippines, 1941–1945*, ed. Lynn Z. Bloom. Madison WI: University of Wisconsin Press, 1989.

Santo Tomás Internment Camp. *Internews*, ed. Russell Brines, Assoc. Press. January 1942–June 1942. New York: Relief for Americans in Philippines, 1942.

Savary, Gladys. *Outside the Walls*. New York: Vantage Press, 1954.

Shimada, Koichi. "The Opening Air Offensive against the Philippines." *The Japanese Navy in World War II*, ed. and trans. David C. Evans. Annapolis MD: Naval Institute Press, 1986, 71–104.

Sneed, Bessie. *Captured by the Japanese: Being the Personal Experiences of a Miner's Wife Caught in the Philippines, at the Outbreak of World War II*. Denver: Bradford-Robinson, 1946.

Stevens, Frederic H. *Santo Tomás Internment Camp 1942–1945*. Foreword by Douglas MacArthur. N.p.: Stratford House, 1946.

Terry, Carol. *"Kept."* Kedgaon, India: American Council of the Ramabai Mukti Mission, 1945.

Tomibe, Rokuro. "The Secret Story of War's End." N. trans. *Bulletin of the American Historical Collection* 7, no. 4 (October–December 1979): 37–45.

Utinsky, Margaret. *"Miss U."* San Antonio TX: Naylor Co., 1948.

Vaughan, Elizabeth. *The Ordeal of Elizabeth Vaughan: A Wartime Diary of the Philippines*, ed. Carol M. Petillo. Athens GA: University of Georgia Press, 1985.

Whitesides, John G. *The Economics of Internment: Life in a Japanese Internment Camp in the Philippines in the Second World War: An American View*. Papers in Southeast Asia Business History. Ann Arbor: University of Michigan Center for South and Southeast Asia Studies, 1988.

Williams, Denny (R.N.). *To the Angels*. N.p: Denson Press, 1985.

Wills, Jane. "Autobiography," in *Interrupted Lives: Four Women's Stories of Internment during World War II in the Philippines*, eds. Lily Nova and Iven Lourie. Nevada City CA: Artemis Books, 1995, 15–30.

Woodcock, Teedie (Cowie). Questionnaire, 1990.

Secondary Sources

Agoncillo, Teodoro A. *The Fateful Years: Japan's Adventure in the Philippines, 1941–1945*, vols. I and II. Quezon City, Philippines: R. P. Garcia, 1965.

American National Red Cross. *Far Eastern Prisoners of War Bulletin (for the Relatives of American Prisoners of War and Civilian Internees in the Far East)*. 1, no. 1 (August 1945).

———. *Prisoner of War Bulletin (for the Relatives of American Prisoners of War and Civilian Internees)*. Washington DC: Review and Herald Publishing Company, 1958. Three volumes. Vol. nos. 1–7 (June 1943–December 1943).

———. *Prisoner of War Bulletin*. 2, nos. 1–12 (January 1944–December 1944).

———. *Prisoner of War Bulletin*. 3, nos. 1–6 (January 1945–June 1945).

Arthur, Anthony. *Deliverance at Los Baños*. New York: St. Martin's Press, 1985.

Bailey, Maxwell C., Major, USAF. "Raid on Los Baños." *Military Review* 63, no. 5 (May 1983): 51–66.

Baldwin, Hanson W. *Battles Won and Lost.* New York: Harper, 1966.

Blacklock, D. M., and T. Southwell. *A Guide to Human Parasitology for Medical Practitioners,* 4th ed. Baltimore: Williams and Wilkins Co., 1940.

Bloom, Lynn Z. "Afterword," in Margaret Sams's *Forbidden Family,* ed. Lynn Z. Bloom. Madison WI: University of Wisconsin Press, 1989, 305–314.

—— and Ning Yu. "American Autobiography: The Changing Canon." *A/B: Autobiography Studies* 9, no. 2 (fall 1994): 167–180 ["Canon"].

——. "Autobiography and Audience." *Journal of Advanced Composition* 4 (1987): 119–131 ["Audience"].

——. "The Diary as Popular History." *Journal of Popular Culture* 9, no. 4 (1976): 794–807 ["Popular"].

——. "Escaping Voices: Women's South Pacific Internment Diaries and Memoirs." *Mosaic* 23, no. 3 (summer 1990): 101–112 ["Escape"].

——. "Introduction" in Margaret Sams's *Forbidden Family,* ed. Lynn Z. Bloom. Madison WI: University of Wisconsin Press, 1989, 3–20.

——. "Introduction: Diarists, This Diarist, and Her Diary," in Natalie Crouter's *Forbidden Diary,* ed. Lynn Z. Bloom. New York: Burt Franklin, 1980, xi–xxvi.

——. "Reunion and Reinterpretation: Group Biography in Process." *Biography* 13, no. 3 (1990): 222–234 ["Group"].

——. "Single-Experience Autobiographies." *Autobiography Studies* 3, no. 3 (fall 1987): 36–45 ["Single"].

——. "Till Death Do Us Part: Men's and Women's Interpretations of Wartime Internment." *Women's Studies International Forum* 10, no. 1 (1987): 75–83 ["Death"].

——. "Women's War Stories: The Legacy of South Pacific Internment." *Visions of War: World War II in Popular Literature and Culture,* eds. M. Paul Holsinger and Mary Anne Schofield. Bowling Green OH: Bowling Green State University Popular Press, 1992, 67–77 ["War"].

Brackman, Arnold C. *The Other Nuremberg: The Untold Story of the Tokyo War Crimes Trials.* New York: William Morrow and Co., 1987.

Burgers, H. A. "Memories of Manila." *Rotarian* 61, no. 6 (December 1944): 31–33.

Butler, Allan M., M.D., Julian M. Ruffin, M.D., Marion H. Sniffen, and Mary E. Wickson. "The Nutritional Status of Civilians Rescued from Japanese Prison Camps." *New England Journal of Medicine* 233, no. 22 (November 29, 1945): 639–642.

Cannon, Donald Q. "Angus M. Cannon and David Whitmer: A Comment on History and Historical Method." *Brigham Young University Studies* 20, no. 3 (spring 1980): 297–299.

Carpenter, Ronald. *History as Rhetoric: Style, Narrative, and Persuasion.* Columbia SC: University of South Carolina Press, 1995.

Castelnuovo, Shirley. "Review Essay: Internment and the Rules of War." *Oral History Review* 9 (spring–fall 1991): 115–120.

Chapman, Sondra Rees. "American Civilians as Japanese Prisoners of War (1941–1945)." Thesis, M.S., Pittsburg State University, Pittsburg KS, 1994 ["Sondra Chapman"].

Clarke, Alice, R.N. "An Army Nurse Returns to the Philippines." *American Journal of Nursing* 45, no. 3 (March 1945): 177–178 ["Army"].

———. "Guerrilla Nurse: The Story of a Nurse Who Served with the Philippine Army." *American Journal of Nursing* 45, no. 8 (August 1945): 598–600 ["Guerrilla"].

———. "Thirty-seven Months as Prisoners of War." *American Journal of Nursing* 45, no. 5 (May 1945): 342–345 ["37"].

Condon-Rall, Mary Ellen. "U.S. Army Medical Preparations and the Outbreak of War." *Journal of Military History* 56, no. 1 (1992): 35–56.

Cook, Charles O. Jr., Captain, USN (Ret.). "The Strange Case of Rainbow-5." *United States Naval Institute Proceedings* 104, no. 8 (August 1978): 67–73.

Corbett, P. Scott. *Quiet Passages: The Exchange of Civilians between the United States and Japan during the Second World War.* Kent OH: Kent State University Press, 1987.

Cully, John J. "Trouble at the Lordsburg Internment Camp." *New Mexico Historical Review* 60, no. 3 (July 1985): 225–248.

Danquah, Francis K. "Japan's Food Farming Policies in Wartime Southeast Asia: The Philippine Example, 1942–1944." *Agricultural History* 64, no. 3 (1990): 60–80.

Daws, Gavin. *Prisoners of the Rising Sun: POWs of World War II in the Pacific.* New York: William Morrow, 1994.

Dower, John W. *War without Mercy: Race and Power in the Pacific War.* New York: Pantheon Books, 1986.

Evans, Jessie F. "Release from Los Baños." *American Journal of Nursing* 45, no. 6 (June 1945): 462–463.

Falk, Stanley L. "Douglas MacArthur and the War against Japan," in *We Shall Return! MacArthur's Commanders and the Defeat of Japan, 1942–1945,* ed. William M. Leary. Lexington KY: University of Kentucky Press, 1988, 1–22; 245–246.

Feuer, A. B. "Introduction." *Bilibid Diary: The Secret Notebooks of Commander Thomas Hayes, POW, Manila 1942–45.* Hamden CT: Shoe String Press, 1987.

Flanagan, Edward M. Jr., Major. *The Angels: A History of the 11th Airborne Division, 1943–1946.* Washington DC: Infantry Journal Press, 1948 ["Angels"].

———. Lt. General (Ret.). *The Los Baños Raid: The 11th Airborne Jumps at Dawn.* New York: Berkley Publishing Co., 1987 ["Jove"].

Fletcher, Angus, ed. *The Literature of Fact: Selected Papers from the English Institute.* New York: Columbia University Press, 1976.

Garcia, Mauro, ed. *Documents on the Japanese Occupation of the Philippines.* Manila: Philippine Historical Assoc., 1965.

Gibson, Charles Dana. "Prisoners of War vs. Internees: The Merchant Mariner Experience of World War II." *American Neptune* 54, no. 3 (summer 1994): 187–193.

Gilmore, Allison B. "'We Have Been Reborn': Japanese Prisoners and the Allied Propaganda War in the Southwest Pacific." *Pacific Historical Review* 65, no. 2 (May 1995): 195–215.

Gleeck, Lewis E. Jr. *The Manila Americans (1901–1964)*. Manila: Carmelo and Bauermann, Inc., 1977.

Graff, Harvey V. "Using First Person Sources in Social and Cultural History: A Working Bibliography." *Historical Methods* 27, no. 2, (spring 1994): 87–93.

Halsema, James J. E. *J. Halsema, Colonial Engineer: A Biography*. New Day Publishers: Quezon City, 1991 ["E. J."].

———. "The Liberation of the Los Baños Internment Camp." *Bulletin of the American Historical Collection* 15, no. 3 (July–September 1987): 86–89 [*"Biblio"*].

———. "Japanese Internment Camps for Allied Civilians in the Philippines 1941–1945." *Pilipinas* 23 (fall 1994): 1–37.

Hartendorp, A. V. H. *The Japanese Occupation of the Philippines*, vol. I. Manila: Bookmark, 1967.

———. *The Japanese Occupation of the Philippines*, vol. II. Manila: Bookmark, 1967.

———. *The Santo Tomás Story*, ed. Frank H. Golay. New York: McGraw-Hill, 1964 [*"Santo Tomás"*].

Harvey, A. D. *Literature into History*. New York: St. Martin's Press, 1988.

Haughwout, Frank G. "The Intestinal Diseases in the Japanese Prison Camps in the Philippines: A Preliminary Note." *Journal of Technical Methods and Bulletin of the International Association of Medical Museums* 25 (1945): 123–147.

Hayase, Shinzo. "Forum to Survey Records of Japan's Occupation of the Philippines." *Philippine Studies Newsletter* 20, no. 1 (February 1992): 7, 12.

Hayashi, Saburo. *Kogun: The Japanese Army in the Pacific War*, trans. Alvin D. Coox. Quantico VA: Marine Corps Assoc., 1959.

Health, Education and Welfare. 84th Congress, 2nd Session. House Document No. 296. "Effects of Malnutrition and Other Hardships on the Mortality and Morbidity of Former United States Prisoners of War and Civilian Internees of World War II: An Appraisal of Current Information." *House Documents*, vol. 1. Washington DC: Government Publishing Office, 1956 ["HEW"].

Hibbs, Ralph E., M.D. "Beriberi in Japanese Prison Camp." *Annals of Internal Medicine* 25, no. 2 (August 1946): 270–282.

Holsinger, M. Paul, and Mary Anne Schofield, eds. *Visions of War: World War II in Popular Literature and Culture*. Bowling Green OH: Bowling Green State University Popular Press, 1992.

Horner, Layton. "Japanese Military Administration in Malaya and the Philippines." Dissertation, Ph.D., Department of History, University of Arizona, 1973.

Hunt, Ray C., and Bernard Norling. *Behind Japanese Lines: An American Guerrilla in the Philippines*. Lexington: University of Kentucky Press, 1986.

Ienaga, Saburo. *The Pacific War: World War II and the Japanese, 1931–1945*. [Japanese title: *Taiheiyo senso*]. Introductory note by Frank Baldwin. New York: Pantheon Books, 1978.

International Military Tribunal for the Far East. *Documents*, vol. 176. Chicago: University of Chicago Center for Research Libraries, n.d. Negative no. 3,187.

———. *Index of Exhibits*, vol. 177. Chicago: University of Chicago Center for Research Libraries, n.d. Negative no. 3,187.

———. *International Prosecution Section*, Doc. No. 6913, "Opening Statement of the Associate Prosecutor of the Philippines [Pedro Lopez] on Class C Offenses in General and Class B and C Offenses in the Philippines." December 4, 1946. Microfilm Publication 1663, Roll 42, RG 331.

———. *International Prosecution Section Records of the Chief Prosecutor Relating to Preparation for and Conduct of Cases Tried by the IMTFE, 1946–48*. Preliminary Inventory NM-11, Entries 316 and 317. Microfilm Publication M1668, Roll 8, RG 331.

———. *International Prosecution Section Staff Historical Files, Relating to Cases Tried before the IMTFE, 1945–1948*. Microfilm Publication 1663, Roll 42, RG 331 ["*IPS*"].

———. *Record of Proceedings, 1946–1948* (IMTFE, *Record*). 36 Reels. Washington DC: Library of Congress Microfilm, 1964.

"In the Hills of Panay." *Time* (June 11, 1945): 90.

Karnow, Stanley. *In Our Image: America's Empire in the Philippines*. New York: Random House, 1989.

Kawasaki, Ichiro. *Japan Unmasked*. Rutland VT: Charles Tuttle Co., 1969.

Keats, John. *They Fought Alone*. New York: J. B. Lippincott, 1963.

Lael, Richard L. *The Yamashita Precedent: War Crimes and Command Responsibility*. Wilmington DE: Scholarly Resources Inc., 1982.

Leary, William M., ed. *We Shall Return! MacArthur's Commanders and the Defeat of Japan, 1942–1945*. Lexington KY: University of Kentucky Press, 1988.

Lensink, Judy Nolte. "Expanding the Boundaries of Criticism: The Diary as Female Autobiography." *Women's Studies* 14 (1987): 39–53.

Linderman, Gerald F. *The World within War: America's Combat in World War II*. New York: The Free Press, 1992.

Long, Gavin. *MacArthur as Military Commander*. London: B. T. Batsford Ltd., 1969.

Lucas, Celia. *Prisoners of Santo Tomás: Based on the Diaries of Mrs. Isla Corfield*. London: Leo Cooper, 1975.

Mahoney, M. H. *Women in Espionage: A Biographical Dictionary*. Santa Barbara CA: ABC CLIO, 1993.

"Manila Infamies." *Newsweek* 26 (November 19, 1945): 52–53.

May, Glenn A. *A Past Recovered*. Quezon City: New Day Publishers, 1987.

———. "Review of Stanley Karnow's *In Our Image*." *Journal of American History* 77, no. 1 (June 1990): 326–327 ["Review"].

Miller, Edward S. *War Plan Orange*. Annapolis MD: Naval Institute Press, 1991.

Mitchell, Richard H. *Thought Control in Prewar Japan*. Ithaca NY: Cornell University Press, 1976.

Mojica, Proculo L. *Terry's Hunters: The True Story of the Hunters ROTC Guerrillas*. Manila: Benipayo Press, 1965.

Morton, Louis. *The War in the Pacific: The Fall of the Philippines*. Washington DC: Office of the Chief of Military History, Department of the Army, 1953.

"The Nature of the Enemy." *Time* 43 (February 7, 1945): 12–13.

Nitobe, Inazo. *Bushido: The Soul of Japan; An Exposition of Japanese Thought,* 10th ed., enlarged. New York: G. P. Putnam's Sons, 1905.

Nolte, Sharon H. *Women, the State, and Repression in Imperial Japan.* Working Paper #33, September 1983. Women in International Development Series, ed. Rita S. Gallin.

Nova, Lily, and Iven Lourie, eds. *Interrupted Lives: Four Women's Stories of Internment during World War II in the Philippines.* Nevada City CA: Artemis Books, 1995.

Onorato, Michael P. *Forgotten Heroes: Japan's Imprisonment of American Civilians in the Philippines, 1942–1945—An Oral History.* Westport CT: Meckler, 1990.

Pearson, Emmet F., Lt. Colonel, M.C. U.S. Army. "Morbidity and Mortality in Santo Tomás Internment Camp." *Annals of Internal Medicine* 24, no. 6 (June 1946): 988–1013.

Petillo, Carol M. *Douglas MacArthur: The Philippine Years.* Bloomington IN: Indiana University Press, 1981 ["Mac"].

———, ed. *The Ordeal of Elizabeth Vaughan: A Wartime Diary of the Philippines.* Athens GA: University of Georgia Press, 1985.

Piccigallo, Philip R. *The Japanese on Trial: Allied War Crimes Operations in the East, 1945–1951.* Austin TX: University of Texas Press, 1979.

Pomeroy, William J. *The Philippines: Colonialism, Collaboration, and Resistance!* New York: International, 1992.

Rasor, Eugene L. *General Douglas MacArthur, 1880–1964: Historiography and Annotated Bibliography.* Bibliographies of Battles and Leaders, No. 12, series ed. Myron J. Smith Jr. Westport CT: Greenwood Press, 1994.

Reyes, Jose G. *Terrorism and Redemption: Japanese Atrocities in the Philippines,* trans. Jose Garcia Insua. Manila: n.p., 1947.

Russell, John F., M.D. "The Captivity Experience and Its Psychological Consequences." *Psychiatric Annals* 14, no. 4 (1984): 250–254.

Russell of Liverpool, Edward Fredrick, Baron. *The Knights of Bushido: A Short History of Japanese War Crimes.* London: Cassell and Co., 1958.

"Santo Tomás Is Delivered." *Life* 18 (March 5, 1945): part 1, 25–31.

Sato, Ryuzo. *The Chrysanthemum and the Eagle: The Future of U.S.-Japan Relations.* New York: New York University Press, 1994.

Schaller, Michael. *Douglas MacArthur: The Far Eastern General.* New York: Oxford University Press, 1989.

Shaplen, Robert. "The Freeing of Bilibid." *New Yorker* 21 (March 3, 1945): 62ff.

Siebenschuh, William R. *Fictional Techniques and Factual Works.* Athens GA: University of Georgia Press, 1983.

Syjuco, Maria Felica A. *The Kempei Tai in the Philippines 1941–1945.* Quezon City: New Day Publishers, 1988.

Taylor, Lawrence. *A Trial of Generals: Homma, Yamashita, MacArthur.* South Bend IN: Icarus Press, 1981.

Vaughan, Elizabeth H. *Community under Stress: An Internment Camp Culture.* Princeton NJ: Princeton University Press, 1949.

Waterford, Van (pseud.) (Willem F. Wanrooy). *Prisoners of the Japanese in World War II: Statistical History, Personal Narratives and Memorials Concerning POWs in Camps and on Hellships, Civilian Internees, Asian Slave Laborers and Others Captured in the Pacific Theater.* Jefferson NC: McFarland and Co., Inc., 1994.

Wickizer, V. D., and M. K. Bennett. *The Rice Economy of Monsoon Asia.* Stanford CA: Food Research Institute, 1941.

Williams, Peter, and David Wallace. *Unit 731: Japan's Secret Biological Warfare in World War II.* New York: The Free Press, 1989.

Willoughby, Charles A., Maj. Gen. (Ret.), comp. *The Guerrilla Resistance Movement in the Philippines, 1941–1945.* New York: Vantage Press, 1972.

Wolfert, Ira. *American Guerrilla in the Philippines.* New York: Simon and Schuster, 1945.

Zinsser, William, ed. "Introduction," in *Inventing the Truth: The Art and Craft of Memoir.* New York: Houghton Mifflin Company, 1995, 3–20.

Reference Works

Dull, Paul S., and Michael Takaaki Umemura, eds. *The Tokyo Trials: A Functional Index to the Proceedings of the International Military Tribunal for the Far East.* Ann Arbor: University of Michigan Press, 1957.

Halsema, James J. "Japanese Internment Camps for Allied Civilians in the Philippines 1941–1945." *Pilipinas* 23 (fall 1994): 1–37.

National Archives and Records Administration. *American Prisoners of War and Civilian Internees.* Reference Information Paper #80. Washington DC: National Archives, 1992.

Netzorg, Morton J. *The Philippines in World War II and to Independence: An Annotated Bibliography.* Ithaca NY: Department of Southeast Asian Studies, Cornell University, 1977.

———. *The Philippines in World War II and to Independence: An Annotated Bibliography,* 2nd ed., enlarged. Detroit: Cellar Book Shop Press, 1995.

Office of the Chief Counter Intelligence: Philippines Research and Information Section, GHQ AFPAC. *The Philippines during the Japanese Regime, 1942–1945: The Annotated List in the Literature Published in or about the Philippines during the Japanese Occupation.* October 10, 1945, n.p.: Biblio-Filipino Report, 1988 ["CCI"].

Panganiban, Consuelo T., ed. *English-Pilipino Dictionary,* updated ed. Metro Manila: National Book Store, 1994.

Pineda, B. P. Ponciano, ed. *Diksyunaryong Filipino-English,* unang ed. Quezon City: Olph Printers, 1993.

Tutorow, Norman E., comp. and ed. *War Crimes, War Criminals, and War Crimes Trials: An Annotated Bibliography and Source Book.* Bibliographies and Indexes in World History, No. 4. New York: Greenwood Press, 1986.

Webb, Herschel. *Research in Japanese Sources: A Guide.* (Center for Japanese Studies, the University of Michigan.) Ann Arbor: University of Michigan Press, 1994.

Index

Filipinos, discrimination against: and corruption and *compadre* obligations, 20–21; *ilustrados* preferred, 19–20; and integrated clubs, 15–16, 18–19

first-person narration, 1, 5, 7; accuracy of, 280–281, 332–324, 324–325, 329–330; narrative models of, 323–324, 327; need for multiple, 331; persona in, 323, 325; and self-selection, 47–48; as sources, 323, 325, 327. *See also* sources

food, in civilian camps, 147–206 *passim*; availability of, 112, 147, 187; camp fare, 150, 155, 156–158, 159, 183 (*see also* menus *and entries for specific camps*); confiscation of, 196, 201–202; as dependent on commandant, 112, 197, 203; extra for sick, women, children, 169–170, 171–172, 206; foraging, 192, 244, 194, 196, 198, 204; "Japanese soldier's ration," 148–150, 186, 189–190, 194; lack of transport for, 186; lugao, 150; not provided, 61–62, 136–137, 193; preservation of, 190–191; as punishment, 147–148, 168–169 (*see also* starvation); during and after rescue, 205–206, 275; and room monitors, 239; stockpiling of, 156, 171; submarine activity's effect on, 186, 197; typhoon's effect on, 180, 181. *See also* diseases in camp, deficiency; gardens; rations and rationing; rice; starvation

Fort Santiago, 263, 267

funds, 78, 152, 180, 254

gardens, 122, 123, 125, 137–138, 154, 157, 191, 194, 196, 234, 244–245, 253, 254

Greater Asian Co-Prosperity Sphere: freeing from, 307; hypocrisy of, 77, 103, 104, 262; missionaries pledge support for, 223

guards, 112, 138–139, 197, 198, 199, 201, 217, 273, 273–274

guerrillas: American, 36, 48, 64, 98–99; Chinese 48th squadron, 293–295; Fil-American, 293, 295; Hukbalahap, 293, 295; "Marking's Guerrillas," 293, 295; Philippine, 96–97, 105; pity of, for internees, 304; PQOG, 290, 293, 294; and rescue from Los Baños, 205, 288, 290, 293–294, 295, 296–297, 298, 299 (*see also* Los Baños internment camp; rescue from camps); submarine rescue of, 99–100; "Terry's Hunters," 289, 293, 295, 296–297, 298

guidelines, 109, 114–115, 118, 120–121, 141–142, 153, 207

"Harvest Struggle," 188–189

health: of children, 162, 196; and climate, 91–92; as dependent on commandant, 113, 167–168; decreasing, 186; demographics as influence on, 167; dysentery, 148, 150–151, 162–163, 166, 200; and edema, 199–200; and fitness, 92–93; inoculations for, 175, 181; and medical staffing, 136, 200–201 (*see also entries for specific camps*); and mosquitoes, 92, 131, 219; and nutritional requirements, 150, 168, 200; "Oriental" diets, 168–169; public, 122, 130, 131, 133, 181; and Red Cross medical supplies, 183–184, 254; and tropical ulcers, 178, 179–180, 183; and weight loss, 160, 193, 194, 195. *See also* dentists; diseases in camp, deficiency; doctors; hospitals; nurses, civilian; nurses, military; postwar effects, on internees; sanitation; starvation

hiding out, on Cebu, 63; and atrocities against civilians, 77, 79 (*see also*